Dina
Ritz

WHAT GREATER
SIN

A Novel

ISBN: 978-0-9989264-8-3 (Paperback)
ISBN: 978-0-9989264-9-0 (eBook)

This book is a work of fiction. Any references to historical events, real people living or dead, or real places are used fictitiously. Names, characters, and places are products of the author's imagination.

Front cover image by Jeff Bringle

Printed in the United States of America.

First printing edition 2020

For Luauna Schmidt
and all free-wheeling, free-thinking,
dancing-naked-to-the-song-of-life-loving
human beings
who continue to have faith and hope in humanity,
even when it seems all hope is lost.
May you soar with angels my friend,
Always

From the speech by Senator Warren Turnouer,
head of the Founders Preservationist Party.
Defense of the Union Rally, July 4, 2028,
Capitol Building,
Washington, DC

"Our great country has suffered four years of disgrace, influence peddling, and corruption at the hands of a kleptocracy. The cronyism and blatant oppression of the personal freedoms that we as American citizens of all faiths and cultures enjoy have torn our beloved country apart and poisoned its very soul. This administration has set brother against brother and sown the seeds of division for its own power. No more will we allow this greedy, criminal regime to subjugate and oppress the free people of this great country. Today, we take back our nation from the Kings of Corruption and return it to the free will of the people. We will fight to make our country whole. We will fight to keep the United States of America united. A nation divided against itself CANNOT STAND!"

PART 1

A Fallen Angel in the Garden

Venus De Milo

It was cold and quiet; that was what she recognized first as the buzz wore off. Dead quiet. Not the quiet of her bedroom back home or the couch in her best friend's apartment. In those places, traffic buzzed at all hours and the nightly freight train thundered in the distance, emitting obnoxious blasts from its air horn at every intersection. It would sing to her like a lullaby as it faded into the distance, taking her consciousness along with it. That was the wonderful quiet of her world. The quiet of this world was absolutely dark and desolate. Wherever she was, she could hear the eaves of the building creak and groan against the wind outside. A mournful wind devoid of life. It blew in long, flat gusts not unlike the wind across the Kansas plains of her birthplace. It howled like a lonely specter in a graveyard searching for its final resting place.

Her mind was foggy. Was she back in Kansas? Had her drink been spiked? That had to be it. The gorgeous guy she'd been dancing and flirting with all night must have slipped something into her whiskey and carted her off. *Stupid waste of good drugs*, she mused. She'd already decided to spend the night with him. Had actually been looking forward to it, considering the amount of heat he'd been packing. He was older than her usual pickups; she liked them as close to eighteen as possible. But judging by the soreness in her muscles, he must have had a pretty good time with her. *Selfish bastard. Just like a man to have all his kicks and leave a girl high and dry.*

A shiver ran over her, and she realized her clothes were gone. At least he'd put her La Perla's back on when he was done. It was all she had covering her most obvious attributes. The cold was tolerable, wherever here was, at least until that damned wind kicked in. She shook her head to clear it, but there was something around her neck. Some light came in from the full moon outside, but the place was still shadows, all made worse by the clotted mascara sticking to her eyelids.

She raised her hands to rub them and saw that they were tied together with coarse rope tethered to an iron ring on the floor. Her ankles had likewise been tied to keep her from standing. *Terrific*, she thought. *Kinky and completely selfish. What the hell next!* Judging by the aging machinery

1

around her, she had to be in a factory of some sort. It was filthy and smelly, and the floor was covered in some sort of crusty film.

"Hey!" she yelled out. "I'm not really into all this kinky role-playing stuff, so could you untie me?" The space stayed silent. "Anybody out there? This really isn't my thing, dude!"

"I find that unlikely," a voice said calmly from the shadows. "For you are a woman of Sodom. You haunt the city of sin and revel in its taverns, leading the innocent astray."

The chill that had crept up her spine in the cold suddenly turned to ice. She'd heard Sodom mentioned before at the church she and her husband attended. He'd been dragging her there for years hoping it would save their marriage, but it hadn't done much good. She went along with it because she loved him. The only thing that kept her from leaving were her semimonthly charity visits to her great aunt's house, which provided an opportunity for her jaunts to nearby Funville. She'd get all the sinning out of her system and then toddle on back to hubby to play the dutiful wife, and no one would be the wiser. It had worked up until now: not a perfect life but a secure one.

"Look, my husband is going to be wondering where I am," she said. "He's a pretty big guy, you know, doesn't like people screwing with his wife. Kinda takes it personal."

"If your poor husband had any idea of how many men had been screwing his wife, he would no doubt suffer a stroke. Your husband is a good man. He is kind and forgiving, a man who would show hospitality to a stranger without expectation of reward and follow his God's commands without question, the very embodiment of Lot." The voice hesitated and then said, "He's also five foot six, physically weak and slightly pudgy, not to mention afraid of heights."

Shit! she thought. This guy knows Al! If he told Al the truth about her little trips, it would destroy him. And she really did love the guy. She just couldn't take living like an Amish housewife twenty-four seven. "Whoever you are, maybe we could work this out. I really don't think it's in either of our best interests to tell Al about this. I'm sure you don't want to hurt him any more than I do, so just let me go and we won't tell anyone about this."

The man stepped out from the shadows. He looked the same as he had on the dance floor when she'd been grinding up on him, with mature good looks and tight blue jeans. But his southern drawl had disappeared, and his eyes no longer had that lustful cast. He stared at her like a bug pinned to a board. He walked over to her and knelt. "I would never seek to intentionally harm your fine husband," he said sympathetically. "He does good works in his community. You both do."

"Do I know you from somewhere?" she asked in a shaky voice.

"Jessica Flynn Glick, wife of Albert Glick, a deacon in the church. You volunteer in the local elementary school since you are unable, or should I say unwilling, to have children of your own, and you twice monthly assist in the care of your elderly great aunt since everyone else in your family lives too far away. You're well-liked and respected and considered among your peers to be a fine example of a virtuous, wholesome wife."

She pulled her limbs in closer to her body as he detailed her closeted existence. She had fought hard to keep her two lives separate. She never hit on anyone she might know and steered clear of places she knew certain male members of her husband's church frequented. Yet here she was, practically naked and wearing a pound of makeup and hair streaks while a stranger she picked up in a dive bar described her daily life in glowing terms. Her face colored with shame.

"Don't look so embarrassed," he told her. "Despite your many faults you've done a great deal of good in your community. I'm sure God will forgive you for whatever sins you've committed."

She watched him as he approached. Maybe the guy had a fetish about having sex in weird places while tying people up. A lot of churchgoing guys these days did things like this or like praying before and after sinning. She even slept with one guy who asked her to beat him with a whip after they'd had sex just so he could go back to his wife with a clear conscience. "Look, I'm up for just about anything, so maybe we can work this out. I mean, it's not like I've never been tied up before." Her voice was shaky, but she put as bright a come-hither look on her face as she could muster.

"Jessica, I'm not here to inflict pain on you," the man told her. "I'm here to help you. You see, I know you're a good person inside. You've helped a lot of people. And I'm going to do the same for you."

"I . . . I don't understand. Why am I tied up here if you're going to help me?" she asked. Her mind slipped slowly into terror mode as he looped a long, wool-lined leather strap around her neck. "Please don't hurt me," she whimpered. "I promise I'll go straight, honest. No more booze and no more men."

"We both know that isn't true, don't we, Jessica," he said compassionately. He took her head in his hands. Tears were flowing steadily down her face as he leaned forward and kissed her tenderly on the forehead. "Would you believe me if I told you that you have one great act left to perform in the service of God?" She shook her head but was so terrified that he couldn't tell whether it was in agreement. "You will be remembered as a vision of God's eternal glory, Jessica, and you will be revered and loved as no one has ever loved you before."

He smiled tenderly and caressed her cheek, whispering, "No more tears now." His gentle touch and tender expression would be the very last moments of compassion she would ever experience.

Centurion

The hum of the morning religious broadcast gave way to the five a.m. news report, jolting Deacon MacNair from a troubled sleep. The show had a theme song that somehow managed to be irritatingly cheery and urgently psychotic at the same time, and it never failed to wake him. The house was warm and dark. The only light came from the video screens in his mother's kitchen. Anna MacNair never missed the sunrise worship program, even though it typically aired two hours before sunrise. It had changed significantly over the years, evolving from a televangelist's freak show to a wartime propaganda broadcast and eventually a state-run hour of sermonizing, but Anna's dedication never failed. Deacon once asked her why she continued to watch the money-grubbing faith healers who used the Lord to line their pockets and steal from the poor. Anna informed him that the Devil could quote Scripture to suit his needs, but that didn't change the Lord's message. You only had to be smart enough to see the truth of it.

He crawled out of bed and walked to the bathroom. As he passed his mother's bedroom, he whispered, "Morning, Mama," and transferred a kiss from his fingers to the door. Anna MacNair had died in that room five years earlier, but the kitchen television still ran twenty-four hours a day just as it had when she still breathed. It kept her ghost alive and well for Deacon, who hated silence. One lingering lesson of the Civil War was that in silence there was only waiting: waiting for the next cry of attack, waiting for the next bomb to drop, waiting for the next crack of artillery. The sounds of Anna's house protected his soul from the silences that haunted him still. He went into the kitchen and made coffee while the reporters detailed the news from across the country, carefully filtered for consumption by the citizens of the Ecclesiastical Republic of the United States. He pressed a button on the table and split the screen to bring up the federal broadcast, and the news went from watered-down to in-depth. Coverage of the upcoming elections was heating up, and the report went live to Capitol Hill.

"With the last of the presidential debates only two weeks away, Senator Wallace Milton of the Ecclesiastical Republic State of Georgia is campaigning hard for reinstatement of the Territorial Representation Act. Permanently repealed after the assassination of President Warren

Turnouer, the act guaranteed the representation of both territories of the United States within the executive branch. However, with Vice President Cahill's conviction and execution last year, it is doubtful that Senator Milton and his party will be successful."

"That's what happens when you shoot the president, dumbass," Deacon muttered as he left the kitchen.

He lingered under the shower long enough for the water to run cold while he inventoried his scars. Mortar fragments and stray bullets had taken a few chunks out of his otherwise fit physique, but it was a pressure cooker bomb slapped together by a couple of dimwits in a double-wide that had nearly killed him. In true southern fashion, they used whatever they had handy to repel the advancing Yankee horde, and it worked. Unfortunately, it also exploded before they could get out of the trailer they were holed up in, and it vaporized them. To this day they were still known locally as the heroes of Ruckersville.

When his chest turned to gooseflesh, he toweled off and dressed for duty. The traffic report showed heavy congestion along the Federal Corridor, guaranteeing the sun would be up before he reached Huntsville, so he refilled his coffee mug. Even on the world's most efficient highway, traffic was still unavoidable. Grabbing his jacket and badge, he headed for the garage. A police Smart Cruiser now occupied the space where his beloved Dodge Charger once sat. The cruiser went from zero to a hundred in less than three seconds and handled like a dream but was far too smooth and quiet for his tastes. He missed the rumble and roar of a gas engine under the hood.

The onboard avatar registered his biosigns and scanned his identity. When complete, it said, "Identity confirmed, Lt. Deacon MacNair. Please set course."

He could have easily opted for his usual manual control but instead said, "Huntsville HQ," and the car went into autodrive.

The garage door retracted, and the cruiser took off. Multidirectional sensors on the vehicle's skin read the city traffic and navigated the car to the Federal Corridor. Once there, they raised the wheels and the cruiser settled into the slowly moving pack, announcing, "Time to destination at current congestion levels: forty-seven minutes."

Deacon settled back, said, "Play personal playlist, Coltrane," and sipped his coffee. The cruiser filled with the "Speak Low" track and he closed his eyes. He hadn't slept well the night before, and a forty-minute nap on a glass-like highway was just what he needed. By the time the first notes of "Blue Trane" flowed, he had drifted off.

Ten minutes from the Huntsville exit, Coltrane's horn was replaced by the voice of the avatar. "Attention, incoming alert. Course correction required."

Deacon sat up, rubbing his eyes, and said, "Display alert." The holographic display rose along the curve of the windshield. A body had been discovered in Gadsden, and local authorities were on scene. He read what few details there were. "Correct course to crime scene and connect me with Det. Bachman, personal line."

The avatar complied by switching to emergency mode. The hazard flashers lit up as the vehicle veered southeast. The Corridor itself responded by rerouting all autodriven vehicles from its path and audibly alerting and threatening any noncompliant vehicles. Inside the shielded interior, Joyce Bachman answered the call.

"Deacon, what's up?"

"Breakfast is served," he said as cheerily as he could.

"It's not even eight o'clock yet," Joyce complained. "What's on the menu: coffee and donuts, or are we talking omelets?"

"Pigs in a blanket today. We have a dead body in the Federal Corridor in Gadsden. I'm on my way there now. Tell Burke and Digger to get their butts in gear, grab that new rookie from Charleston and meet me there. Time for him to get his feet wet."

"Will do, boss," Joyce responded and switched off.

The trip to Gadsden would add another hour to his commute even with the hazard flashers, but there was no point in trying for more sleep. The siren was already reorienting his body to alert mode, a holdover from his wartime service. His mind, however, drifted, replaying the messages from the Ecumenical Affairs Council regarding his son as the cruiser sped on. He'd written numerous letters escalating from requests for clarification to demands for transparency about their rehabilitation methods. At first there had been a couple of cursory condolences for his loss and canned Bible passages about redemption in Heaven, each curated to cater to the territorial recognition of his Baptist upbringing. They prided themselves on their denominational sensitivity. Eventually, their denials and refusals escalated from polite refusals to outright threats from their embassy. Neville had been an adult at the time of his penance; therefore, his rehabilitation records were sealed from everyone, including family members, unless prior permission had been secured before his sentencing. It hadn't. Neville had been furious with his father for handing him over, and although she'd objected strenuously, his mother eventually consented to treatment. Even after he returned from rehab a clean, sober and content individual, his animosity toward them floated like pond scum, tainting their familial waters and eroding any semblance of trust. Neville killed himself before that film could be cleared away.

The day he put his father's honorary service pistol in his mouth, he wrote a letter to his mother, forgiving her and stating his undying love. Deacon's letter had been terser. Neville understood why Deacon did what he did but didn't forgive him outright. He said he loved his father for caring enough to be tough on him but not more than that. His last words were that he hoped his father would never know the hell he had been sentenced to. That he no longer wanted to see ghosts everywhere he looked or live in fear that the Destroyers would come for him as he'd been shown. He told Deacon to remember him as he was before the drugs and alcohol and signed the letter "Goodbye, Dad."

Deacon knew about ghosts. He'd acquired more than enough of them on the battlefields. He knew about the quiet places they haunted. They huddled in the dark recesses of your soul, waiting for those moments of calm when everything was on track and life was good. They rose up into those moments to remind you that your contentment had come at a high price, the interest was astronomical, and God was a mean fucking loan shark.

The Destroyers that Neville feared were another matter. He first mentioned them after returning home from penance during his reassimilation into society. His sponsor had warned Deacon there could be aftereffects that would diminish over time, latent flashbacks like LSD users once experienced. Deacon assumed these Destroyers to be one of them, but instead of diminishing they became stronger and evolved into a paranoid delusion. A delusion that killed his only son.

Deacon's personal mission to discover the truth had uncovered only one reference to the Destroyers, a biblical reference from Exodus about the plagues of Egypt. Speculation about what the Destroyer was ranged from an avenging angel, an angel of death, or possibly even Jesus himself. Whoever it turned out to be, it had but one purpose: to deliver God's wrath and punishment. How such a deadly concept found its way into the mind of his son drove Deacon to learn everything he could about E-Rep territory and its ruling Council, creating a Destroyer they could not anticipate with a mission of its own.

The cruiser turned south onto Highway 431 and headed for the Tennessee River. The federal government had gone to great lengths to erase the battle scars and restore the natural countryside. Everything was lush and green and shimmering in the late summer showers that floated through. It was beautiful but still only a facade. Like every state in the Republic, Alabama and Georgia still bore deep scars that would never heal. You only had to look at its people to see them. Every face held a smile that gleamed just to the right of sincerity beneath a veneer of southern manners and hospitality. Their eyes lingered on you long after you passed by, hoping in vain that you would notice the fear they contained. There were, of course, those who had embraced the new reality. They were the ones who channeled their hatred and superiority into tools of worship. They preyed on the weak with prayer and damnation. They trumpeted their superiority through bigotry and oppression clothed in Scripture. They were the maligned and misguided, the ignorant supremacists, the rebel veterans of an ongoing civil war they had at long last finally won

2033 - Welcome to New Eden

1

Gadsden Shores sat along the eastern border of federal territory, just twenty miles from the Ecclesiastical territorial border and the new Georgia state line. Decades ago, it had been a local quarry until the limestone deposits petered out. It was then converted into a dive lake and sporting hangout for the less experienced. Dense brush had grown along its high ridges and surrounding woodlands due to a battle-induced rerouting of the Coosa River. The water itself came from underground springs and glittered like a deep blue jewel. The New Coosa tributary trickled down from the northwest, bringing with it all manner of spotted bass, bluegill, and catfish. The winter runoff streamed south, flooding the local forests and turning the nearby land to swamps. The cliffs were beautiful in the setting sun and tended to glow, thanks to trace minerals. It was a beautiful and peaceful place to relax. At least it would be if not for the body sprawled along the sandbank.

Deacon crouched down and pulled the woman's hair back from her face. There were no scars other than a couple of minor cuts from where her chin had scraped the rock. Her hair showed no roots, indicating she was a natural brunette. High cheekbones and a pert little nose made her look particularly striking. Identification would be quick and easy, given that the body was still intact. *Pretty girl*, he thought as he looked into her graying eyes. Or she would have been if the rest of her hadn't sustained so much damage. Her skin was covered in large, purple bruises and in some places had split. One arm appeared completely crushed and her left femur had snapped, leaving the bone protruding from her leg. He lowered his head and whispered a prayer for the victim.

Standing up on the makeshift shoreline, he sidestepped quickly as a barrage of gravel cascaded from the hillside. The forensics team had arrived with the coroner, and paparazzi littered the ridge, trying to get pictures. If his team had found the body, they would have cordoned off the area to avoid setting off an avalanche and contaminating the scene. The local talent, however, were more interested in protecting their own asses than the crime scene, which meant this investigation was sure to be a shit show.

"Who found the body?" he called out to a group of local cops. They were E-State by the look of them, all southern swagger and righteous attitude. Every one of them wore khaki with a red over black, double-layered, five-pointed star on their shoulder. And all of them were entirely out of their jurisdiction. The group looked toward Deacon, but none answered. It would seem that being questioned by a six-foot two-inch black cop wearing a Federal Eagle was an affront to their authority. After an array of incredulous looks, the oldest of the group finally walked over to Deacon and introduced himself.

"Sheriff Caleb Markham," the man said, oblivious to the professional courtesy and respect of a handshake. Instead, he indicated a trio of shivering young men grouped at a makeshift pier as far from the body as they could get. "Those young boys over there were scuba diving. They found the victim."

Deacon moved to walk toward them but was stopped short by the sheriff's left hand on his chest. "And just who might you be, son?"

"Lt. Deacon MacNair, Homeland Security Services." He let his title hang in the air for a few seconds as he stared into Sheriff Markham's condescending gaze. "I shouldn't have to point out that this crime scene is in the Federal Corridor, and that makes it my jurisdiction, Sheriff Markham." Deacon dropped his eyes pointedly to where the sheriff was restraining him.

Markham lowered his hand to his belt loop, tucking it snugly under a considerable beer gut. "Those fine young men over there happen to be E-State citizens of my jurisdiction."

"Who happen to be standing in, and are material witnesses to, a crime scene in federal territory." Deacon eyed the sheriff without blinking. "And until I decide otherwise, they are potential suspects." Markham was solidly built, but Deacon had at least ten pounds of muscle and fifteen years of bad attitude on him. "We aren't going to have a problem here, are we, Sheriff?"

Sheriff Markham puffed out his chest and unwillingly stepped aside. Deacon left him stewing on the shoreline and walked toward the young men. His partner was already there speaking to them with an E-State deputy hovering nearby. He joined them and listened as Det. Joyce Bachman questioned a young man named Pete Milton.

"I was driving the boat, and we were dragging the Argo behind us. Parker, he rode in it to keep it steady." Milton pointed to one of his associates, a scrawny young man with greasy hair who fought to keep from vomiting every time he looked toward the body. "We got here around eleven this morning and hung out for a while, then went diving."

"Did you see anything unusual while you were submerged?" Joyce asked him.

"No, ma'am," Milton responded. His eyes dipped to her chest with every pause. "Nothing other than what we expected. Just old cars, old air pipes, a plane, and sunk boats. People dump furniture down there too sometimes."

Deacon looked over at the pontoon boat tied to the dock. It was littered with dive equipment, junk food bags and at least three six packs of empty beer cans. Turning back to the young man, he asked, "You own the boat?"

"Yes," he answered, eyeing Deacon warily. The lack of an honorific in his response told Deacon all he needed to know about Pete Milton.

"Then this must be your beer in your boat," Deacon remarked as Pete swallowed visibly. Deacon recognized the name Milton. There was a Senator Wallace Milton in the E-Rep General Assembly, which would explain the illegal presence of the local law and why they had been notified directly instead of the federal police.

"You do realize that boating under the influence is as serious as drunk driving, don't you?" Pete didn't answer but crossed his arms across his chest and cast a quick glance over to Markham, who suddenly became very interested in Lt. MacNair. "And that regardless of your E-State citizenship, if you violate the law in federal territory, your incarceration is solely at *my* discretion."

Pete began to shift back and forth, and Sheriff Markham interceded. "Now hold up here, Lieutenant," he said to MacNair. "These boys are not federal citizens and aren't guilty of anything. They reported the body to the police as soon as they found it, which makes them witnesses, not perpetrators. You appear to have no justifiable cause to hold them."

Deacon rounded on Markham and said, "Until I decide that these boys had nothing to do with the victim, they are suspects and will remain in my custody. You, on the other hand Sheriff, are free to remove yourself and your deputies from my crime scene." He turned back toward Pete and continued to address Markham. "And you may inform High Senator Milton that his son will be free to return home once I am satisfied that he is not involved and has told me everything I need to know."

Bullseye! The effect of dropping High Senator Milton's name was immediate. Sheriff Markham corralled his deputies and sent them scurrying back to HQ. He then informed the boys that their attorneys had already been notified and would meet them at the precinct. This was clearly a warning to the boys to keep their mouths shut, which Deacon fully expected. Sheriff Markham retreated to his cruiser and relocated it to the top of the quarry, where he could observe from a safe distance. He paced the edge, sending more scree and rubble onto the scene, and started making calls.

Turning back to the boys, Deacon found Pete wearing a rather smug smile, something else he had expected. He held the young man's gaze for a couple of seconds and then said, "Det. Bachman, please have these vessels stripped and searched down to the gunwales and take everything into evidence."

"Yes sir, Lieutenant," she responded and began giving instructions to the rookie in tow. Pete's smile suddenly cracked, and a trace of panic skittered across his eyes.

Deacon returned to the body just as the forensics team unloaded. HSS coroner Arthur "Digger" Tidwell hopped down out of the van, breathed deeply and grinned from ear to ear. Tidwell was a shaggy-haired mole of a man with a stocky body and short legs, but he was inexplicably fast and agile. No one could get to the bottom of a case like Digger Tidwell. He just kept digging until he found whatever he was looking for, and nothing stopped him. To Deacon, that made him the best coroner in the five-state corridor. His van mate Jeremy Burke was a different story altogether. Jeremy was young, opinionated and in love with his own reflection. It served him well as the face of the field forensics team. His handsome face and flashy smile on the evening news endeared him to an audience as easily as Digger's made them cringe. He was also overeducated for the job and completely loyal to his tech gear. He had long dreamed of a future where human investigation would become obsolete and criminal investigations would be totally automated. His end game was to be the first digital detective in the federal service, and he saw Deacon as the ultimate challenge, an investigator with an unrivaled record of successful cases, the mastermind to set his tech against, Boris Spassky to his Bobby Fischer. Jeremy hadn't won yet.

As Deacon stood over him, Jeremy took temperature readings and samples of tissue from the victim. The man had a tendency to whistle that drove Deacon crazy. After listening to him whistle through Ravel's *Boléro* and run his gear over the body, Deacon knelt down and asked, "What's the verdict, J?"

"Definitely a body dump," Jeremy explained. "Hardly any water in the lungs, according to the density tests, and there isn't enough bloat to indicate she's been here for more than twelve hours." He pressed a few buttons on his evidence pad and continued. "Liver temp confirms the twelve-hour limit."

"Cause of death?"

"Extreme blunt force trauma," Digger said from behind them. "You can tell by the deep tissue bruising and broken bones. Although I must say that a fall from any of the rocks surrounding this quarry wouldn't be sufficient to cause this amount of damage. These look more like crush injuries."

Deacon looked at the body's purple hue as Jeremy snapped photos on his evidence pad and uploaded them for identification. "So, are we talking a high-velocity fall?" he asked Digger.

The portly man thought for a moment and then said, "Doubtful. If she were pitched off of, say, a building, moving the remains would have been extremely messy and there would be definite signs of impact trauma."

"In other words, she probably would have exploded like a grape and they would have to sponge her up and haul her here in a bucket," Jeremy interjected.

"Thank you, Mr. Wizard," Deacon replied sarcastically. "So, if there's no impact trauma, Doc, what could have caused these injuries?"

Digger looked closely at the crushed arm and said, "If I didn't know better, I'd say the poor girl was run over with a paving compactor."

Jeremy's control pad began to beep wildly as an image was received. The picture was a reproduction of a travel visa granted only five months prior. A pretty face with smooth skin and bright blue eyes filled the left of the screen while her citizenship details scrolled on the right. She was an E-State citizen with a federal visa. The visa had been issued to an Ellory Bainbridge of Atlanta, Georgia, a graduate of Bainbridge State College (no relation to the namesake) with a degree in education, thirty-three years of age and married to one Allen Bainbridge for the past ten years. She had no priors and no warrants, and there was no missing person's report on file. A picture-perfect citizen. Deacon stared into the twinkling eyes on the screen and then back at the naked body lying in the dirt and felt his stomach turn. An E-State school teacher murdered in federal territory was a nightmare of paperwork and political red tape that was bound to be front-page news, especially with the crowd lining the quarry. And the front page was one place Deacon MacNair loathed to be.

Joyce Bachman bundled the three young men into the SUV she'd arrived in and had the rookie take them back to the HQ for processing. Their lawyers would no doubt beat them to the building and demand to collect their clients before any interrogation could take place. She hated lawyers, but they were a necessary evil in law enforcement. Deacon hated them too, almost as much as he hated politicians, but that didn't explain his current mood. She could tell something was bothering MacNair but wasn't about to question him at a crime scene. Whatever it was, it could wait until they were alone in the car. She joined him as Digger and Jeremy were carefully bagging the body. Deacon was indirectly observing Sheriff Markham as the man paced the ridge talking animatedly into a cell phone.

"You certainly know how to charm the locals," she said. "You should know Markham didn't interfere with me at all when I questioned those boys." He was very polite and professional."

Deacon stared directly up to where Sheriff Markham now sat on his cruiser hood. "When a man introduces himself to me and then lies to my face within two minutes of that introduction, I definitely consider that to be interfering."

"Markham lied?" Joyce exclaimed. "About what?"

"He said those boys reported finding the body to the police immediately. If they had dialed 911, they would have been connected directly to the Federal Emergency System, and ten squad cars would have had this place cordoned off in fifteen minutes. How many Feds did you see here when we arrived?"

Joyce thought back and then answered, "None. We were first on scene and called backup. Markham was already here with his bunch." Then she began to understand.

"Three cars full of Georgia sheriff's deputies and not one federal patrol cop," Deacon pointed out. "Those boys didn't call the cops; they called Daddy. And Daddy sent Markham to protect their asses."

"But how did you know the kid was Senator Milton's son?"

"Didn't. But the name and the looks matched up, and as long shots go, it wasn't a bad bet. It takes influence to send a squadron of cops outside of their jurisdiction to impede a federal investigation. And that means money and political clout."

"You figured all that out in two minutes?"

Deacon turned to her and smiled. "Actually, I called dispatch on the way here and had them trace the initial call. They told me it came through the territorial exchange; wasn't a direct call."

"Remind me never to play poker with you," she declared as she took the evidence pad from his hands. "Anything turn up on the victim?"

"No wants, no warrants, not a single blemish on her record." Deacon lowered his eyes to the smiling image. "How can a married woman this pretty go missing and no one file a missing person's report or post so much as a 'has anyone seen you' blip on social media?"

Joyce scrolled through the information on the victim. "Says here she has a travel visa. If she's visiting friends or relatives by vehicle, she may not be expected yet. Body couldn't have been here very long."

"According to Jeremy no more than twelve hours, but this took a while. Someone took their time doing this kind of damage, and that means at least a couple of days."

"You're thinking this is personal?"

Deacon looked over to where Digger and Jeremy were carefully stowing the bagged body in the coroner transport. "I sure hope so," he told her. "Because if it isn't personal, we have one hell of a sick monster on our hands."

2

It was early evening before the crime scene was completely secured and examined. Jeremy had an entire crew of evidence bots hovering over the quarry, scrutinizing every pebble and collecting a thousand samples. By the time they were through, he had a three-dimensional reconstruction of the scene mapped out, with chemical compositions of everything within thirty yards of the body. Confident that his minions had retrieved every bit of evidence there was to find, he guided them to their pods in the van and packed up his gear. Pausing to take in the scene one last time, he smiled, until he saw Deacon enter the crime scene and start giving it the once-over. It was well known that MacNair didn't trust technology and always investigated the scene for himself to see if the techs had left anything behind. Jeremy shook his head and called out to the lieutenant.

"We're heading back to HQ. I should have the full reconstruct on the wall by the time you get there."

"Thank you, Mr. Burke. That will be a pleasant surprise," Deacon responded, waving toward the van without taking his eyes off the scene. The gauntlet had been thrown down and graciously accepted once again. Jeremy took the bait like a hungry carp. So far, it was a game that Deacon had won on all but a single occasion, and that one instance had involved another detective suppressing evidence. Maybe one day the kid would get the better of him, but he doubted it.

A full hour later, the first drops of evening rain began to fall, forcing Deacon to call it a day. Joyce had already retreated to the cruiser, waiting for him to finish. Deacon slipped into the passenger seat and they drove off, leaving the ominous quarry behind. The area around Gadsden was typical of southern cities: an odd mix of aging historical buildings and new construction made to look like they belonged to the same era. The population was overwhelmingly white and dwindling with each generation.

It was typical of outliers. Eventually, the graded roads gave way to smooth asphalt and then suspensor highway. As the car tires hit the immense Corridor throughway, the suspensor systems engaged, and Deacon felt himself relax. The quarry itself was within federal territory, but it had been close enough to the territorial border to see the reflective white proximity signs bearing the Georgia Stars and Bars. The Georgia state flag had largely remained intact after the war, but the state's coat of arms no longer bore the word "Constitution" on its arch. It now read "Ecclesia Divinum," the motto of the Ecclesiastical state governments. And the three columns representing the branches of government were no longer wrapped in their defining purposes. Instead of "Wisdom, Justice, and Moderation," their purposes had become "Scripture, Judgment, and Devotion." He watched as the disturbing signs marking the nearby entrance to E-Rep territory faded into the darkness.

Most of the surrounding countryside had been devastated by artillery fire during the war, leaving it a wasteland. It was no surprise that the secessionist states had ceded it to the federal government so easily—one less reconstruction headache for the state budgets to bear. The area had bounced back in the ten years since. The Corridor had been restored and the neutral national highway built to provide access between the territories. Most of the residents who called the Corridor home were DC employees, executives or corporate fat cats, all eager to play both sides against each other as the winds of profit changed. It was definitely upper middle class and climbed higher the closer one came to the ultimate seat of power in the country.

Huntsville HQ was where the witnesses would be questioned under the watchful eyes of their overpaid attorneys. The digital evidence was already on its way to both Langley and the central mainframe. The body and any physical evidence retrieved would remain at Huntsville until the investigation was completed. As forensics labs went, Homeland Security Services had one that was unmatched anywhere in the modern world. Its mainframe power was connected via the most secure sealed network in existence to every regional federal hub. They also shared the mainframe facility with the FBI, CIA, and Pentagon and employed the very best technicians and investigative personnel available. Investigations were still conducted in the field by peace officers like MacNair and Bachman, but the cases were built at regional centers like Huntsville, and their resolution rate hovered at ninety-nine percent. Crimes were assigned to investigative teams by the Detective Sergeant on duty. On this particular night Deacon's call was answered by a very restless DS Agnes Chen, and he couldn't have been happier.

"Agnes, old girl, wake up! I got a live one coming in."

"Old girl?" she retorted. "You've got four decades and at least one bypass on me, pal. Your twenties are nothing but folklore."

Deacon laughed loud enough to startle Bachman and then said, "Chen, explain something to me. You are second-generation Chinese American. How the hell did you get a name like Agnes?"

"Mom got to name the first kid and named my older sister Tiffany. Sis got the cool American name and then ran off with a hard rock musician from Seattle. After that, Daddy took charge of naming the kids, so I got the ugly name because he thought it would discourage all those liberal white boys at MIT from sniffing around after me."

"Did it work?" Deacon asked.

"My girlfriend thinks so," Chen told him mischievously.

"How is your sister, by the way?"

"She's divorced, working as a stripper now and has three kids. What have you got for me?"

"Murdered female found in a quarry lake by recreational scuba divers. The body's fairly fresh and should be there within the hour. Four IDs confirmed: the victim and three witnesses. Burke's on point."

Chen opened a secure uplink and punched in Jeremy Burke's badge number. The digital imaging evidence had already begun to arrive, and the physical evidence was thirty minutes out. "It's coming in now, Deke. What's the play?"

"Full court press on this one, Agnes. My gut says this isn't an isolated incident."

Chen watched the images as they tiled onto the evidence wall and winced. "Looks like we have two watercraft coming into the garage. What's the story?"

"Witnesses were drinking pretty heavily. The boat's owner was a pretentious little prick with political ties. Run it through the resonance scanners but don't strip them down unless you find anything illegal. Any trace of narcotics or controlled substances on either one, get an e-warrant and notify the intake officer to detain all three witnesses and administer blood tests. Then dismantle them both."

Chen smiled as Burke's preliminary synopsis of the crime scene began to scroll up one side of the image bank. She scanned it quickly and said, "Prelim indicates a single-victim standard body dump."

"Is that Burke's expert opinion?" Deacon asked.

"I refuse to take sides," she responded. "Standard bet? Loser buys the beers for a month?"

He thought about it for a second and then said, "My liver's had enough of that European craft shit he likes to drink. Let's make this one dinner."

"Done," Chen told him. "Although you might regret that bet. Burke's a vegan."

"Aw, shit," Deacon muttered. "Too late to change the terms?"

"Not a chance, sunshine. You set the wager and you know the rules. Now get off this line and let me get to work."

"Thanks, Agnes," Deacon told her and disconnected.

As Agnes Chen rallied the troops, Deacon looked to his left to see Joyce struggling to hold in her laughter. "What the hell's so funny?"

She looked at him and said, "I think you better say goodbye to those Kansas City ribs and your sister's fried chicken. You won't be seeing them for a while."

3

Deacon groaned and leaned back to watch the highway markers flash by, each one bearing the insignia of the Federal Corridor: the red star of the Ecclesiastical states centered over the much larger blue star of the

Constitutional states, both embedded at the center of a Sun Cross. To the world, it had become the symbol of a new, balanced idealism in the United States of America. To him, it was a symbol of something sacred that had been fractured beyond repair. In today's world, schoolchildren were taught that the Second War between the States had achieved what the first could not: the restoration of the sovereign rights of the dissenting states from a federal government run amok and the freedom to choose a predominant way of life. Everything wrapped up in a neat economic and political bow explaining how the two sides rose above their differences to compromise and work together in peace and respect.

But Deacon knew better. The injustices, the racial unrest, and the unraveling of the middle class were symptoms of a disease that had been eating away at the country since that first recession in 2007. Years of economic and financial drought had left the country as dry as a tinder pile. Then some idiot in Washington decided to light a fire. Within ten years, the country began to roil and bubble, yet the political machine just kept turning the flames higher. The fearful found a savior in a bombastic, Hollywood con man who put P.T. Barnum to shame, ingesting his fevered rhetoric that pandered to their suffering. They aimed their fear at whatever target their false prophet declared was to blame for their lot in life. By the time the elections took place in 2020, the Great American Melting Pot finally boiled over. All it took was one carefully placed bullet at an historical church on H Street two years later to ignite the war that split the country in half permanently.

Before the assassination attempt, no one really believed war would erupt, but there were those who speculated. They were the ones who saw the big picture, the thinkers on the outskirts of the fray. They warned the country of the dangers of giving in to fear and hatred. They saw the fracture of the parties and the rise of despots, but no one believed them. The United States was suffering from a cancer with no cure, and it required the amputation of a few limbs to save the whole. Eventually peace had been achieved, but the country was never the same. The ideological divide was now an ugly scar stitched across the chest of the nation, a reminder of the widow-maker that had nearly killed it.

"Everything we fought and died to achieve for over two hundred years. It's a damned shame," Deacon muttered to himself. He didn't recognize his own country anymore. Old Glory was now relegated to second place on the flagpoles of the Constitutional states beneath the double star banner bearing the symbol of a fractured nation. The Ecclesiastical states had burned them all and replaced them with their own above the Blood-Stained Banner. It broke his heart.

Joyce glanced at the distant signs and said, "You know you can't stop people from being ignorant if that's what they choose to be, Deacon. This way of life is what these people chose for themselves."

"That's just what both governments want everyone to believe, that these people were ignorant and racist. Makes acceptance of the system easier," he grumbled. Looking over at Joyce's profile he asked appreciatively, "What are you, thirty, thirty-five tops?"

"Didn't anyone ever teach you that it's impolite to ask a woman her age?" she countered. When Deacon continued to stare, she answered, "Twenty-nine."

Deacon smiled. "You're too young to remember the political turmoil before the war. After decades of poverty, race riots, police brutality, foreign wars and terrorist attacks, these people weren't ignorant, they were tired. Tired of the endless arguing. Tired of the constant battle over morality. Tired of being used and having their lives extorted from them by the people they put their trust in. They wanted stability any way they could get it, and they were scared to death. Scared of social progress they weren't ready for. Scared of losing everything they and their forefathers spent a lifetime working for. Scared of losing their identity. Scared of losing their children in combat, helping countries that despised us. Scared that even if their kids did manage to survive combat, they wouldn't have a home to return to or a future worth living for. It made them easy targets."

"You're saying they're all victims being held captive by the Ecclesiastical government?"

"The conservative leaders couldn't stop the country from progressing beyond their ability to control and couldn't manipulate it for their own personal gains any longer. They preyed on people's fears and frustrations, blamed progress and science for all their ills, then put a face to the evils in the world in the form of liberals, gays, atheists, minorities and anyone that didn't subscribe to hardcore Christian beliefs. They preached the wrath of God and the pit of hell awaiting every one of us if we didn't change and promised their followers a garden of Eden to await eternity in."

"And the people fell for it," Joyce offered.

"Of course, they did. Then once the real fighting started, those same leaders waited until the right moment and took power. Promised people paradise if they bought into their new vision for a righteous country. The war left them destroyed and broken, and the despots promised them everything."

"Sounds pretty ignorant to me," Joyce told him.

"Worked for Hitler."

"Come on now, Deacon," Joyce chided. "This isn't Nazi Germany, and we're not a dictatorship."

"That wasn't the point. You've worked enough abduction cases to know if a kidnapper tears away at a victim's self-esteem long enough, eventually they'll believe what their kidnappers tell them. Politicians taxed everything they had, bankrupted every parachute, kept their wages at poverty level and left them with nothing. Religion applauded them for their poverty, offered them a safe harbor filled with absolutes, absolved them of the responsibilities of citizenship and the inevitability of progress. No more endless legal arguments and congressional hearings over what is or is not legal. No more constant campaigns of hate, doom and gloom. No more having to wrack your brain to failure just to figure out who was the lesser of the evils fighting for control of the country. No dispute over who can marry who, what's right, what's wrong. Just the ability to go about their consistent, unchanging lives secure in the knowledge that God had it all in hand and all they had to do was follow the rules."

"Sounds like heaven on earth," Joyce mused.

Deacon looked at her slyly. "That was the point."

Joyce thought about the implications of Deacon's point of view, that somehow half of the country now suffered from Stockholm syndrome. She only had bits and pieces of stolen conversations between her parents about what was happening in the world during her childhood. They never discussed world affairs in front of their daughter. She'd grown up in a country at war with itself, safely tucked away in the hills of Malibu far from the fighting. For her, the war had been reality TV, the subject of endless speculation by her teachers and elders. She had friends whose brothers and sisters had volunteered to fight and several whose families had been torn apart by their geographical ideologies. But at that age, it hadn't seemed real to her. Not even when one of them was killed. By the time the war had ended in 2027, she'd graduated high school a year early and immediately joined the federal service as a trainee officer. A career that had shown her the world she never knew and an existence she'd been trained to tolerate.

Unlike his partner, Deacon was a child of the past. At sixty-one, he'd lived through the most progressive and innovative periods of the country and experienced all the turmoil of the conflict firsthand. He'd watched the country rise and then fracture into chaos. He'd served as a marine during Operation Iraqi Freedom and survived to become a Chicago cop. When the new civil war broke out in 2023, he was recalled to service and remained there for its four-year duration. Most of his colleagues and fellow officers were youngsters born into the world, knowing only what they had gained since the war. His generation knew all too well what they had lost and what had been sacrificed in the name of peace.

The country had been split in two. A theocracy had taken control of half of it, and old prejudices thought long vanquished had once again found a purpose. After the Second Civil War, the Federal Corridor was just a no-man's-land of war-torn acreage that more closely resembled the Korean DMZ than a neutral throughway. And it would have stayed that way had it not been for the genius of an obscure Indian American kid from Queens whose name had so many syllables no one could pronounce it. A scruffy teenager who went by the name Ringo and spent his spare time digging in trash bins for recyclables to supplement his family's income.

The postwar economy struggled after the truce since ninety percent of the country's energy production rested solidly within the Ecclesiastical Republic. Oil revenues skyrocketed, which was hailed as proof that God had blessed the territory and was on their side. Ringo changed all that. Thanks to a full engineering scholarship to NYU, rabid addiction to social media, and commitment to environmental issues, he invented the world's first self-energizing, intelligent solar roadway system. Composed of a mash-up of discarded plastics combined with a crystalline polymer of his own creation, the new roadbed could withstand the pounding of constant traffic for years.

Its prismatic qualities allowed it to soak up sunlight from any angle and conduct electricity seamlessly. It powered everything from the buildings and homes in its designated territory to the smart cars that traveled its route. Its creation heralded the dawn of a new age of technology, and Ringo became the new cult hero of the Constitutional states. Down in the Republic, people just called him "Wonder Bob."

With a worldwide abundance of waste to draw from, Ringo's invention could be constructed for next to nothing. And thanks to hefty research investments by Google and Microsoft, the roadbed transmitted data and information faster than any internet connection. It possessed enough redundant storage systems to ensure that no section of it would be without power so long as any adjoining section continued to function. Queens was the first borough to officially go off-grid and become self-sustaining. Brooklyn followed, and within six months the entire state of New York. Within a year it had spread to DC, and within five the entire northeast had been converted. Plastics became the new black gold, and recyclable waste was imported from every part of the globe, giving the third world a booming export trade. The oceans hummed with ship captains who'd abandoned competitive market fishing for trash mining, leaving the smaller outfits to prosper with less competition. Recycling and processing plants sprang up across the Constitutional states as jobs exploded, and Detroit switched over auto manufacturing from fuel to electric. But while the Constitutional and federal governments flourished in the wave of renewable energy, the Ecclesiastical government could only watch as its prosperity withered. Evangelical politicians declared the creation of the Corridor to be the work of an Islamist bent on destroying their Christian sovereignty. They fought its extension from the Corridor into their territory, keeping the population gas dependent. But poverty eventually won, and the technology slowly spread. Utility companies outpaced oil refineries in growth, and the oil barons of the South were forced to tap into third-world markets to salvage their dwindling empires. The loss of the oil industry was also touted as the work of Satan, and the faithful ate it up as long as they had someone to blame for their failure to thrive.

They rode in silence until Chen called them with an update. "Agnes, my love, what have you got for me?" Deacon cooed.

"The mother lode, Deke. Scanners just confirmed trace amounts of cocaine along the boat floor and two very suspicious-looking pouches inside the left pontoon of the Argo. Confirmation of the contents indicated it is most definitely marijuana but with synthetic trace chemicals to enhance its potency. I won't know exactly what until I have hands on it. This should be enough to get a body warrant."

"It most certainly is," Deacon responded. "Thanks, Agnes, I owe you dinner. And I promise, no rabbit food."

Chen laughed and said, "You're on. I'll have the warrant by the time you arrive."

4

The Huntsville Regional Headquarters for the Homeland Security Services was a sprawling marvel of law enforcement. Conveniently situated in the former Marshall Space Flight Center, the complex had been repurposed into an information and security hub for the entire southeastern region of the Federal Corridor. Since the space program had been declared a national security enterprise, all space flight operations had been shifted to secure locations in the Constitutional states. The Huntsville facility was deemed too close to hostile territory, even though legally no state of hostility existed. It now served as a regional headquarters for the new HSS, which arose during reconstruction. With its massive information facility at Langley, the Homeland Hub became the lifeblood connecting all levels of law enforcement into the most effective agency in the world.

Bachman pulled into the entrance but slowed as they encountered a commotion at the main facility. Half a dozen high-end luxury vehicles, all with flashing lights and bearing congressional markings, were parked in front. Bachman drove toward the far end of the parking lot where they could watch unnoticed. An entourage of black suits exited the vehicles, and the facility director, John Pittsfield, greeted them. As he shook hands and introduced himself, the driver of the last car emerged and opened the rear doors to allow its passenger to disembark. MacNair didn't recognize the man's face but he definitely recognized his clothing: a shiny, dark suit that glittered menacingly under the parking-lot lights. The man was an archbishop of the Ecumenical Council, and he did not look happy.

"You have got to be kidding me," Joyce muttered. "What the hell does all this mean?"

"It means my hunch was right," Deacon answered. "You don't pull an archbishop and his entourage away from the dinner table on a Friday night unless you've got some serious money and powerful connections."

They parked under a large southern oak discreetly out of sight of the entrance and got out. After waiting to ensure that no one in the group remained in the lobby, they went in through the back entrance. The desk officer saw them come in and waved them off to the side. Apparently, some of the entourage hadn't been escorted in yet. Five minutes later, they were taken to a conference room well away from the hustle and bustle of a Friday night police headquarters. The desk sergeant gave them the all clear and checked them in.

"Sorry about all the cloak and dagger, but I figured you wanted to avoid those guys," Officer Myers told them.

"I take it they were looking for us," Deacon said.

"Oh yeah, they called ahead, demanding to see you two the moment they arrived. When I told them you were still on your way in, they ordered the director to meet with them. Ordered, mind you, not requested."

"Thanks for the heads-up," Deacon answered and then turned to Joyce. "Let's check in with Chen and find out where we are. I want some ammunition before we have to face those assholes."

As police facilities go, Huntsville was considered a topflight training center. Junior investigators, forensic technicians, even desk jockeys vied to complete training and hoped for eventual placement there. Agnes Chen was considered the best investigative trainer outside of the capital, with a superb instinct for creating "dream teams" when it came to field support. She had a sharp eye for where the pieces fit and where they didn't, and she never wasted time trying to fit a square peg into a round hole. If Agnes Chen said you didn't fit in, it was game over. You either waited until she found a team where you did fit, or you moved on to another line of work. She had a reputation for being cold-blooded when it came to teaching procedure and suffered no breach of security or protocols. For the duration of your session at Huntsville, your life was no longer your own. It belonged to Agnes Chen twenty-four seven.

With such a fearsome reputation to her credit, candidates arrived at Huntsville expecting to meet a large, menacing man-eater who spent her evenings picking the remains of discarded officers from between her deeply clawed toes. What they got was an even bigger shock. Agnes was only five-foot-three, four at best if she wore heels. Her eyes were bright and sparkly, outdone only by her infectious smile. At thirty-three years of age, she was the youngest trainer on the force but never looked a day over twenty-five. Her makeup was always minimalist yet extremely flattering and her hair neatly trimmed just below the shoulders. Her attitude was always cordial and welcoming, and her sharp wit served to defuse any fears or doubts planted by the rumor mill—at least until day two. Day two always began with the same phrase: "Police work is not an occupation where one can simply say, 'Oops, I'll remember next time.' The stakes are far too high." She was there to make sure that they never forgot it. Once training began, she became their teacher, mentor, life coach, spiritual guide, and mother confessor as they learned what detective work in the real world was like. But when a major case hit and the heat was on, Agnes was all business, and she expected no less than someone's absolute best. If you didn't know something, you asked. If you couldn't do something, you spoke up. If you hampered an investigation because you dropped the ball, you were out. There were no second chances.

This year's crew was relatively young. Nearly all of them had graduated barely two years prior, and all were academy rookies. Only one had any sort of true investigative experience. His name was Corbett. He had a deeply perceptive mind and a knack for seeing around a problem, attacking it in ways that most techs would never consider. His one weakness was a significant lack of self-confidence brought on by shyness, poor eyesight, and a weight problem. For all his intuition and ability, he found it gut-wrenching to offer up his ideas and suppositions; it took a superhuman amount of courage for him to do so. Agnes took an instant liking to him. He was the only member of the group that she went out of her way to prop up.

Deacon and Joyce found Agnes calmly ordering her techs around with her usual efficiency, adding more and more information to the evidence pile. She met Deacon with a smile and handed him an e-reader.

"Warrant just came in. You're good to go on your witnesses. I have them stashed in three separate interview rooms: two, four, and seven."

"Have they been well taken care of?" he asked.

"Watered, slopped and sufficiently amused. They shouldn't be hard to handle." A call came in on her earbud and she said, "Deke, the director wants to see you in his office right away. Seems we have a major storm brewing upstairs."

"Wonderful." Deacon turned to Joyce and said, "This should be fun."

5

Deacon sat in the interview room across from Pete Milton and his attorney, Daniel Carter. At the far end of the table sitting quietly was Archbishop Caulder Henry Wirz of the Ecumenical Judiciary Council, the ruling body of the territory. Dressed in a finely tailored silk suit and impeccably groomed, he insisted he was present only in an observational capacity to assess the severity of the offense and ensure that his citizen's territorial rights were protected. But even if his gunmetal gray suit did blend in with the steel desk and institutional walls, the red emblem on his lapel was glaringly obvious. A band of seventeen gold stars embroidered as a halo above it signaled his position in the hierarchy. There were seventeen archbishops on the Council. This made him the second highest-ranking official in the territory. *Pretty impressive representation for an overprivileged brat like Pete*, Deacon thought.

The archbishop remained stoic as the attorney put on a show. Carter brought along two junior assistants from the law firm of Upshaw, Brigham and Curtis, one of Atlanta's biggest and most prestigious firms. They stood off to one side and quietly watched as Mr. Carter attempted to intimidate Deacon into immediately releasing his clients. Deacon remained attentive, quiet and respectfully composed, sipping coffee from a steel tumbler while the man made his speech.

"The level of disrespect my clients have been shown is reprehensible, Lieutenant. These boys were visiting this region in good faith and with all the necessary visas and identification. They have cooperated with law enforcement at every opportunity from the moment they discovered that poor woman's remains. They have been decent and polite and forthcoming as good citizens and witnesses to a horrific crime scene. Yet they have been treated like common criminals, arrested and dragged into this station like garbage and subjected to inhumane conditions that show the utter contempt this institution has for the E-States and its citizenry."

Deacon set down his coffee, favored the man and his client with the greatest concern, and exclaimed, "My apologies, Mr. Carter. Were the accommodations and coffee not to your clients' liking? Perhaps we could arrange a good French roast and some beignets to make them feel more comfortable."

Behind the one-way mirror in the adjacent room, Joyce snickered at the remark. She always admired the way Deacon could find just the perfect turn of polite phrasing to tell someone to go fuck themselves. The director was not as amused and shot her a very irritated look. His eyes were trained directly on the archbishop, and he could see the man composing a vitriolic letter to DC about his team's handling of the case.

"Sheriff Markham happens to be one of the finest officers in the state of Georgia with several commendations for service to his credit!" Carter thundered. "He offered you his officers' complete support and conducted himself as a true professional despite your Neanderthal professional courtesy and bullying of these witnesses. I don't know how they do things here in the Federal Corridor, Lt. MacNair, but we are not in the practice of jailing witnesses to a crime who are doing their civic duty."

Deacon drained his tumbler and set it down rather loudly on the steel table, causing it to ring. He'd allowed this performance to continue as far as he could stomach. Carter and the boy jumped slightly, but the archbishop only turned his head directly to where Deacon sat. Joyce whispered to the director, "You might want to start taking notes, sir. This is where the shit gets interesting."

"Mr. Carter," Deacon announced, "please accept our deepest thanks to all three of your clients. We truly do appreciate their willingness to help us find the person who murdered one of your citizens in our territory. The information they provide will no doubt lead us to a swift and positive resolution to this horrific crime." He said this with the utmost sincerity, and then his voice took on a razor's edge. "What we do not appreciate is your clients crossing our borders and violating laws that put our citizenry at risk. Your clients were far beyond the legal limits of being intoxicated and high while operating a vessel at high speeds, which endangered other citizens on the lake."

There had been no other citizens on the lake that day except for the unidentified killer, but Deacon didn't elaborate. It was enough to point out the specifics of the law to get the lawyer's attention.

"The vessels in question were impounded as the law requires, and subsequent resonance scanning of both uncovered a substantial quantity of illegal and dangerous drugs hidden within the interior. That constitutes interterritorial trafficking and violation of federal law under the jurisdiction of Homeland Security and the DEA."

Deacon pulled out an evidence pad and slid it across the table to the attorney as Pete Milton's face went completely white. When the attorney finished reading it, the archbishop held out his hand without a word and Carter handed it to him.

Deacon cast a glance toward where the archbishop sat reading and lowered his tone. "In accordance with treaty discovery laws, a warrant has been issued for DNA and substance testing for all three of your citizens, to be conducted immediately and, of course, in your presence to assure that the tests are conducted and sealed by you as legally allowed." He then turned back to Carter. "As for the esteemed Sheriff Markham, if I truly wished to be the unprofessional barbarian you purport me to be, I would have Markham here in handcuffs as we speak. He was operating outside of his jurisdiction, failed to secure an obvious crime scene, and allowed his deputies to walk all over said scene, possibly contaminating any evidence that would help us find the killer. And he chose to use his exceptional skills to coordinate and fine-tune the statements of the only witnesses to this crime that we have, thereby obstructing a federal investigation. Had he done even the minimal amount that his sworn duty required, he would have identified the victim as one of your own citizens and afforded her the respect and dignity of shielding her naked body from a bunch of onlookers and news reporters instead of covering his own useless, redneck ass."

Carter's two associates melted into the walls as Deacon checked their boss. From behind the glass, the director cringed and shook his head with every word. Deacon was renowned for his utterly contemptuous turn of phrase when it came to dealing with lawyers and politicians, but he could have toned it down a notch. There was, after all, an archbishop present. Still, this was an interrogation and not a policy meeting, and Deacon definitely owned the room. It was worth catching hell from DC if this went his way. Joyce just smiled. She loved watching the dance, and with Deacon leading the floor, it was always a heart-stopping performance.

Deacon turned to the archbishop as he concluded reading the warrant and addressed him most respectfully and quietly. "Your Excellency, I assume the warrants are acceptable and in proper form, as was the certification of chain of evidence."

"Quite properly executed, Lieutenant," Wirz said closing his eyes.

"Then may we proceed with the testing, as indicated?" Deacon asked.

Wirz nodded, but Pete Milton suddenly found his voice. "This is complete bullshit!" the boy thundered. "If there are drugs on that boat, you planted them there to frame me." He pointed his finger at Deacon and hissed, "You're just pissed because you can't touch me. Do you know who my father is, boy?"

"Silence, you irreverent fool!" Wirz hissed loudly. He then turned to Deacon and asked, "Lieutenant, would you please allow me the opportunity to confer with Mr. Carter and Mr. Milton privately? I believe there are certain aspects of this situation that Mr. Milton needs to be educated on."

Deacon nodded politely and said, "Of course, Your Excellency. Just contact us when you're ready to proceed." He gestured graciously to the intercom embedded in the table and left. Joining Joyce and the director in the observation room, he plopped down into a chair and threw his feet up on the window ledge to watch. The director stood with his arms crossed, staring down at his officer. "Something on your mind, John?" Deacon asked.

"Just wondering how far up shit creek you intend to paddle this boat," he replied.

Deacon grinned and said, "To the falls of Hell itself! Relax, John. Sit here and watch the show. I promise it'll be worth it." He looked around and then muttered, "Dammit, left my damned coffee mug in the room."

John poured three cups from the sideboard, then handed one to Joyce in passing and the other to Deacon as he sat down. She looked into the cup. "You know, studies have shown only psychopaths drink their coffee black," she said, walking over to the cream and sugar.

The two men laughed. John informed her, "You have to be a psychopath to do this job, sister." He raised his cup and clinked it to Deacon's as he muttered, "A hundred bucks says we have her taking it straight by her fifth anniversary."

Deacon smiled and turned back to watch the spectacle in the other room. Although the sound was muted as required by client privilege, Deacon had no trouble narrating the events. Pete Milton was waving his hands wildly and shaking his fingers at both his attorney and the archbishop. Carter was trying desperately to interject, which obviously wasn't going well. "What you are witnessing," Deacon explained, "is the explanation of just how far up the aforementioned shit creek young Master Milton is at this juncture. Chain of evidence was attested to and confirmed, so there's no doubt that the drugs were in the boat before we impounded it. So that little outburst amounted to bearing false witness against a peace officer. That's a one-year sentence at best for perjury to us. In E-Rep terms, that's a violation of the Ninth Commandment." A trace of loud, barely intelligible voices caused the thick glass to shake, indicating that tempers had reached a level that exceeded the soundproofing. "Trafficking in illegal substances between the territories carries a minimum ten-year sentence in federal prison for first-time offenders with three years off for good behavior. As far as the archbishop is concerned, there's no exact commandment or passage in the Bible that deals with drug use because pharmaceuticals weren't around back then. But there are a few distinct passages that can be liberally applied here."

"Like what?" Joyce asked him.

"'Or do you not know that your body is a temple of the Holy Spirit within you, whom you have from God? You are not your own, for you were bought with a price. So, glorify God in your body.' Corinthians 6:19. Basically, when you abuse your body, you abuse God." He took a generous sip of his coffee. "And if that doesn't sober you up, you can always count on Galatians to bring the point home: 'Now the works of the flesh are evident: sexual immorality, impurity, sensuality, idolatry, sorcery, enmity, strife, jealousy, fits of anger, rivalries, dissensions, divisions, envy, drunkenness, orgies, and things like these. I warn you, as I warned you before, that those who do such things will not inherit the kingdom of God.'"

"How the hell do you know all that? I never pegged you for a Bible-thumper, MacNair," she asked.

"Baptist, born and raised," Deacon said. "I know how these people think. Combine debauchery through drugs, rape under the influence, and the selling of them to corrupt the innocent with one of the big ten, and that little motherfucker is pretty much fried when they haul his ass home."

"You don't think Daddy will pull him out of the fire?" Joyce asked.

Deacon pointed to the glass behind which the archbishop had just forced Pete Milton to sit down and shut up. The man was dictating what few choices the boy had and was clearly enraged. His voice remained pitched at a level undiscernible to the officers, but as he talked, his face darkened to a plum while Milton's got whiter. "Our witness has just been informed that Daddy's ass is currently on the line depending on how this goes. If he saves his son, his career is over and his reputation ruined. He'll be removed from E-State leadership and excommunicated along with his family, which means instant poverty. There goes the ridiculous annual salary and expensive lifestyle, and he'll never serve in public office again. Not to mention that he will most likely have to relocate to federal territory to save his own skin. And that is something no red-blooded southern politician will allow to happen without a fight to the death. On the other hand, if sonny boy chooses to face federal justice and not return to the Ecumenical Council for judgment, Daddy would be able to disavow his son and be spared any public embarrassment while privately doing a shitload of penance for the Council. Daddy pays a stiff fine and does some serious atonement but loses no amenities or power, and Junior can probably deal his way down to a lighter sentence with some sincere and unrestricted cooperation with this investigation. In any case, Junior is about to be disinherited."

The noises stopped and all the parties on the other side of the glass suddenly sat down. Seconds later, the archbishop pressed the intercom buzzer. Deacon downed the last of his coffee, stood up and proclaimed, "And that, my friends, means it's time to play Let's Make a Deal."

"Son of a bitch," John muttered as Deacon walked out with Joyce in tow. "Should I fire up the defibrillator in case the monsignor needs help?"

"Archbishop, John, archbishop. A monsignor's just a priest with an Eagle Scout badge. In any case, I think we'll be fine without it." He turned to Joyce and said, "Better grab Chen and have her bring the test kit and an officer. I doubt we'll need muscle, but our negotiations will be much more persuasive that way."

Deacon approached the interview room and then paused, waiting for Joyce and Agnes to return from the lab with a rather impressive-looking rookie. When they arrived, he politely knocked on the door and waited for approval from within. "Wouldn't want to behave like an unprofessional Neanderthal," he whispered to the two women.

Pete Milton sat completely subdued and chastised, as did his attorney and the two junior assistants. The archbishop had resumed his place at the head of the table, but it was clear there had been a significant shift in power. The clergy was now calling the shots.

Carter waited until the archbishop nodded to him and then laid out their proposal. "Mr. Milton has decided to waive his right to extradition and remain in federal custody." *Strike one*, Deacon thought. "He has also agreed to accept full responsibility for the contents of the vessels and the implications thereof in exchange for the dropping of all pending charges against his boat mates, Mr. Parker Kane and Mr. Michael Bledsoe." *Strike two.* "In exchange for his compliance, he has agreed to cooperate fully with the investigation and answer any questions you may have in exchange for lesser charges of possession rather than intent to distribute." Deacon raised an eyebrow and waited for Carter to continue. "I think we can all agree that this would be in the best interests of all parties involved."

Deacon smiled and said, "Well, that is a very generous offer, considering that we already have Mr. Milton in federal custody, that we are under no obligation to extradite him whatsoever, and that so far he has offered absolutely nothing in the way of assistance to this case."

Carter bristled a bit but only looked toward the archbishop. The clergyman cast a glance toward Pete, who straightened up and said, "I got a good look at the vehicle that dumped her, and I think I can help identify the driver."

"And you were unwilling to share this information previously because . . ." Deacon asked.

When Pete didn't answer, the archbishop calmly said, "I'm sure, Lt. MacNair, that by now you are well aware of the association of this young man to one High Senator Wallace Milton of the Georgia Electorate, and you no doubt know that his involvement in any way with a homicide would reflect unfairly upon Senator Milton's current election campaign and his involvement with international peace negotiations underway in Botswana." He dropped his slightly cordial smile and cast a hard glance toward Pete. "Not to mention what such enforcement of the aforementioned charges would mean should young Mr. Milton return to face justice in his own state." Pete's tan visibly faded under that frigid gaze. "It would put the Council in a very delicate position. Thus, it would be far more advantageous to all parties involved for young Mr. Milton to atone for his sins among those he hath sinned against."

"And it would save Senator Milton the embarrassment of having to present his rebellious son to the Ecumenical Council for judgment," Deacon said to the archbishop. "We all know how that story ends, don't we, Your Excellency?"

The archbishop's smile returned with all the warmth of a hungry python. He'd clearly underestimated the detective's experience with canon law. "Then we are in agreement?"

"I believe so," Deacon answered. "Provided that the information Mr. Milton does give us is verifiable, valid and independently corroborated by Mr. Kane and Mr. Bledsoe."

Carter was about to say something, but an icy look from the archbishop shut him down completely. The clergyman rose and offered his hand to Deacon, who shook it, noting that it remained dry and cold as a corpse. "Thank you for your cooperation and understanding in this matter, Lieutenant." To Carter he said, "Ensure that these young men cooperate. I'll expect you to report back immediately once this is over." As the archbishop left the room, he gave no notice of Joyce or Agnes and snapped his fingers. His entourage immediately surrounded him, and the group silently left the building.

Agnes came forward and took blood and DNA samples from Pete, then followed Joyce into the adjacent interview rooms to test the other two boys. Carter remained behind to monitor the interview.

"So, tell me what you know," Deacon said, pressing a button embedded in the table, "for the record." A red light began flashing beneath the glass, indicating that all conversations within the room were now being recorded as evidence.

Deacon watched Pete carefully as he detailed everything he and his friends had seen on the lake and how the drugs came to be in his possession. He'd watched the boy's alcohol buzz burn away as Wirz laid out the consequences of extradition. Deacon didn't need to hear what Pete had been told. He knew it all too well. Deuteronomy laid out pretty clearly what the elders were required by law to sentence him to. His only legal alternative was to voluntarily submit to reconditioning and rehabilitation. If the rumors were true, the alternative was worse. His mind began to drift, and he no longer heard Pete's testimony. He looked into the boy's blue eyes. All the privileged bluster had evaporated, leaving only angry resignation to keep him from crying. He'd seen that same look in his own son's eyes the day they took him away.

6

As Pete Milton settled into a detention room for the night awaiting his fate, Daniel Carter paced the lounge of A. M. Memorial Hospital, chewing on an unlit cigarette. A nurse the size of a grizzly watched him with cold eyes from his perch behind the main station. Each time he reached for his lighter, the bear-like caregiver radiated the certainty that if Daniel made any attempt to light it, the man would happily chuck the attorney out of the third-floor window. Daniel despised hospitals. An ironic attitude since he'd spent the first year of his professional career camped out in one. Back then, emergency rooms were a wellspring of litigation: car crash victims, slip and falls, domestic violence, and the obligatory accidental shooting, not to mention all the medical malpractice incidents that occurred on a daily basis. There was no specialty of law he couldn't argue, and he had handled each one with extreme success. Hospital administrators throughout the state tried everything they could over the years to have him banned from their premises. One poor bastard went so far as to introduce legislation that he be declared a public health hazard. But as a lawyer he had the absolute right to confer with his clients at any time of the day or night. And Daniel's clients loved him. He had a reputation for ensuring that, win or lose, no one walked away empty-handed, and he'd lived up to that reputation without exception. He'd once roamed these hallowed medical halls like a god, bleeding them of every cent he could. Those had indeed been the glory days. The war had brought that all to an end.

A sour burst of chemicals spread across his tongue as he bit through the worn skin of his cigarette. He pulled the soggy stick from his mouth and threw it in the trash. Walking up to the grizzled nurse he asked, "How much longer is this going to take?"

The man looked up at him without expression and then quietly answered, "Approximately twenty minutes longer than the last time you asked me that question fifteen minutes ago. Go have a seat and be patient and quit pestering me. I have sick people to attend to." The nurse turned away from Daniel and resumed pecking at the crossword puzzle on his lap-pad.

Sick people my ass, Daniel thought as he trundled back to the coffee machine to pour a fresh cup. The coffee was surprisingly good and the cream fresh, not the instant brew and powdered milk selection found in the public wards downstairs. He settled down on the couch, sipped his coffee, and thanked God he had the room to himself for now. The few people here when he arrived had all been hustled off to greet their newborn additions, speak to doctors about diagnoses or, in the case of one poor woman, been taken to the chapel by a priest. He momentarily considered following her to see if he could pick up a case, but he had bigger fish to fry this night. Malpractice would be chump change compared to what the senator was shelling out. He glanced over to the trash can where his broken cigarette had been tossed. Good coffee required good tobacco. He thought about pulling out another one, but Smokey the Nurse would probably add more wait time to the testing if he did. Instead, he closed his eyes and tried to imagine the taste of the fine Cuban cigars stashed in his library desk. He'd acquired the habit from his mentor, a fat, salt-and-pepper son of the South named Maynard Guthrie. The man relished fine cigars in addition to mint juleps, well-aged bourbon, linen suits and mechanical watch fobs, all affectations of a time no one had lived in but everyone craved.

"The law," which Maynard intentionally pronounced as *law-uh*, "is the battlefield on which the South continues to fight the war against Northern aggression to this very day." Maynard held to the notion that the South had never actually surrendered at Appomattox and that Robert E. Lee had been tortured into it. "It is a duel to the death between two mighty gentlemen that hold the future of this great nation in their hands. Only the righteous man may prevail."

Maynard loved to lecture Daniel with his musings on the practice of law as a sport of kings. Lawyers, he declared, were the very embodiment of God upon this earth. That it was the duty of such men to do His work and guide the human race toward divinity through the law. His gentlemanly persona was fueled by his open scorn of liberal attorneys who filed civil rights cases so heathens could indulge their perversions. And he loathed female attorneys. They were an affront to the divine masculinity of his profession. All of it an homage to those good old country values that centuries earlier made the South what it was. The reality was that Maynard Guthrie was simply a misogynistic asshole with an ego wider than his midriff. He routinely hit on his female coworkers, refused to engage any woman higher than a legal secretary, and regarded his more ethnically blended employees as examples of his charity toward the underprivileged. But old man Guthrie had the gift of a world-class shyster. It was a testament to his oratory skills that he hadn't been disbarred or jailed at least a dozen times over. Daniel couldn't believe that someone hadn't put a bullet in him yet or sued him into poverty for sexual harassment, but the old man had stayed clean, a skill that Daniel desperately wanted to learn.

A commotion at the end of the hall startled him from a light doze. Peeking out around the doorway, he could see that Smokey the Nurse was fully immersed in defusing an argument and fully engaged in keeping the two parties separated. Daniel made his way quietly to the nurses' station and typed in the names of his two clients. Both came up immediately. Their exams and tests were not only complete, but the reports had been finalized for more than an hour. He jotted down the room number and glanced down the hall. As he left, he snatched Smokey's coffee cup and dumped the contents across the man's abandoned lap-pad. *Spell that, ya hairy bastard*, he thought as it sizzled and popped.

Ten minutes later, Daniel had both Parker Kane and Michael Bledsoe loaded into a limousine for the trip back to Atlanta. The transport had been supplied by the Ecumenical Council, which meant that anything said within the vehicle would be recorded and immediately conveyed. Illegal in the extreme, but if you wanted to represent the big dogs, you had to play by their rules. Kane and Bledsoe chattered on about defying the morality laws and getting away with it thanks to their parents' money until Daniel pointed to the bright red E-Council star on the upholstery. It took them a moment, but they piped down and allowed Daniel to read the exam and toxicology reports in peace. They had been administered and prepared by a Dr. Elli Hollister. He wondered if she were somehow related to Senator Quentin Hollister. Seemed everyone in the South was related to someone in the Council these days. He flipped to the end of the report and glanced over at his clients. *God, these kids are morons*, he thought, perfect examples of one of Maynard Guthrie's more colorful Rules for Representing Rubes: the richer the tree, the dumber the fruit. These two could keep him in legal fees long enough for his own kids to get through college in the north—if they both lived long enough that is.

The electric engine of the limo gave off a white-noise hum as they traveled, eventually lulling his clients to sleep. Considering the drug and alcohol levels in their blood, they should have been unconscious hours earlier. Daniel watched them with a stab of pity. The Council would no doubt have received the police test results by now. With this independent confirmation, Daniel knew their pain was only beginning. They were going to regret allowing their friend to take the rap and remain in federal custody, where it was safe. Pete knew it too, which was why he'd stayed put. Dawn was still a couple of hours away when they pulled up at the Bledsoe house. The Kanes were there as well, each family giving the other support. They posed all kinds of questions, but Carter was in no mood to deal with emotional parents, especially with one of three state senators' sons facing federal prison. He instructed them to keep the boys on lockdown in their own homes: no phone calls, social media, FaceTime, or visitors, and no one was to answer any questions whatsoever without his direct and explicit consent. They thanked him for his help, and Carter instructed the driver to take him home.

7

Sunday morning, the lab tests had confirmed what Deacon expected: copious amounts of alcohol and drugs. Milton had already admitted that the hidden pot was for later when they'd planned to hook up with a group of local girls from A&M University. He didn't elaborate on whether those girls knew what the weed had been laced with, but Deacon surmised the young ladies had narrowly escaped a night of dancing and date rape. Milton seemed to be the type of privileged asshole for whom consent was an unknown concept. He made his statement, which turned out to be substantial. The story was reexamined and repeated for most of the night and never wavered. His two buddies had been more than happy to talk last night, especially after an awesome meal of pulled pork sandwiches and sweet tea, courtesy of Agnes. They corroborated everything Pete reported and were released into Mr. Carter's custody with the admonition that they were still legally bound to cooperate fully for the duration of the case.

Pete was facing at least seven hard years for possession, considering the type of drugs he'd been hauling, but he knew federal prison was a cake walk compared to what the Council would do to him. Even if his father did somehow gain clemency, Dad was sure to make his life a hell on earth. The drugs in question, along with some seriously hefty diamonds, had been payment to his father from a very wealthy Botswana mine executive in exchange for a series of falsified diplomatic visas. Deacon had managed to squeeze that information out of him as well. There was nothing he could do with it since it was outside his jurisdiction, but he carefully stored the information away for future use. Information was always handy, especially when one needed a favor from another agency. Deacon had Pete moved to a more comfortable and private holding area for drunken VIP's and fed as generously as his friends had been. It would be the last decent meal the kid would enjoy for a long time. He slept the rest of the night warm and cozy and was transferred to formal booking when he woke.

The victim's husband arrived as Deacon briefed the director, so Joyce had him escorted to the viewing room. Deacon was more than happy to let her take the lead with this interview. He'd notified several soldiers' next of kin during the war and had no talent for it. But nothing got information out of a distraught husband quicker than a pretty woman, and Joyce fit the bill perfectly. She was blessed with an admirable bosom and curvy hips to go with her quiet demeanor. People often underestimated her because of her exotic good looks, much to their disadvantage, and she had no reservations about using what God gave her to get that information.

The morgue waiting room was as comfortable as a room could possibly be. Couches upholstered in a smooth cloth and stuffed to exemplary comfort sat around small coffee tables. Soft lighting gave the room a warm glow to detract from the harsh light of the corridors. And set into one wall was a massive window darkened to disguise the receiving room beyond. It was into that room that the bodies would be placed and tastefully covered until the family member was ready to provide the identification. The waiting room itself was heavily soundproofed to keep the wailing of relatives from floating through the facility, and an exit door to a separate hallway was provided for the bereaved to depart in privacy without the gawking stares of strangers or onslaught of the press. Its final emergence point was a closely guarded secret and, thanks to the original purpose of the facility, easily hidden.

Allen Bainbridge sat in the waiting room with a fresh pot of coffee. He was still numb from the phone call he'd received about Ellory, but the coffee helped. He hadn't told the children yet. He hadn't even told her parents, who were keeping the kids amused back in Atlanta. All he'd told them was that there had been an accident and he had to go tend to Ellory. He would call them as soon as he knew her condition. They were not to say anything to the children other than Daddy had to go help Mommy and would be back in time to tuck them in. The authorities hadn't told him much, only that Ellory's body had been found in a nearby lake the day before and they needed him to positively identify her. When he'd asked if his wife had drowned, he was told the investigating officers would provide him with the details. Thus, here he sat on a bright Saturday morning, in a quaint and comfortable room, listening to Muzak and waiting to see his wife's dead body.

Joyce entered the waiting room and greeted Allen. He shook her hand with all the manners of a proper southern gentleman, well-dressed in khakis and boots. Tall, with bright blue eyes and a lean but well-muscled build. His hair was a bit long, but he wore it impeccably trimmed and styled. A hint of very expensive cologne tickled her senses. His appearance was warm and inviting yet she still felt an icy draft as she introduced herself.

"I'm Det. Joyce Bachman, Mr. Bainbridge. I was one of the officers on scene when we retrieved your wife. Please accept my sincerest condolences for your loss."

"Thank you, Detective, but no one has told me anything about what happened to my wife. I'd appreciate some information."

Joyce sensed none of the usual frustration felt by spouses brought in on minimal information. Anger was a common reaction for them. But there was something in his casual attitude that seemed inconsistent. "Let's be positive that this woman is your wife before we go any further. I'll be happy to discuss the information we have after her identity is confirmed." She suspected that he knew a visual ID was merely a formality as any DNA sampling and fingerprints taken would positively identify her.

He nodded and Joyce pressed a buzzer on the wall. A light inside the holding room went on and the viewing window brightened. The body was covered, and an attendant stood by waiting for word to begin. Joyce nodded and the man pulled the sheet back from the body down to the shoulders. As Bainbridge stared at the body, Joyce observed him quietly. He breathed deeply to maintain his composure and whispered something unintelligible while staring blankly at her corpse. He showed no emotion whatsoever. There were no tears in his eyes, and his voice was steady as a rock when he said, "Yes, that's Ellory. That's my wife."

She signaled to the attendant, who covered the body as he darkened the viewing window. Waving Bainbridge back to the couch, she watched him carefully as he sat down and rested his elbows on his thighs. Still he showed no signs of shock or grief.

"Will you please now tell me what happened?"

"Your wife's body was found at the old Cobb Quarry Lake in Gadsden. A group of boaters found her and notified the authorities. We are investigating her death as a homicide due to her injuries."

"What were they?" he asked calmly.

"Preliminary investigation hasn't provided a cause of death at this time, but she appears to have been beaten severely. We haven't ascertained the motive yet. Could you tell me why your wife was in federal territory?"

"She was supposed to be visiting her sister Kate up in Jackson, Tennessee. She runs a women's health center there. Ellory drove out three days ago, said she'd call when she arrived. That was the last time I spoke with her."

"What type of car was she driving?" Joyce asked.

"Her own vehicle, a light gray Chevy Constellation."

Joyce made the notation and sent it back to Chen. She then crossed her knees seductively and asked, "Mr. Bainbridge, it's only half a day's drive at best from Atlanta to Jackson. Did you make any effort to contact your wife or her sister when she didn't call?"

He looked up and said, "No. Kate and I don't exactly see eye to eye, so I avoid causing friction as much as possible, for Ellory's sake. Kate gets pretty irritated when I call, so I just wait for Ellory to call me when she's alone. That way her visit doesn't get ruined."

Joyce waited for him to elaborate, but he merely stared blankly at the coffee cup on the table. When he did speak, he asked, "When will I be able to collect my wife? I need to make funeral arrangements."

"Unfortunately, the investigation is just getting started. We'll need significantly more time with her if we're going to catch her killer."

"Does that really matter?" he asked. "It won't change anything, and it won't bring her back. My children will still have to grow up without their mother."

Joyce was stunned by the question. Usually people demanded the police do everything they could to find and punish the perpetrator; they even volunteered suspects half the time. This was definitely a first for her—a spouse that didn't care if his wife's killer was identified and caught. She flagged Allen Bainbridge's file as a person of interest on her ident-pad and informed him, "It's very important, Mr. Bainbridge. We have to make sure this killer doesn't hurt someone else or tear apart other families. I'm sure you can understand that."

He dropped his unusually dry eyes and then nodded in agreement. "Yes, of course, you're right. This monster should be caught and stopped before anyone else gets hurt." He stood up, indicating that the interview was over, and then said, "If I can think of anything that would help, I'll be sure to contact you immediately, Detective."

That was usually Joyce's line to the bereaved. *He's done this before*, she thought. "We'd appreciate that, sir," Joyce told him. "Please don't hesitate to call at any time, day or night, even if you think what you know is insignificant. Let us be the judge of what's important."

As he turned to leave, she moved in closely and grasped his hand in both of hers, placing her index finger discreetly against the pulse of his right wrist. He didn't pull back. He obviously had no trouble getting close to a woman other than his wife. His palm was perfectly dry, not an ounce of sweat, and his pulse was slow and steady. No sign of stress or agitation whatsoever. "We'll call you just as soon as we have a definitive release date for you. Again, please accept my condolences for your family's loss," she purred and gestured to the door opposite to the one he entered through.

He nodded, gave her a slight smile, and entered the corridor that would take him to the underground exit on the opposite side of the old gantry. When the door closed behind him, Joyce went to the observation room at the end of the hall. Every entrance and exit was monitored and recorded at all times, and she quickly pulled up the tunnels, looking for Bainbridge. He waited for the underground tram to take him to the visitor's parking lot and boarded it quietly when it arrived. He emerged from the tunnels and walked calmly to his vehicle, started it and drove off. At no time did he hesitate or make any attempt to contact anyone. The wireless signals emitted by his car were never activated. He simply left as if nothing ever happened.

The Discipline of the Almighty

1

The body lay on the autopsy table. Bathed in the clear, bright light of the overhead panels, the extensive bruising took on an ethereal glow. Digger found the sight beautiful, as if an angel had landed in his arms. People never understood the beauty that could be found in a dead body, one devoid of emotion or pain, a person at peace as they had never been in life. It was exquisite. Even more exquisite were the tales they could tell. And this young lady had an incredible tale to tell indeed. He adjusted the lighting so that the glow would dissipate, bringing the body into full relief and the bruising into stark patches. The bones protruding at odd angles within her limbs indicated that she'd been struck repeatedly, causing the bone below to splinter. Digger had once helped recover several victims from a steep rockslide in Chile who had similar wounds, but the precision of the breaks troubled him.

Digger left the girl on the autopsy bed and went into the control room to begin the intense scans. He calibrated the imagers for deep tissue resonance and waited for the machine to warm up. A large, rectangular panel descended to within six inches of the body and hummed to life. As the lights in the autopsy room dimmed, however, he noticed a strange pattern on the body below that he had not seen while standing right next to it. Halting the sequence, he raised the scanner and activated a remote camera to photograph the body in low light. The pictures revealed a distinct and unmistakable pattern. MacNair had been correct. This young woman had been killed in a most brutal and personal way.

Deacon, Joyce and Chen entered the autopsy theater. Usually the team would spend discovery sessions upstairs in the pit while Burke took center stage over the evidence, but Digger's summons had been urgent. The four of them now stood examining the body as Digger spoke.

"I thought it was a trick of the lighting at first, so I ran the body through at a lower resonance. The bruising is definitely deliberate," he explained as he pointed to the cross-shaped bruises now highly visible on the victim's torso and chest. "The marks were created by an object with a tapered, blunt edge, which appears to have been hammered into her. The killer went across her chest and then came back and worked his way down from her throat to her abdomen. He basically tooled her like a piece of leather."

"You're assuming the killer is male," Joyce observed.

"The anger and force it took to do this much damage to the body and the nature of the marks themselves tells me that we are definitely looking for a man."

Joyce looked at the rudimentary cross that had been pounded into the body. "And this is what killed her?" she asked.

"No, these marks were made postmortem. She was already dead or mere minutes from it. Her direct cause of death was blunt force trauma to the back of the head." He rotated the skull so that the indentation was clearly visible. "She sustained a skull fracture and some brain damage, but she didn't die straight away. She lingered for thirty minutes or so. There were traces of limestone in the head wound and it's very jagged, as if someone simply picked up a rock and hit her with it. I'm running an analysis on the traces. Maybe the killer left a DNA trace."

Agnes rubbed her forehead and said, "The body was found in a limestone quarry. There are broken boulders and jagged ledges surrounding that lake. She could have been tossed in and bounced down. That could account for the injuries and broken bones."

"It does if you're assuming this was an accidental injury. There are no other marks or bruises on the victim's head or face." He reached down and lifted the body from the table, exposing the back side with a grunt. "If you look here, there's no bruising on her back at all except from where the blood has pooled postmortem." He gently allowed the body to settle back on to the table. "All of the deep tissue bruising occurs on the front of the body only. If she'd fallen, her face would be indistinguishable and the bruising would be circumferential, not localized."

Agnes bent over to stare at the victim's wrists and ankles. "There don't appear to be any indications that she was tied up. The killer must have hit her from behind and then moved her to wherever he maimed her."

"Actually, the head wound happened after the primary trauma and before the marking, almost as this were a mercy killing. But even if she were conscious, it's doubtful she would have felt anything or even been coherent enough to object. Her husband must have been beside himself with grief, having to lose two family members in such a horrific crime."

"Two?" Deacon asked suddenly.

"Yes, the poor girl was pregnant. Barely six months along, but I imagine they were well on their way to setting up a nursery."

Deacon looked over to Joyce, who only shook her head and said, "Her husband wasn't very upset and never mentioned anything about a baby, never brought it up at all."

"That means he either didn't know about it or wasn't too happy about it, and I'm leaning toward the latter," Deacon told them. "Might explain why he wasn't as grief-stricken as he should have been."

Agnes scrolled through the toxicology reports and then asked, "Was she drugged?"

"Heavily," Digger told her. "But that isn't the really interesting aspect of it." He sent the toxicology test results to the overhead monitors. "She ingested a very bizarre alcohol concoction. I couldn't trace it to any commercially known or collectible wine anywhere. It appears to be a homemade brew composed of water, grapes and active yeast sweetened with raw sugar but with none of the usual fruits, flowers, or buttery notes that normally constitute a wine variety. It's like it was completely homemade. Of course, it would take months for something like this to actually ferment."

"That would indicate premeditation," Deacon offered.

"Guess the locals have given up on moonshine and bathtub gin and converted over to sacramental wine," Digger answered with a smirk.

"Why would a killer take months fermenting a homemade wine and pumping her full of controlled prescription drugs when he could just as easily have dosed her whiskey with Rohypnol?"

"Probably for the same reason he rubbed her torso down with frankincense oil," Digger told them. "It's reputed to have calming and healing effects on the nervous system, but given what was done to her, I can't imagine that being the purpose."

"Because she wouldn't have drunk it," Joyce told them. "Not with a baby on the way. That's why he used the low-yield wine. He diluted it with water and added sugar to make it taste more like grape juice."

"My God," Agnes whispered as she stared at Ellory's pale face. "Why would someone do this because of a baby?"

"That, ladies and gentlemen, is what we need to find out," Deacon told them. "Let's get back to work, people."

2

The cruiser rounded the corner and crept slowly down the street. It was a nice suburban community designed as most middle-income federal housing tracts were. They catered to government workers and contractors that made up the civilian workforce keeping the Corridor running. Rows of townhomes surrounded by regimented, repeating landscaping indicated which community you were in. The Tuscany tract was bordered with identical Italian cypress trees. Magnolia Woods was peppered with southern magnolias. Willowbrook slept under—what else—willow trees. The tract they were looking for was called Brookside, a planned community with a prefabricated brook that wound its way through the residences.

They finally found it just past Pine Bluffs, a community that bore a striking resemblance to a Christmas tree farm with little gingerbread-style houses and reindeer trails. There was indeed a brook running through Brookside. It flowed over carefully placed faux rocks and waterlilies along the main sidewalk and cascaded gently over a sculpted waterfall at the entrance, right before it disappeared into a sewer. Deacon didn't want to think about what microorganisms might inhabit that prefab river.

Joyce pulled up a description of Kate Buxton, the victim's sister, and located her address. They parked nearby and walked back toward the unit. As they approached, a man and woman came out the front door. The woman matched Kate Buxton's description, and she was very agitated. The young man with her was pissed and waved his arms in the air as he spoke. Kate did her best to console him, but he only seemed to become more upset. In the end, he threw his arms in the air and turned to leave. She stopped him, laid a hand on his cheek, and hugged him close before letting him leave. He walked dejectedly down the street as Kate returned to her unit.

Deacon and Joyce caught up with her just as she opened her door. "Kate Buxton?" Deacon inquired.

"Yes," she responded as Deacon showed her his badge.

"I'm Lt. MacNair, and this is my partner, Det. Bachman. We need to speak with you."

Kate rolled her eyes and motioned for them to follow her inside. She led them into the kitchen, where she resumed putting away groceries as she spoke. "Look, I already gave a statement down at the center. The whole thing was a prank. Just a bomb threat called in by a bitter ex-boyfriend of one our patients."

"We're not here about a bomb threat, Miss Buxton. We're here about your sister," Deacon explained.

Kate reached into the cupboard and removed three mugs. "Have a seat," she told them. "I'll put some coffee on, but I have to tell you, sending two detectives out here over a few transterritorial speeding tickets is overkill."

Deacon and Joyce looked at each other, and then Joyce said quietly, "I'm sorry, Miss Buxton, but I'm afraid your sister is dead."

Kate froze over the sink with the mug in her hand as Joyce explained the circumstances of her sister's murder. Staring into the steel sink, hands trembling, she asked in a broken whisper, "When did this happen?"

"About four days ago," Joyce answered.

Kate threw the mug into the sink, where it shattered, then hugged herself tightly to keep from shaking. "You're sure it's Ellory?" she asked. "I mean, I suppose you need me to come down and confirm the body is hers."

"That won't be necessary," Joyce offered. "Her husband identified her the morning after she was found."

"What?" Kate demanded as she spun from the sink. Her face was covered with tears, but her expression was one of intense anger.

"I'm sorry, has no one contacted you regarding this?" Deacon asked.

She squeezed her eyes shut as she shook her head. "No," she answered. "Not that the bastard would ever have told me." She looked Deacon in the eye and said, "I warned her over and over to be careful. I did everything I could to protect her, but he must have found out."

"Found out what?" Deacon asked.

Kate turned to the refrigerator and opened the door. Reaching into one of the storage bins, she retrieved a vial filled with red liquid and bearing a hospital laboratory label. She handed it to him. The vial was a blood sample for one Ellory Bainbridge, and it was labeled "pregnancy positive."

"Ellory was trying to hide her pregnancy from her husband? Why?"

"Because it wasn't his," Kate told them.

The coffeemaker beeped, and Joyce waved Kate over to the living room. "Why don't we take this discussion into the living room? I'll bring the coffee."

Deacon led Kate to the couch and sat her down. When Joyce brought the coffee, he told her, "Perhaps you should start at the beginning, Kate, and tell us everything you know about your sister's affair. It may be crucial to identifying her killer."

"You don't think Allen did it?" she asked sarcastically. "I'm not surprised. He's not the type to do the dirty work himself. He's more of an emotional abuser, and he's extremely good at it."

"Is that why she was having the affair?" Joyce asked.

"Yes," she answered.

"Why didn't she just divorce him if she was unhappy?"

Kate gave a sad laugh. "Women don't get divorced in the Ecclesiastical Republic, Ms. Bachman, especially not for adultery. They'd be subject to the death penalty. According to the Bible, women who commit adultery are to be stoned to death. Of course, the Council has much more humane methods of murdering its citizens, but the result is the same."

"You mean reconditioning," Deacon said, watching Kate's face lose some of its color.

"Is that the politically correct term for neurological torture these days?" she sneered.

Deacon took a deep drink from his coffee cup and then looked at Kate. "You sound like a Constitutionalist, Miss Buxton, not a country girl from Georgia. In fact, you maintain dual citizenship between the territories and work here in the Corridor."

"I work at the Women's Center because it's important work and I believe in it."

"Then why didn't you just request amnesty and become a Constitutional citizen?"

She set down her cup. "Are you familiar with the history of the first Civil War, Detective?" Deacon nodded. "Whole families were torn apart by ideological and political beliefs. Families were forced to kill their own, and lifelong friendships were destroyed. It was the worst disaster in the history of this country. It split us apart, and we swore it would never happen again. Then the Second Civil War came along and the whole mess started up once more. Only this time, it was about something a lot more personal than states' rights and more invasive than slavery. People were being forced to choose between their faith and their country by legislators who didn't care about either. I chose not to make that choice."

Deacon looked at her quizzically and then asked, "And just exactly how did you manage to avoid declaring your loyalty? The Ecclesiastical Republic doesn't tolerate dissidents."

"I didn't avoid it. I just sort of sidestepped it. I love my family, Detective. And I would never do anything to destroy them. Requesting asylum would mean me abandoning my sister and bringing public shame to my whole family. So I remained a loyal citizen of the territory and instead became a missionary." Deacon and Joyce sat stunned. "As far as the E-States are concerned, I have dual citizenship that allows me to take the word of God to the Federal Corridor and provide adoption services as an alternative for women who want to kill their children. It's a win-win for everyone. I practice my faith, my family has a daughter they can be proud of, and I don't have to live under a barbaric system that subjugates women and minorities like property."

"Brilliant, I must admit," Deacon told her. "But you do work in a facility that provides abortions. That has to have created some tensions between you and your federal workmates."

"I don't approve of the procedure, Detective, and would never do it myself, but I stand by a woman's right to choose her own future. God gave us all free will, so I'm the one person who won't judge them no matter what choice they make. I offer them alternatives and educate them on what faith mandates, but I never threaten or pressure them. I'm here to support their decisions either way." Her face hardened slightly as she crossed her arms and muttered, "Considering the state of most foster homes and state-run war-orphan registries in this country, I sometimes wonder if the aborted kids aren't the lucky ones. I've said many a prayer for their souls over the years. Lately I've wondered if I'm praying for the wrong ones."

Deacon looked at her appreciatively and said, "It's fairly obvious why Ellory came to you for help."

"I was the only one she could come to. She didn't have anyone else who understood what she was going through."

"Perhaps you could elaborate on that a bit more," Joyce asked.

Kate grew uncomfortable but then told her, "Ellory fell in love with Allen practically at first sight, but I always thought he was a bit too perfect, too much of a Prince Charming. My parents adored him, but I don't trust a man without a dark side, and I especially don't trust a man who hides the one he has. He did the whole proper courtship thing—asked my father for permission to date her and then to marry her. They had a beautiful wedding with half the county in attendance. The first two years of marriage seemed idyllic, and Ellory was perfectly happy, so I just swallowed my concerns and was happy for her. Then she got pregnant. That's when everything changed. Allen started to treat her like a prisoner. We barely even saw each other. She made it through the first one, but then when she got pregnant again a year later, she called me and said she didn't know if she could go through it again. I went to see her, and when I got there, she was arguing with Allen. She hadn't asked his permission to go out with me, and he was furious. He slapped her hard enough to leave his handprint on her face, and it wasn't the first time. When I confronted him about it, he said it was his right as her husband to discipline his wife and I had no right to interfere."

"Is that why you and he don't get along anymore?" Joyce asked.

"We don't get along because the last time he raised a hand to her in front of me, I broke his perfect jaw with a right hook and told him it was my right as her sister to defend her from brutality. He never laid a hand on her again. Unfortunately, he found a more insidious means of abusing her."

"Emotional blackmail?" Deacon asked.

"Of the worst kind," she answered. "He knew Ellory was faithful but threatened to turn her in to the Council as an adulterer. She lived with that fear for seven long years. She knew she would be presumed guilty on Allen's word alone. Then she found someone who loved her and could help her and her children get away from Allen for good."

"Was that the young man we saw you speaking with earlier?" Joyce asked.

"Yes. His name is Avi Simmons. He's a doctor at the clinic. They met when Ellory came to visit. She was having some female issues and was considering sterilization. Avi treated her and talked her out of doing anything permanent. He was supposed to meet with her the day she disappeared so they could plan her escape. He hadn't heard from her and was really upset. He thought Allen might have found out and wanted to go down there and take her, but I talked him out of it. I told him I'd go and find her for him." She paused and looked at the small picture of her and Ellory that sat on the shelf nearby. "How am I going to tell him that she's dead, that his child is dead?" Kate gave in to the tears her anger had held back and broke down.

Deacon and Joyce looked at each other and then said, "We would appreciate it if you left it to us to inform Mr. Simmons of the situation, Miss Buxton," Deacon told her. "His involvement with your sister makes him a person of interest in this case. If you speak to him, you could hurt any efforts to eliminate him as a suspect and make it impossible for us to prosecute Ellory's husband."

Kate nodded, but Joyce could tell it was eating her up inside. She had no one to confide in as long as this case was in limbo. Joyce took Kate's hand and said, "You've been a great help to us, Kate. If you need to talk to someone, please feel free to call me at any time. I know how difficult it will be to keep this confidential."

Kate thanked her as they got up to leave, and Deacon told her, "As soon as we have any updates on the case, I will personally let you know. And I hope that if you can remember anything that will help us, you'll contact us immediately."

"Of course," Kate whispered.

3

That night in Huntsville, Joyce read through the file on Dr. Avi Simmons that Agnes had put together. His picture was a far cry from the distraught young man she'd glimpsed briefly. His dark, wavy hair framed two warm, brown eyes. His engaging smile was made all the more brilliant by his smooth, copper skin. She could certainly see why Ellory found him attractive. He was the third son of two middle-class, California-activist parents, now deceased. He received his medical degree in gynecology from Stanford, eventually landing a job with Sloan Kettering in New York. He volunteered for service during the war as a doctor taking care of the many women who served. He had apparently inherited some activist genes because when Kettering opened up a series of satellite clinics along the border states, he volunteered to run the program. That was where he met Ellory Bainbridge. Her sister Kate introduced them, and a long-distance relationship sprouted.

Agnes uncovered no hiccups in his medical career. Not even a reprimand. He'd been detained on a couple of occasions during anti-war rallies and protest marches but never charged. He enjoyed southern cooking and frequented a nearby mom-and-pop called Clay's Kitchen. He rarely drank due to his on-call status and had a very close-knit circle of medical friends. In short there was nothing extraordinary about Avi Simmons. What made him unusual was that he appeared to be the complete opposite of Allen Bainbridge. Ellory's blond, blue-eyed, buttoned-down husband was about as uptight and self-important as a man could get. Avi, however, was a passionate professional with an outgoing personality and the conviction to live as an example to others.

Joyce logged off the file and looked over at Deacon. He'd been quiet ever since returning from Kate Buxton's interview. She walked to his desk and sat on the corner.

"Good news, Simmons is coming up clean," she told him. "Just your average, hard- working gynecologist."

"Who happens to be sleeping with one of his patients," Deacon quietly remarked. "That doesn't exactly speak to his ethics."

"Maybe not, but it certainly gives him every reason to want to save Ellory from an abusive marriage."

"Alleged abuse," Deacon told her. "So far we have no evidence of said abuse other than testimony from a very hostile witness, and E-Rep certainly isn't going to give any evidence up without a fight. That's if they even bothered to document it at all." He leaned back in his chair. "In their eyes, what we have is a husband who is a victim of his wife's infidelity, which, if he did kill her, makes this a crime of passion at best. At worst, justifiable homicide."

"Crimes of passion aren't premeditated, Deacon. You know that. Whoever did this took a lot of time to plan it out, find a place to do it, and then execute it. There's no way this is anything but a straight-up revenge killing regardless of the circumstances."

"Take it easy, Bachman, I'm not the one you have to convince." Deacon waited until she simmered down and then said, "You need to learn to think like they do if you expect to get any cooperation from Ecclesiastical citizens."

"If thinking like they do means assuming the victims are responsible for whatever happens to them, I'll pass. It's barbaric and unfair."

"The world ran steadily under that assumption for damned near seventeen hundred years. Even now most of the Middle East still labors under that presumption," Deacon told her.

"I used to think we'd evolved beyond such backward thinking as a country. How do they expect any kind of a justice system to function if they don't believe in justice for the innocent?"

Deacon laughed softly and shook his head. "Innocence is relative, Joyce. Think about it for a minute. How many cases of justifiable homicide get prosecuted in the Constitutional territory every year? A man wakes up to find an intruder in the bedroom of his child. He's just standing there, and the only crime he's committed as yet is breaking and entering. The father shoots him anyway because he might harm his kid. A woman defends herself from a mugger using deadly force because she fears for her life. The man only tried to steal her purse, and she could have just given it to him. But she took him out anyway because she's afraid he'll do more than just take her wallet. These people get off on a daily basis simply because of the fear of what a criminal might do, not what he did do."

"A B&E or a mugging isn't a mutilation double murder. And those people had valid reasons for their fears," Joyce told him.

"True. However, the argument could be made that if the man had simply held the intruder at gunpoint and waited for the police to arrive, the criminal would still be alive. He would be convicted and sentenced, and justice would still prevail. Or if that frightened woman had just given that mugger her purse and let him run off, she'd only be replacing a few credit cards and changing her locks instead of facing two to five for manslaughter."

Joyce pulled up a chair and sat down heavily. "So, what's your point? You think Bainbridge had every right to mutilate his wife?"

"My point," Deacon explained, "is that we're dealing with a people who consider God to be the victim of every crime committed within their territory. If you steal, you steal from God. If you lie, you lie against God. If you kill, you kill for or against God. It's not about the people involved, it's about the sins involved in the crime they committed. Ellory violated the eighth commandment. Now, that's one of the big ten and in a roundabout way considered one of the seven deadly sins. To the Ecumenical Council, her crime wasn't just committed against her husband; her crime was against God. As such, what her husband did to her, if he did it, makes him an avenger carrying out God's wrath, at least according to Romans 13 in the Bible."

"There are also a dozen passages in that same Bible that declare thou shalt not kill," Joyce told him. "They don't come with contingency clauses."

"And yet if you read through the Old Testament, you'll find a dozen detailed and pretty damned gruesome methods of execution for what we today would consider minor offenses."

"What can I say? We Jews had an eye for detail," Joyce responded with a smile. Deacon smiled back but said nothing. He just kept staring at Ellory's picture. "I'm heading out. Want to join me for dinner?"

Deacon thought for a minute and said, "No, I'm going to keep digging here. Haven't been sleeping much."

Joyce said goodnight and left Deacon brooding at his desk. Half an hour later, Deacon left HQ but didn't head home. Dropping the cruiser into manual mode, he drove until he could no longer see the sprawl of Huntsville. Streetlights gave way to moonlight, and a hundred roads led off into the Alabama night. He made his way along the Tennessee River. The deeper he went, the darker and poorer the population got. A dozen or so underground jazz clubs had sprung up along the northern shore after the war. Places where the faithful could still enjoy all the debaucheries of old without judgment and still make it to church on Sunday.

T-Bone's wasn't the most popular joint, but it stayed true to its roots. There was no jazz fusion or contemporary renditions of old standards on the menu. Only purists took the stage at T-Bone's, and the youngest musician was usually north of fifty. Deacon opened the door, letting the blue haze of smoke envelop him, and then stepped into the dark club. Taking a table in a distant corner, he ordered whiskey and took off his coat. True to his reputation, T-Bone never watered down his booze, and the first sip hit Deacon like a freight train. By his third double shot, "No 'Count Blues" rang through the maze of small tables and he began to relax. He didn't recognize the slight, gray-haired lady on stage, but her voice was superb. She channeled Sarah Vaughan like a psychic, and the ghosts of his sins disappeared in the blue haze of southern tobacco and soul-wrenching music.

4

The late night at T-Bone's had eased Deacon's mind enough to let him sleep. By morning, however, it was taking a toll on his head, and there wasn't enough asoracaine in the entire region to stop the hangover pounding in his brain. The cruiser's autoshade kept most of the sunlight out, but when they arrived at the clinic, he walked quickly into the shadows like a panicky vampire.

Joyce shook her head. She'd seen the vampire polka before and knew what it meant. "Late night?" she asked, basking beside him in the bright Tennessee sunlight.

"Case research," Deacon growled.

"What was it this time: Billie, Ella or Charlie?" she asked, holding the door for him to enter.

"Sarah," he answered, angry and embarrassed that Joyce knew he hadn't been working. "And how the hell do you know about T-Bone's?"

Joyce just smiled and followed him in.

An hour later in the soft light of the Kettering Clinic, Deacon closed his eyes as Avi Simmons silently cried. The DNA results for Ellory's baby had not been a match to Allen Bainbridge, and it had taken only moments to compare the professional DNA profile to the man grieving before him.

"Dr. Simmons, you have my deepest condolences on your loss," Deacon said quietly. "I am a bit surprised, however, that you were unaware the child was yours."

Avi stared blankly past Deacon. "She was still sexually involved with her husband, unwillingly, of course. Wives don't have the authority to refuse their husbands' demands in the Republic."

Deacon nodded in agreement. He knew all too well what few options women had in the Ecclesiastical Republic. Assault of a wife by her husband wasn't considered a crime unless it resulted in life-threatening injuries or crippled her ability to have children. Even then a husband was given the opportunity to defend his actions, and more often than not, the wife was found to be at fault somehow.

"I didn't care whose child she was carrying, Detective. I loved her," Simmons told him. "We were going to take her other two children with us when she left her husband. I have relatives in San Francisco. We were planning on moving there before . . . before . . ."

Simmons stared at the evidence pad in his hands, then hurled it against the clinic wall, causing Joyce to jump as it shattered and sparked. When he was in control enough to speak, he said, "Just please tell me you've arrested that monster she was married to."

"We're still investigating all possible suspects at this time, Doctor." Deacon gave him a minute more and then asked, "As indelicate as this may sound, I need you to confirm your whereabouts for last week, Dr. Simmons."

Avi stared at him in shock and asked, "You think I did this? You think I would kill the woman I loved, kill my own child?"

"We have to eliminate every possible suspect, Doctor, if we're going to bring Ellory's killer to justice."

"That jealous, controlling bastard of a husband is her killer! Why aren't you arresting him instead of harassing me?"

Joyce could see Deacon's patience wearing thin beneath the hangover, and Avi's anger was the equivalent of waving a red cape at a wounded bull. She slowly moved away from the two men as they spoke, positioning herself behind Simmons just in case.

"Calm yourself, Doctor," Deacon warned him. "I assure you we are investigating every possibility, and we will find the person who did this."

"I just told you who did this," Simmons insisted. "Why would I lie about it?"

"Because, Dr. Simmons, you were having an affair with, and impregnated, the man's wife!" Deacon bellowed. Avi flinched at the accusation, but Deacon didn't back down. "I'm a churchgoing man, Doc, and I can tell you we tend to take things like that rather personally." Avi dropped his eyes in shame as Deacon began to circle him. "Jealousy is a two-way street, Doc. We only have your word that Ellory was leaving her husband. Who's to say she didn't change her mind and decide to stay with him? You know what, Avi? Maybe you're the one who can't take rejection, and that gives you just as much motive to kill." Avi swallowed hard as Deacon stopped in front of him and stared him down. "So, unless you wish to be publicly arrested in front of your patients, I suggest you simmer down, have a seat and answer my questions calmly and completely."

Avi sat down hard on the waiting-room couch. "I'm sorry, Detective," he muttered, cradling his nose between his hands as the tears began to fall again.

Deacon waited for him to regain his composure and then sat next to him, speaking quietly. "I know how hard it is to lose a child, even one you didn't yet know. But believe me when I tell you I will find the person who did this, whomever that turns out to be." He waited until he had Avi's full attention and then said, "You know how hard it is to extradite an

Ecclesiastical citizen for a capital crime, so don't make this any harder for me than it already is. Tell me everything I need to know."

Avi took a deep breath and detailed his entire affair with Ellory from the time her sister Kate introduced them to the last time he'd kissed her goodbye. By the time he finished, he was once again reduced to tears.

Joyce excused herself to upload the interview to the team at Huntsville. She had only once heard Deacon speak of his son, and that had been in private after a particularly bad case. He'd been hungover then too, and he'd never mentioned Neville since. Whatever demons still haunted him about his son's death had obviously made an appearance last night, and they weren't quite done yet. She spent the next hour confirming Dr. Simmons's hours at the clinic and his on-call appearances. By the time she finished, Agnes's team had confirmed his off-duty whereabouts through his digital trace and cleared him as a possible suspect.

When Deacon emerged from the clinic, Simmons was once again in control, and he shook Deacon's hand as they parted. Joyce knew that, beneath the hard-ass exterior he presented to the world, Deacon MacNair possessed a very caring and supportive nature. It was one of the reasons she trusted him so deeply. No matter how upset, pissed off or belligerent MacNair got, he always had your back, body and soul. You could count on that, and everyone in Huntsville knew it.

"Simmons checks out," Joyce told him.

"I thought he might," Deacon said, getting into the cruiser. "But we had to be sure."

Joyce climbed in after him. "Well, that leaves us with Bainbridge and a clear motive. I think it's time we requested that extradition warrant."

"You're awfully sure he's guilty of mutilating his wife," Deacon said as the cruiser started.

"You mean you're not?" Joyce asked. "Listen, if you'd talked to this cold-blooded asshole, you wouldn't doubt it for a minute."

Deacon grinned and said, "Being a cold-blooded asshole doesn't make you a murderer. Take it from one of them who knows."

5

As they made their way back to HQ, Agnes called Deacon and Joyce with news.

"A patrol vehicle just called in an abandoned car at a rest stop on I-65 near Ardmore. The description matches the car Milton gave us from the quarry."

"Have them secure the scene and get Burke out there with a team. We'll go there directly."

"Will do, boss, but you should know that the car came back as registered to Ellory Bainbridge."

"Understood," Deacon told her and disconnected.

"So, he kidnaps the victim, holds her hostage for a couple of days, kills her and uses her car to dump the body. He has to have left his own vehicle somewhere nearby," Joyce said.

"Then we'd better get there before this weather turns," Deacon responded, glancing at the incoming cloud cover. He switched on the emergency lights, shifted into manual override, and gunned the engine. It hardly made a sound as they sped out onto the highway, and Deacon found himself pining for the growl of a 707-horsepower Hemi Hellcat V-8.

Half an hour later, they arrived at the rest stop. The area had been cordoned off for at least half a mile in every direction and traffic was being rerouted to a side road, allowing no unauthorized persons, including the press, to approach. Deacon parked outside of the rest stop area. Ellory's SUV sat next to the public restrooms under a large tree. The doors were locked, but the windows were cracked open. A subtle odor seeped from within as Deacon and Joyce circled the vehicle, peering through the unusually clear glass. It appeared spotless inside as if it had been detailed and never driven, but in the cargo compartment behind the rear seat, a large canvas tarp lay balled up.

Pulling his badge from his belt loop, Deacon waved it in front of the car's tailgate lock. The HSS ident-chip sent a signal to the lock to override the owner's DNA coding. The lock clicked three times and then opened. The tailgate lifted, sending out a cloud of industrial-strength cleaner fumes, but nothing could disguise the trace odors clinging to the tarp: blood and body waste. Joyce signaled for the evidence bots, and Burke sent two forward. They grasped the tarp, pulled it into a metal bin and loaded it in the van. It was too big to be unwrapped at the scene without cross-contamination, so Deacon and Joyce accompanied it back to the morgue, leaving Burke in charge.

Ordering everyone to stand clear, Burke sent in his evidence warriors. They combed every inch of the vehicle for an hour but came up empty. The interior had been meticulously scrubbed so that not a single fingerprint remained. What little DNA they could locate was highly contaminated with chemicals, which would make it inadmissible as evidence. Burke, however, wasn't going to accept being outfoxed by a maniac, especially with his professional reputation and a bet with MacNair on the line. He set about examining the outside of the vehicle and then turned his attention to the surrounding grounds. There were footprints everywhere in the drying mud that no doubt belonged to local kids since the tourist season was over, but he meticulously imprinted each one and uploaded the data to HQ. I-95 and the rest stop had been paved over and embedded with the same road tech as the Corridor so vehicles could stay in suspensor mode and quickly rejoin traffic. But the sporadic rains and wind had left the surface covered with enough mud and debris to trigger the full-contact wheels to engage. Tire tracks crisscrossed the site, but only one set had allowed the killer to escape. Ferreting out which one was going to take time. He set the bots for deep resonance imaging and turned them loose. They made one final sweep of the entire site down to half a meter below the surface as Burke coordinated their movements and sorted the data for uplink. They reached the far side of the site just as the first afternoon shower moved in.

Rain was falling steadily when the tow vehicle arrived to impound the victim's car. It beat on the roof of the command van as Burke sat inside sorting and stowing all the images, samples and data. The other technicians would accompany the victim's car back to HQ, so Burke had the van all to himself, just the way he liked it. He accessed the data from the highway's roadbed software as the autopilot drove him back to HQ behind the tow rig. Twenty-two vehicles were tracked entering and leaving the rest stop in the eight days since the murder. Sixteen of the tracks, including the victim's car, belonged to fully automated late-model transports. These were isolated on one of the multiple screens in the cargo bay. The six remaining tracks belonged to pre-autopilot, uncoded vehicles that still ran on gas. That made them local. He put these on a second screen. As the tracks synced to the highway data, algorithms separated them and matched each to a vehicle description, a timeline, and its driver. The second screen was where the real work lay. Since no tracking data was available, only visual comparison to the resonance scanning would work. He opened the camera data at the off- and on-ramps to the rest stop, creating a grid on a third screen while separating the depth impressions left by the tires and weights of the vehicles on a fourth. He remained fully engrossed in his examination as the caravan was directed past the backed-up interstate of angry drivers and one calm individual in a truck with blacked-out windows. By the time he arrived back at HQ, all but four of the vehicles and their drivers had been generally identified.

The Wolf of Sheol

1

The rest stop and its legion of flashing red and blue lights faded slowly into the distance. By the time the he reached the turnoff, it had vanished in the afternoon storm. Still, he wouldn't be able to relax until he saw the familiar tree-lined streets of home. An hour later, well ahead of the storm, the truck tires left whirlwinds of orange and red leaves in their wake as he turned left onto the asphalt road that served as his current place of residence. The sight of it usually calmed him, but not today. The road was narrow and densely lined with tall northern red oaks, breathtaking at this time of year. But beauty wasn't what had drawn him to the house. The density of the trees hid the house from the nearest road for a good half-mile and served as a natural noise buffer. The house was also the only one for five miles on this side of the small lake. He could see the houses on the other shores, all built within shouting distance of one another. They all fronted a much busier road than the one he traveled. He had no idea what the name of the lake was. He suspected it didn't have one. Many had sprung up as a result of the war. Artillery had wreaked havoc with the local landscape, leaving huge craters where homes once stood. Rains had filled them in and left them stagnant until the rivers and tributaries found them again. Eventually some became viable habitats for the largemouth bass, crappie and bluegills the locals loved to catch once the Chattahoochee found them. He wasn't interested in fishing.

He counted the landmarks until he found his driveway. It was exceptionally hard to spot because of its sudden turn and dip toward the lake. His first day he'd passed it twice before actually spotting it. Perfect. The house itself was a long box seated on a raised foundation to protect from flooding. The roof peaked over the white wood siding and green shutters, sheltering a wraparound porch that creaked when he walked on it. Intruders would not go unseen. After pulling into the detached garage, he locked the automatic door from the inside and opened a large trap door in the floor. He unloaded the contents of the truck, taking one of two large tote bags into the subterranean space. He stored its cargo of chemicals and cleaning rags carefully in the dimly lit bunker. Each of the tools he had used on his trip he hung on evenly spaced hooks. He wished he'd kept the crucifix the woman had been wearing. It was a custom piece of unusual workmanship, though, and would have been remembered, so he'd left it around her neck. Eventually everything in this room would go into another lake with some very heavy weights, but that was only after all the work was done.

The interior of the house was as country as a lakeshore house could get. The walls and floors were covered in knotty pine, and only the bedrooms had carpeting. The electrical system had been modernized along with the appliances, and all the windows were double paned. They unfortunately muted sounds from outside, but the creaking porch still allowed him to track the movements of anything or anyone on it. He opened the closest windows to allow in the warm late-summer storm. Opening the second tote, he pulled out a sleek camera and touchscreen pad. He plugged the camera into the pad, started the upload and then poured himself a stiff drink. The good Kentucky bourbon steadied his hands. The first martyr had been proclaimed. Now was a time for rest and reflection.

The last of the light brought the rain eastward, and he settled down in front of the cold fireplace to scroll through the pictures he'd taken. The rest stop and the car in the midday sun, the platoon of police descending on both, all taken from safe distances with the highest-power magnification lens available. He studied them as he sipped his drink, noting the most prominent faces. He would have to watch for them as the work continued. The pictures of the woman began to scroll across the pad. She was beautiful. The sort of woman he'd always pictured himself with when he retired, well-tended and neat. She wore just enough makeup to smooth her appearance yet still looked as alluring as a model in a magazine. And she had a dazzling smile that had nearly caused him to rethink his plan. In the end, he really had no choice. They put her name on the list, and that had sealed her fate. He watched as the pictures of her slowly progressed, pictures of her naked, bleeding and bruised. The photo of her skull caved in and her eyes, incoherent and finally dying. He saw nothing sexual in these images. That would have been degenerate. Instead he took solace in the fact that the death he had given her would serve a much higher purpose than the one those who made the list had in store. They had assigned her the death of a criminal. He had anointed her a sacrifice. He said a prayer for her immortal soul and closed his eyes.

2

Director Pittsfield read the warrant and then looked up at his detectives. Bachman was perfectly satisfied, but MacNair looked a little pensive. "Are you two sure you've eliminated any other possible suspects? I don't want this turning into a bureaucratic nightmare."

Bachman confidently replied, "We've eliminated the victim's lover and her sister as suspects, sir. The only one with a clear motive for killing her is currently her husband. Until we can interrogate him, we have no other suspects."

He thought for a minute and then said, "Okay, I'll put it through. You should have an answer in twelve hours, so go get yourself a strategy. I don't want this guy slipping through the cracks if he's our perp."

He handed Bachman the warrant, and she practically bounded out of the office. Deacon turned to follow her, but Pittsfield held him back. "Take a seat, MacNair."

Deacon sat down and said, "Don't worry, John. I'll make sure she doesn't get out of hand."

"Bachman doesn't concern me—you do." He leaned forward to rest his arms on his desk and looked at Deacon. "You look like ten miles of bad road, and your left eye's twitching from too much asoracaine. I know this case hits a little close to home, so I'm here for you, but you need to tell me right now: do I need to put you in a time-out?"

Deacon looked at him wearily. "No, I'm fine, John. No noises, no panic attacks, no pangs of guilt, just not sleeping. Needed something to put me out. Just went a little too far."

Pittsfield took him at his word. He knew there were things in Deacon's past that he couldn't talk about, things classified even to this day. The damage those secrets inflicted had been spectacular, so he didn't begrudge the man an occasional binge. But the last thing he needed was his best investigator having a meltdown in the middle of a high-profile cross-territorial murder case.

"Try meditation next time," he said with sympathetic grin. "Now, tell me what's bugging you about this case, because you don't seem all that sure Bainbridge is your guy."

Deacon sighed. "There's something wrong about all this, John. The evidence points directly at him, the guy has more than enough motive and, from what Bachman tells me, he's just the kind of egomaniacal prick who would do something like this, but . . ."

"But what?"

"He's too uptight, too proper. The man walks around without a wrinkle in his clothes or a hair out of place. He had a manicure, for God's sake. This is the kind of guy who's too cowardly to get his hands dirty. His method of torture is mental, not physical, the more humiliating the better."

"So, he's a pussy in addition to being a bully. That doesn't mean he didn't want her dead," John offered.

"A man pissed off enough to kill his wife will make sure she suffers. Even if he plans out his revenge, he does it in anger. He's not gentle or compassionate about it; the more tore up she is, the better. But our guy went out of his way to make sure she didn't suffer long, that she wasn't in a lot of pain. Almost as if it was a mercy killing."

"Well, even egomaniacal pricks can have compassion, Deke. Hell, you've been calling me an egomaniacal prick since you got suspended back in twenty-nine and I got promoted. But I've still been consoling your sorry ass every Saturday night since your wife left."

"And my sorry ass appreciates it," Deacon replied with a slight grin. "I just hope Bainbridge is the sick bastard Bachman believes he is."

"Then go get the little prick and let's find out."

3

Abel sealed the heavy door to the studio and set the alarm for the gallery. The intricate system required several passcodes to activate but guaranteed that nobody would get within spitting distance of the art before someone could intervene. Especially his most precious works, which he kept securely locked behind the hidden steel door within. It seemed comical that the only thing holding the front doors shut was an old-fashioned deadbolt, but one shouldn't advertise the value of one's possessions he told himself as he spun the lock. Old world wisdom. Also, modern technology was frowned upon in the artsy enclave of West Park Square. Only unscrupulous Yankees would insult southern integrity with such devices, and he needed southern hospitality to stay in business. He tested the solid lock, then scratched at the long scar that ran from just left of his nose down to the curve below his ear. It always itched when the humidity was high. With his gallery secured, he picked up his cases, holding the one in his right hand lower to allow for a slight slump. His shoulder ached nearly as much as his scar on days like this. He crossed through the park to the north side of the square. There, a quaint restaurant that served outstanding coffee, spiced peach cobbler and Georgia biscuits sat under blossoming magnolias. They were still blooming late in the season thanks to the humidity and prolonged rainstorms of global warming.

The owner of the café was a stout, pretty woman named Charlene who never missed greeting a customer with a smile, a wave and a "How do." Today, however, Charlene was very distracted. She waved to him as he entered, but her usual smile was absent, and she kept turning back to the TV.

"Your guests arrived a little early, so I set 'em at the large table in the corner. I'll bring y'all over some coffee."

Abel watched her scurry off, wondering what news was so disturbing that the entire place was on edge. The widescreen buzzed as people sat at their tables, watching the news while food grew cold. Unheard of in a place like Charlene's. People tore into her cooking like hungry wolves within seconds of it landing on the table and rarely left a crumb. He made his way to the large table only to find his client as thoroughly engaged in the broadcast as everyone else.

"Afternoon, Marshall. Do forgive my tardiness. I had a client that ran long in the gallery." The man rose slightly but Abel waved him down. Charlene appeared and poured two steaming cups of glittering black brew. She smiled graciously but then hurried off without giving her customary speech about every delicious thing the café had to offer that day.

"Don't worry, my friend, Charlene has had me well taken care of, considering . . ." Marshall tipped his cup toward the widescreen.

Abel set his cases down and turned toward the broadcast. A reporter was standing at the edge of a pristine lake, the entrance to which was blocked off by hazard barriers. He spoke with the typical haughtiness of a son of the South.

"It's been over three weeks since Jessica Glick of Montezuma vanished on the way to visit her ailing aunt in Peachtree. Jessica is the wife of Pastor Albert Glick of the Mennonite Church, whose parish has offered a reward of twenty thousand dollars for any information on the poor woman. No one has come forth with any information, and not so much as a sighting has been reported since her disappearance. The family remains hopeful that she will be found safe, but with the discovery of a body just two days ago, their hopes on this Sabbath day have dimmed. The nude body of a young woman found in this very lake by local police was the victim of a vicious beating. Identified as Ellory Bainbridge of Atlanta, this young housewife and mother also disappeared on her way to visit a relative."

He changed his tone as he walked down the access road.

"The involvement of federal authorities in this case is of particular concern to the Ecumenical leadership, as is the involvement of an E-Rep high senator whose son is a primary witness in the investigation. As fears mount that a serial killer from outside our beloved territory may be preying on our gentle citizens, the Council asks that everyone remain vigilant and report any unusual individuals to local authorities."

The broadcast switched back to the newsroom, where the anchors discussed the situation among themselves for the public.

"Thank you, Jeff, for that unsettling report. For such a revelation to come to light on this solemn day is just heartbreaking. As you all know, it was three years ago on this very day that we lost our beloved Archbishop Harrison Meeks when his limousine was driven off the Bull River Bridge to Tybee Island. The vehicle burst into flames before launching into the river, and the hit-and-run assailant has never been found."

"I remember that crash," Marshall told Abel. "Terrible thing to happen to such a good man. Body was so badly burned they had to identify him from dental records. Son of a bitch that hit him was probably a Blue Stater just like the one that hit you. Those soulless bastards drive like maniacs. I suppose I don't have to tell you that, hey Abe?" he said with a slight grin.

"No, not at all," Abel answered, scratching absently at the scar on his face once again. He remembered the Meeks crash as well but from a much different perspective. Charlene returned with a steaming plate of fresh biscuits with spiced peach jam, and Marshall dove in as expected. Abel relished his at a much slower pace, savoring each bite and washing it down with a sip of excellent coffee. The conversation turned to business and Abel removed the pieces from his case, setting them on easels for Marshall to review. There were three portraits of his wife, each from a different angle. Meant to be displayed as a set, each portrayed her with a different perspective of light, giving the display a sense of three-dimensional depth. Marshall loved them.

"My friend, you have outdone yourself," he congratulated Abel. "Sara is going to love them. You will, of course, be at her birthday unveiling. I won't hear of you not showing up. It's going to be great for business."

"I wouldn't think of refusing," Abel responded politely as he sipped more coffee and repackaged the paintings. It wasn't his best work. In fact, painting wasn't even his first love. As meticulous as he was, he seemed to lack the skills necessary for rendering a true one-dimensional face. He made up for it by depicting subjects from side views and adding softening rays of light to disguise the lack of detail. It was a trick he often used in his more lucrative passion, photography. The result was a more emotional and soulful depiction of a person's inner beauty which was always far purer than their exterior facade.

They finished the afternoon meal, and Marshall left entirely pleased and several thousand dollars poorer. Abel remained to finish his coffee and watch the broadcast, which seemed to be repeating. That night on the bridge had been harrowing. People could see the flames for five miles when the car exploded, and the territory had gone into mourning for a year over the loss. Harrison Meeks had been much beloved. But that was another life. A life of service rendered wholesome solely by a trick of the light in which it had been cast. A life cleansed by the fires to which it had been consigned. A replay of the aftermath appeared on the screen as Abel unconsciously scratched at the scar again.

4

Wallace Milton turned off the broadcast and paced the floor like a caged tiger while Caulder Wirz sat quietly reading the warrant. The senator's eyes were red and watery and bounced back and forth in their sockets. He typically looked this way when he was thundering on about some injustice or lobbying for a particular bill on the Senate floor. His charismatic fervor was often attributed to a passion for the Republic and his sacred calling as a leader. Wirz knew it was just too much damned cocaine. He'd been snorting the stuff like a vacuum cleaner as if the Feds had come for him instead of his son Pete. News of the arrest had spread like wildfire despite Wirz's best efforts and, to his credit, old man Milton had been playing the dishonored parent ever since. He'd attended prayer circles set up in local family centers by his constituents. He railed against the ease with which young people bought drugs within the heathen territories and made speech after speech about removing the ineffectual leaders in federal government. And at every appearance the man had been high as a kite.

"How the hell are we supposed to spin this?" Wallace yelled. "I have people at every damned rally asking me about my son's drug habits and how he knew the victim."

"And you've done a masterful job of explaining it," Wirz told him calmly. "I must say that bit about the Lord using even the sinner to do his bidding was masterful. You actually have people believing that God gave Pete his addiction just so it could lead him to the Bainbridge woman."

"Yeah, well, people are just as stupid today as they were before the war," Wallace grumbled. "But that shit isn't being swallowed in the rest of the country. The Constitutional states aren't one-tenth as bad as they used to be. They've cleaned up a lot more than we can afford to publicly admit. They're outpacing us in industrial and technological advancement despite what you hear on TV, and I'm going to need their support if I'm going to make it to the House of Representatives this year, not to mention the White House in four."

Wirz watched him stalk over to the liquor cabinet and pour himself a drink. The way Milton was snorting and drinking, his liver wouldn't survive long enough to reach the presidency, and his prospects for the House were dimming every second.

"I'll deal with the federal investigation. Once we have it under our control, it won't be an issue. Unfortunately, we have a much bigger problem than your son's legal entanglements," Wirz told him. "Your activities in South Africa have created a situation that threatens the overall agenda."

"Bullshit," Wallace snapped as he threw himself into his chair. "Those agreements will be buttoned up by the end of the week. In a month the treaty goes before the national government and the Republic will have an oil-dependent African partner, the first of many, and a new stream of physical wealth to play with." He gulped the contents of his shot glass and smiled smugly. "That should move your agenda along."

"It would if you weren't using it to traffic in blood diamonds and cocaine."

Wirz threw a picture across the desk and watched the flush of alcohol and coke slowly drain from Wallace's face. The image was of a black man in a torn uniform. His eyes had been gouged out, and a large bullet hole marked his forehead. Blood and gray matter formed a halo around the back of his shattered skull.

"You should be more careful who you do business with, Wallace," Wirz told him coldly. "We've had Makunbe under our thumb since he first joined the Namibian Guerrilla Brigade." A bead of sweat fell slowly down Wallace's face. "Those visas you supplied him with were used to smuggle a couple of terrorists into South Sudan, where they were responsible for the bombing of a hospital in Juba last week." Wallace gulped visibly as Wirz walked calmly up to the desk and said, "We were able to track them down them before U.S. involvement was discovered." Wirz tossed two blood-stained visas onto the picture of Wallace's business partner and Milton's face went white.

"Makunbe told me their lives would be in danger if he agreed to sign the peace treaty," Wallace explained. "I agreed to provide them safe passage to the Republic in exchange for his cooperation."

"So, you agreed to give two international terrorists safe haven in the Republic on diplomatic visas to fund your extravagant lifestyle?"

"Shit! We had Bin Laden's whole damned family holed up in Massachusetts while we hunted that bastard down. How many Saudis did the Feds fly out of the country to cover their own financial asses the minute those twin towers fell?"

Wirz stared at him coldly. "And it never occurred to you to make sure they actually got on the plane instead of disappearing into the African bush?" Milton dropped his eyes and stared into his empty shot glass. Wirz said, "Tomorrow morning you will publicly announce that you are turning over all diplomatic negotiations in South Africa to Senator Hayes."

The color rose in Wallace's face and he started to object, but Wirz's stare turned to a block of ice that shut him down as he leaned down close to Wallace's face. "You will tell the country that Pete's arrest has made clear to you that the issues facing the country's citizens in all territories must come above all other concerns, and you henceforth are dedicating yourself to being the voice of the Republic and a champion for this country's young people. You will do this, Wallace, or the next crime scene a Milton appears at will be your own."

He watched the color drain from the man's face again and put on his coat. "We've invested a great deal of time and money in you, Wallace, but you're becoming a liability and you know how we deal with liabilities. Finish off the coke, dry out, and get your shit together, Senator." He looked down at the bloody visas and the ghastly photograph. "Feel free to keep those as an incentive." replay of the aftermath appeared on the screen as Abel unconsciously scratched at the scar again.

5

Wirz climbed into his limo and watched the Milton estate disappear behind him as they headed back to Atlanta. There were only two possible outcomes of tonight's meeting, but only one truly gave relief. Wallace Milton was probably drowning his terror in a vat of whiskey at this very moment, ensuring he'd be dead of alcohol poisoning by morning. If so, Pete Milton would be found hanging in his cell from an apparent suicide within twenty-four hours, allegedly atoning for the disgrace he'd brought to his family. It would entirely solve the Milton problem. On the other hand, if the senator managed to sober up, he'd make his speech on the steps of the state capitol tomorrow morning looking as if he'd spent several horrendous nights in agonizing reflection. If he stayed clean and played by the rules, he could still be a powerful asset, and the threat of his only son's sudden demise would keep him in line in the future. In any case, Wirz would know by tomorrow morning which path the senator had chosen to take.

Kane and Bledsoe, however, were loose ends, and that was something the Cadre tolerated even less than liabilities. That meant a trip to the Monastery for the two young men for a little R&R. Since its implementation, the Rehabilitation and Reconditioning Protocol had been a tremendous success. Participants in the program emerged far more contained and reflective, less prone to the temptations that led them astray. Reconditioning would have the dual benefit of saving their lives while still silencing them. They might need help eating and bathing for what remained of their lives, but it was deemed one of the more acceptable side effects of the program. They most likely wouldn't live long enough to experience the others.

That left only the murder investigation itself to deal with. The warrant for Allen Bainbridge was based on more than sufficient probable cause. Homeland was a doing a first-rate job of building a case against him. Unfortunately, the bastard was a well-known prep school buddy of Caulder's, and any federal investigation that could compromise his carefully crafted history had to be avoided. He'd scheduled a trip to Washington to formally request control of the case, but the situation with Milton's African connections had to be dealt with in person. That meant a suitable substitute would have to be assigned by the high archbishop. Even though they knew nothing of the corruption Milton was involved in, the Ecumenical Council understood the urgency of keeping Milton in check through the upcoming elections and gladly left Caulder to deal with Milton in whatever way he felt necessary.

The limo dropped him off, and he climbed the marble steps to his door. Hanging up his coat and undoing his tie, he wondered if he should simply end Wallace Milton instead of waiting for him to snort and drink his way into an early grave. It wouldn't be the first time the Cadre had sacrificed one of its protégés. Vice President Cahill had been the last but most certainly not the first. A death had to serve the Agenda as much as a life. Waste was not an option. He poured himself a brandy and made several calls. By the time he'd finished his second snifter, adjustments had been made and everything was in place. All that was needed was for Wallace Milton to make the next move.

In the Shelter of the Most High

Margot Turnouer walked down the hallway to the Oval Office. She opened the door with a tired nod to the Secret Service agent standing guard and quickly entered. It was early yet, and the gray dawn cast no light through the tall windows. The motion sensors had been deactivated at her request so that one had to physically turn on the lights. She left the room in darkness and leaned back against the door. Waking daily long before the sun was a habit from the old days when her mornings were dedicated to predawn training. Those days were long past, but that first hour was still hers. That was the rule. No meetings, no calls, nothing short of a nuclear war was to disturb her. She stared into the emptiness of the room. It was fitting, this emptiness, with her husband gone. It echoed how she felt, empty. She communed with him in darkness until the first rays of the sun lit the Resolute desk. Only then did she turn on the lights.

When she'd first walked into this room with Warren eighteen years ago, the walls had been garishly adorned in gilt trimming and obnoxious red wallpaper that made the room look like an abattoir. The carpet had been a disturbing blood red, giving the eagle's gaze that of a vicious predator and not the symbol of calm strength and just resolve of the greatest country on earth. It had sickened her nearly as much as the man who commissioned it. Thankfully, it had been burned on the White House lawn during the 2020 uprising, along with the gold trim and whorehouse wallpaper. She stared down at the new carpet as she crossed it, a serene cobalt blue with the great eagle emblem of the Presidential Seal on a pale gold background. Its majesty restored and all hostility removed. The border of the carpet bore the words "A nation divided against itself cannot stand," the last great speech her husband had given before his assassination.

She sat down and logged into her communications pad. As usual, messages were prioritized as each incoming one was decrypted, cleaned, scrubbed and secured. The Secret Service and NSA had learned well from history, and nothing suspect ever got through these days. Even the invitations to the Secretary of State's wedding had been thoroughly screened. She'd finished reading about a tenth of the incoming e-mails when several high-priority messages appeared at the top of the list. They were from FBI Director Seacomb, and they were not good news. She read them slowly and felt her stomach turn. A knock at the door startled her from her reading. She closed the pad as her personal secretary, David Hines, entered.

"Good morning, Madam President. I have your itinerary and the briefings from the security meetings you requested."

"Thank you, David," Margot replied, arranging them on her desk. After a minute she took a deep breath and asked her customary first question. "So, first fire of the morning?"

"Straight out of hell, I'm afraid," David replied carefully. "Senator Blumberg and Archbishop Spurlock of the Ecumenical Council have requested an urgent meeting. The Secretary of State thought it best to grant them the time, considering the nature of the urgency."

Margot dropped her head and rubbed the back of her neck. "When are they expected?"

David took a deep breath and said, "They're here."

"What?"

"They arrived thirty minutes ago. They've been waiting in the reception room."

"Oh, sweet Jesus," she muttered. Not even eight in the morning and already the day had gone to hell. "Did they give you any idea what this impromptu urgency was about?"

"They wouldn't say anything, but the Secretary of State said it had something to do with a jurisdictional matter presented to their embassy."

"Well, let's get the sideshow started."

David went to the adjacent study while Margot tried to get her head in the game. A fresh tumbler of her favorite espresso latte was delivered, and she gave orders to have it refreshed in another forty minutes. He retrieved the Ecclesiastical Republic Flag from its currently designated resting place in the closet. Its official position was behind and to the left of the president with the Double Star Flag of the new Constitutional Republic on her right, both surrounding the flag bearing the Presidential Seal in the center as its peacekeeper. President Turnouer, however, was a dedicated

Constitutionalist and current leader of the Founders Preservationist Party. She despised the sight of the E-Rep flag almost as much as the Double Star Flag. She insisted on having Old Glory at her right hand and the Presidential Seal on her left as it had been before the war. The new flags she relegated to opposite sides of the Oval Office near the middle, like two relatives at a family dinner table. Siblings who couldn't stand one another but were obligated to respect peace in the house of their matriarch. The placement mirrored the existence of the two territorial embassies now occupying opposite sides of the Ellipse, staring each other down like enemy combatants. A family divided, just like her country.

She reread the most detailed of messages from the FBI while the Oval was restaged and when all was ready said, "Show them in, David." Her secretary left, and she signaled to the agent standing guard at the door. The man had been with her husband before and during his terms in office and was loyal to a fault. "You know what to do," she told him, and he left to secure the room.

Five minutes later, David returned with her guests. Each one she greeted with a reserved smile and a firm handshake before inviting them to sit before the Resolute desk. This was not a cordial visit by any means, and she intended to remind them precisely who was in charge.

"Gentlemen, I understand you have an urgent matter you wish to discuss. How may I assist you?"

The senator spoke while the archbishop sat quietly observing. "Our embassy has been contacted regarding an interterritorial incident involving one of our citizens within your Federal Corridor. A young mother was brutally murdered, and her family is considerably distraught. Apparently, your Homeland thugs are refusing to release her remains to her husband, thereby infringing upon his rights to give his wife a swift burial under Ecumenical law. Such an insult is inhumane and unprofessional, not to mention a complete violation of our citizen's rights."

Margot folded her hands. "Gentlemen, I'm sure you are aware that any crime committed within federal territory falls under the jurisdiction of Homeland Security by treaty. If the body is being held, I'm sure it's as necessary evidence for solving the crime and not meant as an insult to your religious practices. As to any violation of rights, the family will be kept fully informed of any progress made, and I'm sure the case will be resolved quickly."

Blumberg leaned forward and sneered. "I find that scenario unlikely, considering the treatment of the witnesses who found the body. All three are sons of Ecclesiastical Republic senators. They performed their civic duty as United States citizens by reporting the crime and, as a token of thanks, were each subjected to intense interrogations and accusations of involvement in the crime itself." He handed Margot an e-reader with the criminal complaint of police brutality.

"It's widely known that Homeland is currently staffed by appointees known to have Unification Party ties. This is obviously another example of their disdain for our territory," Blumberg remarked.

Margot had heard this rhetoric before. Any time the E-Republic didn't get their way, it was attributed to Unification Party terrorists. She read the complaint. Senators Robert Kane and Thomas Bledsoe were minor players. Wallace Milton, however, was up for appointment to the House of Representatives. She'd been following his speeches that demonized the lack of representation for the Ecclesiastical Republic. He often accused the White House of snubbing their citizens for high-level positions as proof of their underground support of the often-violent political organization called the Unification Party. Politically speaking, his success would defuse that opinion and go far in healing some very volatile wounds in the nation. Personally, she hoped he would rot in hell. His predecessor had made a similar meteoric rise, eventually attaining the vice presidency. That man had put a bullet in her husband's head on a Sunday afternoon.

"As yet there is no evidence that the crime was committed in federal territory," the senator explained. "Your federal police have ascertained that the body was dumped there and the crime committed elsewhere. As such, we are demanding that jurisdiction over this case and the woman's remains be returned to us immediately so that the Ecclesiastical Republic can investigate her death under our laws."

His condescending tone irritated Margot. One did not barge into the Oval unannounced and make demands of the president. E-Rep senators usually reserved their disdain of her presidency for full media occasions, not private meetings.

"I believe the support of the Unification Party leaders was quite instrumental in your appointment to fill your husband's post after his assassination, and to your current bid for reelection," Archbishop Spurlock remarked. He raised his eyes, keeping his gaze along the length of his unnaturally sharp nose. "It would be embarrassing to find that they were involved in this attack on our territorial rights. The ramifications for your candidacy and you personally would no doubt be devastating, even if the allegations were subsequently proven untrue."

Margot eyed Spurlock evenly. It took balls to march into the president's office and openly threaten to smear her publicly. But that was par for the course with the Ecumenical Council. To them, women were a commodity to be possessed and controlled. The gall of having one in a position of power greater than their own had brought out the worst in them these past two years.

Spurlock looked around the room, casually noting the emergence of Old Glory and the distant opposing positions of the flags of the new America. "I must say that your disdain for our freely elected way of life is quite disturbing. People might consider such disrespect very unpresidential."

Margot smiled slyly at him. "I have the utmost respect for the choices of our citizens, Your Excellency—when they are not based on lies and deception, of course." She watched Spurlock's face darken. "Then again, where would politicians and clergy be if not for the ignorance of their respective constituencies?" His face darkened even further. She smiled, waving her hands toward the standards, and remarked, "I see this arrangement as more of a reflection of the current state of affairs in our country and the role this government plays in making sure the peace treaty is respected and adhered to by both sides. This office is, after all, the supreme governing authority of this country and its territories." She let that fact sink in for a moment and then sat up straighter.

"I will review the situation with the Director of Homeland and let you know my decision." She waited until the two of them rose to leave and then said, "While I have the two of you here, there is an issue I should address that directly involves national security." The two men exchanged a curious look and then took their seats once again.

"We recently detected several systemwide communications disruptions emanating from your dedicated networks. The overload was substantial enough to interfere with communications along the Federal Corridor and into federal territory. Is there a problem we should be aware of?"

"We recently detected an intrusion into the E-Republic cyber systems from sources outside the country," the archbishop told her. "The hack targeted several classified Council communications and election candidate files. It appeared to originate from Western Europe, possibly the United Kingdom or France."

"An obvious brute force attack like that seems more like the work of dissidents or rogue hackers than an ally. How certain are you of the origin?" Margot asked quietly.

"Quite certain," Spurlock told her. "And it was a subtle but sophisticated attack, not some WikiLeaks stunt to get attention. It had all the earmarks of a well-coordinated invasion, considering the specific information they targeted; hardly the work of cyber martyrs or bored dissidents looking for their next big social media post."

His condescending tone irritated Margot. She possessed a "master's degree in network systems security", so Spurlock was hardly in a position to argue, but he had no reservations about his own superiority to anyone outside the Ecclesiastical Republic.

Margot put her irritation aside and adopted an air of concern. "If what you say is true, it's fortunate that we began investigating it as soon as we detected it a month ago." Blumberg began to shift uncomfortably as she turned to him. "Why you never alerted us to this attack is rather curious, but we assigned a full contingent to track down the perpetrators as soon as it was detected." She turned her attention back to Spurlock. "We, too, noted the possible origin as Western Europe; however, when we traced the act to its source, we discovered the location to be a misdirection." She let Seacomb's revelation hang in the air for a moment. "We were able to pick up the actual trace and follow it back to the United States. I believe that makes this a matter of domestic terrorism, and that, gentlemen, falls securely within the jurisdiction of the FBI."

The two men exchanged a worried glance that told Margot all she needed. The hack hadn't been reported because it had originated within their territory, and the story they'd just told her was fodder for the next debate. Play intercepted. But there was much more going on here than they were letting on.

"My agents are narrowing the location as we speak. I assume that, wherever this investigation takes us, we will have your full cooperation in bringing these cyberterrorists to justice?"

Blumberg cleared his throat. "Of course, Madam President, we will cooperate to the best of our ability with your agents, and we thank you for the superior efforts of the FBI. It would, after all, be disastrous for both territories if it were known that our systems were compromised by entities within our borders so close to the election."

Margot stood, indicating that the meeting was over. The senator and the archbishop rose as she called her secretary to escort them out.

Once they left, the agent she'd dismissed reappeared. He carried with him a small portable drive on which a hologram of the conversation was recorded. He had made many such recordings, each one personally handed to Margot with a very solemn look.

"Is something wrong, Calvin?"

"No, ma'am. It's just . . ."

Margo closed her eyes and then said, "You don't approve."

"I don't believe your husband would approve," he explained quietly. "The major general was an honorable man. He believed in the sanctity of his duty as president and the trust that all of the people placed in him, regardless of their affiliation. I believe he would consider this a violation of that trust."

Margo looked at Calvin with sympathy and placed a hand on his shoulder. He'd been at her husband's side that day, and he still bore the scars of the attack, both seen and unseen.

"Warren was an honorable man. A man of integrity and principles, committed to making this country whole again. And what did it get him? A bullet in the head while he stood over the grave of our son at Arlington." Leaning forward, she said, "I am not going out like that."

Agent Harris nodded in agreement. He had failed her husband, even if Margot would never say so. He wouldn't fail Margot.

She dismissed him and resumed her morning readings but couldn't concentrate. It was clear that her visitors hadn't anticipated the involvement of the FBI and that they already knew the hack originated domestically. If it had truly been an international attack, they would have been trumpeting the FBI's failure to protect the country and using it to campaign for her rivals. Well, two could play that game.

We Are the Clay, and You Are Our Potter

The small sculpting tool slid over the damp salt, its thin, tapered end etching small lines around the contours of the face. He looked at the image on the pad hanging from a swing arm next to him as he carved. It was important to get the details right. Expression was everything if the piece was to be truly representative of its purpose. A flight from danger that resulted in the loss of a life not easily abandoned. It had to be just the right combination of fear, irritation and regret. It was, after all, representing the consequences of embracing a life of sin. The awl skittered across the surface, encountering resistance. He dipped his fingers into a container of ionized water and carefully placed the drops in its path. The tool resumed its smooth forward stroke. It was important to keep the surface as smooth as possible when working in such a soluble medium. The studio was kept at a crisp and dry forty degrees at all times to preserve its integrity and strength during the creation process. It allowed him to work without damaging the piece. He knew once it was placed it would be at the mercy of the elements and wouldn't last long, but it didn't have to. His art was transitory, as was all life. It was his trademark as an artist, and his clients appreciated his creations all the more for their brief existence in this world.

It was quiet in the frigid studio as he always worked alone. Occasionally he would sculpt to music but not often. He found it more inspiring to work listening to his own thoughts. He wore thermal silks under his work clothes and a thick heat wrap over his right shoulder to ward off stiffness. The old wound was a nasty reminder of his former life. The lined, second skin gloves he wore wouldn't impede his delicate sense of touch as he worked. The cold never bothered him. It was merely a condition of his trade. He'd been in tougher conditions, harsher temperatures and far messier and more hurried situations. Assassins liked to plan meticulously; however, those plans rarely went off without a hitch. Assassination had been as much an art form to him then as his sculpting was to him now. Still, he greatly preferred the exquisite delicacy of creation to the performance art of an assassin. The gruesome, often tawdry methods of execution he'd employed had been necessary, whether destroying a reputation or decimating of a life of virtue. Some required only the appropriate "accidental" death, but those had been rare. In every instance, an assassination had to serve the Agenda.

He poured himself a glass of chilled wine and pondered how the Agenda had changed but the job hadn't. He was no longer a member of the Cadre, but his new Agenda was no less ambitious. That it employed many of the same tactics to achieve its goal was a perfect irony. Breaking into their network had been a dangerous move that could have revealed his continued existence, but it had been necessary and extremely fruitful. Mining their classified edicts and security measures had given him the tools necessary to expose the true nature of this new Eden and send up a flare to the outside world about the serpents who now controlled it.

He set down the thin awl, picked up a wooden tool with a metal loop and drew his wet fingertips across the face of the statue. Stroking it gently, he smoothed the cheeks and neck with even movements, creating a swan-like effect down to the sloping shoulders. Definitely the most erotic part of any woman in his opinion. He glanced back to the pad, confirming that he had the look right. It was obvious why the woman found it so easy to seduce men. She had fine, smooth skin and a delicate aspect easily missed under the tons of makeup she wore. He reached out for the glass of wine to his right and sipped. The cold kept it crisp and refreshing. He'd never been able to take the time to appreciate his work during his tenure with the Cadre. One didn't hang around to enjoy the results after slitting someone's throat or putting a bullet into their skulls. The appreciation of such skills was in not being discovered, of having no one even suspect anyone other than the intended responsible party, be it a jealous spouse or a cheated rival. Your anonymity was your glory, but it was hollow praise. But now there was awe and praise, shock and surprise, revulsion and reverence in equal measure, and they were all expressed solely for his art. His many exhibitions and shows around the world gave him the adoration he sorely needed.

His current body of work would never be part of a traditional showing, but it had a purpose far more important than the massaging of his ego. A purpose that required a combination of his skills both old and new. It was still art, to be sure, and it would still produce the shock and awe that any of his formal pieces could but to a more targeted audience. It also carried a public service message, something none of his previous compilations had done, a task both challenging and exhilarating. He finished the glass of pinot noir and altered the lighting within the sealed studio. The muted beams of light were directed carefully at the statue of the wanton harlot pining for her lost life of debauchery. A tiny rivulet of red seeped from the corner of one sculpted eye where the proximity of the body was close to the surface of the medium, giving the statue a touch of finality. It was his best work ever.

PART 2

For I Am the Lord, Thy Healer

Go and Heal the Sick

1

Behind the glass partition in a busy Georgia hospital, the machines beeped quietly as Toby Holmby slept fitfully in the large hospital bed. The oxygen mask on his face fogged lightly with every breath the boy took, but it was steady, and for that Dr. Elli Hollister was grateful. Thank God the school nurse had known CPR and called an ambulance immediately. Toby had come very close to death. It was early evening as Elli detailed the boy's status to his parents. His mother sat rigidly in a soft chair clutching her purse in one hand and her husband's palm in the other. She shed no tears and showed no emotion other than an obvious desire to be anywhere but in this room. Her husband, on the other hand, was devastated. He fought hard to hold back the tears glistening in his eyes and listened patiently as Elli described his son's condition.

"The adenocarcinoma is significant, which is why Toby collapsed. The pain combined with his loss of strength due to his low weight is most likely why he passed out." She paused in her explanation. Experience told her that this was the point where caregivers began asking questions. But although Toby's father finally lost the battle with his tear-filled eyes, neither of them spoke. The boy's mother merely closed her eyes and exhaled. "May I ask why Toby wasn't brought in to see a doctor before now?" Elli asked. "His physical condition indicates he's been ill for quite some time."

Toby's father managed to find his voice and answered. "We did our best to feed him healthy and make sure he got his rest. It always worked before. We thought this was just a really bad stomach flu or virus he picked up in school. We prayed the Lord would give him the strength to fight it off, but . . ." He choked before he could finish and looked as if he were on the verge of collapse himself.

"Well, there is good news despite his condition. We were able to locate the tumor in time before it spread further. I believe we can remove it and, with an aggressive approach to chemo and radiation, that Toby can make a full recovery. The methods of delivery are far more advanced these days and much more targeted, so the side effects will barely be noticeable. It's not liked the old days where the cure was worse than the disease."

Toby's father looked into Elli's eyes with a desperate gratitude, but before he could say anything, his wife clamped down hard on the hand she was holding. The man visibly winced in pain, and Elli could see the woman had dug her nails deep into his skin.

"Thank you, but that won't be necessary. Please just get Toby ready to return home. We'll care for him there." The woman delivered her remarks with all the compassion and emotion of a corpse, which was what her son would be if he left the hospital without treatment.

"Mrs. Holmby, you do understand that this isn't a virus. Your son has stomach cancer. It's very aggressive and very painful. If he isn't treated, he won't last but a few days and those days will be agonizing for him."

"I'm very well aware of that, Ms. Hollister." The woman couldn't even give Elli the respect of addressing her as Doctor. "But we are devout Christian Scientists. We believe that our son's fate rests with God and that to interfere with His plan would be blasphemy. We simply cannot approve of any treatment that alters that plan. My own father contracted the same disease when I was a child, and I nursed him through it. Prayer will suffice."

"Mrs. Holmby, your son is going to die painfully unless you let me help him," Elli told her, but the woman wouldn't back down.

"We raised our boy in the church. He knows the Gospel of James. If that is his fate, then so be it. We will not interfere with the Lord's plan but ask for his divine intervention."

Elli could tell by the look on her face that Toby's mother had no intention of allowing her son to be treated in any way. She looked at Toby's father cowering next to his domineering wife, wanting desperately to do something to at least ease his anguish. "We can make him comfortable here. We can at least make his remaining time . . . peaceful." She nearly choked on the words.

"You can do that for him?" Toby's father asked meekly. His wife dug her nails into his hand even harder, and Elli saw a thin trickle of blood wind its way down her wrist. This time, though, he squeezed back, causing her to let go. "If my son has to die," he said, "then he should be allowed to meet his maker in peace. I'd appreciate that, Dr. Hollister."

"We'll do whatever we can to make Toby comfortable, and you can spend as much time as you wish with him."

Mr. Holmby sighed in relief and resignation as Elli left the room. His wife jumped from the chair with eyes like daggers as she snarled, "How could you let them keep our boy? You know it's against the faith to allow them to keep him!"

"I've read the bloody Bible, Margie. Jesus sent his apostles out to cure the sick and ease their suffering. That's all we're doing—easing Toby's suffering."

"It's wrong, Carl. It's wrong and you know it. He should be home with his family when he goes to meet God."

"And he will be with his family, Margie. We'll be here with him."

Margie looked at her husband with obvious disappointment. "I knew you would be too weak to make the right decisions. Lord knows I tried to guide you in this, Carl, but you are bound and determined to condemn that boy to hell."

"Dammit, Margie, he's my son!" Carl thundered through tears. "My only son . . . Try to act like you actually give a damn."

"He's my son too, Carl, and I care more than you know." She walked over to her husband and put her hands on his shoulders. "I'll never stop caring about him. Not in this life or the next."

The Holmbys stayed long enough to sign the necessary papers to withhold life-saving treatments and then left to attend to their other children, two young girls that needed care. Elli assured them that Toby would be fine for a couple of days at least and that she would call if there was any change in his condition. She checked the IV drip carrying the nutrients and morphine to Toby's frail arm. His breathing was less labored, and his face showed fewer signs of stress now that the dosage had been properly adjusted. A slight flush of color was even returning to his cheeks even though his eyes still bore the hollowness of a starving child. Her own anger churned just below her professional threshold for bullshit. She was a doctor being forced to watch her patient wither away and die horribly when she had the necessary expertise to save him. It went contrary to everything she believed in. She made the notations on Toby's chart with instructions that she be notified immediately of any changes to Toby's condition or if his parents tried to remove him from the hospital. She didn't realize how upset she was until the pen snapped under pressure as she signed her name.

Elli was Savannah born and raised in a solid Christian home. Her parents had tended to her spiritual education with as much fervor as they had her academic education. She knew what it meant to have faith and to use it to guide your actions. The words of Matthew 10:8 were written on the inside of her locker right next to John 3:16. So why was this boy so different from the many patients she'd given end-of-life care to? She'd done it on numerous occasions. It was their choice whether to fight or accept their condition and receive palliative care, and her obligation as their doctor was to abide by their wishes. But her patient hadn't made this decision. Someone else had made it for him, and it was tearing her apart inside. Calm down and think this through rationally, she told herself. The patient is a twelve-year old boy with a family history of this type of cancer. He is underage, and therefore his legal guardians, in this case his parents, have the right to make those decisions in his stead. But Toby was not barely conscious or in agonizing pain. He was perfectly lucid and completely aware of his situation. He should have a say in whether he wanted to live, just like any other patient. His age didn't make him any less deserving of that respect.

Elli had seen Toby's mother drawing blood from her distraught husband as she sentenced her boy to death. Not so much as a tear or twitch of concern. As cold as a slab of iron in low-slung heels and drab gray. Her husband, at least, had shown grief and gratitude. She was sure that if she'd been able to speak to him alone that she could convince him to allow the treatment. But pitting one parent against another was severely frowned upon by hospital administration and was just plain cruel. A doctor's oath was to first do no harm. That included causing undue emotional distress to the families of the patients in her care. Yet every fiber of her being was telling her that she had a moral obligation to save what lives she could. Surely God wouldn't have given her the skills and abilities to save those lives if he didn't intend for her to use them. It's a moot point, Elli. You have your orders.

The sound of Toby stirring in his bed pulled her from her cauldron of frustration. He was breathing deeply now. The room was quiet and the halls empty. The dinner hour usually saw most of the visitors going home or to the cafeteria to feed their families while the patients were fed their bland meals.

She leaned over the bed and smiled into Toby's brown eyes. "Hey, cowboy, you fall off yer horse?" she said quietly. Toby was too tired to laugh but managed a slight chuckle. "My name's Dr. Hollister, but you can call me Elli. Do you know where you are?"

Toby turned his head slightly and then said, "Looks like a hospital room."

"Very good," Elli told him. She ran Toby through some cursory tests to make sure his eyes were functioning, and his speech wasn't impaired. She asked him if he remembered what happened and what day it was. He passed the tests with flying colors. Luckily, twenty years of medical research had pretty much stripped away the more psychotropic effects of the morphine, which made patients far more lucid during treatment. "You're a really sick little boy, you know."

"I know," Toby answered. "Been sick a while. Guess God must be mad at me."

Ellis bristled at the idea, knowing full well who must have put such nonsense into his head. "Why would God be mad at a cute little boy like you?"

Toby's chin began to quiver as his voice cracked. "I didn't know Eddie was going to hurt that girl, honest. I thought he was just going to tease her a bit." His heart monitor started to beep faster. "I should have stopped him, but I didn't know how. He's bigger than me."

"Calm down, cowboy. I'm sure you didn't mean any harm. When did this happen?"

"About a month ago," he muttered.

"Did you tell your teachers or your parents what happened?"

Toby dropped his eyes and whispered, "Not until later. Eddie is really scary when he's angry. I was afraid he was going to beat me up too if I talked. Now God's punishing me and I'm going to die."

Toby began to cry, and Elli cradled his head between her palms. "I want you to listen to me very carefully, Toby, and pay attention. I'm here to help you, but I can't if you won't trust me. Do you understand?" He wiped his eyes and nodded. She took his small hands in hers and said, "You have a tumor in your tummy, Toby, and it's been there a very long time without you knowing it, a lot longer than a month. Your granddaddy had the same illness, so you probably got it passed down from him. You are not being punished by God."

"But Momma said when boys and girls do bad things that go against the Bible, God punishes them for it."

Elli could remember hearing the same warnings in Sunday school from her teachers and her own mother, so she could understand how his child's mind had made the connection. She smiled gently and very carefully explained, "I suppose that's true. God does punish us for the things we do that are bad. But he also forgives us when we atone for our sins and ask for forgiveness. Did you ask God to forgive you?"

Toby nodded as hard as he could. "Every day for a week and every night before bed, no matter how bad I hurt."

"Well, then," Elli told him. "You have done all that God has ever asked of us, and He wouldn't want you to die thinking He didn't love you." Toby stopped shaking and calmed a bit, but he still looked distressed.

"Am I still going to die?" he asked her.

Elli thought for a moment and then looked into his eyes. "That's up to you, Toby. Do you want to die, or do you want to get better?"

Toby didn't hesitate for a second. "I don't want to die."

Elli brushed his hair from his eyes and said, "Then I won't let you."

2

Deacon sat at his desk, absently watching his crew. In the two weeks since Ellory Bainbridge had been found, the actual crime scene had not been located, no other suspects were uncovered, and the warrant for her husband had still not come through. Agnes Chen and her team were working day and night fine-tuning evidence and tightening their case, but nothing new came to light. Bachman clung to Allen Bainbridge's profile like a hungry tick, frustrated by the wall of diplomatic protection he currently enjoyed. Burke was still hunting down the killer's vehicle trace with only marginal headway. Everyone was pushing themselves to the limit to solve the case. Everyone but him. He couldn't get Neville's death off his mind, and he didn't know why. There was no comparison between the two: Ellory had been murdered, Neville's death had been a suicide. But something about the two pulled at Deacon, some common thread that begged to be unraveled. Whatever it was, it would have to wait.

Burke was oblivious to Deacon's dilemma as he sat and stared at the four sets of tracks on his screen. He was sure the killer had driven away in one of these vehicles. The tires were limited to the gasoline-powered trucks called Swamp Monsters that predated the war. They were notoriously noisy, emitted a tire whine that sounded like an angry swarm of killer bees, and contained no current tech to identify them. Fairly common in rural areas, over ninety percent of them had since been upgraded with bootleg tech to make use of the federal highway system and its free charging panels. The engine kits were marketed online as untraceable by the Feds, which appealed to those E-Rep citizens who bristled at Big Brother's watchful eye yet suckled his teat when he wasn't looking. Burke had cracked and tracked these babies six months after the hardware hit the market, which established his reputation as a technical genius. His doctoral thesis on the ease of locating these so-called untraceable conversions landed him his current position in Homeland. Unfortunately, his expertise had reached its limit. That meant going old-school, as MacNair was fond of saying. He would have to wait for an interterritorial warrant to access E-Rep computer files and conduct physical searches or have one of Agnes's nerds illegally hack into the local traffic cams. He looked over to where MacNair sat lost in thought and knew it was going to be a long night.

Chen's personal protégé was a chunky young man named Corbett. Immersed in the case evidence, he tuned out everything else and reveled in his own happy little world. The conference table at the center of the pit could accommodate fifteen people and housed a computer hub station below the glowing surface that doubled as a touch screen. It allowed the detectives to arrange and rearrange evidence, timelines, testimonies and any other bits of electronic evidence to form their case. When he'd mined every possible bit of information he could, he began researching external sources. Langley had a direct, secure connection to the Smithsonian, and he was able to run simultaneous searches with blinding speed. He translated every possible subject into a matrix and settled in to look for patterns. This was where he lived, moving and rotating the pieces of a gigantic electronic jigsaw puzzle, immersed in an onslaught of information, searching for that elusive connection no one else could see.

Burke walked by on his way to the cafeteria and asked Corbett if he wanted anything, but Corbett only muttered, "Naw, thanks," and kept staring.

Agnes sure has some strange pets, Burke thought as he went downstairs.

Corbett liked the detectives, especially Bachman. She was kind, funny, sassy and smelled nice. That she was a knockout wasn't lost on Corbett, but even though he didn't work for her directly, she was still his superior and he knew he had no chance. Her status as "off-limits" actually let his professional relationship with her flourish free of any sexual tension or mind games. And it boosted Corbett's ego to know that he had achieved something even the great Jeremy Burke could not. He had gained her respect.

Although he enjoyed interacting with Bachman and the others, Corbett preferred to pay Burke as little attention as possible. Burke used to tell him to keep hope alive and nudged him to give it a shot whenever Joyce walked by, that the department's rules on dating coworkers didn't apply in his case. But Corbett knew it wasn't an encouragement. Burke enjoyed seeing people embarrassed, especially Corbett. He had a nasty sense of humor when it came to those he deemed less worthy, and that included nearly everybody.

Joyce put a hand on Corbett's shoulder, and he finally looked away from his screens. "Hey, Tim, how goes the discovery?" she asked quietly. She was wearing that perfume he loved, but this time he barely noticed it. Corbett was onto something unusual.

"Pretty fascinating, actually," he responded. "You have one twisted individual on your hands."

"Hard to believe a man could be that upset over an affair, huh?" Deacon remarked from his desk.

"Oh, this guy was more than upset," Corbett told him. "He's taking the sixth commandment to a whole new level of depravity, or the seventh if he happens to be reformed."

"How so?" Deacon asked, turning his chair to face them.

"Well, it all goes back to the Old Testament. You know, when God was in a seriously pissy mood for about fifteen hundred years before Christ arrived? You just can't beat Leviticus for mayhem," he said with a giggle. Joyce was used to the giddiness he displayed when he was really into something, even if it was inappropriate, but Deacon only blinked. "See, the Bible built heavily on Talmudic law, so the punishments for sins against God were derived directly from it." Corbett pulled up a section of text from the Smithsonian archives and expanded it as they gathered around. "The methods for carrying out executions for the various sins are heavily detailed. Adultery was punishable by stoning." He reached over and pulled a section of an ancient text, lining it up in front of them and watching it translate into English. "Originally, those who bore witness to the crime carried out the sentence. The condemned was pushed from a ledge at least twice his own height, and they had to push him in just the right way so he landed facedown. If that didn't work, the second witness was supposed to drop a stone onto his chest to stop his heart. If that didn't work, the whole congregation went to work on him until he died."

"That's barbaric," Joyce told him.

"Actually, it was considered to be the most humane method of stoning," Corbett explained. "They figured the height of the fall would kill anyone instantly. If not, the secondary blow was considered a mercy. They also did things like cover the genitals to preserve the dignity of the condemned during the long walk to the execution site. They'd rub them down with oils and give them wine to make them relax. You should see some of the other methods of execution these guys invented. Believe me, this pales in comparison."

"Wait, go back! What was that about the wine?" Joyce interrupted.

Corbett backtracked and explained. "The wine was used to relax the condemned, and the oils were a calming agent. That way, he or she wouldn't be making a scene all the way to the execution site. That would have been considered embarrassing and undignified."

Deacon pulled the autopsy report from the corner of the display table. "Digger said the body had been rubbed with frankincense."

"This would definitely explain why," Corbett said. "Your killer was trying to follow the old execution rites for an adulterous wife."

None of them noticed Burke walk up with a steaming tumbler of hot tea in one hand and a protein bar in the other.

"That means the murder was religiously motivated," Deacon said.

"Or made to appear that way," Corbett offered. "There are plenty of places to push a body off a roof or high place, but it would have to be done someplace with no more than a twenty-foot drop, if we're going by the book. And it would have to be done in such a way that the body didn't split apart."

"You couldn't do that from a rooftop in the city; they're too high," Joyce pondered. "And too many people would see it. It had to be someplace secluded where he could hang onto her for a while, drug her, kill her, and then maim her without witnesses."

"Hair and fiber analysis didn't find any of the usual things we'd find in a home or urban location," Corbett read aloud. "No fabric traces other than the victim's clothing, no trace chemicals or household cleaners, not even pet hair. Nothing that she didn't have on her already from her own home."

"Limestone," Burke chimed in, startling them both. "Digger said there were traces of limestone in the head wound and she was dumped in a quarry lake, so she was covered in limestone sediment. There are a hundred old processing plants and cement factories around here. Start with those."

Deacon looked up at Burke and lifted an eyebrow. "Nicely done, Jeremy. I may have to make good on that bet after all."

"I'm counting on it, boss," Burke said.

"Uh, I hate to throw ice water on your little revelation but . . ." Corbett called up a map of the surrounding area showing any factories or plants where limestone was processed within a fifty-mile radius. "Most locations within the Federal Corridor affiliated with limestone processing were razed during the reconstruction since everything is made out of fibroplast now. That leaves only these locations currently standing." He transferred the map to the wide overhead display. Three red lights glowed along the border.

"These plants are still in heavy use, so the chances of them being the crime scene is slim, but these others"— he pointed to the twenty red lights glowing outside the Corridor—" are abandoned, making them prime candidates. And they're all in the E-Republic territory of the great state of Georgia."

Joyce grasped the back of her neck and muttered, "Terrific. It'd be easier to just get Bainbridge to confess."

"That would involve actually interrogating him," the director said as he walked in, "but it doesn't look like that's going to happen." The entire pit went into a frenzy of complaints as he waved them all to silence.

"I just got word from the E-Rep Justice Department. Apparently, the archbishop was a bit more pissed off at you than he let on," he told MacNair. "The Council contacted DC directly via their ambassador and made an official request through channels. They are demanding that we turn over the victim's remains and all case files to them on the grounds that both the victim and the suspect are their citizens. They're claiming jurisdiction over the case."

"But the murder happened in federal territory," Deacon objected. "They're still bound by treaty to waive jurisdiction."

"Not if you can't prove the murder actually occurred here. So far, the only thing we've been able to ascertain is that the body was dumped in federal territory. If you guys can't prove that the murder took place here as well, we may have to turn over the case to avoid a nasty political fight."

Deacon growled. "We'll file an injunction, then. Federal courts would shred that argument in a split second."

"Not this time, pal. The White House was petitioned directly, and the president has asked for a special meeting as soon as possible. They want you in DC within forty-eight hours to brief the president personally."

Deacon's frustration bubbled to the top. "Dammit, I don't have time to play these games. I have a killer to catch! Tell the president to have the Secret Service pull out whatever bug crawled up her ass. Isn't that what they pay them for?"

"Sorry, Deke, but my hands are tied on this. You'll be on an official flight to DC tomorrow night. And for the love of God, please bring your best manners this time," the director begged. "It's the fucking White House, and our budgets are being voted on in three weeks"."

"Terrific. Got any greater news for us?" Deacon asked sarcastically.

"Yeah, Daniel Carter, attorney at law is suing you for police brutality."

"Perfect."

3

Caulder Wirz paced in his study as he replayed the testimony of Spurlock to the Ecumenical Council. He personally reviewed all communications among the Council members, and this one had his blood boiling. The meeting at the White House should have been smooth and polite. Blumberg was to respectfully request the White House's approval for jurisdiction over the murder case. He was to do so with the utmost consideration and assurances that the Republic would resolve the case and prosecute the criminal involved. Nothing more, nothing less. Instead, the fool had turned it into a campaign speech and thrown accusations at the president, egged on by that idiot Spurlock. To make matters worse, after the president informed them that a recent hack was being investigated by the FBI, Spurlock insulted her and leveled false accusations of collusion against two of the country's biggest allies. Spurlock's crowning failure was waiting until he could inform the Council in person, which meant that the FBI had been operating within their borders for nearly forty-eight hours unchecked.

Wirz downed his brandy and threw the glass against the fireplace. If he hadn't been busy propping up a hungover Wallace Milton in front of a live national audience, he would have been there to control Blumberg. He should have anticipated that the high bishop would send that jealous prick Spurlock in his place. Spurlock had been licking the old man's ass for years, but when the bishop was raised to lead the Council, he'd chosen Wirz to serve him instead. Spurlock had been fuming about the demotion ever since, and he'd used this meeting as an opportunity to advance his own status. He'd riled up Blumberg and turned an annoying intrusion into an international incident. To make matters worse, the fool had threatened the president to showcase his talents as a political player. A mistake he would soon pay dearly for.

The Cadre would not be pleased. Regardless of the circumstances, Wirz would ultimately be responsible for any failures within his region of influence. If his failures threatened the Agenda, he would be replaced, and every operative knew what replacement within the Cadre meant. It was not a demotion or a reassignment: it was an erasure. It was also how Wirz had attained his current position, and he was determined not to suffer the same fate. He contacted his field personnel immediately, but time was not on his side. All he could do now was wait.

The comm line chimed as he filled another brandy snifter. "Wirz," he answered.

"There's been a complication," the voice on the line said. "We were unable to warn the team at the farmhouse. Their communications are being blacked out, and the authorities already had them surrounded when we arrived."

"Have they been apprehended yet?" Wirz asked.

"Security forces have moved into the main house, and their arrest is imminent."

"Make a clean sweep of it before anyone can leave," Wirz said. The voice clicked off, and the line reset. It was heavily encrypted, rotating ciphers after every communication.

On the other end of the encrypted line, the order was carried out without question. The voice monitoring the federal police communications noted that they had the terrorists in custody and would be processing identification on-site. Before those identification requests could be sent, a remote command was transmitted to a web of detonators embedded within the walls of the farmhouse, and the entire structure blew apart. The explosives were military grade, which ensured that all evidence would be vaporized, as well as anyone within one hundred fifty yards of the structure. The USGS registered the shock on its seismographs in Knoxville as a magnitude 3.5 temblor, and the fireball lit the night sky clear to Charleston thirty-five miles away.

Wirz took a deep breath to clear his mind and downed his second brandy. One problem solved. It had cost him the lives of seven of his best associates, but that was an accepted risk. He needed no confirmation that his order had been carried out. Cadre personnel didn't debate orders. They did as they were told, unlike those buffoons on the Council or the Senate. The explosion would have caught the attention of every news service in the country by now, and it was crucial that the information be controlled. He dictated several directives and sent them out to various Cadre operatives conveniently placed within the media. The preconceived statements would be transmitted to the press at the appropriate times.

The brandy did its work, and he felt his tension fade away as he lay down on the thick sofa. By tomorrow, the death of the task force at the hands of terrorists would be front-page news. The failure of the federal government to protect a United States territory from an attack on its infrastructure would be trending across the net within minutes. Spurlock's failure would become Wirz's stroke of genius, and the ruling bodies would be relieved. As for Spurlock, he'd be meeting an untimely end as soon as Wirz could arrange it. He would have preferred to do the deed personally. Power over someone's life and death had always been his preferred cocktail. But he could not risk the suspicion. In the morning he would begin research on Milton's successor, the Honorable Senator Quentin Hollister.

4

The sun set as Deacon brushed the lines of dust from the folds of his dress uniform, checked his best manners, and departed for the flight deck, leaving Joyce in command of the investigation. The flight from Huntsville to DC was short and sweet, only an hour and a half from HQ to the White House lawn thanks to an unmarked, jet-powered UH-89 Black Hawk provided by the army. He hadn't been inside one since the war. Converted strictly for clandestine domestic runs, this one was as plush as it was fierce. Comfortable leather seating had replaced the jump seats and cargo netting, but it could still cut through an advancing enemy like Swiss cheese with its side-mounted rail cannons, a first-class killing machine. The public outcry over its use on American citizens during the war had kick-started the cessation of hostilities, which led to the eventual peace treaty. They were now restricted to military use on foreign soil only, but a select few had been retasked to each of the federal services for special missions.

Within the main cabin, banks of video screens broadcast the news from every corner of the globe in real time, but a breaking report of a massive explosion in South Carolina dominated the feed. The pilot chimed in that air traffic was being rerouted as a precaution and they'd be about twenty minutes behind schedule. Deacon muted this channel as well. He knew the Milton case was airtight. His team had left nothing unresolved. The evidence, along with the fully represented suspect's freely given confession, guaranteed that Pete Milton would be spending time in federal prison regardless of who his father was. The police brutality charge was utter bullshit, but if Carter pressed the issue, Deacon had no problem introducing him to what real police brutality entailed. He'd served through the Chicago riots of 2019 and was more than willing to give Carter a personal lesson.

The Bainbridge murder was another matter. He needed to see it through, had promised Kate that her sister's murder wouldn't go unpunished. If jurisdiction was returned to E-Rep territory, it would never happen. In cases such as these, Ecumenical Courts usually focused on the sins of the victim before prosecuting the criminal. If the victim's death was warranted under religious law, the criminal would be given an opportunity to confess and state the reasons why he felt his crime was just. There was a running joke about E-Rep criminals. No matter how inept they were at committing crimes, they knew their Bible well enough to justify damned near anything they did. Most got off with sizable fines and some serious penance, but it amounted to nothing in the end. The victim was left to take the blame for whatever befell them. The fact that Ellory was guilty of adultery and carrying another man's child would be enough to exonerate her husband of any criminal act if he were arrested and tried. Ellory's family would thereafter suffer public humiliation as their daughter's sins were publicly detailed at his acquittal. Deacon couldn't let that happen. He'd hoped to have definitive evidence to keep control of the investigation before he touched down, but Agnes and her team had found nothing to tie the killer to the Corridor. Even Burke had come up empty. All he knew for sure was that the killer had entered the Federal Corridor from one of the surrounding territories and had returned to it the same way. The only thing Deacon had in his favor was the timeline. Digger's autopsy and subsequent discovery had provided a time of death so close to the witnessed body dump that there was no way to tell what side of the border the murder had been committed on. All he had to do was cast enough doubt to leave the question unanswered.

By the time the Black Hawk reached DC, it was full night in the capital, and the whisper-quiet engines of the bird slipped through the night sky heading for the South Lawn. Deacon was not used to such door-to-door service. Whatever was going down in Washington, it was clear that the president wanted his presence to be kept from prying eyes. Deacon marshaled his argument as the craft circled for clearance. He hated political mind games. He'd been offered the directorship of Huntsville three times in his career and had passed on it each time for just this reason: a gut loathing of politics and zero tolerance for bullshit. The president undoubtedly wanted to hear his justification for maintaining control before handing over jurisdiction to the territorial authorities so she could appear cooperative for the upcoming elections.

It was well past the dinner hour, and his stomach growled loudly as he disembarked. It rumbled embarrassingly as the Secret Service escorted him to the president. Outside the Oval, he was handed off to an agent whom he recognized. Calvin Harris waited until the other agents departed and then gave him a warm smile and a handshake.

"Welcome to the White House, Lieutenant." The man had aged since that day at Arlington. The whole country had. But it was more evident in the brutal scar on this man's cheek and the edge in his eyes.

"Good to see you again, Agent Harris," Deacon responded. An incredible aroma was lingering in the hall and his stomach rumbled again, getting Harris's attention.

"I think we can take care of that," Harris said quietly and opened the door, allowing a wave of mouth-watering scents to surround him. "Go right in, sir."

Deacon entered the Oval Office and pulled himself to attention. The last time he'd been in this room, a man had pinned the Medal of Honor to his chest for his service during war time. That man now lay in Arlington National Cemetery next to his son. The man's wife now sat in his place.

"Lt. MacNair, welcome to the White House," Margot said as she approached.

"Madam President," he responded, extending his hand.

Margot Turnouer had changed considerably since his last visit. Back then she had been a distance runner, much to the chagrin of the Secret Service. She'd only been forty-nine at the time. Her runner's frame had softened since then, leaving her with a pleasant set of feminine curves. But that was the only part of her that had softened. The rest had hardened like a diamond. The immense pressure of burying a son in front of the nation and a husband one year later had forced a change in her. She was no longer the sweet and confident First Lady that had charmed the nation in both territories and earned their sympathy with a public display of grief. She was now the fierce, take-no-prisoners leader of what was left of the free world, and it showed.

They exchanged a friendly but hurried handshake as she breezed past him toward a dining table. "Please forgive the lack of decorum, Lieutenant, but my day has consisted of fourteen cups of coffee, a bowl of oatmeal and two energy bars. And I have two more meetings after this one." She indicated the chair opposite her own and said, "Please join me."

Deacon was thrown off guard by the informality, and she wasted no time sitting down and serving out food. The table was set with heaps of spicy roast beef, seasoned potatoes, greens and light, buttery biscuits. No alcohol had been brought in, but ice-cold sweet tea was poured. The aroma set his stomach to rumbling again. "Is that Cookie's roast beef?" he asked as he sat across from her. "I thought he retired."

"He did," she told him. "This wonderful meal is courtesy of his son, Curtis. He may be a four-star Michelin chef, but he kept his daddy's teachings." Deacon smiled as he let the roast beef melt on his tongue and bit into a biscuit. "I'm surprised you remember Cookie," Margot told him. "That was years ago."

"We served together in Iraq, ma'am. He kept us alive and well fed. He was a great admirer of your husband and was honored to be here as the White House chef."

"Believe me, the honor was all ours," Margot told him. "Warren declared every Sunday dinner at the White House to be one of Cookie's hometown specialties. He didn't care if the ambassador to France was joining us. The man would get corn bread and barbecue if that was Cookie's choice."

"Your husband had excellent taste, Madam President."

They ate in silence for a few minutes, and then Margot said, "I apologize for calling you here so late. I hope this will make up for my inconveniencing you."

"I didn't come here expecting a dinner date, ma'am," Deacon replied. "And I am grateful for the meal. But you should know my team is certain that the case against Senator Milton's son is as tight as it can be. The evidence is spot-on and corroborated in full by Milton's confession and his two companions. All the interviews were conducted in the presence of the E-Republic legal establishment and countersigned by an archbishop for good measure. Turning over the accompanying case to the territorial police would be a major mistake."

Margot stopped chewing and gave him her full attention. "Make your case, Lieutenant. I'm listening."

Deacon did so to the best of his ability, remembering the director's admonition to be on his most respectful behavior. He detailed what they knew of the murder and the pending classification of the crime as a double homicide due to the unborn child. She listened without interruption as he detailed the investigation until his comm link chirped urgently.

"It's my team with an update, ma'am. May I?" he asked politely.

She nodded in agreement and excused him. She resumed her meal, but an urgent message came over her own data pad as she waited. The news was devastating. The field reports listing the casualties uploaded along with the status of the mission. There would be hell to pay in the press tomorrow, but tonight she had to find a way to use this jurisdictional dispute to her advantage as it was now her only way in. When Deacon returned to the table, he was visibly upset. "Not good news, I take it," she said.

"We haven't been able to pin down the exact location where the actual crime was committed. The evidence indicates that the location can't be more than an hour's distance from where the body was disposed of in the Corridor. Unfortunately, that means the murder could have been committed either inside or outside of federal territory. There just isn't enough evidence yet to pinpoint it."

Margot took a sip of tea and patted her lips. "What you are telling me, Lieutenant, is that you have no definitive evidence to support denying the return of jurisdiction to the Ecclesiastical Republic Territorial Police and every reason to suspect that they may be within their rights."

Deacon's chest went cold. He could see where this was going and blurted out. "If we turn this investigation over to them, we'll be ignoring the rights of the victim and her family. They deserve to know who did this to their daughter. E-Rep will smear her reputation, vilify her publicly, then sweep it under the rug as a just punishment, and her family will suffer the shame."

"Take it down a notch, Lieutenant," Margot warned him in an even tone. They may have just shared a meal, but this was official business and she was still the president.

Deacon got himself under control and lowered his eyes. "My apologies for my outburst, Madam President. It's just . . . this woman was brutally murdered. I've never seen anything like this in my years in the service, not even during war time, and people did some pretty heinous shit back then. Her sister maintains dual federal and territorial citizenship, and I promised her that I wouldn't let her sister's killer go unpunished."

Margot sat back and looked at Deacon. He'd been with Homeland for more than a decade, but he was still very much the honorable soldier she remembered. "Sit down, Lieutenant," she said quietly. When he had relaxed, she said, "I sympathize with your situation, and personally I stand behind your commitment to this investigation and the victim's family one hundred percent. That being said, with an election coming up in less than six months, I can't afford to appear insensitive to the rights of the territorial authorities."

Oh no, here it comes, Deacon thought.

"So, you and I are going to do a little horse trading." Margot rose and walked over to her desk to retrieve a digital file. "I don't have enough grounds to deny E-Rep any jurisdiction in this case, but I can keep you in the game as the quarterback. I can declare this to be a joint investigation with you calling the shots. E-Rep will have to assign personnel to assist in your investigation and ensure that all territorial rights are adhered to, but they will have to answer to you when it comes to pursuing this case and its leads."

"You know they don't like bad press when it comes to religiously motivated punishments. And with an election coming, they need to appear as righteous as ever to the nation," Deacon told her. "They'll do everything they can to obstruct us."

"I'm sure they'll try," Margot replied. "And I expect your team to do everything they can to keep that from happening." She handed him the secured comm pad. "I'll supply you with ironclad federal warrants that guarantee you and your team unrestricted access to E-Rep territory, its citizens and property. You'll have full authority to run the investigation as you see fit, provided you are accompanied by their representatives at all times. That should move things along. And if they try to obstruct any part of this case, you are to report it to command and to me personally."

"And the horse I'm supposed to provide in this horse trade?" Deacon asked.

Margot sat across from him and said quietly, "What I am about to tell you does not leave this room, Lieutenant. It is for your eyes and ears only."

Deacon was used to handling classified information, but the expression on the president's face sent a chill up his spine. "Understood, ma'am."

Deacon listened as the president outlined the threat and what the FBI had uncovered. As she spoke, he scrolled through the documents she summarized on the data pad. The most recent report was from the task force sent to apprehend suspected domestic terrorists. "That business in South Carolina—that was part of this?"

"We believe so, but the building and its occupants were incinerated in the blast."

Deacon scrolled through the names of the officers on the task force. "I know these men. Most of them were bomb detail during the Virginia invasion. They wouldn't have walked into a building without clearing it first."

"They didn't. The explosives were hidden too well to be detected, and they were remotely detonated. Whoever did this made sure there was nothing left behind, not even their own operatives."

Deacon read through the FBI synopsis and exhaled heavily. "This has to be coming from somewhere in E-Rep leadership, maybe even the Ecumenical Council itself. There is no way this could be happening without a few of them being in on it."

"My thoughts exactly," Margo responded.

"No disrespect intended, Madam President, but how the hell am I supposed to get within spitting distance of the Council or the Senate? They aren't exactly color-blind. They hate me almost as much as they hate you!"

Margot smiled. "Well, as of right now, you are the lead investigating detective on a coalition murder case wherein the sons of not one but three high-ranking E-Rep senators are involved. They can hate you all they want, but they have no choice but to cooperate, and that means giving you access."

He examined her sly smile for a minute and then said, "You were going to ask me to stay on this case before I even begged you to."

"I hadn't planned on asking, Lieutenant."

"So, is this an executive order?"

"I need you, MacNair," Margot told him.

Deacon shook his head. "I'm not a spy."

"You're all I have."

An hour later, with a comm pad securely coded to his DNA and a direct line to the president, Deacon was hustled back to Huntsville with a series of legislative warrants and a bad case of heartburn. He'd flown to DC to keep control of one case and left with a national crisis on his plate. His stomach clenched in pain. He hadn't felt this terrible since drinking that holistic, antioxidant, microbrew crap Jeremy Burke foisted on him at last month's summer picnic. The Black Hawk banked away from the Atlantic, and he pushed the pilot's intercom.

"Captain, could you break south a bit? I want to have a look at that blast site in South Carolina."

"Sure thing, Lieutenant," the pilot told him.

One of the conditions he'd been able to secure was total access to the Black Hawk whenever necessary. It had been retasked to Huntsville by the end of the meeting. Since it was originally registered as an FBI transport, it had no problems entering restricted airspace of the Ecclesiastical Republic, given the situation on the ground. It flew low and quiet in the dark and within forty-five minutes was hovering over the site of a crater in Dorchester County.

5

The sound of an ambulance arriving below broke her from her memories. She watched it pull in and unload a patient, followed quickly by another as it left. *Must be a car accident,* she thought and felt the urge to race down to the ER. But she'd been pulled from rotation and summoned to the administrator's office. She was to stay put until he said otherwise. Elli left the window and paced the mundane office. The walls bore the standard medical charts one would expect a doctor to have. The bookshelves contained a fair number of medical texts and an equally unassuming number of hospital policy binders and labor codes. Even the couch was a nondescript beige. The only piece of furniture in the room that bore any hint of ornamentation was the antique wooden desk. Several family photos nestled beneath a flowing Boston fern. A coffee cup bearing the words "World's Greatest Dad" held the remnants of the morning's coffee as it congealed into sludge. There were colorful paper trays and sorters and a rubbery clown with accordion arms hanging from the corner of his monitor. The hand carved name plate declared the desk to be the domain of Oliver Morton, MD, PhD, and on the far corner of the desk sat a row of old books that were neither medical nor corporate in nature. Seven different versions of the Bible sat between two carved wooden bookends depicting clasped hands in prayer. Elli's father had much more expensive and fully illustrated versions of these same books, along with many from other religions in his library at home. But these were far more worn and creased.

Elli stared out of the window and thought of Toby. She thought about how emaciated he'd been when he was first brought in the ER. She remembered the moment he opened his eyes and smiled. She remembered how brave he'd been during treatment and how grateful and happy he'd been when his parents took him home healthy once again. She thanked God her last sight of him had been a grinning twelve-year old boy bouncing out of a wheelchair and scrambling up into his father's pickup. She froze the image in her mind and held it.

The door opened as the administrator came in. He'd been pitching in downstairs and was still wearing dirty scrubs. Unusual for a paper-pusher, but he still practiced and liked to keep his skills sharp. He also knew the importance of understanding how an ER and its staff functioned under pressure, and the best way to accomplish that was to be one of them when it counted. It made him one of the best admins in the system and Angel's Mercy Memorial one of the tightest and most successfully run hospitals in the country.

Oliver Morton threw a case file onto his desk, knocking over one of the pictures there. He was extremely upset, and Elli knew she was the cause. He settled into his chair and placed his hands flat on the desk with the file between them. When he deemed himself under control, he clasped his hands and regarded her with the stern disappointment of a father figure. Elli blushed and crossed her arms defensively, diverting her eyes to the toppled photograph.

"I suppose I don't need to tell you why you're here," he said and waited patiently for her to respond.

"The Holmby boy?" she asked meekly.

"The Holmby boy," he repeated sternly. "Little Toby Holmby."

"It was a judgment call, Oliver. I made a decision in my patient's best interest, and it was a mistake!" she stammered.

"A mistake?" he asked, cocking his head. "A mistake? Giving penicillin to a patient who's allergic to it because you couldn't understand the attending's handwriting, that's a mistake. Accidentally leaving a sponge inside of a patient during surgery, that's a mistake. Accidentally cutting off a man's testicles during hemorrhoid surgery, that's a big mistake. What you did was criminal!" he exclaimed as he slammed his hand down on the thick file, causing Elli to jump.

"Defiance of a patient's directives, concealing treatment from the parents, falsifying patient records, drug theft? The only reason you're not in custody right now—"

"Is because my father's a high-ranking senator?" Elli interrupted.

"Is because the boy's parents refused to press charges," Oliver finished. "Mr. Holmby spoke to the district attorney and the Ecumenical Council on your behalf. They've agreed to leave all disciplinary action up to the hospital board, and by extension that means me."

Elli was shocked. She never expected the Holmbys to speak up for her. In fact, she'd fully expected old iron-hearted Margie Holmby to petition for her crucifixion. Toby's poor father must have finally put his foot down. In the end, even in his grief and pain he'd managed to forgive her. She felt profoundly guilty for lying to him.

"How did you treat him?" Oliver asked.

"Targeted tri-phase Gemcitabine and five Flourouracil administered over three days to shrink the tumor after the family went home at night."

"How'd you remove it without them knowing?"

"I told them I had to re-suture his biopsy incision overnight because it tore. Went in with a micro scalpel and removed it along with the surrounding tissue."

Oliver looked at her carefully as he twirled a stylus in his hand. "How'd you acquire the surgical team to assist?"

This was the moment Elli had been dreading. She could withstand any punishments leveled at her, but she wasn't about to ruin anyone else's career. "I borrowed a surgical team of residents from pediatrics. They weren't familiar with the case."

"Names," Oliver demanded.

"It doesn't matter," she answered.

"I'll be the judge of what matters in this hospital, Dr. Hollister."

Elli dug in her heels. "It doesn't matter because I misled them. I engaged them under false pretenses and phonied up the charts. I let them think the tumor was a benign anomaly."

Oliver could tell he wasn't going to get an answer from her, but the question was merely a test. It had been one of those unknowing residents who let slip to him about the surgery. The file in his hand contained the names of everyone involved. The fact that Elli refused to name them told him

112

everything about her character, which was why he asked. "Tri-phase is a tightly regulated and expensive chemo treatment. How'd you get it without a formal requisition?"

Elli cleared her throat and answered, "Mr. Cummings. Rural patient forty-three scheduled for in-home infusion next week."

"You stole cancer meds from a residence-bound patient?"

"Not at all, sir. Mr. Cummings passed away two days prior to Toby's admission. The paperwork hadn't gone through channels yet, and his doses were already requisitioned for remote treatment." Oliver raised an eyebrow but said nothing. "Those meds are write-offs," Elli explained. "They're donated by the hospital to impoverished, home-bound patients under a state grant. The hospital gets reimbursed for every treatment and the drugs aren't cross-checked, so no one can ever trace it to a specific patient. They just get lost in bureaucratic red tape and are buried in the budget."

"Well, thank you so much for thinking of our bottom line," Oliver offered sarcastically. He drummed his fingers on the file and then sighed heavily. "Do you have any idea the damage you've caused to this hospital's reputation? We have a duty to respect the wishes of our patients regarding their treatment."

"I was respecting his wishes!" she cried.

"His parents specifically told you that treating him would violate their faith covenant, and they refused life-saving treatment, which is their right under the law."

"They weren't my patients," Elli countered. "Toby was. And he said he wanted to live."

"He told you. A twelve-year old boy dying of cancer told you he didn't want to die."

"Yes," Elli answered.

"What pain meds was he on?" Oliver asked.

"Enomorphine."

"Terrific!" Oliver exclaimed, throwing up his hands. "The kid is high as a kite and you ask him for permission to treat him."

"Oh, come on, Oliver. That's not fair and you know it. Enomorphine has no cognitive impairment side effects. The patient stays lucid."

"Elli, the patient was a CHILD."

"A child who wanted to live," she said. "Am I supposed to just say, 'Tough luck, kid, your parent insists it's God's will that you die, so you're up shit creek,' just because he's twelve?"

Oliver dropped his head into his hands and rubbed his eyes. He regained his composure and glanced at the row of Bibles on his desk.

"Oliver, someone had to be that child's advocate. I couldn't just ignore what he wanted."

He looked at Elli compassionately and said, "Sit down." When she hesitated, he pointed to the couch. She reluctantly threw herself onto it, and he rose to join her. As they both sat staring at the floor, he said, "I know what it means to fight for the life of a child. You weren't here in the old days before the conflict. Back then, a doctor anywhere in the country could countermand a parent's wishes if it put the child's life at risk. There were laws that protected us and gave us that option." He paused and looked at Elli. "In federal hospitals, those laws still exist, and they're only implemented in extreme circumstances and with the approval of a federal court order. But this isn't federal territory, Elli. This is the Ecclesiastical state of Georgia. We cannot disregard the faith-based choices of any patient, his parents or legal guardians, no matter how it may fly in the face of reason or as a betrayal of our Hippocratic Oath. It's what the citizens of this state fought for: the right to decide their own fates without the intervention of government."

"Just the intervention of God," Elli muttered.

"To them, it's not intervention but divine purpose. We have to accept that."

Elli shook her head. "I have no problem with accepting divine purpose. I grew up accepting it. But I don't consider telling a child that God is killing him for ditching school and getting into trouble, something every kid under the age of fifteen has tried at least once or twice, to be divine. What kind of parent tells her son that he's going to die because played hooky? That's not divine purpose, that's child abuse."

Oliver stared at the floor, thinking about what Elli had just told him. After a minute of silence, he stood up. "You're suspended pending further investigation from the board. All your hospital privileges are hereby revoked."

"What!!" Elli thundered.

"Just until the board can convene to review the situation," he told her. "Elli, I have no choice but to suspend you. I can't let this go unanswered." She started to protest, and he cut her off sharply. "It's just until I can present your case to them in its full context. There are obviously extenuating circumstances that led to your decision, so allow me the chance to present them."

Elli huffed in frustration but backed down. She could see he was caught between a rock and a hard place. "So, you believe me."

"I believe you were in a tough position and you acted in the best interests of your patient according to his direct wishes. However," he cautioned, "those circumstances do not excuse theft and breach of ethics. There are going to be consequences, Elli. I can't protect you from that, especially not with such a high-profile case like this. You can't turn on a television anywhere without hearing about the miraculous recovery of Toby Holmby. The boy saved by God."

The intercom buzzed, breaking the mood. Several ambulances were on their way with patients from a structure fire. The burn ward was about to be inundated. "Go on, get your gear and go home," Oliver told her.

"My patients—"

"Charlie Guthrie can take over your patients. I'll see to it that they're attended to. Now get going so I can deal with this overload."

He escorted Elli into the hall, and she headed off to the staff lounge while the administrator ran down to the ER. She yearned to be in the thick of the crisis, but she'd just been effectively fired. It wasn't an actual termination, but she knew the chances of her returning were next to nothing. As she stuffed her clothes and personal items into her duffel bag, she looked into the small mirror on the inside of her locker door. *Was it worth flushing your career down the toilet?* the mirror asked her. Her reluctant answer was yes. It had been worth it.

"Totally and completely worth it," she said aloud as she slammed the door shut.

6

"How could such an atrocity happen to one of our citizens?" the high archbishop asked. The brass nameplate in front of him read Theodore Gideon. "Who is responsible for this act?" He looked around the Council chamber, but all of the archbishops appeared equally appalled at the contents of the federal evidence report. Wirz had read it already and had been stonewalling the Feds for a week.

"Her name was on the Sanctioned List, Your Excellency," he reminded Gideon. "Her husband petitioned this Council for punishment two months ago."

"You above all, Wirz, should be aware that we would never have ordered such a penance while the woman was with child. She would have been cloistered with the holy sisters at the monastery until she gave birth. It would be an unthinkable abomination to murder an innocent child."

The members of the Ecumenical Council all voiced their agreement as the session devolved into isolated discussions of the fate of Ellory Bainbridge. Wirz found it all highly amusing. None of the members of the Council seemed aware of the sanctimonious irony of defending the sacred life of an unborn child while casually discussing the execution of its mother. He wondered if their compassion for the infant would have been so robust had they known of its biracial nature.

The high archbishop rapped on his desk to call the gathering to order. "Do the police have a suspect in this killing, Wirz?"

"They currently suspect her husband of the crime and not unreasonably so."

Gideon scowled. "He would certainly be within his rights to do so. Is he guilty?"

"The evidence seems to support it," Wirz said. "However, several witnesses have come forward to provide him with an alibi. Only two of them have been found to be reliable."

"Could he have solicited a third party to do so in his stead?"

"No, Your Excellency," Wirz answered. It was not unheard of for victims of transgressions to hire professional executioners to act on their behalf, but they had to be present at the time of penance for it to be considered legal. "I personally reviewed all of his finances and contacted all licensed professionals in the area. No such action was legally contracted. And we do have witnesses to support his presence elsewhere. At this time, we believe this to be an unsanctioned penance by persons unknown."

"Then we have a devil in our midst." The high archbishop thought for a moment and then addressed the Council. "In light of the threat this agent of Satan poses, it is in our best interests to cooperate with the federal officers in this matter. It is our sacred duty to protect the citizens of the Republic at all costs and show the nation that we are indeed a just and lawful society in the eyes of God." He rapped his gavel twice. "Dismissed."

The archbishops filed out, all chattering among each other. Gideon tapped his nameplate impatiently as he waited for them to leave. Archbishop Wirz remained seated. He did not need to be told there was more to discuss.

When the chamber cleared and the doors were secured, Gideon tossed a transcript of the meeting between Spurlock and the president toward him and spat, "How could you let this happen, Wirz!" His face darkened as he spoke. "You assured me that your security forces could fend off any intruder. Now we find that our leadership and our very judgments have been compromised and that the federal government knows of the break-in."

"The individual responsible for the intrusion was stopped before he could gain total access. We have his digital footprint now and know what to look for. He won't get in again."

Gideon looked at him grimly. "You indicated that the Bainbridge woman had been sanctioned. Is there any possibility that this case is connected to the Judicii Poenitentiae that was compromised?"

Wirz looked at him curiously. "It's doubtful as they were heavily encrypted, Your Excellency. But the list is merely a record of the judgments handed down by the Ecumenical Courts. Legal, humane sentences dictated by law. Hardly worth worrying over."

"It is not our judgments that worry me. Our judicial system is a beacon of biblical truth. We have a crime rate less than a fourth the rate of the Constitutionalists thanks to the new rehabilitation protocols you've instituted. But the heathen territory has been painting us as barbarians since before the war. The Unification Party zealots have publicly compared our system of justice to sharia law and branded us hardliners and terrorists. They call us the American Caliphate. They would not hesitate to use this murder as proof that we are monsters."

"We'll find him long before he can decrypt any of the data he stole. My associates are actively pursuing him as we speak," Wirz assured him.

"As is the White House, from what Spurlock has indicated." Gideon slouched in his chair. "That woman has led this country astray as Eve did Adam, and now she has sent her serpents into our paradise."

"Those serpents paid a heavy price for their entry into paradise. I'm told none of them survived." Wirz watched as a satisfied grin crept across Gideon's face.

"Then in this service to our Republic, they have no doubt redeemed their souls for obeying the commands of Satan."

"Margot Turnouer is a formidable leader, but I would hardly consider her the equal of Satan, Your Excellency."

"Then you underestimate her, my friend," the man said grimly. "We suffered heavy losses during the Civil War. The procreation laws arrested those losses, but our citizenry still diminishes every year. Many who go to universities in the Constitutional territory refuse to return. They seek asylum as refugees of religious persecution, and it's granted without question. We've had to suspend all travel visas not related to humanitarian missions, even the educational ones, to stem our losses. It's been especially difficult for those with family across the borders. The leadership tells me that if we do not increase the birth rates of our population twofold, we will lose our ability to be self-sustaining within fifty years."

"The survivability rate in our neonatal units is the highest in the nation, and our birthrates are increasing," Wirz replied. "The average family currently supports two to three children, and the able-bodied male workforce is ninety-seven percent employed."

Gideon cast him a sideways glance. "You know as well as I do that close to half our population was on public assistance when we seceded. They were cut off from those programs when we formed our own nation, and we've had to create jobs and force them into working for minimum wage. Of the sixty-five or so percent left, those lucky enough to be highly educated professionals work more than sixty hours a week and use such determination as an excuse to shun the idea of children or marriage altogether."

"God will not allow his kingdom to be destroyed, Your Excellency. We have worked too hard to achieve it. The Marriage and Family Mandate will be brought before the Senate after the elections. It will ensure that we keep our male population procreating and free up more employment opportunities for them."

The old man looked at Wirz as if he were a child. "Thank you, my friend, for being our warrior for God. Now, how are we going to deal with Bainbridge and these federal police?"

"I've known Allen for many years, Your Excellency. I can guarantee that he'll behave. And cooperation will not be a problem. I shall assign a police deputy to escort the federal authorities during the investigation. That should protect the rights of our citizens and give us access to all of their evidence. If they determine the murder location is within our territory, we'll know it immediately and can seize control. And if they step out of line at any time during the investigation, we'll have a viable witness and be well within our rights to expel them from the territory. That will leave us to assume total control of the investigation, no matter what the president has ordered."

"Then I will leave it in your capable hands," Gideon told him. "You may go."

Wirz cleared his throat. "There is another matter pending summary judgment that I wish to address, Your Excellency. A situation that I believe could be used to our advantage."

"What is it?" Gideon asked.

"The incident with the Holmby child. I believe the doctor in charge of his care is facing permanent censorship and revocation of her license to practice."

Gideon groaned. "That poor boy. A ridiculous loss but one that cannot go unanswered."

"I understand, sir, but the Christian sect his family belongs to shuns medical intervention. They are devout, but physicians of Hollister's caliber are rare. She's considered one of the best physicians in the state and has saved many children's lives. We should consider that her devotion to her calling as a healer no doubt prompted her to act to save the boy's life at any cost. In light of the continuing exodus of our professional citizens and their diminishing birthrate, we cannot afford to lose her expertise."

"Her disrespect for the edicts of our Lord God cannot go unpunished, Wirz."

"Understood, but she is also the daughter of Senator Quentin Hollister. As you know, he is one of our brightest candidates for promotion to federal service. Any judgment rendered against her would no doubt sabotage his chances. Thus, it would also be in our political best interests to give her the opportunity to atone rather than face punishment."

"You have something in mind, don't you?"

Wirz smiled. "Yes, Your Excellency. Appoint her as one of the liaison officers to the murder investigation. She can fulfill her penance on the team throughout the investigation by informing us of their every move. Her lack of any real investigative experience will hamper their efforts and buy us time. Let her serve the Council and the Republic in the name of God to atone for defying God's plan. Send her forth as a sheep in the midst of wolves."

Gideon considered Wirz's suggestion and ultimately agreed. He would have preferred a harsher punishment for the woman, but Wirz was right: they could not afford to lose citizens of her expertise. He sat back and sighed. "I long for the days when we were simply men of God and politics was left to those who have no share in the world to come."

Wirz nodded in sympathy and then left the man to his delusions. Religious leaders had been ravenously interfering in politics since the birth of organized faith. They grew powerful by fostering the belief that only they could dictate laws by divining them from Scripture. Any law not in line with doctrine was an abomination against God, as was any government not dedicated to God's purpose. He shook his head as he walked down the marble staircase. Even the Gospel of John recognized the holy war continually being waged against any leadership not founded on divine worship. And one had only to read Revelation to realize that religion always served the Beast in its quest for power over humans. It was the one true failing of all organized faith, that power was addicting, and holy leaders were far more susceptible to its siren song. Self-appointed men of God were not agents of peace; they were agents of destruction, something Wirz had accepted long ago. Faith and politics were nothing more than pieces on a chessboard in a game of domination, one side concerned with life on earth and the other with life after earth, each as brutal as the other in their moves. And both had the same objective: total dominion over mankind.

He went down to his office and called the hospital administrator to arrange a meeting with Dr. Hollister. He would enjoy delivering the assignment of her penance himself.

7

"Can I get a refill?" Elli asked, waving her finger at the bartender.

"Sure thing, Doc," he answered pleasantly. He lifted a bottle of Jack Daniels and poured it liberally over the ice melting in her glass. His name tag identified him as Harlan.

"What gave me away?" she asked, lifting the glass to her lips and swallowing a goodly amount.

"We don't get too many professionals in here wearing surgical scrubs, ma'am." He avoided mentioning the blood stains peeking out from under her jacket. He watched her take another long swill of the fiery liquid and leaned in close. "You might want to try sipping that instead of slugging it back. You might last a little longer."

Elli peered at him through the heel of the glass and then lowered it with a wry smile. "Some things shouldn't be drawn out," she told him. "I'm a doctor; take my word for it. Better to just get it over with." She waggled the glass at him, and he politely took it from her to refill. This time, he doubled the ice before returning it to her. "Thanks, Harlan."

"We aim to please, ma'am." He wandered to the far end of the bar to attend to a group of executives no doubt staying in the hotel upstairs.

She liked Harlan. He was a sweet young man with all the proper southern manners of a good old boy. In here, he hid his roots under the uniform of a proper servant. He was all spit and polish with a red bow tie and brocaded vest under neatly trimmed hair. This was, after all, a place for corporate fat cats, not some shitkicker bar in the burbs with sawdust on the floor and Hank Williams on the juke. She could imagine him burning up the wood decks on Saturday nights, surrounded by wholesome young women and bouncy waitresses. Those were places people went to drink, have fun, and dance until your feet swelled so badly you had to sleep in your boots. This was a place for networking and business meetings, adorned with polished nickel, glass and elevator music. It was the perfect place to be invisible, and that was what she needed, invisibility. Not the camaraderie of friends or the consolation of her peers. Just fucking invisibility. Her scrubs were the perfect turnoff to the jet set. The bags under her eyes and the unruly hair that spent most of the day imprisoned under a surgical cap kept the professionals at a respectable distance.

She sipped her Jack. It was vile. It burned going down and lit her up inside like a brush fire. And it tasted like turpentine, at least until the numbness took over. She'd never understood how her father could sit in his study every night sipping this stuff, but she was beginning to. It wasn't about the taste; it was all about the burn. The scourging away of all the shit life heaped on you that day so you could sleep through the night and wake up empty, ready for the next dump truck of shit to arrive. It was all about survival. Surviving. That's what she was doing here, surviving. She tipped the glass and took a bigger swallow, inching the brush fire up to a firestorm. Better to do it quickly. Burn the kid's face away from her memory before it could etch itself into her mind permanently. *Too fucking late,* she thought as she set the glass down on the bar.

"That looks serious," a voice said from behind her. "Do you mind?" Charlie eased himself onto the barstool next to her and smiled. She didn't return it.

"How the hell did you find me?" Elli asked him.

"Little bird called the hospital and told me where you were. You're lucky I picked it up instead of the hospital administrator."

She picked up the glass and drained the remnants. "The little bird wouldn't be named Harlan, would it?" She shot a vicious look toward the bartender, who blushed and busied himself with restocking bottles.

"What the hell did you expect?" Charlie asked. "You're the daughter of the next head of the Regional Senate. Your face is about as well known as the president's. He probably did you a favor. The last thing you need is the press to catch you getting hammered on duty."

"I'm not on duty," Elli said flatly. "I'm suspended pending outcome of a hearing to decide my status as a doctor at Angel's Mercy Memorial."

"And the dirty scrubs?"

"Keeps people away. In case you hadn't figured it out, I want to be alone."

Charlie studied his hands and then humbly asked, "Has there been any word from the Ecumenical Council?"

"Actually, yes. They made me an offer and politely advised me not to refuse. So, rather than sentencing me to a reconditioning camp, they are assigning me to some police investigation as a consultant, starting tomorrow. As long as I spy on the Feds for them and don't heal anyone, I don't lose my license. All the charges will be dismissed, and I can resume my duties as a doctor who lets her patients die when the investigation is over."

Charlie signaled Harlan and whispered for a cup of coffee.

"That better be for you because I have no intentions of staying sober tonight."

"It is," Charlie replied. "The downtime will probably do you good, give you some time to regroup." Harlan set the coffee down in front of him, and he grasped the cup in his hands. "You know we all lose patients, Elli. You're too good a professional to come unglued like this."

She slammed her empty glass down on the bar, catching the attention of a few stray patrons. "I didn't lose a patient, Charlie. My patient lived. I saved his life. But that was a mistake according to his church. That was interfering with God's plan, and they killed him for my mistake."

"It was a suicide, Elli. No one killed him." Charlie reached out and cradled her arm in his hand, but she pulled away.

"He was twelve. He was in remission. The gene therapy worked. He wanted to live. *They* wanted him to suffer God's judgment." She closed her eyes, trying to swallow her fury and lower her voice. "They made him do it; his mother guilted him into it. And you know the really sick thing? They aren't even condemning it as a suicide. The church council said he was just putting himself back on the path God set for him, so he's completely absolved of any sin. They're even giving him a hero's funeral next week."

"You're not his minister, Elli, and you're not that boy's mother. Saving him wasn't your decision to make."

Elli pulled a plastic card from her pocket and threw it on the bar as she rose. "You're right. I'm not his mother or his minister. I'm just his fucking doctor."

The Lamb of the Praetorium

1

"You have got to be kidding!" Bachman told the director. She looked over to Deacon, who only confirmed the orders that had come down. "We have to chauffeur around a couple of E-Rep flunkies everywhere we go?"

"Not only that," the director explained. "You'll have to keep your presence to a minimum, two to one. All tech team and medical personnel are to be dispatched on an as-needed basis only. They don't want it to look like the Feds are sending in an army to harass their citizens."

"But they still want us to catch a criminal?" Joyce asked.

"Whether they want us to catch this person or not is debatable," Deacon interjected. "It's also irrelevant. The victim's family has asked us to find her killer, and we are going to catch him regardless of where or who it turns out to be. And we will proceed as if the prosecution and incarceration of this individual will be a federal matter. We'll leave the legal and political arguments to the team in DC after we've done our job."

Deacon shared a look of frustration with Joyce as she paced like a caged mountain lion. She was upset, but he knew she would funnel her frustration into the case, which made her more formidable. Agnes's tech team was used to working in-house, and with the body already stored, Digger's work could proceed without a problem. Burke was another matter. He considered himself on equal footing with the detectives and crime scenes to be his personal domain. The idea of backwoods cops contaminating his crime scenes and second-guessing his abilities was pissing him off to distraction.

"Fifty bucks says we get Sheriff Markham and his band of white knights crawling all over us," Burke grumbled. "Those idiots couldn't secure a pay toilet without contaminating it."

"When can we expect these locals to arrive?" Joyce asked.

"The E-Republic Senate has asked for at least forty-eight hours to assign the appropriate personnel from their territories," the director announced, and they all began to object at once. "Put a sock in it!" he yelled. "I know that time is critical to catching a killer. We're already three weeks in, and this guy could be halfway to the Caymans by now for all we know. But our hands are tied on this. We don't set one foot inside E-Rep territory until that assignment is in place. In the meantime, hunt down every possible lead in the Corridor and make sure the crime scene isn't right under our noses. Tighten up your case and make a plan to hit the ground running when those assignments come through."

He looked toward Agnes and said, "Chen, as soon as you have things in hand, I need a couple of your guys to help with the investigation out of South Carolina. A lot of our fellow officers got incinerated, and I want to know everything I can before Director Seacomb has to face their families with an explanation."

Agnes muttered a "Yes, sir" as the director left.

With the director gone, they all resumed their collective objections, all except Deacon. He closed his eyes and tried to blot out the South Carolina operation and the faces of the men they had lost. Ellory's killer needed to be caught. If the victim's husband was indeed responsible, he wasn't going anywhere but he wouldn't face much justice for what he did under E-Rep law. If that happened, Deacon would take all manner of pleasure in making sure the details of the murder were nationally known. If he couldn't make this man pay, Deacon would leave him nowhere to hide. Allen Bainbridge would remain a stain on the reputation of God's little kingdom and never be able to set foot outside of E-Rep territory again. *But what if it wasn't him? How do you catch a killer no one wants to catch? How do you protect people who don't want your protection, and how do you get secrets out of people whose lives are shrouded in secrecy and fear?*

Forty-eight hours stretched into seventy-two with no word. Deacon's team spent the time targeting the three processing plants within federal territory. They were owned by locals, which meant southern money that didn't take kindly to federal cops showing up and disrupting their daily operations. The Old South sentiments still ran deep. However, they all had lucrative federal contracts, and the fact that the Feds were hunting a killer that had brutally murdered one of their own provided an added incentive to cooperate fully. Every location was scoured and examined, and in each case, the plants came up clean. Even Burke's miracle bots came up empty.

With no further leads to pursue, Chen and her team were temporarily reassigned to the Dorchester raid. The incident had been classified, but details of an explosion that large couldn't be kept from the public for long. The news broadcasts had started out with speculations about stored fertilizer on the farm. After reporting on the loss of seven FBI agents, however, this quickly evolved into rumors of a secret, high-level drug lab. The owner of the property had sought refuge in a foreign embassy, so public paranoia took over. People in both territories were seeing terrorists everywhere despite the representatives of both reassuring them they were safe. The president did a masterful job of reporting that, with the cooperation of the Ecclesiastical Republic Territorial Police, a threat to the nation had been uncovered and averted. She praised the lost agents and awarded them the highest possible commendations. As to the details, the ravenous press was informed that they would have to remain classified due to the ongoing investigation. The Ecclesiastical Senate wasted no time in jumping on the bandwagon with High Senator Wallace Milton himself praising the efforts of the FBI and thanking the federal government for protecting the territory. He, of course, took credit for the collaboration, which gave him a solid boost in the polls. The president gave no comment on his involvement.

2

The photographer relaxed beneath a tree, watching two men sitting on a bench highlighted by a ray of afternoon sunlight. One was young, only months away from adulthood, while the other was far older. The older man wore the uniform of a pastor and kept an arm wrapped securely around the younger man's shoulders as he spoke. The younger man's eyes were dry and red, but the pastor's eyes were swollen, and tears fell openly as he spoke. The photographer watched the two, taking pictures for an hour before the pastor rose, gave the young man a warm hug, and took his leave. He thought the old pastor looked much older than the last time he'd seen him. The man walked as if the weight of the world had crushed his desire to live now that his only child had died. The photographer took more pictures and wondered if the pastor would have been so compassionate in his ministry had he known that the young man he'd been consoling only moments before had been directly responsible for his daughter's death.

Once the pastor was gone, the young man known as Kevin Dockweiler sat back down on the bench and pulled out his smartphone. Kevin appeared to be an innocent, ordinary teenager. An illusion that, to the outside world, was nearly perfect. As he scrolled through his messages, Kevin began to scowl, never looking up and never stopping. The photographer didn't need to know what the boy was looking at. He'd hacked into the kid's social media page days ago. The discussion was an intense and somber memorial by Kevin's fellow students. The posts reflected shock and dismay at the disappearance of two of their classmates. Many posted pictures in memory of a young man named Paul, in his football uniform. They praised his performance on the field and his loyalty to friends. Others were of his fiancée, Janine, the editor of the school paper. She had just received a journalism scholarship to Auburn University, and the two of them had planned to marry after graduation. A picture-perfect couple.

Kevin read through the posts, growing more irritated as he did so. The endless adoration made him sick. Everyone in the senior class knew why they had disappeared. The daughter of a pastor had engaged in unlawful sex with her fiancé, and both had been given penance for the crime. Their friends were appropriately shocked and dismayed that it had happened. If anyone knew they had been intimate, no one spoke of it. Even their closest friends said they knew nothing. But the boy knew their claims of cluelessness were hollow because all social media in the Republic was monitored. If any of them had any knowledge, they would never admit it publicly. What happened among teenagers, stayed among teenagers, a survival ethic they learned from their parents. There were several posts speculating about how the affair had come to light. Many assumed they had been caught in the act. A few, however, believed someone had turned them in but wouldn't name names. They knew that Ecumenical law dictated that, without proof, no one could make such accusations publicly, and these posts were quickly censored. It made Kevin smile. His friends could speculate all they wanted, but in the end, it would amount to nothing. Paul would never have Janine, and that satisfied the boy.

The photographer snapped away, every picture telling the story of a young man angered by the loss of a girl he deeply loved yet perfectly content that she would never belong to another. A handsome face with dark, brooding eyes that masked a monstrous soul. Kevin turned off his phone and headed out of the park back to school. He knew he was in the clear. Had he been four months older, his scheme would never have worked. He would have been required to face those he had accused and take part in their execution. But his identity had been protected due to his status as a minor, and his testimony had been handled remotely. The couple had been innocent, of course. The most contact they'd had involved some serious kissing and heavy petting, but it didn't matter. The implication, along with a few secretly taken photos of their close encounters, had been enough to sway the Council. Against those, no one could defend Janine's chastity, not even her father.

Kevin was a student of LaGrange, the local academy that had been molding the state's young people for over sixty years. It became part of the Federal Corridor after the war and the interterritorial tuition was now astronomical, but the locals didn't care. The South had finally won its war. Publicly, the locals proclaimed themselves proud and defiant Republic Georgians, and the federal government overcharging them was just an act of economic oppression regularly trotted out as propaganda. Privately, however, those same citizens knew the worldly and science-centered curriculum of the now-federal academy was far more extensive than the restricted education offered in standard Republic schools. It would open doors not available to average citizens and give their children a possible avenue of escape. A smart Republic parent would rob a bank if necessary to send their kid there.

Kevin returned to the campus and watched his classmates return from lunch. A group of younger girls paused to speak to him but didn't linger. Once they were gone, he retrieved his motorcycle and headed off. The photographer followed him at a respectable distance as they headed out of town toward the local foothills. He watched the kid stop to buy beer, which was legal in the Republic for anyone over sixteen, and then go through a greasy fast food drive-through. Thirty minutes later, they turned off onto Roanoke Road and made their way toward The Falls.

The Falls were a natural formation that had been uncovered after the war. The shelling and heavy artillery cratered the area, opening up shallow caves over which the waters of West Point Lake fell in sheets. The spot had become very popular with the local youth and provided ample privacy for forbidden activities. What few drugs or various illegal indulgences made their way into the Republic could usually be found at The Falls. The local sheriff knew about the trafficking but never acted upon it without an explicit complaint. No parent wanted their child to suffer penance, so such things were handled discreetly within communities far from the watchful eyes of the Council.

The photographer watched as the motorcycle pulled off the highway just past the old saloon and onto a grass-covered trailhead. He gave the boy enough time to reach The Falls at the end and then drove his truck down the trail, deep enough to conceal it from the highway. He sat listening to the breezes off the lake for a time and then walked down to the shoreline. He found Kevin finishing the last of his beer and texting his feigned heartbreak to his friends. Forty minutes later, the motorcycle lay at the bottom of the lake and Kevin began to atone for his sins.

3

Deacon watched the Sunday news anchors, shaking his head. He'd spent the week reading the actual FBI reports provided by the White House, which revealed that the entire investigation was the result of an accident. The farm in Dorchester belonged to some telecommunications bigwig, so no one questioned the large satellite equipment and intricate networking system he installed. With programming in the territory heavily restricted to only wholesome content, the entertainment vacuum seemed like a guaranteed success, and he was determined to create the Hollywood of the South. He traveled regularly in pursuit of this goal, and it was during one of his European trips that the farm suddenly begun sucking up enough power to light up a nuclear plant. It overloaded bandwidth across territorial lines and was noticed by a junior NSA analyst who piggybacked himself onto a remote access request. The request executed seamlessly, so he had no idea that the login was unauthorized. Eventually he found himself looking at a series of heavily encrypted files with E-Rep Classified designations and an insignia he had never seen before. Curiosity got the better of him, and he forwarded the files to a buddy in cryptology before he lost the connection. The cryptologist thought it was his buddy's usual midnight dare until he cracked them open. Within minutes the content was forwarded up the chain of command, and an hour later said junior analyst had been sanctioned for illegal surveillance and reassigned to the task force, and the entire FBI Cyber Division was mobilized. In the month that followed, cryptology had learned that Dorchester was only one cell of a much larger operation. The insignia remained a mystery, but whatever organization it represented had a worldwide reach and was playing a very long game of shadows.

Deacon's attention was disrupted by a rather high-pitched "Excuse me." He looked up to see a very young sheriff's deputy from Markham's district standing at his desk, attempting to look official.

"I was told to report to a Lt. MacNair for special duty. I'm Dep. Kyle Tanner." Deacon noted the Georgia star on his uniform as the kid handed him a document pad. "These are my temporary transfer orders. I'm to report to you on the Bainbridge case."

Deacon looked the kid up and down. He couldn't be older than twenty-three and was wearing a gun belt at least two sizes too big for him.

"I'm Lt. MacNair," Deacon said, offering his hand. The kid didn't expect a handshake, but he returned it. His hands felt soft and uncalloused.

"Pleased to meet you, sir," Kyle said, pulling his hand back.

Deacon scanned through the orders quickly. "You're one of Markham's boys?"

"Yes, sir. Been assigned to his division for the last six months."

"And before that?" Deacon asked.

Tanner cleared his throat. "Academy class of 2035. Top of the roster, sir."

Deacon stared at the kid and then looked over at his dumbstruck team. "Det. Bachman, would you and Sgt. Chen please get this young man settled in? Show him around the pit and give him a place to work while I retrieve his access badge and clearances."

"Sure thing, Deacon," Joyce said as she watched him leave. Agnes could easily have had them run off in the pit in minutes, but Joyce knew this was just a diversion. And she knew exactly where Deacon was going.

"A ROOKIE?" Deacon thundered at the director. "A MOTHERFUCKING, WET BEHIND THE EARS, STILL LIVING IN HIS MAMA'S BASEMENT ROOKIE!"

The director sat quietly while Deacon exploded and paced. He knew from experience that there was no stopping the MacNair Express once it left the station.

"He's probably spent the last six months since the academy writing traffic tickets, pulling over teenage girls and frisking waitresses!"

The director chuckled.

"This is NOT funny, John. They're doing this intentionally, trying to mess with this case. This kid has no practical experience handling evidence and no street sense whatsoever. And he has no training as a profiler. He stands a better chance of shooting himself in the foot than taking down a suspect!"

The director composed himself and said, "Look, Deacon, his only job is to shadow you and Bachman while you are in E-Rep territory to make sure we aren't violating any local laws. That's it. We give him full access to any evidence or progress you make on this case, and it's his responsibility to report to his superiors, not ours. We are under no obligation to utilize his skills or protect his ass. He's a ghost as far as you're concerned. If he shoots himself, let them do the paperwork."

Deacon rubbed his forehead where a migraine was threatening to emerge. "That still limits the investigation team to me and Bachman."

"We haven't received the assignment of the forensic personnel yet. They are, and I'm quoting here, still sourcing someone with the necessary qualifications to assist with the handling and analysis of forensic evidence.'"

"What, the local Walmart ran out of stock boys?" Deacon snarked.

"I know this is a major pain in the ass, but by law we're stuck with whomever they assign to us. You just do your job, make sure your team does their job, and catch this bastard no matter how long it takes." He poured a shot of scotch from a small flask in his desk and handed it to Deacon.

"You know you could be arrested for just having this in the building, don't you?" Deacon said as he accepted the glass.

"Just take a deep breath and get your head in the game. And don't worry about the politicians. The president was nice enough to assign us a legal team ready at a moment's notice. Any bullshit happens out there, you report it to me immediately. I'll have federal warrants and the National Guard out there so fast their heads will spin." He handed the deputy's authorization passes and access badge to MacNair. "You must have really made an impression on Madam President," the director teased.

Deacon downed his scotch, scowled and left.

When he arrived back at the pit, Joyce was updating Dep. Tanner on the status of their one and only suspect, the victim's husband.

"Couldn't have been him, ma'am, he has an airtight alibi," Tanner told her, pulling up a list of all the interviewed witnesses on his personal evidence pad. He handed it to Joyce, but Deacon intercepted it. Sheriff Markham had warned Tanner that MacNair was a hard-ass with a strong dislike of E-Rep cops, especially white ones, and ordered him not to let the son of a bitch get under his skin.

"Who interviewed all these people?" Deacon asked.

"I did, Lieutenant," Tanner responded confidently.

"And did you corroborate their individual statements with evidence of their whereabouts?"

Tanner was momentarily confused but then said, "No, there was no need to."

Deacon looked at him sharply. "No need to?"

"They all said the same thing, that they saw Mr. Bainbridge and his kids at their school fundraiser in Marietta on the night in question."

"And you did nothing to confirm that any of this was true?" Deacon asked him as Tanner tried to puff himself up.

"I checked with the event organizers. The fund-raising carnival was in full swing just like they said it was. Practically the whole town was there, so I didn't see the need."

"Did it ever occur to you that they could be lying? That maybe they are just protecting one of their own? I don't know how you do things in Atlanta, but we don't just assume someone is telling the truth."

Tanner didn't like being called incompetent, and it showed. Screwing up his courage, he stared up at Deacon and said, "And I don't know how you people in the Federal Corridor do things, Lieutenant, but in my territory you're still innocent until proven guilty. We don't doubt a person's honesty and good faith without evidence."

Deacon turned away and said, "Agnes, I want every one of these statements cross-checked and verified. Get an electronic trace of everywhere those witnesses went within forty-eight hours of that fundraiser."

Agnes set her team to work without question. Deacon watched Tanner's face redden in anger.

"Hey, you don't have the authority to just investigate E-Republic citizens that haven't been accused of a crime!" Tanner blurted out. "These aren't suspects—they're witnesses, and we sure as hell don't accuse them of lying without a damned good reason."

Deacon pressed his comm link and called the morgue. "Digger, pull Bainbridge for me. I'm on my way." He looked Tanner in the eye and said, "You need a damned good reason? Come with me."

By the time they arrived in the morgue, Digger had Ellory Bainbridge's body on an exam table, completely covered with a sheet. Unimpressed, Tanner said, "If you think you can intimidate me with a dead body, Lieutenant, you're wrong. I've seen dead bodies before."

Deacon said nothing, just pulled the sheet from Ellory's body and let it fall to the floor. Nearly four weeks in Digger's cryofreezer had kept the decay from setting in, but death still left its mark. The shattered bones left her body misshapen as it settled around them, and the horrifying crucifix that had been beaten into her torso was now a sinister blue-black.

Tanner looked the body over, breathing deeply. In the end, it wasn't the broken bones and bruises, the condemnation of that black cross on her chest, or the look of tragic disbelief on her face that shattered his resolve. It was the slight rise and visible contour of the hand of the dead child in her belly. Tanner staggered back from the body and vomited heavily onto the floor. Deacon waited patiently for Tanner to get himself under control and pulled the sheet up over Ellory's torso, covering the ghastly tattoo.

"What happened to her?" Tanner asked between dry heaves.

"She was pummeled to death and then had a crucifix pounded into her chest as she and her baby lay dying," Deacon told him quietly. "We only have one suspect at this time, and he has a very compelling motive." Digger handed a towel to Tanner. "But as you said, he's still innocent until proven guilty. In fact, you could be right about him, and the killer could still be unknown."

"What kind of monster would do that to a pregnant schoolteacher?" Tanner asked, wiping his face.

"That's what we're here to find out, preferably before this happens to anyone else," Deacon said quietly. "That a good enough reason, son?"

Tanner lowered his eyes and nodded in agreement.

4

Deacon returned from the morgue to find a woman lounging in a chair in front of his desk. She had a mop of brown curls pulled into a messy bun. Several loose strands framed a face of creamy skin with a splash of freckles. He pegged her at about five-foot-seven, judging by the way her socks hung out past her faded jeans and she huddled under a summer chambray jacket. The woman must have been napping under the dark sunglasses she wore because she jumped when he spoke to her.

"May I help you?" Deacon said.

The woman stood stiffly. "I'm supposed to see a Lt. MacNair. I'm Dr. Hollister." She handed him her encoded orders. "The Justice Ministry assigned me to your task force as your forensic liaison."

Deacon looked at Elli as she rubbed her eyes beneath the shades. He could tell she was squinting beneath the glasses by the way her nose wrinkled when she spoke. "Rough night?" he asked, pointing at the shades.

"Rough week," she muttered.

"For all of us, Doctor," Deacon replied. "I'm Lt. MacNair."

"Pleased to meet you," Elli said, shaking his hand and staring past him as Dep. Tanner wobbled slowly into the room. "Um . . . is . . . he okay?"

Deacon glanced at Tanner as he sat down. "Who, Sunshine? He's fine; just getting himself settled in. Have a seat, Doctor." He indicated the chair she had just vacated and then walked over to the coffee dispenser. He poured two large cups and handed one to Elli as he sat down. "There's cream and sugar if you . . ." He never finished the sentence. Elli was already gulping it down black.

"Thank you, Lieutenant, and it's just Elli, please."

"Okay, Elli. You should know that the case you've been assigned to is a murder case and a rather gruesome one at that."

Elli looked over the rim of her cup and said, "You're kidding, right?" Deacon only shook his head. She set the cup down. "Was the victim a child?"

"One of them was," Deacon answered. "The mother was pregnant when she was killed." He watched Elli's face turn a little green. "Exactly what type of medicine do you practice, Doctor?"

"Pediatric oncology mostly, but I don't know how much help I could possibly be examining a dead child."

Deacon closed his eyes and then laughed softly. "Well, Doc, in case you haven't figured it out yet, the fact that you can't be much help is precisely why they chose to send you and Dep. Sunshine over there." He pointed toward Tanner, who sat rubbing his forehead.

"Look, I'm here as a representative of the Republic to make sure communication is transparent between both agencies and all evidence is interpreted and relayed intact. I'm not here to hold you back."

"You're here because my three witnesses are the sons of rich, powerful Republic senators who transported illegal drugs into federal territory and had the bad luck to stumble onto a murder victim. Their daddies can't afford to have them publicly tied to the crime in an election year, so they are doing everything they can to hinder, and then take over, this investigation and bury it. Why else would they send a rookie traffic cop with no field experience and a baby doctor with no crime scene expertise to shadow my team?"

Elli stared down at the tabletop, embarrassed. The man was right about her lack of experience. She'd said as much to the archbishop when he assigned her, but it was made clear that her lack of expertise was irrelevant and her only other option was unthinkable.

"Both the victim and the primary suspect are citizens of the Ecclesiastical Republic, and I am required to be accompanied by two representatives of their government at all times when I am within their territory until this case is solved," Deacon continued politely. "I requested experienced police personnel so that I wouldn't have to worry about contamination of evidence or putting civilians in unnecessary danger. Instead, I have to catch a killer and babysit the two of you at the same time. Now, I don't know who you pissed off to earn this assignment, and I don't care. My only concern is catching the person who did this and making sure the victim's family receives the justice and closure they deserve. Are we clear?"

"We're clear, but ..." she said and looked back down at the table sheepishly, "you should know the Ministry was pretty emphatic that you wouldn't abide by our laws. They assured me that you would try to withhold crucial evidence and use this case to politically embarrass my government."

"Then allow me to put your fears at ease." Deacon called the case file up on his monitor and turned it to face her. "This is all the evidence, forensic reports and witness interviews we've gathered so far. Help yourself to the coffee. Cafeteria is down the hall, and if you need anything, just ask Sgt. Chen over there." He pointed to Agnes and then stood. "I have a meeting to attend to, but I'll be back in a couple of hours."

Elli watched him leave and absently said a prayer.

5

Sunday afternoon remained clear and warm, guaranteeing a wealth of fellowship throughout the Republic. Even in the Federal Corridor the sounds of church bells rang out, calling the faithful to services. Deacon hadn't attended a Sunday service since his mother passed, but he still brought the usual donations he managed to collect in his spare time. He stopped by the local restaurants to pick up any meals they had to donate. His mother had done this service for the church for many years, and he continued the duty whenever he could. The courtyard of First Baptist was filled with parishioners enjoying the post-mass meal that was always set out for those less fortunate. Pastor Cooper was an old family friend and used to Deacon dropping in, usually before sunrise. His appearance this late in the day could only mean a difficult case. Cooper helped him unload the car and set the food at the buffet tables. Deacon then excused himself and entered the empty church, leaving Pastor Cooper to tend his flock.

Deacon found an empty alcove and quietly said a prayer for his mother's eternal soul, even though such prayers were deemed pointless by his faith. He did this mainly to honor her devotion to the church. He did not pray for his son Neville, and he never left the alcove without uttering one final statement to God. He stood, looked up at the statue of Christ, and quietly said, "I'm still waiting for an answer." The statue remained as silent and indifferent as it had the day Neville died, looking down upon him with vacant eyes full of prefabricated benevolence. When he laid his son to rest, he demanded this very statue tell him the reason his son had to take his own life to show his commitment to God. He'd been waiting since that day. He would have preferred the answer sooner rather than later, but if he had to wait until he stood before God himself, so be it. Until then, there was nothing more he and the good Lord had to say to one another. He left the cold, holy darkness and walked out into the Alabama sunshine.

Pastor Cooper never pressed him to stay for worship. He knew the demons Deacon harbored ran much deeper than the atrocities of war. Those trials had left a crack in his faith that the congregation rallied around when he'd come home. But Neville's loss and his subsequent divorce etched a fissure across his heart deeper than even fellowship could heal. The few times Cooper counseled Deacon had always been private. Deacon was not one to share his pain with a pitying crowd. Cooper could always tell when that pain was becoming unbearable, and it was obvious another session was overdue. He watched Deacon get back into his cruiser and waved goodbye, muttering a prayer for God to watch over his wayward son.

Two hours away in a parish devoid of afternoon fellowship, Pastor Turnbull walked slowly up the stairs of the Church of the Holy Light and into the vestibule to prepare the evening service. It was difficult most days due to his age, but the good Lord had always carried him up. This evening, he climbed alone. The church had remained closed all day by order of the Ecumenical Council out of respect for his loss, but he could not bear sitting in his empty house. The church has always been his calling, but even here he felt cold and abandoned. There was no joy in his heart nor words to convey to his parishioners, no God to guide his sermon. Loss and bitterness clouded his heart as he reached the top of the stairs. The church faced south and a row of ten great stained-glass windows lined the western wall, allowing the setting sun to bathe the faithful in color and the commandments embedded in each one. They had always been a source of encouragement and inspiration as he walked beneath their prismatic glow. Today, they cast a taint upon his soul.

He looked down at the words reflected on the floor before him, proclaiming "I am the Lord thy God," and trod heavily over them. He had never served any other god and had never taken the Lord's name in vain until the day the Ecumenical Council served penance on his child. *Damn your indifference, you heartless God*, he thought as he walked on. He crossed himself and asked forgiveness as he passed beneath the third commandment. Today was the Sabbath, meant to be kept holy, but he felt only futility, unable to remember even the most uplifting passages. His parents were long dead, but he still honored them. Nevertheless, he felt their judgment as he walked beneath the fifth commandment. The long days it granted would be unbearable without Janine. He stopped below the sixth commandment and looked up. The red glass cast a ruby glow that mirrored his pain. *Thou hast killed*, he thought. *You holy men of God called it penance, but still my child is dead.* He fought to keep his seething hatred of them in check as he strode past "Thou shalt not commit adultery." Janine and her fiancé had not been guilty of any carnal sin. Of that he was sure. Their only crime had been impatience for the happiness their married life promised.

A pain gripped his side, and he stumbled onto a pew for support. A tear streaked down his face as he looked up into the words "Thou shalt not steal." "You have stolen my child!" he hissed at it, finally giving in to the blackness in his heart. He made his way beneath the next window but stopped cold. The floor was dark and colorless as something blotted out the sunlight. A foul-smelling pool had stained the carpet and wood railings. He looked up to the service walkway above only to see a body bathed in a shining halo of color. The words "Thou shalt not bear false witness against thy neighbor" formed a banner above dark eyes and an innocent face. The naked body of the young man named Kevin, whom he had comforted and consoled only days before, hung from the gallery. As he stared in shock, the harsh truth of the accusation hovering over the body came crashing down, and the pastor screamed his daughter's name beneath the instrument of her destruction.

6

In the harsh lighting of the basement viewing room, Elli stared down at poor Ellory Bainbridge, unconsciously twirling the tiny crucifix around her neck. In her line of work, she'd seen far more dead bodies than anyone else on the team but was still fighting an overwhelming urge to cry. Beneath the faint rise of this woman's belly lay a child that never had the opportunity to see the light of day. She thought of Toby Holmby as she traced the faint outline of the tiny hand within. Another sacrifice to a God she felt she hardly knew anymore.

Joyce Bachman sat quietly on Digger's stool, giving Elli her space. She read through Elli's bio as the doctor circled the table. An only child to a very powerful, political father and a fashion editor mother. She was educated in the north but returned to Atlanta to practice after graduating. She even belonged to the same denomination as Allen Bainbridge and occasionally attended the same church. As devotees of the same religion, she expected Elli to be as cold and judgmental as Bainbridge. Yet this woman, who had never met the victim, was showing far more emotion at her loss than the victim's own husband had.

"She should have spent the day at church and been home having dinner with her family by now," Joyce said quietly. "Lousy way to spend a Sunday."

"Lousy way for any of us to spend a Sabbath," Elli answered. "I don't often make it to services. Medicine doesn't take Sundays off. Neither does police work, I imagine. You must be used to missing your holy days too, Detective."

"Not my day," Joyce said, pulling the chain with the Chai from under her collar. "But I know what you mean. I've spent plenty of Saturdays chasing suspects when I should have been at temple." She looked at the body and then said, "I'll bet the Ecumenical Council is ready to give her husband a medal and a lengthy absolution for taking care of their dirty work."

Elli looked up in shock. "That's a very ignorant thing to say and not exactly fair. God hates violence more than he hates divorce, especially within a marriage. Those vows are sacred. And there is a provision for divorce in the Bible. If he was as abusive as her family claims, she could have brought her case before the Council and petitioned for her husband's punishment."

Joyce leaned forward on her knees, attempting to appear humble. "My first assignment when I joined Homeland was in a domestic violence unit, Doctor. I've seen firsthand how the church handles these cases, and you know what I learned? That the church's first and only commitment is to preserve the marriage at any cost, even if that cost includes the life and safety of the wife and children. They do this not because they think the woman is lying but because those holy men fear God so much that they would rather allow a woman to be abused for the rest of her life, or even killed, rather than be known as the one who violated the words 'What God has joined together let no man put asunder.' You see, they know the one inescapable truth of faith, Doc—that yours is the only soul you can really save, and in the end it's every man for himself."

Elli was offended by Joyce's opinion. "Our church leaders aren't as cold-blooded and selfish as you paint them. There are counseling centers throughout the territory, Detective. My father personally helped draft the legislation that provides for marriage intervention; it was one of his proudest moments. The Ecumenical Council regularly sends people for assistance. It's part of their mandate to preserve marriage." She looked at Joyce with a sneer. "Maybe being self-involved is how the churches in your Constitutional territory handle their problems, but here in the Republic we do care about our citizens, even if they are women."

141

Joyce appreciated Elli's defiance, but she could also see small cracks of doubt. The kind of cracks that investigators routinely used to break a suspect's defiance. Although Elli wasn't a suspect, her attitude triggered Joyce's cop instincts into overdrive. "When was the last time you heard of a woman in the Republic being granted a legal divorce, Doctor?"

Elli hesitated and then said confidently, "My circle of friends and acquaintances is a bit more devoted than yours. I don't know anyone personally who ever felt the need to ask for one, but that doesn't mean it hasn't happened."

"Well, as luck would have it, marriage and divorce decrees are public knowledge, even in the Republic. Out of three hundred ninety-seven petitions, there have been one hundred forty-seven divorce decrees granted to petitioners in the Republic in the last ten years. Guess how many of those petitioners were women?" Elli didn't answer. "Two, Doctor. Two out of one hundred forty-seven, and the only reason those two were brought before the Council was because their spouses were caught red-handed in full view of law enforcement officers physically abusing their wives in public."

"That means that sixty-two percent of those marriages were salvaged, which only confirms that state-sanctioned counseling works. I think you just disproved your point, Detective."

"Really? Because out of the remaining one hundred forty-five divorces granted to men who petitioned for divorce, none but three of the wives involved subsequently survived the separation. The last one was a year ago up in some flyspeck town in Idaho."

"You're making that up," Elli said nervously.

"The cause of death in every single case was listed as 'natural causes.' Pretty amazing since most of those women were under the age of forty and in perfect health except for any prior physical abuse. In fact, the only common denominator in every case was a divorce decree."

"You expect me to believe they were all executed, that there's some conspiracy to exact revenge on wayward wives?"

"Come on, Doc. You're a medical professional. You know the odds of that many women suddenly kicking the bucket for no reason in that short a time are astronomical."

Elli wrapped her arms tightly around her own body. "There could be environmental factors involved, or even genetic ones for those deaths. Malnutrition and lack of services in many rural counties contributes to hundreds of deaths every year."

"But we're not talking about one particular affliction bubble, Doc. The causes of death range from strokes and heart attacks to aneurysms, even fatal allergic reactions. Things these women never suffered from prior to their dissolutions or had any genetic markers for in their health histories. You can't really believe that's just coincidence."

"That doesn't mean the Council sentenced them to death. Penance is a private thing. You can't possibly know what services or treatment either party was required to perform for their transgressions once their marriages were dissolved, so how can you insinuate that the Council ordered them killed?"

"You're right, I can't. But I do know that within ninety days of each of those dissolutions, a legal death certificate was filed for every one of those women."

Elli's skin suddenly turned cold.

Joyce hopped off the stool and walked to the opposite side of the table as Elli digested what she'd been told. "Those statistics don't even cover the domestic morality laws of your territory. Under that edict, thousands of homosexual citizens, who were only guilty of being born different, were incarcerated and given a choice: they could renounce their lifestyles and submit to conversion therapy, be shipped off to a federal immigration facility for resettlement, or be sentenced to death. Tell me something, Dr. Hollister, are the Ten Commandments the same in your book as they are in mine? Because I distinctly remember the words 'thou shalt not kill' being one of the really unforgivable sins."

"It's the church's job to give penance for any sins committed by its followers and return them to grace. It's the lawful restitution for their failure to God," Elli responded robotically, hating every word.

"You really believe that, Doc?"

Elli felt a wave of uncertainty rush over her. She'd questioned the severity of territorial laws many times but just couldn't accept what Joyce was saying.

"The Council mandated genetic testing for homosexuals and found no scientific markers for their . . . same-sex attractions. It was deemed a personal choice on their part to follow the ways of sin." She stared down at Ellory's corpse, disgusted that she was standing in a morgue spouting government propaganda to defend her beliefs.

"Conversion therapy was outlawed as cruel and inhumane long before the war," Joyce told her. "Yet your people resurrected it because they couldn't accept what those people already knew about themselves: that they were the way God made them."

"The Council abandoned conversion therapy as ineffectual not long after it was reinstituted. They've developed far more successful and humane methods of rehabilitation since then."

"You mean the R&R Protocols?" Joyce asked, watching Elli wince at its mention. "The rehabilitation methods so successful that they've been classified at the highest level as state secrets?"

"Our leaders developed them because they wanted to rehabilitate people while still being bound to follow God's laws. They found a way to arrest their weaknesses to enable them to live free of sin. Considering how much ridicule they were subjected to over the original conversion therapy, you can't really expect them to make their methods public this time, can you?"

Joyce nodded her head. She certainly could understand why it was classified.

"My leaders are not barbarians, Detective," Elli told her.

"Because only a barbarian would murder an innocent child whose only sin was existing," Joyce answered softly, shattering her resolve. Elli stalked away toward the door, shaking with shock and anger. "I'm sure Ellory would agree considering what she suffered," Joyce called out over her shoulder.

Elli stopped and turned, her face flowing with angry tears. "I'm sure she would, Detective, but I find it strange that you do. After all, the method of her murder was greatly detailed in the Talmud, and I believe that's your book, not mine."

Elli left Joyce standing with the body and headed for the stairs. On a landing halfway up to the pit, she stopped and leaned against the wall, shaking and out of breath. She couldn't believe what Bachman had told her. The woman had ridiculed her, hammered away at her, made a mockery of everything her faith stood for, openly accused her government of murdering its citizens. Yet all she could see was Toby Holmby's sweet face beaming with gratitude the day she discharged him. A week ago, she'd been drunkenly raging against that same government for declaring the boy's suicide a just restitution. Had they given him R&R to correct his desire for a life he was no longer entitled to? She'd howled that no one had sanctioned Toby's parents for not stopping his suicide and letting him die a slow and painful death. Instead, they'd landed a spot on the evening news "Heroes of the Republic" broadcast. They'd been praised for taking part in it and blessed by the high bishop of Georgia. Elli, on the other hand, was here because she owed God restitution for Toby. A penance she had earned for saving the life of a child in defiance of His will. What if Bachman had been telling her the truth?

7

Elli returned to the pit looking considerably angry and upset and was surprised to see that Deacon had returned. Bachman had arrived ahead of her and was speaking to the entire team.

"We know that the crime was committed with a blunt object made out of natural limestone," Joyce explained, "but we haven't been able to pin down the location where it happened. We have twenty locations to check and very few resources to do so."

"We need to narrow down these possibilities," Deacon told them. "We know that death occurred within an hour of the body dump, which we are assuming happened before daylight. So let's concentrate on the locations within an hour's distance of Gadsden Lake. Someplace that allowed enough privacy for him to take his time."

Corbett didn't wait for Deacon to ask. He immediately overlaid a circle around Gadsden that encompassed five of the twenty locations they'd identified. "We should start with these," he told them. "I did some checking on the plants, and although twelve are still connected to the local power grid, only these five showed power activity within the last month."

Agnes grinned with pride at Corbett. He was definitely going to make detective first grade someday. "That still leaves us a lot of ground to cover," she added, "but I'll have the warrants within the hour."

Deacon looked up to see Elli standing off to one side, listening and looking very disturbed. "Let's get to it," he said, dismissing the team. He walked over to Elli and took note of her red, swollen eyes. The body must have disturbed her more than she expected. "You okay, Doc?" he asked quietly.

Elli didn't answer at first, but then she said, "I need to get out of here."

Pushing past Deacon, she grabbed her purse and headed down the stairs. Deacon shot Joyce an angry, questioning look, but Joyce merely shrugged. He hurried after Elli and caught up with her as she crossed the parking lot.

"Elli, wait!" he hollered breathlessly.

"I can't do this, Lieutenant," she shot back without stopping. "I don't care what they do to me; I'm not spending the next few months being ridiculed and interrogated for my beliefs."

Deacon reached out and grabbed her arm, pulling her to a stop. "Now hold on, Doc, just put it in neutral for a second." He bent over, clearly out of breath, and said, "You move fast for a baby doc."

"When it's life and death, you don't have a choice, especially when your patient is a child," she said. Looking down on him, she said, "You should probably lay off the bacon and booze if you can't handle a light jog across a parking lot."

"You're right about that," he responded with a slight smile, "but I'm more concerned about you right now." He held his hand out to a nearby bench and gave her a pleading look.

She plopped down on the bench. "What's there to talk about?"

He sat down next to her. "For starters, you can tell me what the Council is using to force you to do this." When Elli didn't respond, he said, "If someone's threatening you, I can help."

"No one's threatening me," she told him and then much more quietly added, "It's my fault I'm here. I did something unforgivable."

Deacon looked at her with a smirk and said, "So you did piss off someone to get sent here."

"If you must know, I saved a child's life."

"That's hardly unforgiveable. Even on the off chance your medical training was fabricated, that's not exactly a sin."

Elli looked at him defiantly. "It is if your parents don't believe in medical intervention."

A scowl crept onto Deacon's face as he began to understand the position Elli was in. "The parents petitioned the courts for penance?" he asked.

"Actually, they pleaded for leniency, seeing as how the situation was resolved to the good Lord's satisfaction."

"Resolved?"

Elli turned to Deacon, and he could see a sheen of tears in her eyes. "Toby hung himself a week after he went home. His parents informed everyone that their twelve-year-old son had decided to follow God's path for him after all."

Deacon remembered the story vaguely. It had slid past during the news feed a few days earlier, but the reporters had been far too involved with the Dorchester explosion to give it more than a blurb in the on-screen footer. Elli wasn't here as a willing puppet for the Council. She was serving a sentence for a crime of compassion and had no choice. He watched her wipe a stray tear from her face as she said, "I always believed that being a healer was what God intended me to be."

"I'm sure that's true," Deacon told her.

"But every day I have to accept that I can't save everyone. Not because I'm not capable of doing it but because God has other plans for them. It's a hard thing to accept, and I struggle with it every day. But now Bachman tells me that it's not God's plan that's killing my people but my spiritual leaders purging them from our society. If that's true, the work He guided me to is meaningless. I can't help anyone."

"Then maybe He led you to us because there was someone here who you could help."

"Ellory and her baby are already dead. I can't help them," Elli told him.

"She has a family that is suffering, Doc. She has parents and a sister who are devastated by her murder. They need closure and justice. You can help them heal by helping me find the man who did this."

Elli searched Deacon's face for some trace of the dangerous, deceptive interloper the Council had ordered her to inform on. She only saw desperation and compassion. "I'm not a detective," she whimpered.

Deacon put his hand over hers. "No, you're not. You're a key. A very important key that can help me open doors I can't open alone. Doors that will lead me to whoever did this. Your people trust their own. They see me as an outsider, an invader. What I need you to do is help me gain their trust so they can help me hunt this man down and stop him from hurting anyone else. Can you do that?"

Elli closed her eyes and let her head fall back as Bachman's derision tapped away at her resolve.

"And I'll put a leash on Joyce to keep her from harassing you as long as you're here."

Elli looked into Deacon's eyes, searching for deception, but only saw integrity. "She didn't exactly harass me, Lieutenant, just told me some things I didn't want to accept."

"She's very good at that. It makes her one hell of an interrogator," Deacon explained. "But she shouldn't have used it on you. I'll talk to her."

"Thank you," Elli said gratefully. They walked back into the building, and Deacon led her to the elevator. As he pushed the call button, Elli said, "Bachman told me that the Ecumenical Council was killing women as penance and making it look like they were just natural deaths. Is it true?"

"There's a great deal of evidence to suggest it. And it's not just women. There are several men who also have suffered what we call illogical deaths, but we don't have the authority to investigate them. The laws of the Ecclesiastical territory govern according to the wishes of its citizens. We do know that they are using those deaths to reinforce the idea that God's judgment is a far worse fate than anything the Council can hand down. They shift the blood from their own hands to God's, and the people see them as their saviors on earth. It's a very dangerous precedent that has a lot of people outside the territory worried."

"We always knew there would be executions," Elli said quietly. "God's punishments have always been pretty absolute with regards to the more heinous offenses, but this . . ."

"I doubt very seriously that God had anything to do with what happened to Ellory Bainbridge," Deacon offered. "My job, our job, is to find the man who did this and punish him according to man's laws. What God does with him after that is His business."

The door opened, and Elli and Deacon emerged to controlled chaos. Bachman was barking orders as Agnes put together a team for Burke. Without waiting for Deacon to ask, she handed him his field gear and said, "We got a call that another body was discovered. It's on the Corridor border, but it was flagged for us. Locals thought it tied in to our investigation."

"What does that mean?" Elli asked.

Joyce handed her a protective vest and her temporary ID. "It means we may have a serial killer on our hands."

8

Markham looked up at the ghastly image emanating from the window and muttered, "Holy shit."

"You might want to get those lights turned off," Deacon suggested as he led the team past him into the vestibule.

The scene inside the church was far more horrific than the apparition being displayed outside. Several deputies stood around staring at the suspended body, but none of them approached. Without taking his eyes off the body, Deacon started giving orders. "Tanner, round up your deputy buddies and lock down any witnesses in the rectory."

"I know that kid," Tanner muttered, frozen as he stared up at the corpse.

Deacon snapped his fingers in Tanner's face. "Focus, Deputy," he said, and Tanner hurried off.

"Burke, you and Chen start documenting everything. I want the scene clear by the time Digger arrives to retrieve the body." They immediately went to work without a word. Elli stood beside Det. Bachman, clutching herself in horror as Burke's bots did their work and Agnes made her way up to the catwalk. Deacon patted Elli on the shoulder. "Come with me, Doc," he said quietly and led her to the rectory.

Inside the rectory, Joyce and Tanner watched as a pair of paramedics gave Pastor Turnbull oxygen. "What happened?" Deacon asked Joyce.

"The old man found the body when he came in to open for evening mass. Got the shock of his life. They're just making sure he isn't having a heart attack or something."

"Elli, would you please see to the pastor? I'm sure he'll feel much better having a real doctor help him." Elli joined the paramedics, eager to have something to distract her from what she had just seen. Tanner, however, was still visibly disturbed. "Tanner, you said you knew the victim."

"Kevin Dockweiler. He's a senior at LaGrange," Kyle told him.

"Personal friend of yours?" Deacon asked.

Tanner hesitated, then replied, "No, but I know he was a personal friend of the pastor's daughter Janine." He swallowed visibly. "She passed away recently."

Deacon looked at him suspiciously. "By passed away, you mean . . .?"

"He means they murdered my child!" Pastor Turnbull cried and immediately began heaving and rubbing his chest.

"Calm down, calm down," Elli told him, then ordered the paramedics to lay him down and give him a sedative. "Do you have a portable MRI with you?" she asked, and one of the paramedics pulled a large scanning pad from his medical bag.

Deacon pulled Tanner out of the rectory into a nearby alcove. "Explain to me what happened to his daughter, and don't leave anything out," he commanded. Tanner relayed what he knew about the alleged affair and the subsequent judgment. As with all executions, the details were kept secret, but the implications were obvious. "Who turned them in?" Deacon asked.

"Nobody knows. The witness's identity was sealed by court order."

Deacon walked Tanner out into the church, then looked up at the body in the window and the words above it. "'Thou shalt not bear false witness,'" he said as Tanner stood next to him.

On the catwalk, Agnes made her way up close to the body with Burke directing her from below. "It looks like he's been strangled by some weird contraption," she called down. "We'll know more when we take him down."

Kyle followed as Deacon returned to the rectory and gave him instructions. "If he's the one who turned in the pastor's daughter, we need to know everything about the victim's relationship with her. First thing in the morning, I need you to start questioning his and Janine's friends. You're close to their age, and they'll relate to one of their own more than my team. And take Dr. Hollister with you. Make sure you corroborate everything you find out."

Tanner shook his head and hurried behind him. When they arrived, the paramedics were strapping Pastor Turnbull's body onto a gurney. "What happened?"

"Massive heart attack brought on by shock," Elli told him. "He'd been having chest pains all day and nearly collapsed just before he found the body. We tried to revive him, but it's been coming on for too long. The P-MRI showed massive damage to the heart itself. No one could have saved him."

They followed the body out of the rectory and up the aisle. As they passed, everyone lowered their heads out of respect, even Burke despite his strictly atheist views. They exited the church to discover that not only had Markham failed to turn off the perimeter lighting, but the crowd had actually grown. The situation had fallen into chaos. destruction.

9

Low light photos are tricky, especially when taken from a discreet distance, but the risks were necessary. The setting sun had created the perfect halo for the body in the window, and he was able to get several shots that would feature perfectly in his next showing. The fun really began when the parking lot lights were triggered, casting pools of illumination into the night. He waited patiently as the police pushed back on the crowd and set up a perimeter. It left him a clear view of the front of the church and the investigators' comings and goings. He watched as the federal lieutenant and his pretty partner arrived and noted that they were accompanied by two newcomers to the team. The photographer took pictures of them as they passed. The young man he didn't recognize, but the young woman seemed oddly familiar. They entered the vestibule, and he relaxed a bit. It would take time for them to investigate, which meant a much greater risk of him being discovered. But the local police were hardly worthy adversaries. They couldn't even secure a large group of spectators and spent a great deal of time chasing down adventurous lookie-loos darting beneath the barricades. He settled in and sipped hot tea from a thermos.

Within thirty minutes the sun had fully set, and the church's interior lighting broadcast the silhouette of the body like a bat signal into the sky. An ambulance had pulled up minutes earlier, which was curious considering that a coroner's transport had arrived with the investigation team. Even more curious was the gurney carrying a body emerging from the church while the martyr was still clearly visible through the stained-glass window. The old pastor must have received an even greater shock than expected.

Timing was everything. He set the speed and exposure and began shooting away mere seconds before the gurney passed through each pool of light. Such a beautiful, haloed effect for the journey of a holy man who'd lost everything to his God, even his child. The photographer waited until the team returned to the confines of the church and then made his way down to the truck parked in a darkened lot nearby. Crawling through the lot with no running lights, he drove the quiet vehicle nearly half a mile along residential streets before entering the highway. No one was the wiser. He turned off at the cemetery where young Janine and her paramour were buried. The section where they lay was a fenced area at the rear of the property reserved for those given penance. The church insisted on publicly shaming dead sinners and their families throughout eternity no matter how much they had atoned for in life. He parked near this unlit section, pondering how the cemetery echoed the dynamic of life in the new South. Everywhere he went, towns and cities had evolved into this very schism. The more wealthy, godly and devout you were, the closer you were to the church. Your economic level determined how close you lived to the seats of power, and your devotion to the faith determined your success. Sinners of all manner now sat in the back of the bus where the coloreds had once been stowed.

Major cities now housed more government entities and cathedrals than they did corporations, and only the citizens who served those entities lived in the city proper. The affluent suburbs encircled these enclaves like a halo housing the wealthy and powerful while the remaining population spread out into increased obscurity, its colors growing darker and darker the farther away they settled. A crown of thorns for the shining new theocracy.

Before the war, those with little more than the necessities of life gravitated toward big cities in search of the long-dead American Dream: a better life, better opportunities, and fifteen minutes of fame to make their mark on the world. The rise of theocracy had reversed that gravity entirely. The price of faith rose exponentially the closer you got to God, as did the cost of disobedience. Thus, people aspired to obscurity and learned to be content with less.

The photographer's neighbors on the lake were a prime example of this new normal. They were an odd mix of those raised with little and those who had abandoned much. The old conspiracy theories and tales of Big Brother were no longer wild fantasies. In the Republic, they were a stark reality. In the fringes, they were free from such intrusions, so things like the internet, web cams, computers, cell phones and satellites held little attraction for them. Wealth no longer meant survival. It amused him that after two thousand years only the very lowest of humanity had finally gotten the true message that Jesus had brought: that wealth of the soul was far more valuable.

The photographer drove back to his lakeside home and stowed his gear in the subterranean workspace. He kept no mementos of his deed this time even though it had been a far greater work of art than his previous subject. The boy had been completely repugnant and cowardly right up to the end, bargaining for his life with the dirty secrets and indiscretions of his classmates whom he deemed far more deserving of punishment than himself. Bourbon was his usual homage to a job well done, but this subject wasn't worthy of such a toast. Instead, he drew a bottle of SweetWater brew and popped the top. Dockweiler had definitely belonged to the Budweiser class, but there were limits to good taste. Besides, the subtle bourbon and chocolate notes of the stout ale tickled his palate.

He uploaded the pictures and pulled up the images from the church. Opening a web browser, he uncovered few articles on Lt. Deacon MacNair. The coverage of his Medal of Honor ceremony portrayed him as a decorated war veteran. The coverage of the Chicago Riots of 2019 detailed how his work on the investigation resulted in a record number of arrests and convictions of corrupt, racist officers. As a reward for his civil rights efforts, he'd been appointed to Homeland Security by the former president. The only other story on the man was from the funeral of his son, Neville. It listed the cause of death as a suicide and hinted that the boy had a troubled past but did not go into detail. The accompanying photo showed MacNair in his full-dress uniform standing beside his wife as they buried their son. There were no stories about his career since his appointment, as such things were typically not newsworthy, but his rank as a lieutenant and the colored notches on his lapel in the photograph told him all he needed to know about Deacon MacNair.

The new young woman on the team turned out to be quite a surprise. She appeared in several stories across the net, but they were all due to the notoriety of her father, Senator Quentin Hollister. His rise and popularity were well known throughout the territory, but his daughter Ellinore kept a very low profile. At least, she had until a couple of weeks ago. A quick search of her personal profile identified her as a pediatric oncologist at Angel's Mercy Memorial. A more in-depth search of her recent career revealed her to be, much to his delight, the attending physician of the recently deceased Toby Holmby. He recalled the news reports on the boy's suicide and his mother's pleas for forgiveness. Apparently, Marjorie's crocodile tears had been taken to heart because Dr. Hollister had not been officially sanctioned—or had she? She wasn't a cop and had no expertise in criminal investigations. Was this her punishment for defying the great plan of God? If so, it made her a rather intriguing adversary, and he would endeavor to make her atonement a much more interesting journey in the future.

10

The following morning saw cold, crisp sunshine as fall seeped into the air. The smell of slash pine and loblolly burning in fireplaces around the lake gave him a tremendous appetite. The photographer considered breakfast to be a lavish affair and filled each day with local delicacies. He usually drove into town and enjoyed his traditional pairing of rich, dark coffee and pastries with strawberry rhubarb jam. The previous night's activities had stoked a creative fire within him, so he decided to skip the trip and make himself a banquet. Today it was buttermilk biscuits dripping with sawmill gravy and smoked trout hash, the ingredients for both generously given to him by his neighbors' wives in exchange for family portraits. He was up well before the sun creating the meal. The aromas of freshly flayed trout simmering in butter, cayenne and caramelized onions set his stomach to rumbling. Making it turned out to be nearly as enjoyable as eating it.

He hummed as he cooked and spread the meal across a traditionally set table when complete. He turned on the news feeds as he ate, anticipating reviews of his activities. He typically ran the four most prominent broadcasts after a long night's work so that he could gauge the progress of his new Agenda. Tucking into his meal, he watched the stories tick by, growing more and more concerned as the shows went on. He dragged the last biscuit through a dam of sausage gravy with a scowl as the six a.m. broadcast began. The reporter on the lead station broke the story he was waiting for as the biscuit made its way to his mouth. Video of the previous night's murder at the church played on all four stations, but in every case, the body in the great glass window was blotted out. That was to be expected with the sense of southern decorum that permeated the airwaves these days. He took a bite and chewed slowly as the reporter droned on. There was plenty of moral outrage regarding what kind of monster would commit such an act in a church and on the Sabbath, but no substance. The details of the murder were carefully omitted as each journalist focused on the bystanders' personal outrage and disbelief, as if such a thing were unthinkable among God's children. The only speculation was that the atrocity had to have been the work of outsiders. A carefully planted shrub in the political landscape no doubt requested by the leadership. The federal police could be seen, but none were interviewed. Only the honorable Sheriff Markham was authorized to speak, and he said practically nothing. That would have to change.

He scanned the crowd as it was broadcast from different angles. A sea of gawking faces all appropriately gasping in shock for the cameras in a quest to be noticed. All but one. The same face in each broadcast stood quietly taking in every aspect of the incident while speaking into an ear mic. The man never approached anyone involved with the case nor pushed his way to the front of the crowd, but everything about him screamed journalist. That meant a freelancer most likely looking for a big story to break back into the game, judging by the way he tried to blend in. The photographer set down his coffee and ran a search of former career journalists covering the Republic. The list was extensive due to government censorship, but he eventually found him. Buck Meisner, an intrepid war reporter whose career was cut short by a nasty bout of alcoholism and several drug rehab visits, courtesy of a lucky shot from a New Confederate soldier. The station he reported for held onto him after he recovered until the Ecumenical Council censored him on morality charges. He'd been kryptonite ever since. No station in or out of the territory would jeopardize its license or access to hire him, and he'd been writing trash for an underground gossip rag under an alias ever since. The man had aged considerably since his last press photo and was carrying at least thirty more pounds, but he was exactly what the photographer needed to kick things up a notch.

He That Increaseth Knowledge Increaseth Sorrow

1

Digger worked intensely on the Dockweiler boy over his morning coffee and blueberry muffin while Corbett examined the apparatus of strangulation on a nearby table. Digger preferred working with Corbett directly more than any of Chen's other technicians as they shared many of the same quirks. Both were quiet and studious unless they found something, at which point either would launch into an inappropriately giddy dissertation of the evidence. And they both had a penchant for drilling through a problem until they hit bedrock. Neither one fit in physically with their peers, both were limited socially, and both seemed to prefer the company of dead people to live ones. Dead people were decidedly nonjudgmental and didn't care about how you looked or dressed as long as you got the job done. They didn't care about your ability to converse or whether you had bad table manners. They just lay there and let you do your thing. Digger's thing was definitely the more macabre of the two but nonetheless revealing.

Corbett's queasiness usually abated once he set his mind to a particular evidence-mining task, and Dockweiler's murder weapon was fascinating. The killer had taken a lot of care in constructing it. The leather straps were thick and sturdy at the center and tapered to a more pliable width at their ends. They were lined with pure lamb's wool for the victim's comfort, which tied into the methodology of the Bainbridge murder. But what made them truly interesting was that they were completely hand-cut and stitched by a very practiced hand.

"This is quite intriguing..." Digger muttered as he often did during autopsies.

"How so, Doc?" Corbett asked.

"The boy bears the same crucificial tattoo on his chest, but it isn't as cleanly defined as the first victim. The lack of feminine curves and breasts should have made the process easier, so it may mean that it was made just after he died. Also, the vertebrae in his neck have been broken by tremendous force and his larynx crushed. I find it hard to believe that a human being could have done this on his own, especially if the victim were still conscious."

"The kid was dead before he was tattooed? That doesn't fit the M.O."

"Actually, it does," Digger explained. "You see, this young man had a significant amount of Coors in his system, which would have made it unnecessary for him to be drugged. He would have been quite easy to subdue. But his method of execution means he succumbed to death much quicker than the first victim, so the killer had to act fast to leave the tattoo. He was then rubbed down with the same frankincense oil as the first victim. Preliminary tests show the substance is identical."

Corbett shook his head as he looked at Kevin's slack expression. "My mom always said never to get falling-down drunk, even around your friends. You never know what they'll do to you while you're out or what you'll wake up to. I've seen some pretty embarrassing stuff posted on the net."

"Well, unfortunately for this poor fellow, his inebriation wasn't long-lasting enough to get him through his execution. There was a significant spike in his adrenaline just before he died. I also found several defensive wounds to the hands and upper torso, indicating that he did at some point fight back."

Corbett looked down at the strangulation ropes. "So the ropes he was suspended with weren't the cause of death?"

"Oh no, my boy, they were indeed," Digger answered, beckoning him closer to the body. Corbett hesitated and swallowed his disgust but inched closer. "You see the ligature marks on the neck? These most definitely match the straps he was suspended with at the church, and there are lamb's wool fibers deeply ground into the skin. That would only have happened before death."

"But if he was conscious, he would have struggled. He definitely would have kicked out that glass window he was suspended in front of," Corbett told him. "And the body was dangling freely between two columns. Nothing in that church could have held up to the force necessary to do this."

Digger smiled at Corbett and in his best Sherlock Holmes persona said, "Ah, dear chap, that is where it gets interesting. You see, wherever this poor fellow was murdered had to allow enough room for him to be restrained and prepared with oils. He was already quite inebriated which made the wine unnecessary in this instance. The bruising at his wrists indicates that he was tightly suspended between two objects and the straps placed around his neck. They were then pulled in opposite directions at the same time to snap his neck. The body was then left in the church as a message."

"That means there's still some murder den out there we have to find."

The doors to the morgue hissed open as Deacon, Joyce and Agnes walked in. Agnes threw an appreciative smile to Corbett as she asked, "Good morning, gentlemen. Are we making any progress?"

"A great deal, actually," Digger responded. "This unfortunate young man does appear to be a victim of the same murderer. He was killed at another location and his body displayed here after death. He also bears the same biblical tattoo as Ellory Bainbridge."

"What do those tell us?" Deacon asked, pointing to the straps on the table.

"They tell us that the killer is either a skilled artist or knows one," Corbett said. "They're handmade and hand-stitched. This kind of work has to be commissioned unless you do it yourself. I'm leaning toward the latter because this guy doesn't seem to be the stupid type. We may get a lead on the materials themselves if they were purchased locally, but we still need to find out where he committed the actual killings."

Joyce crossed her arms and sighed. "Well, that is the million-dollar question. We've secured warrants for all the ore processing plants in the surrounding area, but it's going to take time even with an entire task force."

"I did find traces of unprocessed limestone dust on the victim's bare feet. The odds are good that he murdered them both in the same place," Digger told her.

"Thanks, fellas. Keep it coming," Deacon told them and left. Joyce followed after throwing a wink at Corbett. She caught up with Deacon at the elevator, where he scowled and said, "This guy's killed two people in a month already. We need to narrow down the possibilities fast. Where the hell is Burke?"

"He went back out to the scene," Joyce informed him. "Said he noticed something along a side street and wanted to check it out."

"Yea, I noticed that microbrewery on the corner too," he replied as the doors opened.

"Any word from Tanner and Hollister?"

"Not yet, but the school day just started," Deacon told her and then stood silently as the car went up.

Joyce waited in silence for a bit and then said, "You want to tell me what's got you so worked up?" He turned to see her staring at him with great concern, but he didn't answer. "Come on, Deacon, you and I have worked together for five years now. I've seen the spells come and go, and I know when you're struggling. This case is getting to you." He lowered his eyes but remained silent. She pushed the emergency stop and then softly asked, "Is it Neville?"

Deacon grinned slightly and shook his head. "You always were exceptionally perceptive." She smiled seductively, and he felt something inside him clench. "We've seen so many improbable deaths over the years. If these murders are a result of some form of Ecumenical justice, I can't help but wonder if his was too."

"Neville's death was a suicide, not a murder, Deacon. You know that."

"Except that he wasn't suicidal," he insisted. "And just like a hundred other so-called natural deaths that have occurred after an Ecumenical reconditioning, it just doesn't add up."

Joyce took a breath. "I hate to throw your own advice back at you, boss, but we need to stay focused here. I'll do anything I can to help you get justice for him once this is over, but we all need you here and now, not chasing a personal crusade. One bad guy at a time."

It ruffled him to hear his own words used against him, but Joyce was right. He schooled his investigators to set their personal issues aside when working a case, and he had no right to behave any differently. The director had seen his distraction days ago, and now his team was onto it. He knew he had to put Neville out of his mind, but some part of him kept insisting it was somehow connected to the case.

2

Tanner and Elli arrived at LaGrange to find it surrounded by official Justice Ministry vehicles and parked a discreet distance away. Kevin Dockweiler's murder had become a national news story overnight, and the Council was taking full advantage of the tragedy to show concern for its citizens. The school was full and bustling with students, but no classes were being taught. Every room had been converted into a group therapy session and prayer vigil while the auditorium had been sectioned into smaller private rooms for individual counseling sessions. A confessional had also been brought in for those students feeling the sudden urge to repent. It was typical for the Council to provide support to a student body whenever a minor passed, but neither of them had seen this level of response since Hurricane June made landfall five years earlier. Several squad cars were parked outside the administration building, and Tanner recognized Sheriff Markham as he approached.

"What the hell are you doing here, Tanner?" he asked condescendingly. "I thought you were supposed to be shadowing the Feds."

"MacNair wanted to come down and give the students a hard time about Dockweiler, but I cut him off. Last thing these kids need is some federal fuckwit grilling them about some poor murdered kid," he told Markham.

"That still doesn't explain why you're here," Markham said, eyeing him suspiciously.

"Come on, boss. I'm here because someone has to look out for our own, and MacNair certainly isn't going to do it. I know a lot of these kids. I grew up here with their older brothers and sisters. I'm not going to let him turn them all into suspects," he told Markham rather convincingly.

Markham glanced at Elli, who had remained silent and looking downward as Tanner spoke. "And who's your friend?" he asked Tanner.

"Some government paper-pusher sent to take notes on how well we handle things?"

Elli looked up, stunned, but before she could respond, Tanner said, "This is Dr. Hollister. She's one of ours and came along to help. It was this or let some federal shrink in here to manipulate these kids."

"Then get to it," Markham told him. "And make sure you pass everything you find on to my office before you tell the Feds. I don't want a bunch of angry parents storming my precinct barking about civil rights violations and threatening to sue."

Markham walked off as his collar mic chirped, and Tanner exhaled the breath he hadn't realized he'd been holding. Telling him Elli's real last name had been a calculated risk, but with her publicized connection to the Holmby boy, Tanner couldn't exactly lie. Luckily, Markham didn't recognize her even though she'd been at the crime scene the night before and walked right by him several times. Markham had never been a mental multitasker. It was one reason he took copious notes and delegated a lot of his duties to lesser officers. But with Markham's deputies crawling around the school, it was only a matter of time before someone connected the dots for him. Tanner wanted to be long gone before that happened, so he hustled Elli out onto the school quad.

"You mind telling me why you lied to your boss?" Elli asked as they walked.

"I didn't exactly lie. These kids aren't going to talk to any federal cops. They're too close-knit for that. But if I'd told him the truth, he'd make sure we never got anything out of them." Tanner looked around the grassy area where groups of kids sat around talking. He spotted the group he wanted, relieved that they weren't accompanied by a counselor.

"Come on, and just act like you're part of the support team."

Elli followed him to a group of girls under a large magnolia. A tall girl with long brown hair and a splattering of eye shadow looked at him from a rock bench. "Hey, Tanner," she said with a slight smile and a flutter of her blue-tinged eyelashes. "You here to comfort us poor, suffering little girls?"

Tanner gave her a wink and turned on the southern charm. "Morning, Martha June. You're looking pretty darned good."

She smirked and looked at him seductively. "I'm as good as they get, sugar."

Tanner ignored the bait and quietly said to them all, "I'm just here hoping you girls can give me a hand. I'm trying to find out who killed Kevin, and I could really use your help."

They all exchanged the furtive glances that make up the unspoken language of high school girls, which Elli recognized immediately. They definitely knew something, but none of them would give it up without something in return, and they were sizing up Tanner like a prize bull. The tall girl leaned back and crossed her legs in a not-too-subtle attempt to flash her panties and said, "I don't know what help we could be, but I'm willing to try. No matter how long the interview takes."

A pert redhead leaning on the trunk to her left rolled her eyes, pushed Martha off the bench with her foot and said, "Jesus, Martha June. He's not here to give you a pelvic exam." To Tanner she said, "Kevin was a cool guy. We all hung out with him and his friends, but we never really spent much time alone with him."

Tanner knew the redhead too. Her name was Betsy Reed. Her brother Hank had been one of his police academy bunkmates. "Come on, Betsy girl, didn't you date Kevin a while back?" he asked teasingly.

"Yeah," she said with a sad look. "We all did, but it never really stuck. Guess we weren't his type." This revelation sent a wave of sideways glances rippling around the group.

"Do you know if someone had a grudge against him or might want to harm him?" Tanner asked. "Even if it was just a small beef, it might help us."

Nobody answered the question, but after a few moments of silence a mousy girl with a long ponytail said, "You should talk to Mona Davis. She's the one he's been dating the past few months."

"Like Mona would know anything," Martha June groused as she dusted the dirt from her legs. "All she did was follow him around like a lost dog pretending to be someone she wasn't."

"Shut up, Martha June," another of the girls said. "Mona never did nothing to you, and it wasn't her fault he was stuck."

The atmosphere of the group suddenly became tense as if a deadly secret had been revealed. Tanner leaned close to Martha June and sweetly asked, "Could you perhaps tell me where to find Mona Davis? She may know something that could help us, and I'd be really grateful for even the smallest amount of information."

The offer was enough to break through Martha June's petulance, and she looked around the quad. "There," she said pointing to a blonde walking out of the library. "That's Mona, the one carrying the tote bag."

Tanner watched the girl heading for the school exit and then said to them all, "Thanks, girls, I really appreciate this."

"Just don't forget to stop by and thank us in person," Martha June said, throwing him a wink.

He hurried off to catch Mona with Elli on his heels as Betsy remarked, "Good God, could you be a bigger slut, Martha June?"

When they rounded the corner of the library, Elli said, "I distinctly remember high school girls being a bit more subtle. I hope you aren't thinking of taking her up on her offer."

"Are you kidding?" Tanner exclaimed. "I wouldn't touch Martha June with a ten-foot cattle prod. That girl is practically a rite of initiation at LaGrange. She's been rubbed over more balls than a locker room towel."

"So much for godly living," Elli muttered as they bounded up the stairs.

At the entrance to the school, they saw Mona Davis struggling as she tried to adjust the heavy bag in her hand.

"Let me take the lead on this one," Elli whispered to Tanner. "If she's really Kevin's girlfriend, the last thing she needs right now is some slick southern beefcake putting the moves on her to get her to talk."

"Beefcake . . ." Tanner mused as he watched Elli walk up to Mona.

"Excuse me . . ." Elli said to her quietly. The girl hadn't noticed Elli approach and was so startled she dropped the tote bag, spilling its contents everywhere. "I'm so sorry. I didn't mean to frighten you," Elli apologized as she helped Mona scoop up the contents of her tote, which she suspected contained the contents of the poor girl's locker. There were e-readers, a makeup case that had burst open, one traditionally bound book, and a box of store-bought hair color called Mocha Mahogany. "Pretty color," Elli told her, handing her the box.

Mona muttered "thanks" as she snatched the box and cradled it like a stray kitten. "It's mine," she remarked, tucking a bundle of stray blonde hairs behind her ear. Elli noticed that the blonde had grown out by about an inch as she helped Mona gather her scattered possessions. The box was a clear match to Mona's roots. She also observed that Mona had been crying considerably, which was to be expected. Her eyes were puffy and bloodshot and her nose red and runny. But she also had a sizable ring of bruises around her neck. Bruises that looked very much like finger impressions.

"Can I help you, honey?" Elli asked with concern. Mona looked at her suspiciously, so Elli blurted out, "Oh, I'm with the response team." Mona's suspicion fell a couple of notches as Elli explained, "I was supposed to be in the auditorium, but you look like you need someone to talk to." Mona shook her head and stood to leave, but Elli gently placed a hand on her back and said, "Anything you tell me is strictly confidential, honey, and I'm not here to judge. I'm just here to listen." The caring tone did the trick just as it had in the emergency room, and Mona nodded as a couple of tears slid down her face. "Why don't we just sit down over there and talk, just you and me for a bit." Elli pointed to an empty stretch of grass shaded by the school's hedges, and Mona let herself be led there.

They both sat cross-legged in the warm summer grass, and Elli waited patiently for Mona to speak. Tanner watched from behind a nearby pillar, amazed at how easily Elli handled the girl.

Mona wiped the tears from her face, took a deep breath and said, "I'm not suicidal or anything."

"That's good to hear," Elli said with a compassionate smile. "You must have known the boy who died pretty well. Was he a good friend of yours?"

Mona thought for a moment, pulling her bleach blonde locks behind her ear and exposing those nasty bruises again. "We were dating, I guess, but we broke it off last week."

"I'm sorry," Elli said sympathetically.

"Don't be," Mona told her. "It's kind of a relief," she said, laughing lightly and surrendering to a flood of tears. Elli waited for her to regain control, and when she did, she said, "At least he's with Janine now, and I'm off the hook." She laughed a little more. "I can go back to being just me. I get my life back, and I'll finally be able to look in the mirror and see my own face!"

Mona began to laugh even harder through the tears. Mona Davis might not be suicidal, but her trolley was definitely jumping the track. If she'd presented like this at Angel's Mercy, Elli would have dosed her with haloperidol, but there was nothing she could do now. Her medical credentials were currently suspended, and she was interviewing a potential witness under a patently false pretense of medical confidentiality.

"Did Kevin give you those bruises?" Elli asked.

The question shocked Maniac Mona out of her laughing-crying jag, and she stared defiantly at Elli. "These aren't mine, you know," she said, trembling. "They're hers."

"Hers?" Elli asked cautiously.

"Janine's," Mona told her. "She tempted Kevin even though she was claimed by someone else. She was a bad girl. She didn't treat her man with respect. Didn't take care of him."

Mona's eyes began to bounce back and forth in her eye sockets. "A good woman takes care of her man. Doesn't refuse him. The Lord put us here to take care of them; it's our duty." Elli watched as Mona's gaze shifted to a faraway place. "Daddy says you have to take good care of your man and make sure his needs are met. Otherwise you get punished. God's men will punish you."

That was all the girl said as her eyes drifted away. Whatever streetcar she was riding slid off the rails and crashed into a wall, leaving Maniac Mona humming "How Great Thou Art" quietly in the late summer grass. Tanner caught sight of a group of counselors approaching and rushed to Elli.

"We have to go, right now," he whispered, but Elli pulled back.

"I can't just leave her here like this. Look at her. She's in the middle of a psychotic break." Mona was now rocking and humming "What a Friend We Have in Jesus."

The men could be heard clearly now, and Tanner pulled Elli behind the nearest hedge wall as they rounded the corner. One of them noticed poor

Mona and asked the girl if she needed any assistance. Mona didn't look at him. She just stared and giggled and hummed. The man radioed for assistance, and while they were escorting Mona to a rubber room, Tanner led Elli away behind the hedges.

"Come on. She's in good hands, and we have to get out of here before people start swarming." They made their way back to the parking lot, dodging Markham's deputies, and headed back to Huntsville.

3

Elli said nothing on the drive back to Huntsville. When Tanner asked her what had happened with Mona, she only said, "Just get us back to HQ fast." She was clearly disturbed by whatever the girl had said, so he turned on the emergency lights and blasted down the highway. When they arrived, Elli hopped out of the cruiser before Tanner could even finish parking it. He caught up with her just as she hurried through the doors to the pit.

"We have the necessary search warrants, and I have four teams set up to do simultaneous inspections on the plants," Agnes was explaining. "Hopefully we'll find something that will help tie one to a suspect."

"Considering that we still don't have a suspect, we need to turn up something fast," Deacon said.

"I don't think we should let Bainbridge off the hook just yet," Joyce argued. "Despite the eyewitness statements to the contrary, he's still our primary suspect. He could be orchestrating other killings to throw us off the trail."

"He couldn't have done it," Tanner complained as he joined them. "You already confirmed that at least two of the eyewitness statements placing him elsewhere were true, and you have photographic evidence to back it up."

"That doesn't mean he didn't hire someone else to do it," Agnes offered. "You have to admit he has the ego and the motive."

Tanner shook his head. "It would take an enormous amount of cash to pull that off. We checked his financial dealings for the past year. Nothing out of the ordinary came up. No large, unexplained amounts of money that would indicate a payoff either to or from him or anyone else he was connected to."

Deacon looked at Tanner quizzically. "I thought you didn't doubt a person's honesty and good faith without evidence. Why would you check his financials if you didn't question his integrity?"

"We didn't. The background check was ordered by the Ecumenical Council. They wanted to know if he was involved because of . . ." He stopped and looked at Deacon, knowing that he had just been manipulated.

"Because of what, Deputy? You may as well spit it out because you've just put both feet squarely in your own mouth, and I'm going to find out anyway."

Tanner sighed. "Because of the preexisting penance order." Deacon held his index finger up and flexed it at him, demanding more. "Alan Bainbridge filed charges against his wife for adultery two months before her death. Once you made him a suspect, the Council ordered an internal investigation because of his personal connection to Archbishop Wirz. They went to school together. Senator Milton just about had kittens when he found out."

Deacon folded his arms. "They knew it would look like they were sabotaging the case if it came out that the lead territorial investigator was good buddies with the prime suspect."

"Especially with his wife being on the detainment list. She was scheduled to be sequestered before she disappeared."

"What do you mean by sequestered?" Agnes asked.

"It means incarcerated until your sentence is carried out," Joyce told her as she looked at Elli. "The Council holds convicted sinners in isolation from family members and witnesses. They're attended by enforcement clergy to prepare their souls for penance. They only allow one family visit prior to execution of the sentence to allow the condemned to ask forgiveness of those they have wronged or, if necessary, to say goodbye."

"I take it not everyone ends up sequestered?" Deacon asked.

"No, only persons whose transgressions fall under the seven deadly sins. For the lesser sentences, the local law enforcement serves them and escorts them to rehabilitation centers when it's their time to serve. We handle everything like speeding, petty theft, and drunk and disorderlies down at our level." Tanner turned inward just a bit as he continued. "We've pretty much been reduced to a glorified highway patrol and delivery service. All detective-grade investigators were integrated into the territorial police and sworn in as the Council's personal enforcement unit."

Deacon could tell this didn't sit well with Tanner. "Do you know if Kevin Dockweiler was on that list?"

Tanner shook his head. "I've never heard of him being officially charged with anything. I've only busted him once, and that was for underage drinking out at The Falls."

"I'm willing to bet he was," Elli offered quietly. It was the first time she'd spoken since returning from the school and interviewing Mona Davis. "I spoke to his girlfriend. She was pretty distraught, but not like you would expect."

Deacon waited for Elli to continue. It was obvious she was struggling to put into words what she learned, and whatever it was had been highly disturbing.

"Try to tune out all the emotional baggage, Elli. Concentrate on what she told you," Deacon instructed.

Elli took a couple of deep breaths. "She said that she was finally free to be who she really was now that Kevin was gone. That she could return to her old life because Kevin was with Janine now, and that was who he wanted to be with."

"Janine Turnbull?"

"I don't know. I didn't have time to find out. She had a mental meltdown and the Council cops showed up before I could get her to tell me."

Deacon signaled to Agnes, who jumped on the mainframe searching for school records as Elli spoke.

"She was going to dye her hair back to its original color. She'd dyed it blonde because Kevin told her to. And she had these horrible bruises around her neck that looked like fingerprints." Elli was getting teary, and Tanner reached out to grasp her hand. "She said the bruises were Janine's, not hers. That Janine got what she deserved because she hadn't taken care of her man. That's when she started babbling hysterically."

"Got it!" Agnes shouted and sent the obituary up to the overhead display. "Janine Turnbull passed away on August 24th of this year. No cause of death is listed, but her services were held at the Church of the Holy Light, exactly where our second victim was found last night. AND her father was one Pastor Lawrence Turnbull. The same Lawrence Turnbull who discovered the second victim and died of a massive heart attack during our crime scene investigation."

"That actually makes sense," Tanner offered. "There were rumors that Kevin had a thing for Janine because they grew up together, but she always said they were just friends. She was engaged to Paul Cotton, and they were getting married next year."

"Well, this isn't exactly the work of a jealous boyfriend," Deacon told him.

"That's not what I mean, and anyway Paul's dead too, so he couldn't have done it."

"You lost us, Junior. How does any of this make sense?" Joyce asked.

"Janine and Paul were both convicted over the summer. Their deaths were penance bestowed by the Ecumenical Council after an unnamed source presented evidence of them having premarital sex. Nobody believed it, especially not their parents, and the evidence wasn't of the actual act but the prelude to it. No evidence existed of intercourse."

"But virginity and intercourse can easily be established by a medical examination. Why wasn't one conducted?" Joyce asked Tanner.

"Because it would have been an accusation of perjury against the witness without any substantiated motive. If the parents had demanded the examination and it proved the act, they would also suffer the same fate as their children for maligning the witness. With the photographs of the foreplay already entered into evidence, they couldn't do it without risking their own lives, and they have four younger children between them to still care for."

"How'd you find out about all this if you weren't privy to the details?" Deacon asked.

"Markham confided in me privately but only because he was so upset at having to go and arrest those kids. He knew them pretty well and didn't believe the charges either. He hated the idea."

"But there are no unnamed witnesses in such cases," Joyce said. "Anyone bringing evidence before the Council must by law participate in the sentencing and execution."

"Unless the witness is a minor," Deacon told them. "Children's identities are protected by the Council and not disclosed unless they are convicted. Their participation also isn't required unless they reach the age of eighteen before the sentence is carried out."

Agnes pulled out the bio on their second victim. "Kevin Dockweiler won't turn eighteen until January second. If he was the source, his identity would still have been sealed."

Elli quietly listened to them unravel the tale of the mysterious Janine, but all she could see were the ugly bruises on poor Mona Davis's throat. "It was him," she muttered. When they all turned to look at her, she said, "If you'd seen the bruises and listened to how that poor girl described their relationship, you wouldn't doubt it for a minute." She looked to Agnes and said, "Can you pull up pictures of Mona Davis and Janine Turnbull?"

"Sure," she replied and went to work. Within a minute, she had located the class photographs of both girls—Janine with her smiling face and shiny natural blonde locks and poor Mona in happier times with her thick brown mop and bright eyes.

"Can you make Mona's hair the same color as Janine's?"

Again, Agnes went to work and within seconds matched the two. It was impossible to deny the resemblance.

"He couldn't have the girl he wanted, so he took poor Mona and turned her into his own personal version of Janine. Then he took out all his frustration and rejection on her. He couldn't have the real one, so he made sure no one else could either."

"Shit, what is it with you men?" Agnes groused.

"So Kevin lied about the relationship and took revenge on Janine and her fiancé," Deacon wondered aloud. "That fits in with him being declared a false witness. But since his identity was sealed, that means only one of two things. Either our killer knew him intimately enough to know he lied, or our killer is someone with access to high-level Ecumenical Council business, maybe even a member of the Council itself."

No one spoke as everyone absorbed this revelation. Hunting a serial killer was difficult enough when he was particularly smart and skilled. But accusing someone on or involved with the Ecumenical Council was a guaranteed career death sentence.

Deacon rose. "I think it's time I had a heart-to-heart talk with Archbishop Wirz."

"Whoa, hold on, now," Tanner interjected. "You can't go after one of their own and expect them to cooperate. Even if they believe you, they'll never let you expose the truth. They'll close ranks tighter than a mother superior's crotch."

"Not a visual I need walking into a basilica, Tanner," Deacon said as he turned to leave.

Joyce didn't like the look in Deacon's eyes and followed him out. It was the same look he got whenever he contemplated doing something very risky and utterly stupid, usually after spending a night at T-Bone's. She stopped him at the elevator. "You aren't seriously going to accuse a sitting member of the Council of being a killer," she told him. "All we have is a working theory that fits some circumstantial evidence and no hard facts. "

"I'm not going to accuse anyone, but the only way we're going to get within spitting distance of someone employed in the Ecumenical Seat is with Wirz's permission. So I'm just going to ask him very, very nicely."

"You'd be committing career suicide. They'd publicly crucify you, and you'd need an act of God to come back from it."

The doors opened, and he turned to Joyce's worried face, grinning. "It wouldn't be the first resurrection in history."

4

Kyle offered to drive Elli home that night, but she politely declined. Not an easy thing to do when he was at his most charming, but he eventually accepted her refusal. She said she wanted to do a little research on a medical issue and found a quiet office to work in. But even alone with her thoughts in a dimly lit room, she couldn't get Kyle Tanner out of her head. She felt ridiculous, obsessing over a man ten years younger and far less worldly than herself. She'd spent her entire collegiate and medical infancy in the Constitutional states, broadening her horizons and experiences, while he'd been cruising the streets of Cartersville and Kennesaw hitting on high school girls with his buddies. Her father had been so proud of her when she chose to pursue medicine rather than follow Mom into the fashion industry or Dad into politics. She wanted to be her own woman. Kyle followed in his daddy's and granddaddy's footsteps and joined the sheriff's academy, just like all the other good old boys who couldn't make the grade enough to leave. They were worlds apart in both ambition and experience, yet he stuck to her like a stubborn piece of melted gum on a hot summer sidewalk. She had been pulling and tugging at that gooey mess in her mind all afternoon, but it just kept stretching and oozing, never letting go. Maybe it was his southern charm and respectful turns of phrase, like the way he fumbled between calling her Ma'am or Miss or Doc before finally agreeing to just use her name, something not quite proper until one became "familiar" with a young woman. She tried to convince herself it was all just the swaggering persona adopted by most young men trying to get laid. They cultivate their act long before high school and perfect it over time, but even the most skilled players couldn't keep the act up every minute. They eventually tire, their true natures emerge, the game ends, the lights go up and the music stops. Kyle was different. No matter how the situation shifted or how horrific the circumstances became, his game never changed. Whatever ineptitude MacNair saw in his police work, the manners never went away; the charm and respect never dissipated even when they were arguing. It wasn't an act—it was Kyle's nature, and it stuck to Elli with a vengeance.

She pulled up the case evidence and reread the statements given by the girls at the school and poor Maniac Mona as she collapsed. Mona's words disturbed her far more than her attraction to Kyle. The way she'd willingly abandoned herself to become someone else just to please a boy. The abuse she'd suffered because it was what was expected of a good southern woman. It wasn't the first time Elli had encountered such attitudes in the territory. Her friends had exhibited the same strange willingness to abandon their individuality after they married. She'd always assumed it was just a consequence of relationships. Marriages were exercises in compromise, her mother had said. There were things you simply had to give up to be with someone. The trick was finding that special someone who truly appreciated those sacrifices and was willing to give as much as they received. Elli hadn't seen much giving on the part of her friends' husbands, but none of them was going headfirst down a rabbit hole of personality disorders, so it must be working for them. Or maybe it was the fact that her friends were all professional working women who had a strong sense of identity before they married. Strong enough to carry them through even the greatest of compromises and remain whole.

The pretty face from Mona's high school yearbook hovered on the screen in stark contrast to the demented ravings scrolling beneath it. The poor child was still trying to find herself when Kevin Dockweiler got hold of her and warped her sense of self to satisfy his own unfulfilled desires. Elli wondered how many women in the Republic grew up with these same influences, captured and indoctrinated into a male-driven society before that sense of self could take hold and give them courage and identity. As a doctor, she'd seen her share of abuse explained away as accidents or dismissed as routine. It was common in rural families and communities, where women knew their so-called place. Elli's father had told her early on that she should never ever accept this for herself. She should never let any man or woman abuse her, never forget who and what she was, and above all never be afraid to stand up for herself and speak her mind. He wanted his child to be confident and strong, which was why he had sent her up north to be educated. He advocated for women's individuality and strength in his speeches and encouraged his female supporters to speak up and make their voices heard. His attitudes were rare for a territorial senator: a man who believed women could be mothers and wives and still be leaders. He represented every citizen of the territory equally and never let them forget it. It made him a beloved figure among the citizens and a traitor to his colleagues in the Senate.

She closed Mona's case file and tried to prepare her initial report to the archbishop. It proved to be overwhelming. She knew what they really wanted. They wanted dirt on the investigators as much as any possible breaches of territorial law they might commit during the investigation. But she'd only been there a day and already there was so much detail to the case it was hard to know where to start. The dirt would have to wait. Drawing on her experience as an oncologist, she dictated the sequence of events and the evidence with clinical precision, no emotional suppositions or personal impressions. She reread the report several times, making sure to keep it objective and concise.

Her encounter with Det. Bachman in the morgue swam up from memory. The disturbing statistics of justice that women receive in the territory. She pulled up a search engine on another screen and requested the public records for domestic abuse cases in the Republic and their dispositions. It took a couple of minutes, and the list went on for page after page. She called up the records for divorces granted in the territory since its inception. That much-shorter list came up within seconds. Running a trace comparison, she found that every name on the list of divorce records appeared on the list of domestic abuse complaints at least four times. She stared at the two lists for a moment and then requested death certificate records for the territory. It took a while to compile, but eventually it came up and seemed to go on forever. She ran one more comparison and waited. The new list populated. Every name on the divorce list and a considerable number of names on the domestic abuse list also appeared on the list of the dead. She sorted the compared names by date. The causes of death were never attributed to the cases in question. Each was listed as some sort of accident or previously undiscovered ailment. But in every case, the death was reported as having taken place within ninety days of either a divorce or an arrest, and at least ninety-eight percent of the names were women. Elli reread the list over and over, hoping she was misreading the data, but with each pass the ugly truth of what her society had become was made more apparent.

She didn't realize a tear was running down her face until Det. Bachman quietly said from the doorway, "It's heartbreaking when the truth stares you in the face, isn't it?"

"There has to be some other explanation for this," Elli told her.

"We've been trying to find one for a couple of years now, but we haven't come up with anything. The deaths appear explainable until you add them all up." Bachman walked over to the desk and handed Elli a tissue. "You're a doctor. Maybe you can shed some light on it."

Elli read as she wiped her face. The deaths covered a wide range of conditions: undiagnosed cancers, burst aneurysms, strokes, heart attacks. None of them made sense. The chances of any cancer being undiagnosed even in the territory was slim to none these days. As an oncologist she was well aware of the rates for detection and cure in Republic hospitals, and it hovered at an impressive 98%. Even the most rural patients had access to immediate care thanks to Corridor technology. Strokes and heart attacks were unfortunately nothing new thanks to the intensely fattening diet most southerners still followed, but the ages of the afflicted women were astounding. They were too young to have built up the level of plaque necessary to induce such conditions, and there were far too many of them. The aneurysms worried her most. It was true they were silent killers, often going undetected until they became catastrophic. But they only occurred in roughly ten out of every one hundred thousand people. According to the list in front of her, the number of people dying in the Republic of brain aneurysms each year was nearly five hundred, all of them women.

"The causes of death have all been attributed to known diseases, but they could have also been a result of abuse," Elli said. "Without a recognized family history, we have no way to confirm it. The only other possibility is that there's a large spike in genetic disorders in the Republic."

"Don't they check for such things when babies are born?" Joyce asked.

"Absolutely. When the Territorial Protection Act went into effect, everyone was tested at a genetic level, and every child born since then has been." Elli paused and dropped her eyes before adding, "The government couldn't discredit the scientific theory about homosexuality being a genetic trait, so they instituted the program to assure the people that any propensity for it was detected early enough that the church could address it before it took hold."

Joyce looked at her strangely but said nothing.

"The testing proved nothing either way but gave us a wealth of information about the health of the populace. It helped advance our preventative medicine and cure rates astronomically, which is why these statistics don't make sense."

Joyce stayed silent and allowed Elli to draw her own conclusions. She'd already seen how Elli reacted when an outsider criticized her society. If she were ever going to accept the truth, she would have to come to it on her own.

After a few more minutes of reading in silence, Elli said, "How could we have fallen so far?"

"Well, the good thing about falling is that once you land, you have nowhere to go but up," Joyce told her. She quietly exited the room.

Elli closed the statistical research file and opened the final draft of her report. She scrolled down and deleted her personal conversation with Mona Davis, then sent the report to the Justice Ministry. She also sent a blind copy to Deacon.

5

Deacon sat in the tattered armchair in his mother's living room, staring at the unopened bottle of bourbon on the table. Joyce was right. If he even hinted that someone in the Ecclesiastical government was tied to the killer, his career would be toast. Ordinarily, he wouldn't have cared. If it caught him the killer, he would suffer the reprimand or the demotion, even the forced retirement if that's what it came to. John had been subtly lobbing that suggestion at him ever since Neville's death. But there was more at stake here than anyone on his team realized. If he made even the slightest misstep during this investigation, it would give the Republic grounds to take over the case, which would cost him any chance of uncovering those behind the threat.

He leaned back with his eyes closed and absently wished it was still war time. With the Declaration of War still in place, he would be free to confront the threat by whatever means necessary as it was a threat to the entire country. But peace had broken out and made a mess of his country before it could be brought to its senses. Now he had to treat half of his fellow Americans as if they were foreigners living on foreign soil and behave with the tact of an ambassador. Peace had made him a politician whether he liked it or not, and it made the acid in his stomach churn. As he rubbed his aching gut, the secure comm line to headquarters activated.

"Lieutenant, you have an incoming communication on an encrypted line from the White House," the avatar announced.

"Put the video through and encrypt," he responded, tossing the bottle in the trash. The television broadcast vanished and the holographic face of the president appeared on the display, grinning like a Cheshire Cat.

"Good evening, Lieutenant. I hope I didn't wake you. How goes the investigation?" she asked.

"Getting more complicated every day. Our case of domestic violence has escalated into a serial killing."

"I heard about the boy in the church. I'm sorry you have to deal with this," she said sympathetically. "But there isn't a man in the department more capable of catching him than you."

Deacon shot the image an annoyed look. "You didn't call me up on a secure channel at this hour just to give me a pep talk, did you?"

"Absolutely not," she said with that bizarre grin. "I have some new information on our little project that could be relevant to your case. The FBI decrypted more of those communications they downloaded. They seemed pretty routine at first: notifications to all members of changes in command, introductions to replacement members. But then we ran a cross-check on those being replaced and discovered a disturbing trend."

"They're all dead, I'll wager."

"Very perceptive, Lieutenant, but that's not the disturbing part. They were dated and transmitted subsequent to each death, but forensics discovered that every one of them was composed between forty-eight and seventy-two hours *prior* to the death of the subjects."

Deacon sat up. "You're saying they were eliminated?"

"If they were, it was done by a highly skilled professional. Every one of those deaths was entirely plausible and non-suspicious. They ranged from natural causes to simple accidents or predictable illnesses. Remember the accident two years ago when the Hand to the High Archbishop was killed on the Tybee Island Bridge?"

"Are you kidding? They've been holding memorials down here all week for him. Drunk driver took him out." Deacon's eyes went wide. "Wait, you're telling me Harrison Meeks was one of them."

"They're called the Cadre," the president told him. "We were able to deduce that much about who they are from the communications, and yes, he was one of their senior members."

"But they pulled the other driver from the wreckage on the bridge. Blood tests confirmed he was blackout drunk when he caused the crash."

"And he died before anyone could question him, didn't he?"

Deacon nodded as he remembered the details of the accident, but then his eyes went wide. "If Meeks was taken out, they would have had to replace him with another operative, but the current high archbishop was elevated through the ranks."

"Right on both counts. The current high archbishop may not be Cadre, but his right hand most certainly is," the president teased.

"Caulder Wirz," Deacon said aloud, feeling his gut burn deeper. "The most popular man on the Council."

"And someone you want to be very careful of," the president cautioned. "We examined his entire history. All of it is aboveboard and corroborated, nothing fabricated. Did his theological training in Vatican City among the Catholic elite but left Catholicism when he returned home. He's politically and religiously well connected with an ancestry that dates back to the Confederacy of the first Civil War."

"A son of the South with all the right bloodlines and ties to the wealthiest faith on the planet," Deacon muttered. "And he's in direct control of the leadership."

"I'll send you a complete list of the operatives we've uncovered so far. Watch your step, Lieutenant. The list doesn't contain the names of those they may have groomed, so there's no way to know who could be working with them," the president cautioned and then signed off.

Deacon exhaled deeply as the file downloaded to his PDP. With Wirz at the top of the list, he would have to tread very carefully when dealing with the Council. The killer could be among them and part of a very dangerous organization, one that excelled in well-executed assassinations. He retrieved the bourbon from the trash and poured himself a shot.

6

Wirz quietly tapped his fingers as his operative spoke. The news was exactly what he had expected. The hacker had not been found, a failure that would ultimately be laid at his feet. Such a failure could be fatal, and should a decision be made at the highest levels to remove him, his previous accomplishments would be meaningless. Continued success was the only guarantee of service and the fabulous rewards it offered. He needed to turn this debacle to his advantage somehow.

"We've examined his method of entry thoroughly, sir, and it wasn't an outside hack," the operative, a man named George, reported, intruding on Wirz's personal turmoil.

"We're already aware that the intrusion originated within the Republic," he responded with annoyance.

"What I mean is that it wasn't an intrusion, sir. It was an authorized entry."

Wirz sat up, focusing his icy glare on the man. The operative was used to it, having served the archbishop for almost a year. Nevertheless, he kept his guard up as he continued to report.

"We found a back door into the central systems. It was how he gained access so easily. It appears to have been programmed in several years ago and updated as the system was upgraded. The last access was just over a year ago. This could only have been done from the inside, perhaps by a former operative."

"There are no former operatives, George," Wirz reminded him. "The Cadre is a lifetime commitment with only one retirement plan. You know this as well as any of us."

George steeled himself. "Then we have a traitor among us, sir."

Wirz stood slowly and walked to the window. The Atlanta suburbs spread out under a slight haze of smog. It lingered everywhere in the oil-dependent Republic and increased the further you got from the federal border.

"That is a serious accusation to make, George. One that could have catastrophic consequences if proven inaccurate."

George swallowed. "Agreed, sir. But the evidence points only to these two possibilities. Given that one is impossible, we must consider the unthinkable to be true."

The prospect of a traitor within the Cadre was hard to believe. The recruitment process took years. Even after extensive conditioning and manipulation, the slightest hesitation or resistance at any stage would be met with immediate elimination. Still, there was the possibility of regression. It had happened once before. Operatives tired of the stress and expectations over the years could request removal to deeply isolated positions where they served only as information conduits. If, however, they regressed and began deviating from the Agenda, their permanent removal was imperative. In fact, it was the regression of his predecessor that elevated Caulder Wirz to his current position. He'd carried out the removal personally, a difficult thing to do when one's mentor becomes a threat. But the brilliant execution and subsequent popular reaction to his promotion in office had catapulted Caulder Wirz into a much-beloved representative on the Council and a greatly feared operator within the Cadre.

Caulder's mind went into high gear. If he were to expose a traitor within the organization, it would cement his devotion to his superiors. They might even orchestrate his promotion to high archbishop much sooner than anticipated, although he had far grander ambitions. Why rule one country when you could rule them all? A false sense of security was exactly what he needed his mentors to attain.

"Begin an immediate investigation of all Cadre personnel in territorial service. Monitor anyone who has access to that level of government information and work your way outward from there."

For the first time, George's eyes went wide and he fumbled his words. "Sir, we have hundreds of members in every state. It would take years to investigate them all!"

"We're not looking for some low-level data processor, you moron!" Wirz spat at him. "He'll be among the members with red-level access or at least affiliated with them to a high degree and most likely affiliated with the individual whose access was corrupted in some way."

"Even so, the numbers are significant. Such a mass investigation might alert the traitor and send him into hiding."

"Agreed," Wirz muttered. "We need to mask our search."

He walked back to his desk and stared at the communication screen embedded there. As always, a small window was tuned to a twenty-four-hour news cast. Silently, the story ribbon reported the lack of federal progress in the recent territorial homicides. A sly grin crept across Wirz's face, and his eyes gleamed with purpose.

He looked up at George and said with a smile, "The Feds are looking for a killer, so start with those."

When a Stranger Sojourns

1

One block from the church of the recently deceased Pastor Turnbull sat a taproom in a large brick building. It served craft beer for the more educated southern palates but also stocked some of the more common brands to attract enough local business to remain open. Its proximity to the church wasn't unusual. Prayer and Pilsner went hand in hand in these parts. What made it stand out to Jeremy Burke was the way its corner entrance—with security cameras—stared directly toward the church's main vestibule.

Burke doubted they would be of any value. Most places installed fake systems as a deterrent, but since everyone knew they were fake, they were more of a running joke. Occasionally you'd come across an actual working system, but it usually provided playback of people mooning it or some other drunken snub. And once in a very long while, you hit pay dirt. Burke examined the cameras as he entered the taproom. Definitely a working system, so his odds were improving. He stepped into the darkened lounge and inhaled deeply. Hops, malt, yeast with a touch of citrus; aromatherapy at its finest. He wished he had the time to enjoy a batch, but he was here on business. The bartender was a slender man in his sixties sporting a wiry, neatly trimmed beard. Despite his dapper appearance, his face was deeply lined and tanned, and his hands had thick callouses. This was a man who spent a lifetime doing hard labor, not some entrepreneurial brew master from upstate. That meant, as Deacon repeatedly counseled him, being on his most conciliatory behavior.

"Afternoon," Burke said to him, smiling like a 5th Avenue magazine cover. The man just nodded politely without smiling or speaking. "I'm wondering if you could introduce me to the owner of this establishment."

The bartender stared back at him for a minute without changing his expression. He dropped his eyes to where Burke's federal ID hung from his shirt and then looked up. "I own this place." He pulled a beer glass from the rack and set it disapprovingly in front of Burke. "A little early for a cop to be tossing back beers in a local bar. Besides, aren't you Feds supposed to be investigating a murder?"

"Actually, that's why I'm here," Burke responded, putting on a slightly sad and desperate expression. "I'm Investigator Jeremy Burke. I'm hoping you can help me with the investigation. I noticed your security camera system out front. If it's active, it may just help us catch the guy who killed that poor kid."

The bartender gave him the once-over again. "It's not fake, if that's what you mean. It downloads to an off-site security service as a backup. Data usually gets stored for about two weeks until it rolls over."

"I'd really appreciate it if I could get a look at that data," Burke said with all manner of false humility, "and I'm sure the victim's family would appreciate you helping us catch this sicko," he added for good measure.

The bartender hesitated but then waved to one of the waitresses and led Burke to his back office.

"I didn't get your name, friend," Burke said, following him.

"I didn't offer it," the bartender told him coldly. They walked up to the back office and into an electrical room where a remote display sat next to a bank of recording equipment. The system had obviously been installed by an amateur and cabling ran everywhere, but the replay setup was new and easy to operate. The man opened a desk drawer and pulled a crumpled gum wrapper from the tray. He spread it out and handed it to Burke. The pass codes were written on it.

"You should probably keep these in a more secure location, like a fingerprinted access file," Burke said. "You wouldn't want your passwords to fall into the wrong hands."

The bartender crossed his rough arms and smirked. "I'll keep that in mind in the unlikely event you techno-Yankees figure out how to hack a Juicy Fruit wrapper."

Burke held his tongue and nodded. There was no point in arguing with Neanderthals who scoffed at technology. The territory was full of them. Maybe that's why Deacon felt so at home among them. They were definitely his people. As Burke typed in the access codes, a small part of his intellect whispered, *You never would have thought to look at a used gum wrapper.* He shut the thought down and scrolled back through the last two days of footage.

"I know all the people who come in here," the bartender said. "None of my locals would have done this."

"Then you're probably the most important person in this room right now, sir," Burke told him as he continued to watch. "Mind telling me what time you close?"

"Cutoff's one a.m. I lock the doors promptly at two every morning."

Burke ran the stream to two a.m. three days prior and watched. There was no movement on the street except for an occasional car. Then a black truck stopped in front of the church entrance just out of the glow of the streetlight. The driver rummaged around in his vehicle for a few minutes and moved on. He rapidly scrolled through the feed again to the following morning at closing time. Again the street remained empty, but just before four a.m. the same black truck slowly pulled up to the church. Only this time, the driver pulled into the parking lot. As it crossed beneath the lights, Burke noticed it had no license plate. He watched it turn to the right and skirt behind the trees. It was a full hour before a young woman came walking back from behind the trees, straightening her clothes. Five minutes later, the truck left the parking lot and returned the way it came. Nothing but a hookup, plain and simple.

Burke ran through the feed to the following night, feeling his frustration mount. This would theoretically be the night the murder occurred. He watched the street empty and the lights dim. Once again a black truck pulled in front of the church and turned behind the trees. But this time, it drove across the lot to a side entrance. Burke tried to bring the image into focus, but the truck had parked out of the camera's range. The best he could achieve was a blurry vehicle moving in the dark. He watched as an indistinguishable blob got out and carried things back and forth to the church. The very last one was nearly as big as the blob itself. Pay dirt!

Burke ran the tape back to the day before and turned to the bartender. "Can you identify this vehicle?"

The bartender came forward and looked at the truck while Burke advanced it frame by frame as it passed under the light. The bartender shook his head. "Nope. Don't belong to any of my people. Too damned clean and unscuffed for a work truck. Probably some tourist tooling around, picking up local girls."

Burke sped the feed up until the young woman came around the bushes and stopped it. "Can you identify her?"

The bartender looked closely at her face. His eyes got wide for just a minute, and then he scowled. "Don't know her," he said rather unconvincingly.

Burke knew he was lying. He was just the type of good old boy who didn't trust anyone not wearing Rebel Red and wouldn't cooperate. He dropped all pretense of professional courtesy and patience. "Look, I couldn't care less if she's servicing farmhands off the grid. She's not my concern, but the guy in that truck is. If he's the killer, and from what I see here that's highly likely, she's seen him and that puts her in extreme danger." Burke waited to see if his words had any impact. When the bartender didn't answer, he said, "She could be his next victim." The man still said nothing, so Burke puffed himself. "And I don't think you want it made public that you were too busy wallowing in your southern pride to help save her life. I promise you I'll have no problem blasting that fact to every reporter in the territory."

The threat had an immediate impact. The bartender's face began to darken in anger, and his calloused hands balled up. Burke was calculating whether or not he could take the man when he said, "Susan Shafter. She's a cashier over at the feed store on Bright Star Road."

"Thanks," Burke said with contempt. "I'll have to upload these feeds as evidence, and the detectives will want to interview you."

"Just take what you need, Yankee. Get out and don't come back!" the bartender yelled as he threw open the door.

Burke plugged an evidence pad into the main access port and entered his federal credentials. The device immediately began to pull the information from the feed and upload it to HQ. Within a minute it finished, and Burke sealed off the device with an encrypted code before disconnecting it. He strode past the bartender with a sarcastic "Thank you for your cooperation" and wasn't the least bit surprised when the man spat on him on the way out. When he got back in the van, he stowed the recording device and pulled a sterile pad from his kit. The bartender may not have given his name, but the gob of spit Burke wiped from the back of his head would have him identified in no time. He even toyed with the idea of having the bastard arrested for assaulting a peace officer.

Fifteen minutes later as Burke headed up the ramp to the Federal Corridor, a truck came out of nowhere. It plowed into the van, sending it tumbling down the embankment into a deep ditch. The driver stopped but only long enough to make sure he hadn't been seen, then sped onto a feeder road and disappeared toward Marietta.

The van lay on its side, small sparks crackling along its undercarriage. The communications array on its roof had been crushed during the rollover, and its passenger side bore the impression of a maniacal bite mark where the truck's reinforced grill had slammed into it. Burke didn't see what had hit him. He'd been uploading the evidence to Agnes, and the van was on autopilot. All he knew when he awoke was that he'd been in a serious accident and knocked unconscious. He could smell burning wires and hear the occasional pop of live current, but he couldn't move. Every loose piece of equipment in the vehicle had bounced around and landed on top of him during the impact. The cabin was bathed in the muted orange glow from the emergency backup system, and there were shattered bits of glass and pieces of sharp metal everywhere.

After a few minutes, he managed to get one arm free, shredding it on every edge and bleeding everywhere. He could feel cool air coming from somewhere but couldn't see the driver's cockpit. He pressed the comm link on his collar, but it produced only static. That meant he'd lost the communications array and his ability to reach HQ. He was sure the video upload was incomplete. The sudden interruption would alert his team that something was wrong, but that could take hours. He had to find a way to get clear and get an open signal. A large metal case had landed atop his chest, and he used his free hand to move it. When it slid off his chest and onto his shoulder, he heard a loud crack, and a bolt of pain shot up his arm and into his brain. He couldn't tell which bone he'd shattered, but it was washing the world away in a gray haze.

Fuck! I'm going to die in this redneck shithole, he thought as he wheezed into the pain and passed out.

2

Back at Huntsville Agnes was poring over the video feeds as they came in. They showed the black truck that returned to the church each night, moving closer each time. Burke was definitely onto something. When the final feed came up, showing the driver unloading his mysterious cargo, it abruptly stopped. She checked the connections and tried to reestablish the signal but failed. She pressed the comm link to the van, but there was no answer. Agnes's concern began to mount as she opened a secure, encrypted connection to Burke's personal line and it went straight to voicemail. Burke never ignored a call from her, not even at the most inconvenient times. She'd interrupted him on more than one occasion having sex and each time heard him defusing the moment with how critical his expertise was to his team.

Concern became alarm as Agnes fought to control her emotions. Run the numbers, eliminate the possibilities. There is a rational explanation for everything, and it's our job to find it. That's what she always told her trainees. She ran the systems checks by the numbers and watched as every possible explanation was eliminated. She checked the external networks to ensure they were all operating unimpeded at full capacity. She even called up the weather and determined no natural reason for the communications failure. She was left with only one explanation for Burke's disappearance: human intervention. She hit the panic button and called Deacon.

A light went off in every office in every building in the complex, alerting the entire division that they had an officer down.

"What happened?" Joyce cried out, running into the pit.

"Burke's down," Agnes told her. "He was uploading evidence, and I lost all communications with him."

"Did you run a systems check? Maybe he hit a blind spot."

"I ran every check possible, and all systems are green. I can't raise him," Agnes explained. "I'm running a locator trace on the van right now." She activated the onboard GPS, and everyone watched the overhead map. The beacon should have sounded immediately, but it took a full minute to engage, and even then the signal was intermittent and weak. "There. He's ten miles outside of Marietta near the interstate."

"Pull up the satellites," Joyce told her.

"We can't. Not without an interterritorial warrant."

"Dammit!" Joyce yelled. Turning to Tanner she said, "Kyle, can you do anything?"

Tanner looked at the map desperately and said, "I'd have to go through channels for satellite access, and that would take hours."

Joyce linked into the hanger and ordered a rescue chopper. "I want everybody at the launch pad now!" she said, grabbing her tactical gear and weapons.

"I can get the sheriff out there with EMS to protect him until you get there," Tanner offered.

"No way, pretty boy. You're getting on that chopper right now," she said, tossing him a Kevlar vest. "We need permission to fly in, but with you on board they can't deny us emergency access to their airspace." Tanner blanched and started to object, but then Elli spoke up.

"I'm going too," she said. "If he's hurt, you'll need a doctor."

"Everybody move out. Agnes, get Deacon to meet us at the landing pad."

"He's already there," she called as they all ran out.

By the time Joyce, Tanner and Elli arrived, the rescue chopper was already spun up and waiting. Deacon was perched in the open hatchway. "Get a move on. Tanner, you sit up front."

Tanner hesitated but climbed in nervously next to the pilot. As the chopper took off, he grabbed his shoulder straps in a death grip. Deacon squeezed in behind them and spoke into his mic. "Tanner, get in touch with air traffic control and identify yourself. Tell them you are acting on the authority of the Council and need access to their airspace for a medical emergency." Tanner shook his head but didn't say anything as the chopper lifted off and banked hard southeast toward Georgia. Deacon looked at the sweat beginning to run down Tanner's scalp. "You afraid of flying?"

"Yeah," Tanner answered as warm winds buffeted the helicopter.

"How the hell did you ever graduate the police academy with a fear of flying?" Deacon asked.

"It's not something the academy really cared about since police cruisers don't fly. Choppers are strictly for territorial police."

"Well, close your eyes and make the call before we get shot down," Deacon told him.

While the chopper waited for permission to continue its mission, a light began to flash inside the wrecked van, keeping time with a high-pitched beep. The sound broke through the darkness Burke floundered in. Peering through a pain-fog, he saw the emergency beacon flashing and smiled tightly. "Good girl, Agnes," he muttered and fell back into the dark well of relief.

He didn't stir again until he felt the van shift around him and the metal container trapping his shoulder bore down. His eyes bolted open with pain, and he cried out. Instead of being met with silence, he heard shouting. He didn't recognize the voices, but they seemed to know he was inside. A bright light glowed in the crumpled cabin, and a voice told him to close his eyes and cover them if possible. Seconds later, a welding torch bore down on the van's rear doors, sending sparks everywhere. Within minutes the doors were pulled away and a path cleared through the debris. The voices continued to shout orders as they entered. At one point he could have sworn he heard someone vomiting. He only hoped it wasn't in response to his injuries. The last thing Burke remembered before passing out again was Elli's voice telling him he was safe and that everything would be okay.

3

Agnes watched Burke crack open one eye, wincing at the pain the light brought to his head. He moaned pitifully as Agnes rubbed his arm. Burke was part of her team, her family. And she was, after all, the designated mother hen of the group. She stared at Burke's hair, which inexplicably lay perfect even after a car wreck and two days in a hospital bed. The bruises and tiny scars were already fading and only served to add character to his chiseled, perfect features, in her opinion. He worked his eyes open slowly, mewling like a wet, disgruntled kitten. She just shook her head, marveling at how such an egomaniacal specimen like this turned out to be such a pussy. She slapped his arm roughly, causing him to squeal, and said, "He's coming around, boss."

Deacon walked up on the other side of the bed, scowling. "Welcome back, Sleeping Beauty. You enjoy the vacation?"

"Vacation, my ass," Burke replied. "That son of a bitch tried to kill me. What the hell is wrong with these yokels?" he complained and tried to sit up.

"Which son of a bitch in particular are you referring to?" Deacon asked.

"That damned bartender!" Burke cried. "He was pissed because I confiscated his surveillance system. And before you say anything, boss, I asked nicely. Then he spits at me and throws me out just for doing my job." He tried to look tough but only managed petulance. "I'm pressing charges, and it isn't going to be assault on a federal officer—it'll be attempted murder."

Deacon waited for Burke to finish, then calmly said, "It wasn't the bartender."

"What?" Burke asked, stunned.

"We found the assailant, thanks to Tanner and a few of Markham's deputies. Turns out the young lady in the security feed has an older brother who's a close friend of the bartender. Bartender called his buddy after you left. He was afraid his little sister's secret rendezvous with her boyfriend would become public knowledge."

"So he tried to kill me to protect that little slut's reputation?" Burke snarled.

"He was trying to protect her from prosecution," Deacon snapped back. "She's underage, in love, and a little bit hormonal, but it's still considered a criminal act in the territory, and she'd be subject to arrest and reconditioning. The guy panicked, Burke."

"He could have just asked us to keep her name off the records. It doesn't justify him running me down."

"That would involve trust, and these people don't trust us. They've been fed propaganda about jack-booted fascist Feds all their lives. Trust isn't something they'll give. It's got to be earned." Deacon stared at Burke's scowl and said, "Markham's holding him for fleeing the scene of an accident while intoxicated. He'll be released in a day or two."

Burke sat forward, causing his brain to shift painfully. "Bullshit, boss! I want him charged. It was attempted murder."

Deacon ignored the outburst, leaned against the wall, and sighed. "Burke, I'm going to tell you something you need to hear." Burke sat up and listened intently. "You're one of the best, if not *the* best field investigator I have on the force today." He gave Burke a sideways glance. "But you are by far the dumbest motherfucker I've ever had to deal with." Burke stared in shock at his boss, his ego withering under the blow. All he could do was emit strangled noises as Deacon continued to speak.

"Part of being a top-notch investigator is knowing how to talk to people, and that doesn't mean just being professionally polite. People aren't machines, Jeremy. You have to get witnesses to cooperate. It means being able to relate to them and gain their trust. You have to know everyone involved in your case—your witnesses, your suspects and your victims—better than they know themselves. You've worked this beat with me for four years now and should understand these people's beliefs and convictions inside and out, but you refuse to respect anything that doesn't fit your atheistic view of mankind. It's the reason you're no better than they are, and it's the reason why you'll never be top dog at the agency."

Burke started to vent his defiance, but Deacon shut him down with a solitary finger. He picked up a stool and brought it close to Burke's bed.

"Look, I know you think the Bible is complete bullshit, and you're probably right. The Scriptures were passages written by very human men long before the Bible was assembled. Men who were merely inspired by God to write them, which means they can't be objective or without personal bias. I understand why you reject the Bible, Jeremy. In a way I even agree with you. But you've become so rooted in your disbelief that you're as much a fanatic as any true believer."

"Boss, they tried to kill me. These people think that killing people is okay as long as you do it in the name of God. Just like every other crazy religion out there."

"See, that's your problem right there. You attribute devotion to insanity. We all have faith in something, whether we call it God, science, technology, nature, or humanity. Whether or not it's supported by facts or simply accepted as true, none of it is a sign of mental illness. You need to accept that."

"How can you still accept such lies?" Burke asked him. "After everything you've learned and witnessed, after what happened to Neville?"

Deacon cringed at the sting of his son's name but choked back the pain. "It's because of what I've learned that I can accept it. The words of Christ were all about removing bias and uniting mankind all over the world. He taught us to love our neighbor regardless of what faith he followed. He taught us to respect every man, woman and child regardless of their origins, for we are all God's children. He taught us not to judge one another because none of us is without sin. He taught us to care for the sick and the poor and to shun wealth, not because he wanted us to be poor but because he knew greed would strip us of our compassion, that greed would lead us to reject our willingness to care for our fellow man. These are all tenets of faith that exist in every religious text on the planet. They are the core of every belief system."

"Then why does this holy book of yours dictate the exact opposite of his teachings?" Burke asked.

"Because when it was finally written, the powerful rulers of the time realized that what Christ wanted was a world without war, a world without borders. One world united and at peace. And the one thing a world at peace would not need was them. You can't wage war against your neighbor and take what's his if every man is your brother. You can't rule over a population if they will only recognize God as their one true King. If Christ's vision came true, they would be powerless. And that was a world they couldn't accept. So they constructed a religious system that guaranteed their continued power over men. They edited Scriptures to support their position and used it to subjugate entire races. They used it to suppress an entire gender. They used it to oppress knowledge so that they could never be overpowered by it. And they criminalized anything that didn't serve the goals of their new faith. The faithful were told that if they didn't obey the book, they would suffer eternal damnation. By the time they were done assembling the Bible, they'd set the world on a path of conflict and hate that would rage for the next two thousand years."

"The world's changed, boss. It's been centuries since those words were written. We're not all ignorant peasants and farmers. We're capable of making our own decisions and governing our own lives. We're educated and informed. Their vision came true. We've already proven we don't need them anymore. We've evolved beyond faith," Burke insisted.

"Have we really?" Deacon asked him. "Or is secularism simply your new religion?" He looked at Burke as the man struggled to answer. "You belong to a political party, Jeremy?"

The question caught Burke off guard. "Yeah. Card-carrying Constitutionalist all my life."

"So you believe we should all be governed by a document that was written over three hundred fifty years ago by a bunch of Deists, Protestants and members of other Christian denominations who governed a bunch of ignorant peasants and farmers whom they, too, considered incapable of self-governing? A system for Americans to elect representatives who were educated and informed, to enact laws for them to live by and set punishments for those who broke those laws?"

"The Founding Fathers knew the fighting and chaos caused by organized religion. That's why they rejected it as a form of government."

"And gave you a new religion to follow, one that wasn't based on a particular faith in God, but it's a belief system all the same. It's what you have faith in, Jeremy, and there's nothing wrong with that. But the Constitution was written by men and thus isn't any less flawed than the Bible. If it were, we wouldn't have amended it thirty-three times. And religion may be a whole lot slower when it comes to change, but it is changing. If you'd take the time to listen to the people you're condemning, you'd see that."

He clapped Burke on the shoulder, grinned at his wince, and got up to leave.

"You need to be more tolerant and understanding, Burke. Stop looking down on these people as if they suffer from some kind of mental disorder." He stood over Burke and put on his I'm-the-Boss hat. "But whether you do or not, we can't afford to alienate potential witnesses. So, I'll arrange a meeting with Markham once things settle down and have the man apologize in person." Burke didn't respond. "You will assure that man that the witness's privacy and reputation will be fully protected by us. And I'll expect you to be understanding and forgiving about the entire incident. You hear me?"

That pulled Burke off the pillow despite the enormous pain it caused his head.

"Oh relax, Burke," Deacon said as Burke sat smoldering. "You can go on Facebook, Reddit, Twitter, Instagram or whatever and anonymously blast his shitty beer when the case is over. Drive the man out of business if it makes you feel better. But you will keep your revenge in check until this is over. Understood?"

The smirk that crept onto Burke's mouth worried him, but there was nothing he could really say. He was in no position to lecture Burke on revenge, but there were priorities to consider. They had a killer to catch, and that had to come first. Besides, he knew if Burke's lead paid off, Burke would probably win the bet and forget all about his little Twitter campaign.

Joyce burst into the room with Elli and Tanner in tow, startling them both.

"The director called," she announced. "Apparently, our old friend Senator Milton called a press conference to give an update on the case." She walked over to the bed and grabbed the remote from beside Burke and switched the overhead displays from Burke's CAT scans to an outside feed showing Milton, flanked by a stately looking Sheriff Markham in a dress uniform, surrounded by a sea of press and angrily waving his hands.

"The fact that they have no clue who this killer is or where he is committing these crimes is proof that Homeland Security is using these heinous acts to harass and intimidate our citizenry," Milton said. "Why, just last week, some poor children at the victim's school had to be admitted for psychiatric treatment after being interrogated by federal representatives during their time of grief and pain."

"What!" Tanner stammered as Deacon hushed him. Elli stood silently watching, knowing that the girl in question was poor Mona.

"They insist on looking among our own devout citizens and terrorizing children to hunt for a monster when they should be looking for one of their own. Only someone with the most heinous contempt for our way of life would commit such horrific acts against two of God's innocent children."

The accusation caused a flurry of questions, all of which Milton answered with copious amounts of fire and brimstone peppered with humility and Scripture. Deacon watched the senator and felt his muscles tighten in anger.

"Looks like your good buddy Markham just threw you under the bus, Tanner," Deacon said without facing him. He didn't have to see the look on Tanner's face to know how he was taking it.

4

Milton was in the midst of making a statement about his petition to Washington to seize control of the investigation when a reporter in a shoddy-looking suit squeezed his way forward. Without announcing his name and affiliation, the rumpled man loudly asked "Senator, isn't it true that the two murders committed were actually biblical in nature?"

The question stopped Milton cold and he stared down at the man standing before him. Everyone else in the crowd had likewise gone silent.

"Certain details have come to light that the victims were killed according to biblical practices in accordance with their sins and that the killings may have been sanctioned. Can you comment on this?"

Milton's face went white but turned a healthy shade of crimson as the surrounding press descended on the journalist, asking him questions instead.

"That is a vicious lie cooked up by the federal authorities to justify their mistreatment of our citizens," Milton thundered back, drawing all eyes to him once again. "I will not have the integrity and faith of my constituents slandered by a servant of the heathen media such as yourself. Identify yourself sir."

The reporter was unfazed and politely replied "Buck Meisner, Senator, and isn't it true that the first victim, a Mrs. Ellory Bainbridge, was guilty of adultery and subject to such punishment as she received?"

Milton swallowed his rage and looked out over the crowd sweating. "I will proceed with the petition immediately. This press conference is over." He then stalked off stage followed by a very bewildered Markham and his entourage. The videographers wrapped up their reports and returned their broadcasts back to the main stations while everyone else milled around the journalist asking questions.

Meisner had just thrown gasoline on a low burning flame setting the airwaves on fire. And he loved it. Reporters huddled around him begging for information and details about his sources. He soaked up the attention like a dry, cracked sponge. These people hadn't given him the time of day since he jumped off the wagon after the war. But as rewarding as it was having them begging HIM for leads for a change, Buck was no fool. He'd run his share of informants across enemy lines during the fighting and wasn't about to compromise a source. Dead men told no tales and he intended to keep his source alive, even if that source went to extraordinarily theatrical lengths to remain anonymous. He brushed off the beggars and accepted the occasional "nice move" from the more adventurous of his colleagues. But as he walked away from the podium, he heard an unpleasantly familiar voice.

"Nice nut jab, Meisner. I haven't seen old Milton that flustered since those pictures of him in that DC strip club hit the airwaves."

He turned to see Chip Gorman circling him like a cat. It was his way of disarming his targets and Buck knew it well.

"Just investigative reporting, Chip. That's how it's done," Buck replied confidently.

Chip stopped and grinned down at him. At six feet four he had a good foot on most reporters, and he used it to intimidate everyone.

"Only if your sources turn out to be reliable, pal. Informants can be really skittish, especially in the territory and I'd hate for you to get burned again."

Buck looked up into that lipless grin and said, "Don't worry about me, pal. I'm watching my back this time."

Chip slapped a hand on his shoulder and chuckled. As he walked away, he said, "That'll make a nice epitaph for ya, Buck."

5

Milton grabbed the decanter from his desk and threw the stopper on the floor. Instead of grabbing a shot glass, he tilted it to his lips, gulped the liquid inside, and promptly spat it out onto the carpet. Sweet tea. "Fucking sweet tea!" he howled as he threw the container into the wall. Wirz must have had his handlers replace it while he was campaigning. A sweeper crew had cleaned out his residence of every illicit substance they could detect, but he never imagined they would strip his office. He leaned over the desk, hands trembling as he gripped the edge. God, he needed a drink, something to steady his nerves after that disaster of a press conference. Even more than that, he wanted that reporter's head on a pike for ruining his spotlight moment.

"Milton, are you okay?" a voice asked from the doorway. Pissed that he'd forgotten to shut the door properly, he whirled to see Quentin Hollister looking around at the broken glass and brown liquid staining the rug.

He straightened up, running a shaky hand through his greasy hair. "I'm a little busy right now, Quentin, if you don't mind."

"I imagine so after that press conference," Quentin told him, sniffing the air.

Milton saw him scrutinizing the mess. "Sweet tea. I'm keeping my wits about me these days."

"Good thing too," Quentin said. "Is it true, what that reporter said about the murders being sanctioned?"

Milton whirled on him. "What's true is that some Unification Party asshole is paying to smear us and steal the election. They're more interested in using these sick attacks on our citizens as political currency. I wouldn't be surprised if they're responsible for the attacks themselves." He rounded the desk and threw himself into his chair. "Quentin, I want a special session called. We're going to draft a formal demand to Washington that this investigation be immediately surrendered to Republic territorial authorities with the authorization to pursue the criminal no matter where it leads."

"A resolution like that would be a declaration of no confidence in the executive branch. Do you think it's wise to piss off the very government you're trying to get elected into?"

Milton steepled his hands and looked Quentin in the eye. "They threw the first punch when they sicced that reporter on me at the conference, and I intend to hit back."

"You're assuming they did it," Quentin responded. "I've read the police reports, Milton. That reporter wasn't lying about the details. He's obviously got a reliable source. Discrediting him could backfire on us big time if his allegations are proven true."

Milton shook his head. "Quentin, I'm going to win this election come hell or high water. And when I do, you'll become high senator. Now, I know you're the fair-haired boy, our resident pacifist, but if you don't learn how to play this game to win, the press is going to eat you alive."

"My constituents didn't elect me to play games, Milton. And as I recall, the 'games' played in Washington were one of the many reasons we fought for our independence."

Milton's mood was deteriorating as rapidly as his migraine was expanding. "We fought a civil war to gain our independence because we wanted to live as God intended us to live. The unholy horde threw everything they could at us and couldn't defeat us, not even with bullets. Now they're using the only weapon they have left: the so-called free press, which is anything but free. They use it to twist everything they can, even the truth, to destroy us, so you'd better get better at spinning it than they are, or you'll find yourself selling cars for a living." He leaned back. "Now if you'll excuse me, I have calls to make, and you have a session to arrange."

Quentin left without another word, much to Milton's relief. He despised the man personally almost as much as his popularity. Thankfully he'd be Wirz's problem in a couple of months, if Wirz didn't kill him first. He placed a call to the Basilica and fumed.

In the Midst of the Rebellious House

1

Pandemonium swarmed outside the Huntsville headquarters as Elli and Tanner arrived from the hospital. A department representative was peppering the crowd with the standard reply that "to protect the integrity of the case, Homeland cannot comment on an ongoing investigation," but they weren't buying it. Reporters fruitlessly tried every angle to corner the officer into divulging some clue or other'. Tanner had ditched his uniform after the press conference. His badge was clipped under his jacket, so the two of them easily slipped past the crowd. The commotion was in stark contrast to the scene inside the director's conference room. Except for Burke, who was still hospitalized, the entire team had gathered. All eyes were on the viewscreen from which President Turnouer was demanding answers.

"I just spent two hours facing down a contingent of representatives from both parties demanding to know whether my office authorized the leak of sensitive case information to a reporter to derail the upcoming election. Half of them demanded that I remove you and your team from the case, and the other half demanded I turn over the investigation to the territorial police!"

Deacon stiffened at the prospect of losing the case but kept his cool. "Madam President, I can assure you that no one involved in this investigation on the federal side had anything to do with leaking the details of the case. I personally instituted Quick Quiet Protocols as soon as you authorized my jurisdiction. All personnel involved in any way with the evidence or details of this case have had their personal and professional communications monitored without any objections. No one has had any contact with the press or persons unauthorized to handle this information. Whoever Meisner's source is, it wasn't anyone here."

The president shifted her eyes past Deacon to where Elli and Tanner stood quietly watching. "And your liaison officers? They're not subject to those protocols. What about them?" she said, nodding in their direction.

Deacon glanced back to the two of them. "Officer Tanner and Dr. Hollister have provided valuable assistance in the investigation and were instrumental in discovering the second victim's connection to the first. I'm sure they had nothing to do with this."

"But you can't be certain, can you?" the president asked.

Tanner's reaction to having his integrity questioned hadn't changed since the day Deacon dressed him down about his lack of interrogation skills. Elli could see his temper rising and interjected before he could explode.

"Madam President, the only information that Officer Tanner and I have relayed has been to the Justice Ministry per the conditions of our agreement. Lt. MacNair has received copies of every daily report. Your Quick Quiet Protocols may not be enforceable on us, but we are abiding by them nonetheless out of professional respect."

Margot looked the two of them over for a minute, took a steadying breath and then offered, "My apologies if I've offended you. I'm thankful to you both for your cooperation and your assistance." She then turned to Deacon and said, "Lieutenant, I gave you this case because you assured me that you would do everything you could to find the guilty party and give the victim's family justice and closure." She paused for a moment and then asked sternly, "Can you handle this case or not?"

Deacon could tell by the slight look of desperation in her eyes that she was referring to more than the murders.

"My team and I can and will catch whoever committed these crimes, Madam President."

"You have seven days, Lieutenant. After that, I'll have no choice but to turn over control of this case to the territorial police." She leaned closer to the screen. "And I don't have to tell you what that will mean, not only for the department but for this administration as well, do I?"

The director had stayed quiet up to this point but moved forward to support his people. "Madam President, I can assure you that everyone in this room will do everything in our power to solve this as quickly as possible. Their dedication to that end is absolute, and if information is being leaked, it isn't from anyone in my organization."

"See to it that it stays that way, Director. Now please excuse me. I have a political firestorm to put out."

The president signed off, and the room let out a collective sigh. Everyone except Deacon. He turned a stony expression to Elli and Tanner and said, "I just put my career on the line for you two, so I'm only going to ask this once. Did either of you have anything to do with feeding information to anyone outside the authorized chain of command?"

"No," Tanner told him a little more sharply than he meant to. "The only person I've given any information to has been my C.O., Markham, and it was limited to the reports Elli created for us through you."

Deacon shifted his eyes to Elli, who said, "I haven't made any other independent communications to anyone." Deacon's eyes became slits as he stared her down. "Not even to my father," Elli finally told him.

His eyes closed, and he released the breath he didn't realize he'd been holding. When he opened them, he said, "That's settled, then." He turned to address everyone in the room.

"Let's get back to work, people. We have a killer to catch, and the clock is ticking."

2

When it came to T-Bone's, there was no such thing as the weekend. Jazz poured out in soulful ribbons every night no matter the day of the week. The Thursday night crowd was considerably lighter than the Friday night barrage, which suited Deacon just fine. He needed the solitude. A large woman in worn clothing rumbled through Ella Fitzgerald as the aging band played with muted perfection. The group would have looked at home in any subway or bus station, huddled before an open guitar case filled with change. It was the sound that set them in a place of honor on T-Bone's stage. The music was all that mattered, and tonight it soothed Deacon's jangled nerves as T-Bone's homemade rotgut burned through the day. Distillery booze would have had a smoother effect, but it wouldn't have done the trick. This was liquid napalm for the soul.

No one knew T-Bone's secret recipe, but the ruddy-colored hooch had been known to cause hallucinations and visions if misused. Deacon needed visions tonight. He'd searched quarries and mines and industrial plants, conducted interviews and interrogations, and came up empty. His adversary was still out there and completely unknown. And Deacon knew in his heart he was only getting started. Every criminal had a reason for doing what he did. If it were a chance encounter or a robbery that had gone wrong, it would have been hastily covered up. There would have been more evidence to indicate what had really happened. But the Bainbridge murder wasn't random: it was well planned and carefully crafted to send a message about the wages of adultery. The Dockweiler murder was even more elaborate, as was its message: be truthful, not vengeful before God. But why? Why was the killer sending these messages, and who was he sending them to? Was his message meant for the territory, the whole country, or just Deacon? Were they warnings or revelations? What was yet to come?

Ella's throaty words floated to him from the grizzled angel on stage as she slyly declared she was no longer bewitched and bewildered. If only it were true. He took another sip and felt the fire scorch through his forest of thoughts. His head was swimming and he welcomed it, but nothing came to him. There were no visions or epiphanies to be had, only the scorched earth of his mind.

T-Bone wandered over and refilled the double shot glass, but instead of moving on, he pulled a chair around and sat down. He took a swig from the bottle, capped it again, and stared at Deacon.

"That's not exactly the most sanitary way to serve your customers," Deacon observed.

T-Bone smiled a mouth full of marginally yellow teeth with one blinding silver cap and chuckled. "Show me da germ that can live in this shit."

They laughed together for a spell and took in the music. As Deacon reached the bottom of his second shot, T-Bone grew somber and asked, "It true what dey say about the killings? Those two punished like de Bible say?"

Deacon was about to give him the standard rebuke of not being able to discuss a case, but the knowledge was already out there, and T-Bone was one of the few men in this world he knew could keep a secret. "Yeah, it's true,"

Deacon answered as the shot glass was refilled. "Damned if I can figure out why, though."

"God's will be God's will. Ain't no arguing with de Lord."

"This ain't God's will, T-Bone. This is man's doing. God had nothing to do with this."

T-Bone sighed. "Maybe so. And maybe dat's what dis here boy's trying to tell you."

Deacon looked up from his shot glass and squinted at his friend. "But the people here live according to God's will. That's why they formed the Ecumenical Council to run it in the first place."

T-Bone hoisted his aging, considerable frame from the chair. "God ain't on the Council. Least I ain't never seen his name on no ballot. And I ain't never seen him wearing no red suit on TV on Sunday. Come to think of it, I ain't never seen him vote, neither."

Deacon was puzzled and just kept staring at his friend. T-Bone leaned over close and asked, "You wanna know God's will?"

Deacon shook his head slightly, and T-Bone smiled. Pointing a finger over his shoulder toward the stage, he answered, "Keep listenin'. You find all the God you need right der."

Deacon watched him lumber away, head swimming and wondering if T-Bone had gone senile. He stared down into what was left of his drink as Ella's plea for someone to watch over her wafted through the air.

Someone was indeed watching. Someone who didn't like what he saw. That someone had sent Deacon and the world a message that there was a wolf among the sheep. But which was the greater threat? The wolf or the shepherd?

3

The cruiser pulled out into traffic on autopilot as Deacon asked himself for the hundredth time why he was doing this. He had only circumstantial evidence that someone in the hierarchy was involved in the murders, which meant he had nothing. He had no search warrant, no proof, no hard evidence, not even an e-mail to support his theory. Yet here he was driving into the mouth of hell itself to confront the devil on his home turf armed with nothing but a smile. Joyce was right. It would be career suicide, so why was he still going to do it? Because there was indeed a wolf among the sheep. A wolf with a pack so well hidden and cunning that the herd had no idea they were there.

At some point during his visit to T-Bone's the night before, his intoxicated, suspicious mind started to assemble a theory. It was no doubt a side effect of T-Bone's fiery hooch, so Deacon dismissed it. While he slept off the booze, his subconscious continued to fiddle with the idea, putting the pieces together like a psychedelic puzzle with no primer. He awoke with a fierce hangover and injected himself with asoracaine before stepping into a blistering shower. As the sobering meds went to work, the scalding water burned away the mental fog, leaving only a wild theory that seemed perfectly plausible. Whoever the traitor was, he knew about the wolves and wanted to expose them. There was even the high probability that the killer was a member of the pack itself.

He stopped at a greasy diner near the interstate to grab coffee and a quick breakfast. While he waited for it to arrive, he pulled up the fatality research that Joyce and Elli had been arguing over and created a timeline. It showed that, since the formation of the Ecclesiastical Republic, the bulk of the so-called natural deaths occurred within the last four years. His breakfast arrived and he ate it while Googling the last four years of the territory for major events. The most notable changes had occurred since 2031, when the Republic leadership passed a series of laws intended to cement religious adherence among its citizens. As emigration ground to a halt, the deaths began to rise. The numbers flatlined the year that Vice President Cahill assassinated then-President Turnouer but rose significantly after the death of Archbishop Harrison Meeks a year later. They'd been climbing steadily ever since.

Once back on the road, Deacon tried to reconcile the research with his theory. He was sure that the death of Meeks was the turning point, but the catalyst came weeks later when a relatively well-liked, low-level prosecutorial bishop was appointed to take his place. That man was Caulder Wirz. Within months Wirz assumed duties as head of Ecumenical Law Enforcement for the region, cultivating political connections and power not only within the Council but in the Senate itself. He oversaw the Rehabilitation and Reconditioning Protocols, the so-called R&Rs, for transgressors, which were hailed as a remarkable success in returning citizens to a state of grace. Within a year, he was promoted to Right Hand of the High Bishop, where he currently served. The wolf among the sheep. Deacon knew it deep down in his gut. And this wolf had a pack called "the Cadre" at his command, infiltrating the leadership while the sheep grazed unknowingly around them.

He called up the case evidence on the dash monitor as the cruiser continued into the city proper. There had been no trace of DNA or any fingerprints to track. Each site had been unusually clean. The methods of the murders had been elaborate yet meticulous in their conformity to biblical requirements and theological punishment. The perp appeared to have the skills of a master hit man to go with his attention to detail and access to sealed Ecumenical documents. He had to be a member of the Cadre. A lone wolf who had turned on his pack, but why? A killer with a conscience? Doubtful. More like a killer with a chip on his shoulder. An assassin who wanted to pay back his employers by exposing them to the world in the most brutal way possible. A wolf with a grudge.

The vehicle stopped at a large intersection and awaited a light change to merge into oncoming traffic. His two cases were merging as well, but he was under strict orders not to reveal to anyone the nature of the president's assignment. He couldn't tell his team what he knew, much less how he knew it, and he couldn't let Wirz and the Cadre know he was on to them. Joyce had been right. This was a fool's errand with only two possible outcomes: either a forced retirement or criminal prosecution for interterritorial espionage. Wirz was no fool. He'd see through any attempt to draw out information about the Cadre itself. Deacon had to find a way to manipulate him, and he only had forty minutes to find it.

4

The cruiser exited the highway and glided along the Atlanta streets. The capital had changed much since before the war. A cluster of glass and steel high rises dominating nearby sporting venues and retail centers, all woven together by intricate highways and surrounded by pristine parks with dense landscaping. Its beauty hid the scars of hatred left by the conflict. Before the war, dozens of beautiful mosques had dotted the surrounding area in addition to the numerous Christian churches. The seat of power he now sought was built on the site of one such mosque. The Second Burning of Atlanta had not come at the hands of a Confederate general desperate to keep supplies from the Union army but at the hands of enraged Christians on a lily-white crusade. Fired up by political rhetoric and stoked with fear of any faith other than their own, they had burned and destroyed every non-Christian house of worship in the city and a sizable number of surrounding homes and businesses. Clergy across the country had urged their followers to remember the teachings of love and compassion and hold true to the values of Jesus Christ. But in the end, political demagogues and their hired thugs had succeeded in lighting a wildfire of hate that quickly spread out of control. Many innocent people were killed as the specter of fear branded them an enemy of faith. The loss of so many lives, not by the acts of soldiers but at the hands of civilians, was a sin the country felt to this very day.

The cruiser drew considerable attention as it drove onto the capitol grounds and parked in one of the available VIP spots near the front entrance. Deacon powered down the vehicle and stared at the elaborately carved entrance to the Capitol Basilica. The looks of derision he drew as he entered the building, as much for the cut of his uniform as the hue of his skin, were typical of the new southern society. The faces of color sparsely freckling the crowds bore looks similar in their dismissal but with a subtlety long known to southern blacks and Hispanics. Two hundred years earlier, light-skinned minorities and mixed-race families infiltrated the Klan, hiding in plain sight. They wore the white robes and pointy hats and preached the purity of a race they marginally belonged to while secretly warning their families and friends of impending raids. They were the informers and the double agents of the past. Only a hundred and fifty years later, the Black Klan itself evolved, forming a dysfunctional friendship with their White Klan brothers. Both preached the purity and segregation of their respective races while using the murderous acts of the other to validate their cause. Strange and intimate bedfellows, each killing to support the other's objectives. The territorial blacks that eyed him today were the descendants of these opposing but united forces. Dedicated to equality but still committed to an illogical and desperate purity for their own cultural survival.

He approached the guard at the entrance reserved for peace officers and presented his badge. Unlike the other officers filing through, all of them white, he was subjected to a full body scan and an unceremonious pat-down. Standard procedure for non-citizens, he was told apologetically. *Standard, my ass,* he thought as he retrieved his weapon and identification. He was then escorted up to the Council chambers and into a comfortable office. An usher in official robes greeted him politely and offered him every amenity an honored guest was due. Deacon thanked him as he closed the doors and offered a polite blessing for his meeting.

Deacon had barely finished investigating the room for listening devices when Archbishop Wirz entered alone. In his own habitat, the man presented a very different image than Deacon remembered. In fact, he seemed positively charming.

"Lieutenant, forgive my tardiness. I was preparing for an upcoming Senate hearing and lost track of time." He reached out to shake Deacon's hand, something he had intentionally refused to do at their first encounter.

"Nothing to forgive, Your Excellency. I'm grateful for your time," Deacon replied, shaking his hand cautiously.

Wirz motioned for him to take a seat on one of the opposing sofas and sat down. "I'm only sorry that our first meeting happened under such uncomfortable circumstances. You actually surprised me, Lieutenant. Your unique understanding of our system of justice is nearly as profound and intriguing as your own personal history." Deacon looked puzzled as Wirz poured them both coffee and handed him a cup. "A man born and raised in the territory who chose to fight for the other side despite a profoundly religious upbringing. A conflicted man of honor who now battles injustice for both sides. A modern-day Solomon, if you will. I find you to be quite intriguing."

"I'll take that as a compliment, Your Excellency," Deacon replied although he was sure it was the verbal equivalent of a glove to the face before a duel.

"It must be difficult living and working among the ungodly when you have such an intimate relationship with the Lord's word," Wirz offered.

"I'm not quite sure what you mean, Your Excellency," Deacon replied cautiously.

"I mean your fellow officers, of course. I read their bios. All of them are quite accomplished and impressive—despite their moral and spiritual failings, of course."

Deacon felt his anger start to bubble. "I'm not aware of any failings that would preclude their ability to resolve this case."

Wirz pressed a button in the arm of the couch and a screen slid up with the team bios layered before him. "Your chief evidence technician, Agnes Chen. MIT graduate with a doctorate in forensics, an astounding IQ and several awards for excellence within the department."

"She is a spectacular training officer," Deacon said with a smile.

"She's a Buddhist and openly homosexual," Wirz responded slyly. "Her people pray to strange deities and even demons as a part of their religion. Not to mention that she regularly commits heinous acts of sexual perversion. We would be completely within our rights to arrest her if she set foot on Republic territory and have her convicted and sentenced within twenty-four hours."

Deacon kept his anger in check. "Officer Chen's beliefs offer a unique perspective on how the natural world works and its inherent harmony. It makes her an impeccable scientist, as her doctorate will attest. She also serves as an invaluable touchstone, a sounding wall for objectivity that keeps my people focused on the tasks at hand."

"And her depravity?" Wirz asked.

Deacon sat up straight and looked at Wirz with cold determination. "I'm aware that the Bible considers her lifestyle choice a deadly sin. I'm also aware that it mandates the death penalty, should she engage in such activities within your borders. But I'm also aware that, throughout history, God has conveniently turned a blind eye to such activities whenever his priests, bishops, and popes committed them within the walls of His house. Having trained in Rome, I'm sure you'd admit that if God really considered homosexuality a sin, he would have rained fire and brimstone down on Vatican City centuries ago."

Wirz chuckled. "Touché, Lieutenant," he said and sipped his coffee, but Deacon's face remained tense and tight. "The young man leading your field investigations, Jeremy Burke, is an atheist, is he not?"

"He is," Deacon responded. "But aside from it making him a bit of an asshole, it doesn't impact his impeccable investigation skills."

Wirz coughed into his coffee and smiled. "Well, I've never met the man personally, so I'll take your word for it." Deacon didn't smile back.

"Your partner, Joyce Bachman. She's a staunch liberal, an activist, and vocally critical of our little utopia. Her university dissertation was an extensive critique of the hypocrisy and inherent cruelties of twenty-first century theocracies. And there's the fact that she's Jewish."

"I'm aware of her distaste for your chosen way of life," Deacon replied evenly. "As for her being Jewish, her faith has shed a great deal of light on this case and the application of biblical law. Yours is based on the Old Testament as derived from the Torah itself, from what I understand." Deacon waited for Wirz to respond and then added, "One should always be aware of one's roots."

"It hardly makes her an objective investigator."

Deacon composed himself and replied, "Det. Bachman came to me as a rookie, Your Excellency. She's worked at my side for half a decade, and I can assure you I've gone to great pains to educate her about the intricacies of territorial justice and law. She may not agree with them, but she is as committed to defending them as I am."

Wirz smirked and then passed a finger across the screen. "Which brings me to you, Lieutenant. I must say you've had quite a distinguished career."

A little warning light began to blink inside Deacon's head. He picked up his coffee and inhaled the aroma as Wirz took aim.

"Your son committed suicide, did he not? Neville, I believe, was the young man's name." A lump formed and sank to the pit of Deacon's stomach as he listened. "He was remanded to us by you and your wife for rehabilitation from a rather insidious drug habit, according to the commitment decree."

"He was," Deacon replied quietly. "We had hoped that the church would give him the necessary structure to beat his demons. Instead, he took his own life about a month after he completed R&R."

Wirz studied Deacon's face, knowing he had struck a vital nerve. "And you've been submitting written demands for information about the rehabilitation protocols since his death. I hope you don't believe our treatment had anything to do with it."

"As a detective, I make it a practice to rule out any and all possible contributing factors when investigating a death. Even the unlikely ones. It protects the integrity of the case. I feel it is necessary to know the particulars in order to . . . reconcile the act. To give people closure." He sipped his coffee and tried not to choke on his deception.

"But your son's death isn't a criminal case; therefore, any investigation could only be of a personal nature. Are you searching for closure, Lieutenant?"

Deacon composed himself. "It would put to rest several unanswered questions and provide a personal, spiritual resolution of sorts."

"Then as a detective, one as astute as you obviously are, you know that such procedures are classified and cannot be made public without the permission of the penitent. And since your son signed no preexisting release and is no longer able to give such permission, we must honor his wishes, even in death."

Deacon had heard this before. It was the same line that the government had been giving him for the past five years. Hearing Wirz speak the words made them even more infuriating.

"I apologize for bringing it up at this time," Wirz offered, "but I would be remiss in my duties if I did not question your personal reasons for demanding jurisdiction in this case. I have to be sure your motives and those of your team are clear."

"I can assure you, Your Excellency, that our only motives are the ones that we are sworn to uphold: to bring the guilty to justice and protect the lives of all the citizens of the United States with respect for and regardless of their territorial affiliation."

Wirz steepled his fingers. "A rather diplomatic statement. One that could easily be seen as a political device."

"Did not the Lord say to Zechariah, 'Administer true justice; show mercy and compassion to one another. Do not oppress the widow or the fatherless, the foreigner or the poor. Do not plot evil against each other'?" Deacon replied.

"He did indeed, Lieutenant," Wirz said with a smile. "I suppose we could engage in philosophical banter all afternoon, but let's save that for a discussion between friends when this is all over."

"Is that what we are now? Friends?" Deacon asked him.

Wirz cocked his head and smiled. "Allies, I think, would be a much better description at this juncture. I trust that you have news of the case."

"I do, Your Excellency, and it is somewhat sensitive in nature, which is why I felt it prudent to address you personally and under confidential conditions."

"You make speak freely in this room, Lieutenant. I chose it for its lack of monitoring devices." Deacon was sure the opposite was true but didn't let on. "I've been following the reports of the second victim in the news," Wirz told him, mocking concern. "Please tell me you are making progress in that boy's tragic death."

"We are. However, certain aspects of the case have led us to a very unsettling possibility, one that I require your assistance and wisdom to sort out."

Wirz was caught off guard by Deacon's humility. Only moments ago, he'd looked ready to kill. It was obvious the man was doing his best to contain his volatile nature and disdain for biblical law. Wirz wondered how long it would last.

"We've completed several searches and interviews, and although we've turned up no new physical evidence, certain facts have come to light that I felt should be brought to your attention."

Wirz sipped his coffee. "Go on."

"A common thread has emerged between the victims. Both had recently been involved in legal sentencings handed down by the Ecumenical Council, and it appears that both were guilty of transgressions punishable by death. In Ellory Bainbridge's case, her adultery warranted punishment. In Kevin Dockweiler's case, evidence suggests he bore false witness against his fellow citizens. The young couple he accused may have been innocent and wrongfully sentenced."

Wirz sat quietly for a moment, still sipping his coffee. Without looking up at Deacon, he said, "If I understand you correctly, you are insinuating these were lawful executions, not murders."

"I would never suggest that such acts of inhuman butchery be considered lawful under any circumstances," Deacon responded.

"Nevertheless, you can't deny that the Bainbridge woman deserved her fate, although we would never condone such methods of punishment."

"I'm not in a position to judge the woman, Your Excellency," Deacon told him. "Nor is it my job to pass judgment on the victims. My job is to catch the man who did this and stop him from hurting anyone else."

"I see," Wirz responded, looking at him coldly. He set his cup down on the table between them. "May I ask how you discovered their names were on those sentencings? Such documents are confidential and highly classified."

Deacon could hear Joyce's warning rumbling up in his mind and phrased his response very carefully. "Alan Bainbridge confirmed that his wife was having an affair and had been sentenced by the Council, awaiting penance. Interviews with several of the Dockweiler boy's classmates revealed the volatile and jealous nature of his relationship to Janine Turnbull, who was sentenced earlier this summer along with her fiancé on the word of a sequestered witness. They were all of the opinion that Janine and her fiancé were innocent, which means that, if Kevin was in fact the anonymous informant in her case, his jealousy may have led him to lie."

He waited for Wirz to react, but Wirz just waited silently for him to hang himself, so he stepped out onto the verbal ledge.

"We believe that the killer has access to Ecumenical sentencing decrees and is using them to choose his victims."

Wirz tensed slightly. "I hope you aren't implying that someone on the Council is involved in these killings."

"No, sir, but given that this information is tightly controlled, it could only have been accessed by someone with the highest level of clearance." Deacon adopted a most humble attitude. "If someone is illegally targeting the Republic, we need your help to find the person responsible for accessing this information."

"I'm afraid the answer to that question may already be known, Lieutenant. We recently suffered an intrusion into our government servers, and several files were stolen. The perpetrators were subsequently killed in an FBI raid."

"The explosion in South Carolina," Deacon remarked, taking Wirz by surprise.

"What do you know of the operation?"

"Not much more than what's been reported in the news, I'm afraid. Some of the officers lost in the raid were friends and former colleagues of mine."

"My condolences on your loss, Lieutenant," Wirz offered, though he was sure Deacon knew a great deal more than he let on.

"We have established that the second victim was murdered after the explosion, so our perpetrator is very much alive. He may, however, be connected to them." Deacon adopted a pleading attitude. "Is there any information you can give me that would shed more light on the situation?"

"Unfortunately, no, Lieutenant. Your FBI was able to act much more quickly than we were and located them first. The only information we have about them comes directly from the FBI. If there is anything more, they haven't shared it with us."

Deacon feigned disappointment and then humbly said, "I don't have the authority to investigate members of your government, Your Excellency, but you do. That's why I brought this to your attention. I suspect that whoever this individual is, he isn't finished yet. There are others on that sentencing list who may be his next targets."

"I'm not sure exactly what you wish of me, Lieutenant," Wirz responded.

"As the head of Ecumenical Law Enforcement, I am asking that you launch an internal investigation into the leak in whatever capacity you deem appropriate and that you provide us with any information you discover." Deacon paused and then added, "It may be the key to our stopping him and protecting your citizens."

Wirz sat quietly for a moment and then stood, indicating that the meeting was over. As Deacon rose to leave, Wirz said, "Even though I find the suggestion abhorrent, I respect your logic in this request. I will launch an internal investigation into Ecumenical involvement, Lieutenant. Unfortunately, I cannot release the sentencing decrees to you. The laws of the territory forbid their dissemination to anyone not directly involved in the convicted person's case. However, I will forward to you any other information we uncover as soon as it is vetted."

"I understand," Deacon said. He'd known from the beginning that getting the list was a longshot.

"Don't look so disappointed, Lieutenant. I have no doubt that you will be victorious in your quest. You heart is righteous, and believe it or not, I have complete faith in your abilities. For whatever is born of God overcomes the world; and this is the victory that has overcome the world—our faith."

"I'll keep that in mind," Deacon said. "Thank you for your time, Your Excellency."

"It was my pleasure," Wirz told him as he left.

5

Once Deacon was gone, Wirz poured himself a shot of Tennessee whiskey and downed it quickly. The possibility that someone on the Council had turned into a serial killer was ludicrous. Most of them couldn't get around without assistance due to either old age or dissolute lifestyles. The rest were too busy currying favor with their older colleagues to further their own careers. None of them had the strength, skills, or stomach to perform such grisly executions. They did have the monetary resources to hire a professional to act for them, but such a shift in finances would have triggered the tight surveillance Wirz kept on each of them. The involvement of someone with Council access, however, was a certainty. That MacNair knew it made him dangerous. MacNair had made no mention of the Cadre or any sort of subversive involvement, but if he pursued his theory, he would eventually uncover their existence. That couldn't be allowed to happen.

Wirz poured himself a second shot and read through the internal security reports. His team was still conducting investigations of all Cadre operatives possessing deadly skills, but they had found nothing to tie any operative to the killings or the cyber intrusion. That made sacrificing one of them to halt the investigation an unlikely prospect. Even if they could set one up with enough evidence to portray him as the suspect, there was still the chance that the real killer could strike again.

He lightly swirled the untouched shot in the glass as he stared out across the Atlanta skyline. It was very rare for one of the membership to go native, but it did happen. And it was someone who had the instincts of a killer and the technical prowess of a programmer with access to their most secure networks. That marked him as a high-ranking operative. Whoever it was had to be dealt with quickly and quietly. No scrutiny of the Cadre's existence could be allowed, and that meant eliminating the Homeland investigation team as well, one way or another.

Pulling up the current statistics for the R&R Protocols, he activated the tracking chips and waited. A holographic map appeared above his desk, and one by one, tiny red lights began to populate it. Within a minute, all of the one hundred forty-six living subjects had been located. None of the penitent were currently exhibiting any signs of psychosis or abnormal behavior. The latter usually resulted in the subject becoming uncontrollable and suicidal. No glitches or aberrations appeared on the accompanying graphs. The newly implanted triggers had been fine-tuned to avoid any random activation and remained dormant. His flock was under control. When the Protocols had first been implemented, they'd simply been a means to an end, a way to punish sinners into complete obedience or rid the territory of them once and for all if they relapsed. The Protocols had evolved in the last two years under his direction to become something more: a recruitment tool of sorts, a sleeper mechanism to create an unwitting personal army. An army that would, if successful, propel him to the very top of the Cadre hierarchy and perhaps even world leadership. Lofty ambitions, to be sure, but it was his ambitious nature that had drawn the Cadre to him in his youth. Leading them was merely part of his destiny.

Staring at his clandestine army of little red lights, a smile crept onto Wirz's face. It was time to prove what his little army could do, and MacNair had just given him the perfect field test.

When the Righteous Cry for Help

1

The pictures were coming out nicely. The skies had cleared, and the air was once again filled with crisp, clear autumn breezes. Everything had been washed clean, and the southern landscape shone like a new penny. Even the man he was photographing looked newly washed although he was anything but clean. He'd followed the man from the church in Decatur, Alabama, as he traveled south on Interstate 65. He took pictures as the man drank in a bar while his car charged up in Birmingham. Those pictures would turn out to be dark and shadowed, but they captured the man's anguish beautifully. He followed the man east to Bremen and watched as he ate dinner in a hash house, barely tasting his food. The man settled into a Motel 6 nearby for the night. Tomorrow he would return to his sister parish in Decatur, Georgia. That was his routine. That evening the photographer was able to capture a breathtaking shot of the man staring off at the sunset as angry tears ran down his face. He wondered if the man would cry as vigorously when he finally met his fate.

The photographer took the room next door and settled in to scroll through the day's photos and listen to the man cry and wail next door. At some point the man threw something across the room that shattered against their shared wall. Such a tortured soul. *You won't have to suffer much longer,* he thought with a compassionate smile. He ordered pizza from a nearby restaurant and finished dinner around nine thirty, quite surprised that the food had been pleasantly edible. Washing it down with an expensive lager had certainly helped. The man next door was snoring loudly now. He turned on the television and scrolled through the photos he'd taken three months earlier. Mousy brown hair framed a plain face and dimpled chin. The loosely fitting drab clothing hid most of her substantial bosom, and her shoes were low heeled and well scuffed. He had several shots of the woman as she went about her day in Montezuma. As wholesome as they were, they paled in comparison to the ones he'd taken of her in LaGrange. The lank hair bore streaks of sprayed-in red where it hung from a messy bun. The plain face was spackled in garish makeup and bloodred lipstick. And the concealed bosom had been hoisted into a demi bra that spilled out from a sequined, strapless top over a miniskirt hanging miles above five-inch spikes. It was difficult to reconcile the vision of the plain Amish housewife with this tacky whore that prowled the Cypress Saloon unless you looked into her eyes. The same empty brown gaze stared out of every shot, the eyes of a soul desperately living in one world but incapable of abandoning the other. He drew his fingers across the screen, caressing the image. This was the face of his Venus, his masterpiece. He would restore her virtue and wipe away the sins of men.

He put the pad in his overnight bag and began to undress. Television programming in the territories was notoriously dull thanks to the Ecumenical Council's edicts on morality, but for a significant fee, the motel clerk would have been happy to supply a bootlegged drive of several banned shows from the Constitutional airwaves. He turned on the news instead. He listened with interest to the weather forecasts as it impacted his work, less so to the highlights from the Tennessee Titans game against the Denver Broncos. Any conflict between the two territories, even in professional sports, seemed to be a holy crusade in E-Rep country. The announcers ridiculously praised God whenever Denver suffered a hit as if it had been ordained. The subsequent news story, a follow-up about a suicide, caught his attention immediately. A young boy named Toby Holmby, who had recently taken his own life, was being considered for sainthood by the Council. The reporter was interviewing the boy's mother and pastor. Marjorie Holmby's stoic face filled the screen as the reporter asked why her son would be so troubled by his recovery as to risk his eternal soul.

"My son was dying when we took him to the hospital," Marjorie explained. "We were told there was no hope. So when he recovered, we thought God had saved him. We didn't know the doctors had found a way to cure him until later."

He watched as Marjorie Holmby played the victim for the cameras and shed crocodile tears for her dead son's soul. Any normal parent would have been on their knees thanking God for sending such angels to save their child. But this was Ecclesiastical territory. Angels here were tightly regulated and dispatched only when it suited those in power to do so.

"When my son realized his recovery wasn't God's plan for him, he prayed to be shown the way. In the end, he went home to God because that was what the Lord had intended all along."

The reporter then cut away to the pastor, who explained that the extenuating circumstances surrounding the boy's suicide had prompted the Ecumenical Council to grant the child absolution, and Toby Holmby would be buried with all the ritual befitting any of God's children. The reporter went on to say that the boy's uplifting story was now trending on social media, and support for his eventual beatification was unanimous throughout the territory.

Uplifting story? How on earth could anyone consider a child's suicide an uplifting story? He turned the television off and turned out the lights. As he drifted off to sleep, he wondered how much haranguing Marjorie Holmby had done to get her poor child to hang himself. Perhaps he would pay her a visit when this was over. It wasn't often he found an artist as adept as he was at inflicting such emotional pain.

The next morning, the photographer watched as the man dragged himself out of the motel. The sun was still an hour from rising, but the dim light couldn't hide the red eyes and dark hollows on his cheeks. He knew that by the time the man in the robes reached the parish, he would appear appropriately chaste and humble. The young children he left behind in Alabama, however, would not recover so quickly. They would hide the encounters from friends and family. They would exist in a state of quiet shame because their mentor had chosen to service them as penance for their sins. It wasn't that they were too young to know it was assault. They simply didn't have anyone in authority to go to. Sin most often followed the victim now that the Church had become the supreme law of the land, and they were at its mercy.

The photographer took a few more shots as he watched the priest drive away. His name had been a footnote on the list, which indicated that those in power knew of his activities but were as yet undecided what his punishment should be. The photographer circled the priest's name. He did not need to wait for the Council to declare a sentence. God had long ago detailed the punishment for one who wears the robes of faith and preys on the weak in His name.

2

Deacon's meeting with Wirz left him feeling apprehensive and slimy, as if he'd crawled through a sewer. Baiting Wirz with classified information had been a huge gamble, one that could backfire spectacularly. But he'd known men like Wirz during the war. Men with so much power they didn't believe anyone could fathom what they were up to. Deacon knew all it took was one person to pick up their trail to send them scrambling. That was when they made mistakes. That was when they got caught. *Wirz had better make those mistakes soon,* he thought. Before he had to explain to the president why he tipped off his prime target to an ongoing investigation.

He turned down Hickory Drive toward the old church but stopped suddenly at the corner. A dozen police vehicles and one large transport van surrounded the front and sides of the church, and officers swarmed the place. His heart skipped a beat as he thought of Pastor Cooper meeting with foul play, but no ambulance or coroner's wagons were present. Only sleek, black SUVs bearing the bright red stripe and gold symbol of the territorial police, all of them with red lights blazing. This was a raid, pure and simple. One of many that were routinely conducted on the less hardline congregations that flourished along the federal border. He parked behind a nearby grocery store and waited. An hour later, the vehicles were gone, having turned up nothing. The last one to leave contained the arrogant prick in charge, who gave the old pastor a stern warning and a nasty shove before leaving. It took every ounce of control Deacon had not to chase the man down and beat him to a pulp.

When the officers were gone, he entered the church to find it a disaster area. Doors hung wide open, chairs and pews had been broken, the altar was tossed aside, and there was broken glass everywhere. Pastor Cooper was sweeping debris across the floor. The old man had a slight swelling on one cheek and the beginnings of a bruise around his eye. He gave Deacon a sigh and a slight smile.

Deacon pulled the broom from his hands and turned the pastor's face to his. "I've taken worse," the old man joked as Deacon's expression turned from anger to disgust. "Cop was more upset with himself than he was with me. Failure didn't suit him well."

Deacon pulled off his coat and started moving debris and furniture out of the way. "What the hell were they looking for?" he asked, picking up the broken chairs and tossing them into a pile in an alcove.

"Same thing they always look for," Cooper told him as he swept. "Refugees, asylum seekers, anyone wanting safe passage."

"They didn't find anything?" Deacon asked.

"They never do," Cooper told him confidently. "Don't concern yourself, son. The Underground Railroad ran for over a hundred fifty years under their noses, long before the first Civil War. They couldn't stop it then, and they can't stop it now."

"They're better equipped these days and a hell of a lot more determined."

"So are we," Cooper told him, dragging the trash can across the floor.

Deacon's lips tightened into a menacing line as he righted the altar. "This never would have happened in the old days. Back then, authorities respected the sanctuary of the church."

"The Church is the authority nowadays," Cooper told him, scooping up a pile of debris. "God's house is their house, and you know they like to keep their house in order." He looked over at Deacon scowling over the altar. "You didn't come here to check up on me, and I know damned well you didn't come here for Sunday service. So what brings you to my church?"

"I need your advice," Deacon said hesitantly.

Cooper's eyes grew wide as he laughed. "And they say there's no such things as miracles." Deacon, however, didn't laugh. "What can an old man of God do to help you, Lieutenant?"

"What makes you think I'm here in an official capacity?" Deacon asked.

"Because you wouldn't be here otherwise," Cooper answered.

Deacon felt shame rise into his cheeks and redirected the conversation. "What did that officer say to you before he left?"

Cooper could see Deacon wasn't really ready to talk, so he continued to clean. "He said one day I'd slip up and he'd be waiting for me, and on that day, he'd deliver God's justice to me with a smile on his face." He dumped another scoopful of debris. "Apparently he thinks I'm the new serpent in Eden."

"He might not be wrong," Deacon answered slyly. "After all, you do preach a lot about fighting ignorance and recognizing temptation. Isn't that what the serpent did to cause the expulsion of man from Eden? Get him to eat from the Tree of Knowledge so his children would become as God and know the truth of both good and evil?"

"Nice to know you still remember your Sunday school," Cooper said with a smile. "Let me ask you something. What did you want for your son in this world?" He saw Deacon flinch and added, "More so, what does any parent want for their children?"

Deacon thought about it for a while and then said, "To grow up and be more than they were. To become a better person than they were. To leave them the world and make it better than it was when it was given to them so they can pass it on to their children in time."

"To follow in their footsteps?" Cooper offered.

Deacon shook his head. "Maybe for some people. I never wanted Neville to become a cop. He was too sensitive. I just wanted him to be . . . more. So much more."

"And if you could keep him from growing up and just let him be the innocent child that you could care for and protect for the rest of your life, would you?"

"I suppose we all wish for that at some point, that our children would stay young and innocent forever," Deacon answered.

"Then why do you think God wanted anything different for his own children?" Cooper asked him. "God gave us the world. He gave us a paradise. He wanted to keep us innocent and childlike because he loved us, just like any parent would. The Tree of Knowledge wasn't evil, but its fruit came at a price. The price of that knowledge was mortality."

"The wages of sin is death," Deacon muttered in response.

"So we've been told," Cooper told him. "You see, with knowledge, all children become adults. They learn, they grow, and before you know it they're men and women with new destinies and responsibilities. It's not evil and it's not sin; it's just life. What our Father wants of us now is what every parent wants of his grown children. To be better. To take the world they've been given and make it a better place than it was when they received it."

"And the serpent in the garden?" Deacon asked him.

"A mortal life. Nothing more. And at the end of that life, the faith and hope that we all return home to our Father in paradise as all children do, not as innocents, but as equals."

"You know some would consider that blasphemy—setting yourself equal to God."

"Only those who can't see beyond the Word to the Truth," Cooper told him sadly. "But you didn't come here to ask me about original sin, did you?"

Deacon shook his head. "No."

"I've been following the news a bit," Cooper told him. "This monster you're chasing. I've been praying every day that you catch him before he hurts anyone else."

Deacon righted a candelabra. "I don't know if he's the real threat out there."

Cooper set his broom aside and listened. There was a fear in the man's voice he hadn't heard since the Lieutenant had committed his son.

"I've read my Bible. I know what it says, but people shouldn't live their lives in fear because their slightest transgressions could be used against them out of spite. They shouldn't have to be anything but who God made them to be, and they shouldn't have to do anything but respect each other and live in peace." He looked into Cooper's gentle eyes. "This killer fancies himself a righteous executioner. He draws the sinner's punishment directly from biblical law and performs their penance exactly as is dictated by the laws of God and the Bible."

"Are you asking me if he's innocent?"

"No. I know he has to be caught. But I also know that, if I catch him, the murders won't stop. According to the Republic leadership, nothing he's done could legally be considered unjust except for the brutality of his methods. And even that could be argued away as being biblically appropriate by a good lawyer. They'll just resume condemning people in their sanctioned, so-called humanitarian form. The people of the Republic will go back to their lives feeling safe and secure as if nothing ever happened, blind to the fact that the killing continues."

"You don't believe the leadership is acting as God intended?"

"No." Deacon sighed.

"And the judgments of the Almighty?" Cooper asked.

"Shit, we can't even judge each other fairly in accordance with our own laws. So as far as His judgment goes, it's His to hand to down," Deacon answered.

Cooper smiled and picked up his broom. As he limped past Deacon, he patted him lightly on the shoulder and said, "Exactly."

3

Tanner stomped on the accelerator, but the engine just kept ticking. It was that damned aftermarket conversion kit again. He popped the hood and jumped out ,slamming the door. Muttering a stream of curses, he traced the wiring to the rear junction circuit and began disconnecting and reconnecting the contacts one at a time. He had almost enough money to buy a fully automated vehicle, and as a law enforcement officer, he'd have no trouble getting the import permit. Instead, he'd caved to the good old boy code to avoid taking heat from his buddies and colleagues at the department. Real men drove roaring, gas-engine vehicles that sweat power and exhaust fumes and let the world know they were coming. Sissified quiet cars were for "tree-hugging blue-staters who snuck around like cowards and hid from a fight."

It was all bluster, testosterone and ignorance, and on some level Kyle knew it. But he never truly saw it from an outsider's point of view until now. He'd been working with federal officers and Corridor tech for almost a month and seen how incredible it was for gathering evidence. And MacNair's people were anything but cowards. Even the lab techs that processed the data were dedicated to a fault, often forgoing sleep to make sure things got done. MacNair did tend to condescend to him, but it was due to his lack of experience and not where he was from. The lieutenant had actually shown him more respect than his own colleagues and went out of his way to make sure the team treated territorial laws and citizens with that same level of respect. None of that would matter to his fellow deputies when he returned to his post. They'd just accuse him of going native and make his life and his career a living hell until he either exploded or quit.

Kyle made the last connection and climbed back behind the wheel. The control panel hummed to life as soon as he pressed the button, and three seconds later, the gas engine roared to life below the pedal. He let the truck idle and hopped out. He thought of Elli as he listened to the engine level out and purr. Her delicate face and bright eyes clouded his vision, and his mind wandered up and down her slender, taut frame. He smiled as he thought of how she was always peeking out from behind her unruly brunette waves and the delicate vulnerability she hid behind her sense of right and wrong. He shook it all away before any more of her could swim into focus. Out of his league didn't begin to cut it. Her family had money and influence. She had a decade on him, at least ten years of advanced education, and worked on the front lines saving lives every day. All he had was a high school education, a career chasing shoplifters and drunks, a truck, and a farmhouse on some unworked acres his parents had left him.

He slammed the hood down in frustration only to see Sheriff Markham standing there grinning at him.

"I see time in the Corridor hasn't rusted your skills any," Markham remarked, slapping the rear fender of the truck. "Or maybe it has. You still running this beast on a kit?"

"Puts less stress on the engine," Kyle told him. "Makes the mechanics last longer."

"So they say," Markham said, staring at Tanner. "Your report's overdue. I told the Justice Ministry it was because they were keeping you busy on the latest murder."

Tanner grabbed a rag from the fender and wiped his hands. "Tell them whatever the hell you want," he said, throwing the rag onto the ground. "Better yet, just tell them whatever story they need to hear to tear the investigation apart. That's all they're after anyway," he said, walking past Markham to the garage.

"Don't turn your back on me, Junior!" Markham called over his shoulder. "I'm still your superior officer."

Kyle came to a halt and turned back. "Well, that's a matter of opinion, isn't it?"

Markham's voice took on a hard edge as he faced his deputy. "You've got about five seconds to explain that crack before I bust your ass for insubordination."

"When you assigned me to this case, I actually believed you when you said you trusted me to do the department proud. I told you I was way out of my league, but that was the whole point, wasn't it? You used me to stick it to MacNair and screw things up, all so you would have something for your buddy Milton to campaign about."

"You don't understand, boy."

"I'M NOT YOUR BOY, CALEB!" Kyle thundered back. "I'm not your boy, your son, or your stooge. And I'm sure as hell not your next soundbite on the evening news."

"Is that what's crawled up your ass?" Markham asked.

"MacNair wasn't anywhere near the campus. He sent us there because he didn't want to scare those kids and make a bad situation worse. He was looking out for our people. Half the department saw me at the school with Dr. Hollister, and you and Milton made it look like we were out there torturing children!"

"No one mentioned your name or Hollister's. The only ones who knew it was you two doing the interviews are me and that girl who flipped out, and she ain't talking. And what the hell do you care if Milton slithers up on his soapbox and uses you two to slam the Feds? That's what you're there for—or maybe you've forgotten whose side you're on . . . Kyle," Markham said with obvious contempt.

"I'm on the side of the citizens that I'm sworn to protect. Our people are being slaughtered, and those Feds you claim are the enemy are doing a hell of a lot more to stop it than the Ministry—or you, for that matter."

"Watch it, Deputy, or you'll find yourself washing cars in the motor pool."

"You want my badge?" Kyle asked, ripping it from his back pocket and tossing it toward Markham. "Take the damned thing."

Markham grabbed Kyle's arm as he stormed by. "Kyle . . ."

Before he could utter another word, Tanner's fist connected with his jaw, causing him to stumble back and double over. Tanner had never raised a hand to Markham before, and it left him shaking with rage and disgust. He climbed into his running truck and floored it, covering Markham in a spray of dirt and gravel. Rubbing blood from his mouth, Markham watched him drive down the road. He knew he had it coming after what he'd done to Kyle, but he never thought the boy would have the balls to stand up to him. He picked up Tanner's badge and rubbed the dust off on his arm, smiling a sad smile. His sister Sally's little boy had picked a fine time to grow a pair. He only hoped it wouldn't cost him his life.

4

Kyle took the turn onto Roanoke Road, driving aimlessly into the foothills. His anger toward Markham burned through his emotions as he took the turnoff to West Point Lake. It wasn't until he found himself sitting in the parking lot of the old saloon that he realized where he was. It had been a couple of years since he'd been to The Falls with his friends, but they'd spent entire summers getting into trouble on the lake. He cut across the street and turned onto a grass-covered trailhead and drove as far as the truck could go without getting stuck. From there he walked into the quiet woods, feeling more and more at ease as the sunlight disappeared beneath the canopy of turning leaves. He emerged at the base of the falls, where the water thundered from the late summer downpours.

He breathed deeply, letting the vibrations of the waterfalls beat away at his anger at Markham. He'd known Caleb all his life and Caleb had bullied him the entire time, making a man out of him, so he said. But Caleb had also always been there to take care of him and his mother. When money was tight, it was Caleb who filled the fridge and kept the lights on. When his mother got sick, Caleb had paid her doctor bills. And when she passed on, it was Caleb who made sure she got the Christian burial she deserved. He always suspected there was something between Caleb and his mother, but she denied it. She would only say that Caleb had served in the army with his father and that he was keeping a promise to always take care of them in his father's place.

The memories brought forth angry tears as he climbed over the slick rocks and into the nearest cave. The kids who used it kept it free of debris as a condition of being left alone by local law enforcement, but graffiti covered the cavern walls. He turned on the small penlight he kept attached to his ident cards and scanned the walls. The crude drawings and scrawlings of teenage defiance were everywhere; some of it he'd left himself. He followed the artwork to an outcropping where kids would dive into the lake below and tripped over a stack of cans, scattering them between the rocks. Someone hadn't packed out their trash. The cans were crumpled in the center and still had beer in them. Kyle pushed them back into a pile with his boot and bent down to pick them up. They were sticky but not just from beer. He ran his light over the can, noting the gooey, reddish-brown substance that covered them. He followed the splatter to a large rock at the edge of the outcropping where a round stain was drying. Lying in the dirt below it was a LaGrange Academy jacket with the initials KD embroidered on the chest.

5

Deacon and Elli made the rounds of every active limestone quarry, mine and processing plant between the Alabama and Georgia borders from the Tennessee line south to Columbus. Accompanied by a limited group of field technicians, they interviewed the staff while any potential evidence was collected. It was tedious work, and nothing panned out. Local animosity was running high, and the sight of federal police only made matters worse. The workers were solid, God-fearing loyalists, but despite the occasional racist remarks, everyone cooperated. Elli turned out to be a natural at interterritorial relations, smoothing whatever feathers Deacon accidentally ruffled. Deacon was certain that if she ever decided to follow her father into politics, she'd be a serious contender. Unfortunately, she would have to be beyond her child-bearing years and unmarried to even run. He suspected her superior skills as a doctor were the only thing keeping her free of the marriage mandates, but that wouldn't last. By the end of the day, the sites were deemed clean and the workers reported nothing out of the ordinary. The two of them crawled back into the cruiser after serving the last warrant, exhausted and frustrated. Elli threw her head back and groaned as the car bounced along the dirt drive.

"Outstanding job today, Doc," Deacon told her. "The way you handled the locals, I'd swear you must have inherited Daddy's genes for politics."

Elli let out a sarcastic grunt. "I'm sure you meant that as a compliment, but I did have to bend the truth to get them to cooperate."

"How so?" Deacon asked warily.

"Ever hear of good cop, bad cop?" she asked. "I made you the heavy and gave them the line Wirz gave me when he first outlined my penance: that I was there as a representative of the Ecumenical Council to make sure no federal officers—meaning you—violated their civil rights. I painted myself as their savior and warned them that any act of aggression or non-cooperation would only make E-Rep look like the bad guys in this, and everyone knows how the Council deals with people who make them look bad."

Deacon laughed loudly and shook his head, but Elli didn't join him.

"I just wish all that maneuvering hadn't been for nothing," she finally said.

"This is the tedious part of detective work," Deacon consoled her. "Day after day of digging for clues and coming up empty, no closer to the criminal than you were on day one."

"I don't know how you deal with the constant frustration," Elli remarked.

"The same way you deal with trying every possible treatment day after day only to watch your terminal patients slowly die anyway."

"We drink. A lot," Elli smirked.

Deacon smiled. "So do we."

They arrived back at HQ, where everyone else was just as burned out and on edge. Bachman had Allen Bainbridge detained and had been questioning him for several hours. He didn't bat an eye when she shared the details of his wife's affair and her subsequent pregnancy. When she revealed their discovery of his Ecumenical complaint and Ellory's penance from the Council, he only smirked and thanked Bachman for justifying his actions, for the record. No matter what she threw at him, he continued to deny any direct involvement with his wife's demise. What liaisons and abuse he did confess to he insisted were the result of his wife's affair, even though many occurred well before it had begun. He spat out these indiscretions with the air of a man who felt entitled to them by his society, which only made Bachman more determined to tear him apart. Deacon finally called a halt to the interrogation much later than he should have. The only reason he let it go as long as it did was to allow Joyce to get Bainbridge out of her system. But apart from being a self-involved, abusive dickhead, the only bit of information she confirmed was his longtime relationship to Archbishop Wirz. It was immaterial to the case, but it was political leverage, so Deacon had Bainbridge released. Joyce wanted to interview Mona Davis next but was informed by the Ecumenical Council that she'd been hospitalized after her breakdown.

They went over the evidence repeatedly reaching the same conclusions until no one wanted to do it again. Deacon was about to send everyone home when Tanner called in from the field.

Pressing the open mic for the pit he barked, "You better have a damned good reason for not being at work today, Tanner."

Kyle's voice came through, shouting over a continuous roar. "I found the site where the Dockweiler boy was murdered!"

Everyone shot to their feet, staring at Deacon as Tanner spoke.

"I'm at The Falls. The caves over West Point Lake off of Roanoke. I need the forensics team out here now!"

Deacon pulled up a map of their destination and smiled. If Tanner was right, their crime scene was solidly within federal borders. "Seal off the scene, Tanner. Make sure no one gets anywhere near it. We're on our way." To the team Deacon said, "Hustle, people!" It was unnecessary as everyone had already grabbed their gear and started racing to the garage. Burke stood to follow, but Deacon stopped him. "Hold on, Jeremy. You are in no condition to go climbing around a waterfall."

"I nearly got killed chasing a lead on this case, boss. I'm not about to stop now."

Deacon looked at him sternly, but he needed Burke on this. "Agnes! Keep Burke on your six and make sure he doesn't end up taking a nose-dive off a cliff."

As they rode the elevator down, Joyce said, "This would be a hell of a lot faster if they'd just let us use the Blackhawk."

"Without Tanner on board E-Rep won't give us the air clearance to fly a federal bird over their territory, and even then it has to be a life-or-death emergency." He waved his hands comically in the air. "They're afraid we might spy on them from above."

"Eish Mtometm!" Joyce responded.

An hour later, The Falls were cordoned off and the forensics team was in full swing. Burke's evidence bots scanned the caverns from top to bottom and packaged every trace of an illicit substance they encountered. For once, Deacon stayed clear. If this was, in fact, the location of Kevin's murder, he wanted the confirmation to be crystal clear with no chance of human intervention to contest. He joined Joyce, Tanner and Elli at the shoreline and waited for the all clear.

"This should have been the first place we looked after Kevin was killed," Tanner told her. "If one of those kids had stumbled on this, all hell would have broken loose."

Elli rubbed his shoulder and said, "You couldn't have known, Kyle."

"I should have known!" he snapped back, causing her to flinch. "I'm a cop, for Christ's sake. It's Crime Scene 101 in the academy. But they don't let us local boys investigate major crimes. We just play traffic cop while the E-Rep detectives run the show."

"Judging by the amount of contraband we've collected, I'd say E-Rep wasn't doing a very good job," Deacon said as he approached. "There's evidence of alcohol, drug use, and condoms all over those caverns." He watched as Tanner began to blush. "But they don't know about it, do they?"

"No," Tanner answered, shaking his head. "The Falls are kind of a special place. Someplace where kids can just be kids and do stupid kid stuff before they have to grow up and become proper citizens. All the locals know what goes on out here. They don't say anything. This place belonged to their daddies and their daddies' daddies before them. Back then, it was just a private little beach cove on a lake, before the war dropped cluster bombs on it. The grown-ups stay clear as long as the kids keep the place cleaned up. The only time the law comes out here is if things get out of hand and they start drawing unwanted attention."

"And E-Rep's never raided the place?" Deacon asked him.

"We never gave them a reason to. God's people are very good at keeping secrets," Tanner responded sternly.

Deacon nodded in agreement. "We'll gather up everything we can find. No sense in giving these kids more grief than they've already suffered." Tanner shot him a concerned look, and he quietly said, "I grew up here too, Kyle. We'll only log what we need for the case into evidence. The rest . . . let's just say we'll leave that to the Almighty to sort out."

Tanner exhaled heavily as Deacon clapped him on the shoulder and walked back to the caves. He recalled Markham's warning about trusting federal niggers and now regretted not hitting Markham hard enough to break his jaw.

"He's certainly not what we were told to expect, is he?" Elli asked at his side.

"No, he certainly isn't," Kyle told her. Glancing at Elli, he muttered, "You probably never hung out in places like this, what with those fancy prep schools you went to."

She turned to him and grinned suggestively. "You'd be surprised at what us fancy prep school girls get up to."

6

The tension inside the director's office was oppressive. The president's face on the monitor was tight with anger and frustration as she delivered the news.

"I'm sorry, Director Pittsfield, but I have no choice. With the level of urgency escalating and with all the evidence pointing to an attack perpetrated on and by an E-Rep territorial citizen, I have no choice but to honor the Ecclesiastical territorial ambassador's request to assume control of the investigation as a matter of internal security."

This was a major blow for the department, one that would most likely require his resignation and possibly force MacNair into retirement. The director shook his head. "I understand, Madam President. I'll inform my team and make arrangements to deliver all corresponding evidence to the territorial police."

Before he could disconnect, Deacon burst into the room and said, "I wouldn't make that call just yet, Madam President."

"This is a secure communication, Lieutenant," the director told him sternly.

"I apologize for the intrusion, sir, but there's been a critical development in the case." Addressing the president, he said, "We've positively identified the location of the actual crime scene in the Dockweiler boy's death." He walked to the control deck and uploaded a data stream to the monitor. A map of the location and the details of the forensic analysis began to scroll down. "The location is at the west side of West Point Lake in Georgia, a site commonly known as The Falls and frequented by the students at the victim's school. DNA analysis of blood found at the scene along with the supporting personal evidence confirms without a doubt that this is our crime scene—and it is well within federal territorial borders."

The president scanned the evidence quickly. "This only applies to the second victim. You still haven't found the location of the first murder yet, and the third victim was murdered within E-Rep territory, was he not?"

"That's correct, ma'am, but as you can see, this killer is willing to cross territorial borders. It is therefore in the best interests of both territories to continue pursuing this as a joint investigation." He could tell by her hesitation that the president was weighing the political fallout from denying the E-Rep petition. "For the record, Madam President, it was E-Rep Dep. Tanner who discovered the crime scene. Both he and Dr. Hollister have been instrumental in moving this case forward. I continue to have the utmost confidence in their abilities, and I would ask that you have them irrevocably assigned to my team until this case is fully resolved. I believe that any attempt to remove them at this time would be doing a grave disservice to the victims' families and the sovereign citizens of their own territory." She raised a questioning eyebrow to him. "And you may quote me on that for the record, Madam President."

The president visibly relaxed. "Thank you for your assurances, Lieutenant. I'll make sure they're secured to the team, and please give them my utmost gratitude for their efforts." She cast a sly smile toward Deacon and added, "I trust their continued involvement won't jeopardize our concurrent endeavors in any way."

"No, ma'am," Deacon told her.

"Good hunting, then."

She signed off and Pittsfield asked, "What the hell was that all about? And don't tell me it's just about some jurisdictional battle."

"I'll tell you when you're old enough," Deacon said with a smile and walked to the door.

Pittsfield called out, "If you're banging the president, MacNair, I better not hear about it on the evening news."

Deacon extended his middle finger and left.

7

Along the grand concourse surrounding the Georgia capitol building, people shouted and waved as news crews covered their protests. Milton could see them from his office. The majority of the crowd were a sensible bunch. They just wanted to live good Christian lives and be as far removed from the temptations of the outside as they could be. They stayed well behind the rabid dogs that yelled and protested, vying to be seen by the cameras so their cries would be heard around the world. These desperate protestors had become the heart and soul of God's new Eden, the face of the new Republic. They had no real justification to protest, no real position to argue. They were simply a barking pack of angry hounds that gathered every time an outsider knocked on the gates to paradise. They didn't care who the outsider was or why the outsider was there. Their sole purpose was to snarl and yap and chase them away. Today the stranger at the gate was a team of HSS detectives hunting a serial killer. The stranger was there to protect the pack from a greater threat in their midst, but the pack didn't care. They only knew the duty they had been indoctrinated to perform: patrol the fence line and bark and howl and frighten the strangers away. Milton loathed their ignorance.

He hadn't always felt this way about them. After all, it was this rabid pack of animals that led the charge to form their own country. It was these very same dogged pit bulls that kept the lines firmly drawn between what was divine and what was evil. And it was this pack of fervid believers that had propelled him to the highest position a politician in the Republic could attain without being ordained. And they were about to launch him into federal service and send him out into the world to bring God to the heathen territory. He should have been down there thanking them for their support, assuring them that their cries of anger were heard and would be obeyed. Instead, he sat up in his office counting the days until he no longer had to hear or see them. If it weren't for them, he could have been at home, enjoying his favorite brandy at his desk while reshaping the country for his legacy. If it weren't for them, he could have spent the afternoon with his girlfriend, doing whatever depraved acts they could contrive without a care in the world. If it weren't for them, his son Pete would be home right now where he belonged and not doing time in a federal prison for a stupid mistake.

The voice on the comm line began to cough, forcing his attention back to the conversation. Milton's foot tapped a nervous rhythm under his desk as he listened. Pete's voice was groggy, and he slurred his words. The beating had done that. He said the nurses were taking care of him, and the enomorphine drip kept him out of pain. He didn't remember much about the attack and only knew what the warden had told him: that a group of four inmates had cornered him and beat him near to death. They didn't tell Pete why he'd been jumped, but Milton had a pretty good idea. He told Pete to get some rest and not worry, that he would make sure he was safe from here on out. The boy gurgled his thanks and the line went dead. The beating had been a warning, not to Pete but to him. Wirz found out about his little booze binge somehow, and Pete had paid the price. *Fuck! It was only one minor slip!*

Milton wanted to kick himself for never really believing Wirz had the clout to make good on his veiled threats in federal territory. That arrogance had nearly cost him his son's life. He had to keep it together until after the election. He could stay sober for a couple of weeks. Hell, he'd been sober for nearly two months since Pete's arrest. Two weeks would be a cake walk. He closed his eyes and breathed deeply, imagining the bender he would go on once he won.

Ever since the president's announcement that the interterritorial investigation would remain a joint effort with HSS in control, they'd been making a ruckus. Not a single senator managed to enter or leave the capitol without being questioned, either by an angry mob demanding to know why federal cops were investigating their citizens or by a journalist wanting to know why E-Rep law enforcement was incapable of catching a killer on their own. His colleagues gave only a terse "no comment" as they pushed through. They couldn't afford to have some raw, unfiltered sound bite flooding the airwaves this close to a victory. They were all doing exactly as he'd instructed. All except for Quentin Hollister. Quentin was all too happy to ease the concerns of the general citizenry. He reiterated the commitment of both governments to protecting them and assured them that their rights would be respected. He radiated with the trust and confidence of a true leader and the crowd ate it up, their applause eventually drowning out the howls of the rabid pack before them. Quentin's daughter being on the investigation team only made him look more like a savior, and now Hollister was riding a wave of support, leaving everyone asking if he'd consider running a write-in campaign in the upcoming elections. Quentin evaded the question each time but never gave them a definitive "no," either. As a result, Milton's poll numbers were dropping like a rock against a man who wasn't even running. How could anyone blame him for going off the wagon?

He closed the drapes and dropped himself heavily into the plush chair behind his desk. Dropping his head between his hands, he closed his eyes and drifted off into memory. Memories of Pete as a toddler. A precocious, unruly, tow-headed bundle of energy being chased around the house by his mother. The kid got into everything. If it wasn't Pete's maniacal, childlike laugh piercing the house, it was the lamenting cries of his mother begging Milton to give her a hand controlling his son. Claire. The sweetest soul he'd ever known. Too sweet. She'd had faith, the way all the good ones did, that the deeper teachings of Christ held the answers to humanity. But the assault her morality had to suffer for his success proved terminal in the end. Two years into his first term, the facts of politics shredded her hopes. A year later, the reality of hardline religion destroyed her soul. She couldn't reconcile the sacrifices her soul had to make with the abandonment of humanity and kindness necessary to retain power. The papers declared her death a tragic accident, but Milton knew that she'd just given up.

The door to his office crashed open, startling Milton from his memories. His arms flew across the desk, sending everything crashing onto the floor.

"Wallace! Have you lost your goddamned mind!" Quentin yelled as he barged in, waving a data pad. "You can't possibly believe that this bill has a chance in hell of making it to a vote!"

Milton gripped the desk and growled, "Quentin, you may be my number two and the fair-haired boy of the Republic, but I'm still in charge, at least for now, and you'd better FUCKING DAMNED WELL KNOCK BEFORE YOU ENTER MY OFFICE!"

Quentin had been on the receiving end of Wallace's hair-trigger temper before but wasn't intimidated this time. "You can't introduce a bill that will officially force an entire gender into a life of servitude. It's tantamount to slavery."

"I know a couple of million mothers that would take offense at that statement, Quentin. It's their biblical mandate to serve their husbands and bear children as God intended. The women of the Republic are proud to be wives and mothers. They serve as an example to the rest of the country that family is sacred and deserves their full attention."

"They do it willingly, Wallace. They do it as a matter of faith. You're telling them they now have no choice. That they can no longer be doctors or lawyers or hold any professional titles whatsoever until they no longer have any worth as a wife and mother because men are entitled to those opportunities ahead of them. You're reducing them to the status of breeding stock."

Milton stared at his second in command, feeling every bit of their mutual dislike, and waved for him to sit down. When Quentin plopped into the chair he said, "Let me give you a little history lesson. A little over fifty years ago, China instituted laws to curb its population growth among the more ethnically acceptable members of its society. The result was a limited superior class and a rapidly multiplying peasant population. It gave them a wealth of disposable people as laborers to conscript in the event of a land war, saving the necessity of sacrificing the more desirable citizens in battle. The unfortunate side effect of such a society was that females were unwanted, aborted and even murdered. And without a land war to keep the population under control, it left a large percentage of their male population without acceptable wives. Eventually, they instituted more balanced controls to preserve the necessary female population, but it proved that laws regarding procreation were not only effective but predictable." He sat down in his chair and clasped his hands together tightly. "All we're doing is taking a predictable system of control and making it work for us. We aren't telling women they can't have careers; we're encouraging them to do it, rewarding them for it, even, after they serve their higher calling as mothers."

"By taking away their freedom to be what God intended them to be."

"This IS what God intended them to be!" Milton said, stabbing the desk with his finger with every word. "Our population is in crisis, Quentin. The male population is outpacing the female population every year, and job creation has slowed to a standstill. The men of this country have been emasculated by feminist bullshit for far too long, and it's time we put them back where God intended them to be: as the kings of their castles and masters of their world. That means putting our men back to work and putting our women back in the bedrooms where they belong. It's the only way to balance out this crisis."

Quentin looked at him in horror. "There's no way I'll support this. I won't let this happen."

Milton flew out of his chair and hissed, "You'll do exactly as you're told if you know what's good for you. There's a lot happening in the territory, Quentin, and if you want to continue being a part of its governing body, you'll do everything you can to ensure its survival." He sat back down and muttered, "And yours."

He was trembling with anger when Quentin stormed out of his office as loudly as he'd stormed in. After his tremors subsided, he placed a call to the Basilica.

8

Quentin paced in his office. He had never seen Milton so rattled before, not even during the height of his cocaine habit. Quentin pitied the man, but he had greater concerns than saving Milton's ass. The Ecclesiastical Republic was being led down an all-too-familiar road. The last time they'd taken this route, they were led by an egomaniacal madman with an unmistakable talent for manipulating the most vulnerable with grievous lies. An exterminator in Pied Piper's clothes, entrancing his unwitting victims by playing the music of fear and insanity. The piper was eventually imprisoned for his many crimes, but the brainwashing of his followers only led to an even greater menace and eventually a war that nearly destroyed the entire country. Quentin had lived through it all and devoted his career to ensuring that no demagogue would ever lead his people astray again.

He looked out into the square, where the crowd was still chanting angrily. There was a time when the crowds would gather and sing hymns in joy. Every Sunday, choirs and parishes throughout the Republic would raise their voices in praise, spending the day in fellowship with family and friends, and the world just seemed right. Even in the aftermath of war, every voice found song, and people engaged each other as kindred souls. Today each Sabbath was filled with people trudging into houses of worship and sitting on edge. Their eyes darted back and forth. They remained silent unless it was time to speak, wary of saying or doing anything that might be considered provocative or sinful. Their main purpose in attending was no longer fellowship: it was to be seen by their peers and those in power as being loyal to God, and they couldn't leave fast enough when services ended.

There was definitely something happening in the territory; Milton was right about that. A new wave of extremism had slowly worked its way into the Ecumenical leadership, leaving only fear in its wake. On the streets below, his people were once again hearing the music of a piper. But this time, the piper was no bombastic buffoon in poorly fitting suits. This piper wore the robes of a holy man. His music was not enthusiastic hard rock nor punctuated by the beating of war drums. It was the smothering blanket of hymns and the resolute voices of somber choirs that drew these people to be remade in the piper's own image. Until today, he had not known the seriousness of the threat this man and his organization represented. The look of panic on Milton's face told Quentin that not only was he aware of them but he was also a willing part of their agenda. The fear in Milton's voice told him the man had bitten off more than he could chew.

He called up the text of Milton's latest disastrous bill on the monitor and reread it. As horrifying as it was, he knew it stood an excellent chance of passing the inherently male Senate. Women's rights were rarely acknowledged in territorial law. Conservative women had fought bravely alongside the men during the Second Civil War, many sacrificing their lives for this new dream to be realized. Those who survived were forcibly retired from service, stripped of their rank and benefits, and encouraged to seek husbands. Women were forbidden thereafter from serving in the territorial military, something Quentin considered a grave disservice to their courage and abilities. Mandating marriage and procreation was only the latest affront to their contributions to society.

An hour later, his secretary announced the unexpected arrival of Archbishop Wirz with an urgent matter to discuss. *That was fast,* Quentin thought as he invited the man in. The meeting wasn't scheduled, but with Milton acting strangely he should have expected it. The archbishop greeted him warmly with all the grace of one called to serve God, but Wirz made his skin crawl. The holy piper himself in all his Ecclesiastical glory. This was the man directly responsible for Elli's assignment to the HSS task force. He should have been grateful for her reprieve, given the alternative his daughter faced under the current laws. But that alternative had been the brainchild of this very same madman. A system of reconditioning that, if the rumors were true, had potentially horrific consequences.

"I regret that we have to meet under such urgent circumstances, Senator Hollister, but I'm sure you can understand the need."

"I assume you're here to discuss the situation with Wallace Milton and his proposal, Your Excellency," Quentin stated.

"That is one of many things we need to discuss, Quentin . . . if I may?" he offered.

Quentin wasn't comfortable being on a first-name basis with Wirz but was willing to play along if it gained him the information he sought. He nodded his acceptance and offered the archbishop some coffee. "A little early for an intervention, but I assume the Council is pressuring you as much as my colleagues are pressuring me. Unfortunately, I can't support the bill as written. I won't be responsible for instituting what can only be classified as gender-based slavery."

Wirz accepted the cup and smiled. "I'm not here as an adversary, Quentin. I'm here to assure you that the Council is only concerned with the well-being of the Republic." He took a sip and then added, "In fact, I may be able to assist you in ways you may not be aware of."

Quentin absorbed the sly look in Wirz's eyes. "I'm sure the Council has its hands full with the spiritual health and obedience of the territory. I think the legislature will be just fine."

"And what about you, Quentin? Will you be just fine?"

Quentin bristled at the question, which was more of a threat than an expression of concern.

Wirz set his cup down and assumed an authoritative posture. "Your star is on the rise, Quentin, far more than Wallace Milton's ever was. You have the support of the people and, more importantly, their respect. Have you ever considered running for national office?"

"I have no such aspirations, Your Excellency," he responded carefully. "I have enough work to do right here in the territory, protecting its citizens."

"Protecting them from what, may I ask?"

Quentin stared at Wirz for a moment and then answered. "From those individuals who would use faith to steal power for themselves and destroy everything we've worked so hard to achieve."

"Oh, come now, Quentin," Wirz chided. "You're the second most influential politician in the territory. You are the very embodiment of power."

"I don't use that power to subjugate our citizens," he said. "We are still Americans and have certain rights that transcend faith."

"Rights are a myth, Quentin. The only rights our people have are those granted to them by God through the Church as so declared in the Territorial Charter. Such old-fashioned patriotism doesn't suit someone of your position," Wirz told him.

Quentin stared at him with disbelief and contempt.

"Don't looked so shocked," Wirz continued. "Throughout history, governments have been ruled by religion. Since Emperor Constantine himself, the two have been one and the same. Governments have forced their subjects to worship their declared faith since the third century and fatally persecuted heretics and deviants who opposed them."

Quentin's faced paled slightly. "We aren't barbarians."

"Barbarity is a matter of perception, Quentin. The saints themselves by definition were inhuman monsters. St. Augustine himself cruelly tortured those who would not embrace his faith. Thomas Aquinas, a Dominican priest, endorsed and promoted the execution of all who violated the laws of faith. These men were but a sample of the savagery of the church and had more blood on their hands than Hitler and the entire Third Reich, yet both were canonized for their efforts. Barbarity is subjective, Quentin. Just ask the Iranian Supreme Leader. Even he would agree that the very nature of religion is its own sovereignty, and sovereignty exists only through subjugation."

"Does that subjugation include torturing people into submission and calling it rehabilitation?" Quentin asked. "I wonder how the people would react if they knew how their loved ones were being reconditioned to death?"

"Careful, Quentin. Conversion is a lawful form of penance overseen by the Ecumenical elders of the Church. Given its success, the Council might consider those statements to be sedition," Wirz warned him.

"I'm not afraid to publicly oppose any mistreatment or torture of our citizens by leaders they put their trust in. I've dedicated my life to it."

Wirz sat back and asked, "Does your daughter feel the same way?"

"My daughter has dedicated her life to saving the lives of our people at any cost. Her calling was given to her by God."

"A calling she used to defy that God, and it nearly cost a child his eternal soul. Perhaps I should ask her if she believes her calling gives her the right to act against the Church." Quentin froze as Wirz stared him down. "She's already been convicted of one serious crime. Heresy would require a penance that even my benevolence couldn't protect her from."

Quentin pushed himself out of his chair slowly and glared at Wirz. Only a couple of inches in height separated them, but Quentin's extra bulk made him overshadow the wiry archbishop. "Are you threatening my family?" he hissed quietly.

"I'm only warning you of the consequences of your position. As charming as your naiveté is, there are a few facts you need to accept. You may think you represent the people, but you don't. You represent the Council. You enforce the edicts of the Council, no matter how distasteful those edicts may seem to you. You legislate divine law as written by the Ecumenical Courts and enact similar laws that ensure the citizens act in accordance with the expectations of the kingdom of God. That being said, opposing the recommendations of the Council could have very serious consequences." He turned to leave, then added, "Remember your place, Quentin, and you could enjoy a very long and rewarding future . . . and so could your daughter."

I Send an Angel Before You

Mona Davis returned home from R&R after two weeks of treatment for her breakdown. The Council doctors warned her and her parents that dissociation was a side effect of the treatment that would go away in time. All that was needed was to keep their daughter calm and relaxed and give her time to adjust. Mona spent her first week at home in bed, sleeping fitfully, only emerging from her room to eat or bathe. Her mother fawned over her constantly, which made her feel warm and safe, while her father scowled. Eventually she brightened up, and by the time the second week started, she was up helping her mother make meals and do chores. By that Wednesday, she announced that she wanted to return to school the following week. Her mother was overjoyed. Her father simply said, "Bout time you got yer lazy ass out of that bed and back to school. Can't hide from the world, Mona. When it knocks you down, you gotta take it on and fight yer way through it."

Sometime after midnight Friday during a bathroom run, Mona heard a car pull up outside, followed by a loud thump and slurred voices. Her father must have come home drunk again and been dumped off by his buddies from work. She expected it since her parents had been arguing about money for the last two days. He'd no doubt stomp up the stairs, waking her mother. Then the two would start arguing and he'd whale on her mom until she cried enough to satisfy him. It always happened when he drank. Mona sleepily wandered back to her room before her father could see her and watched him shuffle by, tripping on the rug and kicking it out of his way with a curse. But then something happened that brought Mona fully awake. She watched in horror from behind her bedroom door as her father's face began to blister. It bubbled until he was nearly unrecognizable, and then the blisters began to ooze. His skin sloughed off, and before Mona's eyes, her father became a demon. As she watched him clump down the hallway, dragging a clawed hand along the wall, she stumbled back into her room and crouched behind the bed.

Grabbing the bedspread, she pulled it down over her head and slammed her eyes shut. "It's not real, it's not real, I'm dreaming, it's not real," she kept telling herself, but her mind knew otherwise. During her hospitalization, the

246

therapist had informed her that the sins she committed with her dead boyfriend were the work of demons that Mona had allowed to inhabit her soul, that she had abandoned God, and thus her guardian angel had abandoned her. The only way she could be saved was to embrace the angel of God again and remain his soldier in Christ. If she did that, she would be forever protected and never be a victim of sin again. The litany of her sins was drummed into her head day after day as the drugs had surged in her veins. At some point during the treatment, she actually began to see the demons the doctors spoke of. They crawled out from between her legs and hissed with serpents' tongues. Mona would scream in terror for hours each day while the nurses read Scripture and demanded she face her demons. Several days into treatment, a bright light and a pale face enveloped her vision and spoke to her before she passed out. Every day after that, whenever the demons came, the man in the bright light vanquished them. On the last day, the man in the light demanded that she give herself to the word of God, that she fight the demons wherever and whenever they appeared and vanquish them however possible, and she would be saved. Mona tearfully agreed.

She slept for two days and was then released to her parents. She was told that her angel would be with her as long as she kept her covenant with God, and they were right. She'd seen him as she left the hospital. She'd seen him in the car on the way home. She'd seen him in her house occasionally, always as a fleeting glimpse in her peripheral vision. But she had no doubt that he remained with her as promised. She saw less of him as the days passed until she was nearly convinced she'd imagined the whole experience. Now here she was, cowering under a blanket and praying for an imaginary being to save her. The doctors warned her what would happen if she lost faith, and now the demons had returned, only this time they'd taken her father. She could still hear her parents arguing in their bedroom. Her father's voice had become a guttural snarl and her mother's wails even more terrifying than usual. "God send my angel, I need my angel," she kept repeating, hoping that it wasn't too late. Her mother let out a blood-curdling scream, which was followed by a loud thud, and then light enveloped Mona's mind.

She woke Saturday morning as sunlight bled through the pale curtains. The house was nearly silent, but she could hear faint noises coming from the kitchen below. She was stiff from sleeping in a tight ball and crawled over to the heater vent to relax her muscles in the warm air. *It must have just been a bad dream,* she told herself as she walked out onto the landing rubbing her eyes. She looked toward her parents' bedroom and stopped cold. On the wall were long, dark streaks. The demon had scratched them into the wall the night before. "It was just a dream," she whispered as she held out a shaking hand and touched the marks. They smeared beneath her fingertips. Not scratches, grease. She smelled her fingertips. AeroShell 5. Her father used it all the time when he was repairing engine bearings at the aircraft hangar where he worked. *Just a dream, silly girl.* She made her way silently to her parents' door and peeked in. Lying across the bed, fully clothed, was her father, his deviated septum buzzing like an angry wasp hive with every breath. No demon; just Dad.

Mona relaxed and made her way quietly downstairs and crept into the kitchen. Her mother was rolling out biscuit dough and sniffling. There was a large red welt on her left cheek, and the area beneath her eye had begun to bruise.

"Did he hurt you too bad?" Mona asked quietly.

Her mother looked up suddenly and, seeing the tears in her daughter's eyes, said, "Oh honey, it looks worse than it feels. Been through much worse, you know."

Mona knew. She'd seen it firsthand.

"You mind buttering up that platter, dear?" her mother asked as she cut the circular biscuits with a tin can. Mona complied, running the tube of butter over the baking tray as her mother prattled on. "The good Lord must have been looking out for me last night, honey. Your father looked ready to kill me, practically grew horns and claws. Then all I saw was a bright light, and he fell over."

Mona dropped the butter right onto the floor in shock. Her mother had seen the angel too.

"Mona, watch what you're doing!" her mother gasped, rushing over to clean the greasy floor. Looking into her daughter's pale face, she said, "You don't look like you slept much. Why don't you go take a long, hot bath, and I'll bring your breakfast up."

"Okay, Momma," Mona muttered as she went back upstairs and into the bathroom.

With the bacon frying and the biscuits ready to bake, Mona's mother went back upstairs to straighten up the mess. Passing by the bathroom door, she heard the water stop and Mona step into the tub. Her husband was still asleep and would stay that way until she shook him awake. Nevertheless, she moved cautiously, picking up the broken glass and torn shade from the lamp he'd hit her with. The light from the exposed bulb had blinded her so she didn't know what happened next, but when she opened her eyes, her husband had passed out. She'd gone downstairs to sleep on the couch.

It was nearly a month after Kevin Dockweiler's murder when Mona Davis returned to LaGrange. She wished she hadn't. Her friends were surprised to see her. They gave her all the customary "welcome backs" and "glad to see you're betters" that were expected, along with a healthy dose of "Are you okays?" But to Mona, it was all wrong. The words sounded real, but they held no sincerity or authenticity. They were hollow platitudes echoing from suspicious faces floating in another dimension. Now that her uniform was regulation and her face was makeup free, she no longer looked like she belonged. Her friends stood in defensive groups when she was with them, their hands and arms tucked tight to their bodies as if she had some communicable disease. The only one who made any physical contact with her was Martha June of the loose thighs and blue-tinged eyelashes. When Martha saw her that first day, clean-faced and well-rested, she slapped poor Mona on the shoulder and laughingly said, "Boy, did they fuck you up!" This brought a chorus of laughs from her friends. It was meant to be sympathetic, but not to Mona. Thereafter, Mona spent her days adrift and avoiding them, sitting alone in tight corners or under low-hanging trees, pretending to catch up on her studies. She looked for her guardian angel, but he was nowhere to be found. Now, two days before Halloween, she discovered why.

Biology was by far the most boring subject, and most of the kids in the class spent the hour making sexual comments or innuendos and driving their teacher to distraction. Mona was far more apprehensive than bored. She glanced around the class, watching her schoolmates goof off whenever the teacher's back was turned and remembering how she used to join them in their disrespectful behavior. But things were different now. Her friends were different. She looked over to Martha June, who sat making eyes at the football team, crossing and uncrossing her legs. But when Martha flicked her tongue at them, Mona noticed that it was most definitely forked. She shut her eyes and forced the image away. She then noticed that some of her classmates had red eyes and others sharp fangs when they smiled. More than a few had clawed hands. Excusing herself from class, she ran to the girls' bathroom and locked herself in the largest stall, praying that what she had seen was only a hallucination. She left school early and gave her mother a rather convincing story about having an abominable case of cramps. Her mother sent her to bed and brought her tea.

All that afternoon Mona stayed in bed and prayed. When her mother brought up dinner, she picked at it enough to show her appreciation and returned to bed. She did not sleep and continued to pray. Just as the night was beginning to wane, Mona's prayers were answered. Her cell phone began to chirp as it had back when Martha June would sneak back into her own house after a night of prowling. MJ always texted her to brag. But instead of a message from Martha June, the screen began to flash, blinding Mona and making her head spin. She threw the phone onto the floor and pressed her temples tightly to right herself—and that was when the angel came once more and spoke to her. She listened as he warned her that she had not kept her promise to be a warrior for God, to vanquish evil wherever it appeared. "But I'm just a kid. I can't fight monsters," she whimpered. "You can and you must, or you shall become their servant," the angel told her over and over again until it became an echo in her head. The voice of the angel, the voices of the doctors and nurses all saying the same thing over and over, intertwining until she could stand it no longer. Then a bright light washed over her and she passed out.

She woke minutes later to the sound of her mother's voice calling for her to hurry or she'd miss the school bus. Mona put on her school uniform and brushed her hair quickly, not noticing the dark circles that had formed under her eyes from a lack of sleep. She brushed by the kitchen and gulped down the orange juice her mother offered, muttering that she didn't have time for breakfast. She'd eat something at school. Her mother didn't object and attributed her daughter's haggard appearance to a rough night courtesy of her period. Mona left her mother working on her father's breakfast and opened the hall closet. Pulling the coats aside, she removed the shoulder holster and the Ruger SR9 her father kept in it. Adjusting the straps for her thin frame, she then zipped the sweater up to her chest, grabbed her backpack and headed for the bus.

The ride was typically rowdy, and no one paid attention to her. She stared at the back of the seat in front of her, the Lord's Prayer repeating in her head. She went through homeroom and first period, taking note of the number of demons that surrounded her, and waited. Morning break brought out the sun, and everyone gathered in the quad, laughing and enjoying the day. Spying her friends gathered under a statue of the school's founder, she carefully took note of how many of them had been possessed and then went to join them. Barbara noticed her and muttered, "Watch it, here comes Mona." This brought a round of moans and giggles. Martha June had had enough of Mona's morose mood and turned to say something snarky, but her eyes went wide. Mona swung her arm around and leveled the pistol at Martha June. Time slowed to a crawl as the first shot rang out, but it caught Martha right between the eyes. As she went down, the screaming started, but Mona's hand was steadied by her angel and she made short work of those in the group who were possessed. Kids were running every which way as no one could believe what was happening. The football players from her biology class, in a decidedly macho display, came running and confronted her. "What the hell are you doing, Mona? Put the gun down right now! Don't make us take it from you." Their voices sounded so far away to her, but the angel's voice was loud and clear. "Go, Satan, for it is written you shall worship the Lord your God and serve him only." She cut them down without hesitation.

It took only minutes for Sheriff Markham and his deputies to arrive, but the pandemonium of stampeding children hampered their efforts to get in. When they finally made their way to the quad, Mona had cornered a student next to the building and was preparing to shoot.

"Drop the gun, honey!" Markham screamed. "For the love of God, girl, don't make me take you down. Put it on the ground!"

But Mona couldn't hear him. She only heard the voice of the angel and knew what she had to do. She sighted down the barrel as Markham raised his weapon. Mona tightened her grip and the cowering student curled into a ball, screaming at the top of his lungs. Markham took the shot. The force of Markham's slug slammed into Mona's back, but all she saw as she died was a bright, white light and a gentle voice calling her home.

PART 3
False Prophets and Ravenous Wolves

The Doctrines of Devils

1

Deacon's mouth was parched. Thirst wrapped itself around his throat like a snake, and no amount of water or his usual mud-like coffee could quench it. It was the old thirst. The one that only T-Bone's rotgut could quench. He'd been trying to ignore it for days, but it was unrelenting. With every shift that ended no closer to finding the killer, the serpent tightened its grip. *As soon as the case is over, I promise,* he kept telling himself. It was his go-to mantra whenever he was involved in a stressful case. But this time the beast wasn't listening. It knew that serial killings were rarely solved quickly. Most went unsolved for years, and it wasn't about to wait until some random clue or slipup occurred, breathing new life into a case gone stone-cold.

Deacon tried to console it. Modern advances in technology would get the case resolved. Burke's miracle bots could track evidence nearly to the molecular level, and DNA could now be matched within hours instead of months. *We will solve this case, and we'll do it soon.* But Deacon knew no amount of technology could ever substitute for human intuition. No machine could logically think its way to a conclusion when it came to murder. Murder was personal, whether it was spontaneous or premeditated. It required interaction between predator and victim, an understanding of where each one fit into the world and why such an action was necessary. These were things born of the human mind and heart, things no machine could ever replicate. Burke's bots could scour every trace of evidence and pinpoint the exact details of an act, but they couldn't crawl into the mind of a man and extract a compulsion or look out through the eyes of a victim and feel death's embrace. Some things would forever be the province of humans.

The possible crime scenes had all been investigated. Everything that could be collected had been collected, and his head felt like a snare drum the day after Mardi Gras. The killer had two murders under his belt, the second more ghastly than the first, and they were no closer to finding him than they had been two months ago. The team spent each day in the pit rerunning the evidence and examining the case from different perspectives. So far, their profile consisted of a middle-aged white male in good shape and highly educated in theology, fine arts and history. This set him apart from seventy percent of the territory's male population, but the remaining thirty percent was still vast. The killer's access to classified information unfortunately limited him to the territory's largest employer, the endless bureaucracy that ran God's new Holy Land. Personal, professional, and social media profiles both public and private were researched and, in many cases, hacked by Burke and Corbett. The further back they went, the more clandestine accounts they uncovered. Most detailed a parade of debauchery, racism, violence and corruption that somehow seemed to vanish when one of them was appointed to public service.

A disgusted sigh emanated from Joyce's desk. Deacon rubbed his eyes and looked over to see her shaking her head as she read and munched on a sandwich.

"How the hell did these guys ever get picked to serve in government?"

"Compliments of the Territorial Rebirth Act of 2025," Deacon explained. "All appointed officials must have confessed and been absolved of all of their sins, both physical and spiritual, before accepting tenure of service."

"You mean they passed a law to absolve themselves of any past crimes?" Burke asked. "That must have taken all of a minute to compose. Heh, and they call us corrupt."

"Actually, it took months to draft before it was enacted," Elli countered, feeling her defenses rise.

"What? Did they have trouble finding all the loopholes, like tax evasion, money laundering, criminal conspiracy, collusion, corruption and sex trafficking?" Burke sneered.

"That wasn't the purpose of the legislation," Elli told him with a scowl. "Until the law was finished, the provisional government was only allowed to serve in a temporary, custodial capacity." She then added, "And considering the centuries-long history of corruption in the U.S. government, I'd appreciate you showing a bit more respect when disparaging my territory."

Deacon shot Burke a vicious look of warning, and he begrudgingly muttered, "Sorry, boss."

"What was the purpose behind the law?" Joyce asked her politely.

"It was meant to ensure that only those free of sin would inhabit the kingdom of God and serve as its stewards. Humanity was expelled from paradise for its sins, and it was felt that, in order to be worthy of returning to it, the people would have to return to that state of being. Absolution was a necessity, even more so for those in power."

"But how could they just forgive these men for their past acts?" Joyce asked. "There are some major felonies in these records. Some of the things we've uncovered would require lengthy jail sentences under the law."

Elli sat in a nearby chair. "It wasn't about forgiveness for a criminal act," she explained. "It was about facing God with a clear conscience and going forth with a promise to be better. Are you familiar with the tale of Nicodemus in the Bible?"

Joyce thought for a moment and then said, "Yes, he was one of the Pharisees. He snuck out to see Jesus in the middle of the night and questioned him about being born again."

Elli smiled. "That's right. As a Pharisee, Nicodemus knew everything about God's law but didn't truly know God. His knowledge meant nothing because he hadn't accepted God in his heart. Jesus explained to him that being born again wasn't a physical act but a spiritual one, a matter not of your actions but your soul. If your sins were laid bare to the light and you truly accepted Christ as your savior and lived in service to that belief, then you would be born again and worthy to enter the kingdom of Heaven. Nicodemus eventually accepted Christ and was saved even though he was an old man by then and had lived a man's life of darkness. And just like the Pharisees and religious scholars of old, it was felt that our leaders today had to be given that same opportunity."

"So, they wrote a law commanding everyone to confess their sins so they could be absolved, then just declared them born again?" Burke asked, drawing an irritated look from both Deacon and Elli. Softening his tone, he added, "As you pointed out, Doc, our elected officials have a history of corruption and criminal behavior. And a good number of them were self-proclaimed God-fearing, churchgoing, Bible-thumping Christians. They only confessed their sins and offered to repent after they got caught in the hopes of saving their political careers. That doesn't mean they meant it or that they gave up their criminal behavior. They just got better at hiding it."

"The custodians considered that," Elli explained. "They knew that there would be those who were just paying it lip service, saying whatever they needed to say to retain influence and position in the new government. They also knew that there were some crimes too serious to be ignored. That's why the Ecumenical Council was created. It acts as the check and balance on our own legislature, public servants, and population. For those with serious offenses, the Ecumenical Court handed down penances, which had to be served before anyone could be granted tenure in the leadership. The territorial police monitored their conduct for a time, sort of like parole. If they kept their oath to God, they would be deemed born again. If not, they would be remanded to the Council for summary judgment. We have faith in the oaths our leaders take."

Burke shook his head. "People swear on the Bible or whatever holy book they adhere to in every court in all three territories to this day, and they lie under oath all the time. If history has taught us anything, it's that human beings will lie to save their own asses, and it's impossible to legislate faith or morality. It's just something you have to have in your heart."

"So you assume everyone is guilty of lying based on this statistical probability but without any proof whatsoever?" Elli shook her head sadly. "Even your beloved Constitution declares a person's innocence until proven guilty. But on behalf of all humanity, Mr. Burke, allow me to forgive you for the insult."

Burke bristled but didn't respond.

"Forgiveness is a beautiful thing." Deacon chuckled at him. It wasn't the first time he'd caught his teammates sniping at one another. In the ten days since the president's announcement, the case had become a footnote to a greater circus. Citizen protests and prayer gatherings, unheard of since the days before the Second Civil War, were becoming a daily occurrence in Atlanta, and every state in the Ecclesiastical Republic was erupting. The hardline groups with the loudest and most xenophobic views got the most news coverage, even though they represented a mere fraction of the territorial population. The presence of federal officers operating within their borders had become the major topic of every political broadcast. Incumbents preached cooperation with the investigation while challengers across the territory took advantage of the hostility to bolster their own campaigns. And the more audacious and self-righteous the candidate was, the more airtime he was afforded. The reporting was purely for ratings appeal. Not once did anyone cite the lack of progress on the case or ask for updates. No mention was made of the poor victims or how their families were doing. All anyone seemed interested in was the imaginary invasion of the federal government into their sovereign territory. The fascist Yankees were on the march again, and delusions were spreading like wildfire.

Half of the video feeds in the pit were kept tuned to the broadcasts but muted. The lack of sound, however, did nothing to mute the emotions on the crowds' screaming faces.

"You'd think we were armed troops invading the territory," Joyce said, looking up from her meal at the screens. "I've never seen this level of crazy before."

"That's because you were just a kid when the war started. By the time you were old enough to understand what the fighting was about, it was all battles and bloodshed. The rhetoric had already done its job," Deacon told her.

"You mean they acted like this before the split?"

Deacon laughed. "This? Ha, this is nothing. These clowns are amateurs compared to their predecessors. Look up some of the historical videos from the 2016 and 2020 elections and you'll see crazy."

"I thought they'd all been removed from mainstream media and relegated to the Smithsonian."

"They were. Nowadays, schools use them for sociological and clinical teaching tools on mental disorders and societal dysfunction studies."

Joyce took a bite of her sandwich and said, "Hard to believe in a country where freedom of speech is so sacrosanct that Congress and the states would have agreed to it."

"It was known as the Second Great Compromise," Deacon told her. "Before the forty-fifth term, no other president in the history of this country had ever created so much hate and hysteria that it threatened our national security at home and abroad, and that includes during both World Wars. When people couldn't take it anymore, they marched on Washington and ransacked the White House. A hundred and fifty thousand out of a couple million civilians were either killed or wounded by military and Secret Service officers defending it. The carnage of American civilians was so bad that, by the time they dragged the man out of office, the media vowed to remove his face and his rhetoric from the airwaves. They held tight to that promise, and Congress followed suit. He is the only president in history to have his official portrait removed from the National Portrait Gallery. They don't even talk about him in school anymore other than to refer to him by his number. He was a national embarrassment and one that we never wanted to repeat."

"Rewriting history to suit their purposes?" Joyce asked.

Deacon looked at her sadly. "At least this time they did it for the right reasons."

Burke hobbled up and sat on the edge of Joyce's desk, munching an energy bar. "There's never a right reason," he told them. "If there were, Germany would have burned the camps and erased Hitler from the history books. Instead they used his legacy as a history lesson and the camps as a warning. They embraced their Nazi past as a cautionary tale."

"And yet, nearly a century later, you can still get ten years in prison for publicly using the swastika, making the Nazi salute or displaying the symbols of political organizations that have been declared unconstitutional, according to Germany's current criminal code," Deacon reminded him.

The remark caught Burke off guard. Deacon looked up solemnly and said, "Sometimes you have to do something wrong in order to do something right." The look unsettled both Joyce and Burke, who sensed that he had more to say. Deacon took a moment and then announced, "I paid a visit to Archbishop Wirz a couple of weeks ago to see if we could gain access to the sentencing documents."

Joyce's face went white. "You didn't . . . Tell me you didn't actually do it."

"If you mean did I tell him that someone in the Ecumenical leadership was complicit in the murders, yes I did. Although I was quite a bit more circumspect than that."

"So, when's the funeral?" Burke chuckled.

"Your confidence in my abilities is astounding, Burke. In any case, I didn't get us access to the list, but Wirz did interrogate me about all of you. He made a point of bringing up each of your anti-Christian viewpoints and lifestyle choices. He was concerned that it would create significant bias in the investigation. I assured him that no such bias would occur and that each of you would remain as professional, objective and vigilant as always."

"Thanks, boss," Burke responded.

"Don't thank me yet. There can't be so much as a hint of impropriety or personal bias for Wirz to latch on to, or he'll use it to publicly discredit you and remove us from the investigation permanently."

"I thought that wasn't a possibility any longer," Elli said.

"We have clear jurisdiction, but that won't cover negligence. I managed to secure your and Tanner's participation for the duration, but E-Rep could still chip away at the rest of the team and cripple it."

He walked over to Agnes and said, "I don't want you going anywhere in the field without an armed escort. Wirz intimated that your very presence within the territory was grounds for an arrest warrant. He doesn't actually have the authority to prosecute a federal officer, but he could make things very dangerous for you. From now on you don't set foot inside Ecclesiastical territory without Burke or myself at your side."

Agnes shook her head but kept her disgust to herself. She had more accolades for field experience and expertise than most officers in the region, including Burke, and now she would have to be escorted around like a rookie. "Understood, boss."

Deacon looked around the room and asked, "Where the hell is Tanner?"

"He didn't swing by to pick me up this morning," Elli told him. "He didn't answer his comm link, either, but there was a lot of police activity today. He must have been called back on an emergency."

"Until he shows up, see if you and Agnes can put together a list of names from the school roster of the Dockweiler boy's friends. Make arrangements with their parents to have them interviewed formally and in the presence of their personal attorneys. You can start with Mona Davis."

"Mona Davis is dead," a shaky voice told them from the doorway. They looked up to see Tanner standing there, looking devastated and white as a sheet. "There was a shooting at LaGrange," he explained, his voice cracking as he spoke. "Most of our potential witnesses were shot. Only a couple survived, but they won't for long." His voice cracked as he said, "Markham had no choice. He had to take her down."

"Take who down?" Elli asked. "You mean Mona?"

"If he hadn't, she would have shot even more of those kids." Everyone stared at him in shock. "She just took a bead on them one at a time. Like she was shooting targets at a shooting range. Just as calm as ever, like she was in some sort of trance. She'd take one down and then just move on to the next like it was nothing."

Burke tapped into the territorial news feed, which mentioned a disturbance at a local academy involving significant police presence for the protection of the students. The announcer promised that an update would be forthcoming on the nightly news.

"They aren't even reporting it yet," Joyce commented.

"They won't," Deacon told her. "Not until the news can't be contained any longer. The moment it leaks to the national networks, they won't have a choice."

Tanner took a long pull on a water bottle Elli handed him and said, "She was fine. Her parents said she'd just completed rehab and wanted to get back to school." He looked up at Deacon, searching for answers. "Those kids were her friends, and she just executed them."

Deacon had no answers and could only say, "I'm sorry, Kyle. I know these people were close to you." Tanner nodded but fell silent, staring at the walls without really seeing them.

The team's entire pool of witnesses had just vanished in the blink of an eye. It wasn't until midnight that the news reports could no longer contain the story that a shooting had occurred at LaGrange Academy and several students had been killed. The story was woefully thin on details, saying only that a mentally disturbed student had brought her father's gun to school and begun randomly shooting people for unknown reasons. Sheriff Markham addressed the press briefly but couldn't maintain his composure when pressed for details.

Deacon could tell the man was a wreck. He'd just been forced to shoot and kill a child he knew personally, and it was obviously eating him alive. However big a prick he considered Markham to be, Deacon had only the greatest sympathy for him as a fellow officer and silently sent him prayers.

As the shooting victims were identified, their yearbook photos were displayed in three rows. Tanner couldn't bear to watch. Elli teared up as the faces floated above their birthdates. She and Tanner had questioned every one of them about Kevin Dockweiler the day after he was killed, and it had made them targets.

"Those are all the kids we interviewed at the school," Elli whispered to Deacon.

"That means this wasn't a random attack. Someone is cleaning up their tracks," Deacon told her quietly.

"How?" Elli whispered. "I saw that girl mentally break down in front of me. There is no way she would just suddenly turn into a highly trained killer."

"Not unless she had help," Deacon told her.

As the news droned on with interviews from students and teachers who miraculously survived the shooting, a call came up from dispatch. Agnes listed to it carefully and then called out, "Deke, we just got a call from the sheriff's office in Marietta. They found another body."

2

The sun hadn't risen yet and the buildings lay deceptively bathed in predawn light before the team was fully deployed. The abandoned processing plant sat ghost-like under the fog still clinging to the ground outside. Within the mist, a gathering of red and blue lights flashed wildly. The local sheriff set up a perimeter half a mile out to keep the site secure while federal officers descended on the main plant with their weapons drawn. Joyce found the security guard who made the call. He was currently doubled over and shaking, unable to contain his breakfast. The suspect had been leaving the scene when the call was made, so the guard was able to provide a vehicle description: a truck painted black with no plates. Joyce would have liked him to show the team exactly where he'd seen the body, but in his present condition there was no way they would get him to go back into the plant. The best he could manage was to show them where to go on a set of plans.

Deacon and Chen were standing by with an entire squad of officers. Looking around at the dim lights surrounding the building, Agnes asked, "If this place is abandoned, why does it have power and a security guard?"

As Joyce arrived with the floor plan, she said, "The plant was recently sold. The new owners wanted to chase away any trespassers to avoid liability. A patrol company swings by twice a night." She nodded over her shoulder. "The guard's out of commission, but he says we need to follow the south entrance downstairs to the smelting pots, third level. All the other ways down are rusted and unsafe. This is the only clear way."

Deacon reviewed the floor plan on the pad and then sent his officers out in pairs to secure all the known entrances and exits on each level. He took the lead, followed by Bachman and Chen, each one sporting a large flashlight. Tanner stayed close to Elli, who refused to stay outside. The facility was crisscrossed with iron catwalks that were covered in rust. They groaned under the weight of every step but held fast. Flakes of rust rained down in the air, and everything smelled old and neglected. After clearing the first level, Deacon proceeded down to the second floor and left two officers on standby at the top of the stairs. The second level was even gloomier than the first and lined with makeshift offices overlooking the open floor below. As they descended to the lower level, they could make out a massive conveyer belt with several enormous buckets suspended overhead. When the plant was in full operation, the buckets would swing out and pour molten metal into forms along the belt, bringing the facility to a sweltering and impossibly hot condition. Now it was cold and dead but no less unsettling.

Walking out onto the ground level, the first thing they noticed was a change in the way the air smelled. A barn-like odor permeated the stale, metallic air and grew stronger as they moved deeper along the smelting floor. To the far right, a pipeline allowed burning metals to flow from the raging furnaces and into the large buckets overhead. At evenly spaced intervals, holding tanks were positioned so that the metals could be stirred and tended before being piped in the forms. All the doors were closed, but the pipeline grew progressively warmer. As they rounded a corner, the temperature in the air began to change.

The barn-like odor grew more intense and became nearly unbearable by the time they reached an open holding tank. On the floor at their feet, a trail of manure ran up to the open door. Stepping carefully around it, the three detectives stood staring at the open hatchway. All had completely forgotten the cloying odor as they stared at the body propped within the tank. The bottom of the tank had been filled with several feet of shit, and a man was suspended in it up to his knees. He was naked except for a cloth wrapped around his groin, and his arms had been tied with ropes to two very large hooks drilled into the metal. Along his torso, the faint red bruising of a cross was forming.

Unlike the serene countenance of Ellory Bainbridge or the slack face of Kevin Dockweiler, this man's face was a road map of agony. His head lolled on his shoulders and his mouth lay open wide beneath distended eyeballs. Tendrils of smoke flowed out of his mouth, bringing with them a stomach-churning smell of cooking meat, and there were trails of a silvery substance running down his chin and onto his chest.

Joyce fought to keep her stomach down by covering her mouth with her free hand. Chen was breathing rapidly through her mouth but keeping her cool. Deacon turned away and walked to the far wall. He pressed the intercom in his ear and called to Huntsville. Jeremy Burke was connected within seconds.

"Burke, I need you and Digger here now. Got another body for you. It's bad this time."

"We're five minutes out. Can you upload to the van?"

Deacon called over his shoulder, "Chen, send Burke an image of the crime scene, please." Luckily Agnes had already shifted into forensic mode in an effort to disconnect from the horror of what she saw. She had a panoramic shot on its way within seconds. As Burke drove, Digger fussed over his instruments and watched as the pictures filled the screens in the vehicle. He gasped as the body resolved and the face came into view.

Burke turned off the siren but kept the emergency lights on as they reached the turnoff. He was having trouble keeping a steady hand on the wheel after his accident, but Digger was so engrossed in the video he barely noticed. Burke was a bit of a wild driver at the best of times, so getting knocked around occasionally was something he was used to. He set the image into a repeating loop and called Chen.

"Agnes, it's Digger. I need you to examine the body for something for me."

Chen couldn't believe the request coming over her earpiece. "The victim's not going anywhere, Digger. Are you sure it can't wait until you get here?"

"I need you to check something before it stops," he told her. "Get a close-up of the victim's face. He's got some sort of smoke coming out of his mouth."

Chen moved in closer, holding the pad out in front of her with one hand and her nose and mouth closed with the other. There was indeed smoke coming from the victim's mouth, and the smell of his insides cooking made her stomach lurch. "How's that, Digger?" she snorted as she finished her sweep and retreated.

Digger looked closely at the screen and said, "That's perfect. Can you see what's causing it?"

"There's some sort of liquid in his mouth. It's starting to cool but must have been really hot when he swallowed it. It smells as if he's being cooked from the inside."

Digger grinned. If his suspicions were correct, the substance would be molten lead and the victim a member of the clergy.

3

Buck Meisner watched from atop an operations bank as the officers made their way down into the plant. He'd been camped outside for nearly two days waiting for something to happen. Unfortunately, he'd chosen Jim Beam as his personal assistant and passed out just before sundown. He'd been out cold under the loading platform when the black truck arrived and was rudely awakened when a spray of gravel hit his face as it left. The security guard had given chase on foot, as much as his extensive gut and knock-knees would allow, but soon doubled over gasping for air as he called dispatch. The guard was armed, so Buck stayed put. If he was going to die, his epitaph sure as hell wasn't going to be "shot by a startled, overweight security guard."

The guard drew his weapon and flashlight and went into the plant. Buck quickly rolled everything but his camera into his sleeping bag and shoved it further beneath the platform. He then crawled out and stood listening by the door, stretching his cramped muscles. About ten minutes later, he heard a high-pitched squeal and the protests of the rusty staircase as the guard scrambled toward the entrance. He dove back under the platform just as the guard came wheezing through the front door, white as a sheet. He stumbled about five feet away from where Buck lay and puked up his substantial dinner.

The stench of it was horrendous, and Buck struggled to clamp his jacket over his mouth and nose. The salt pork in the guard's Brunswick stew smelled just as bad coming up as it had going down. Eventually the guard stopped heaving and called dispatch to report a body and call the police. The minute Buck heard "body," his mind tore through his hangover and he went into action. His source had been dead-on, as promised. This would be the scoop of the century, and his days of begging for editorial scraps would be over. He checked his gear, threw dirt over it to make sure it wouldn't be seen, and snuck into the plant. The stairs complained as he descended, so he climbed over the railings to avoid them wherever he could. The guard had run out to the main road to wait for the sheriff, well out of earshot, but there was still the unlikely possibility that the intruder hadn't been alone.

He made it to the catwalk over the third level down when he heard the wailing of sirens approach. He jumped down onto a control unit tall enough to conceal him but with a clean view of the machinery below and waited. Lying in the shadows with his camera ready, he watched the officers deploy around him. He recognized the tall, black lieutenant from the church parking lot where the Dockweiler boy had been killed. He looked mean enough to beat the shit out of anyone messing with his crime scene, so Buck stayed put.

The cops discovered the tank where the body was suspended. They were too far away for him to see personally, but their shock and disgust were crystal clear through his zoom lens. He snapped away quietly, taking every opportunity to photograph the body. *This shit is pure Pulitzer,* he thought as he filled the memory card with images. He was so involved in his impending notoriety that he crawled forward to get a better angle. He didn't notice the tactical officer quietly drop down behind him until he felt the cold muzzle of a rifle at his neck.

"Drop the vid and go facedown, or I splatter your brains here and now," the officer told him.

"No problem," Buck replied, dropping the camera and spreading his hands flat on the metal unit beneath him. "I'm with the press. My ID's in my back-left pocket," he stammered as the nose of the barrel pushed into his ear. He'd never been so happy to have an empty bladder as when the cop yelled out, "Lieutenant, we have an intruder." Buck looked down to see MacNair striding toward him with a stunning brunette at his side.

The cop threw down his ID and said, "Isn't this that journalist everyone's looking for? I hear the E-Rep's put a bounty on his hide big enough to feed southern Kentucky."

Buck swallowed deeply as Deacon read his ID and said, "Send him down."

Buck breathed a sigh of relief. The big guy wanted to talk to him, and that was fine with Buck. It beat a bullet in the eardrum. But when he pushed himself up, the cop gave him a solid kick with a steel-toed army boot that sent him rolling off the operations bank and onto the concrete floor below. He howled as his shoulder hit the pavement. The cop that kicked him hopped down off the equipment and landed squarely next to him with a smug smile. Buck rubbed his shoulder and launched into his all-purpose, canned speech on police brutality, demanding to see his lawyer. No one was impressed.

After he'd run out of steam, Deacon asked, "Are you finished?" The question was purely rhetorical as he gave Buck no time to respond. "Because I doubt you'll be needing a lawyer. You just might need a coroner though, which, as luck would have it, should be here any minute."

"You can't kill me! I'm a reporter. Freedom of the press!"

"Until HQ confirms your credentials, you're a suspect found near a murder victim at an active crime scene, intentionally hiding in the shadows and stalking my team. That makes you an imminent threat, so we would be well within our rights to shoot your ass."

Buck looked around as more officers joined the circle, which was now composed of both federal and state police. "You fellas aren't going let him get away with this, are you?" he implored. His pleas were met with hostile silence.

Deacon let him sweat for a minute and then said, "You beginning to get the picture, Mr. Meisner?" Buck knew he was hanging from a very narrow ledge and nodded. "Good. Now you and I are going to have a very in-depth discussion about how you knew about this place before we did. You're going to tell me everything you know because, if you don't, I will leave you in the custody of these fine Republic deputies who will be more than happy to interrogate you under territorial laws as an accessory to murder."

Buck's face went white. Thanks to a bumper crop of police corruption stories he'd written, he was already censored in E-Rep territory. If these good old boys got hold of him, they'd make sure he ended up as gator shit somewhere along the Mississippi. Worst case scenario, he'd undergo reconditioning in an Ecumenical retreat in the Okefenokee. Deacon extended his hand toward an exit, wrinkling his nose at the man as he walked by. The guy was sweating whiskey, and his red-rimmed eyes told Deacon he'd been staked out here for a while. Turning to the lead deputy he said, "I need your boys to comb every inch of this place. If this ass-clown can get in here, so can someone else. And look sharp because the killer could still be here." To Joyce, he said, "Make sure our tac team covers these boys, and stay in direct contact."

4

Outside of the plant, Meisner paced like a caged tiger. The crime scene was being documented and discussed by the team of police in the building behind them. The method of execution was being painstakingly documented inside, and he was missing all of it. He tried to convince Deacon to conduct the interview inside where it was warm so he could still pick up information, but the old detective just dragged him further away into the cold night air. Rather than be incarcerated as an accessory to multiple murders, Buck detailed everything he could about the mysterious source as Deacon listened, not that there was much to tell. His source's anonymity was airtight even from him.

"So, you get this anonymous call from a person claiming to have unreleased details about these killings, and you agree to meet with him alone in a very dark, abandoned boathouse?" Deacon asked.

"You know how the game is played, man. People who don't have authority to speak on the record are paranoid."

"Awfully risky move for you, not telling anyone where you're going. Place like that, far from emergency services. Your source could be our killer, and you could have ended up his next victim."

Meisner puffed up a bit and said, "I covered the war from behind both sides of the enemy lines, pal. Ever been stuck in a Georgia swamp? It would scare the shit out of the legendary Viet Cong. Some crumbling boathouse on a backwater lagoon is child's play." He paused and then added, "Besides, I'm not his type. My sins and their repercussions are well documented."

Deacon could see that Meisner's self-proclaimed courage as a war correspondent was his weak spot. The man clung to his glory days like an Alabama tick. But he was also a little scared of his mysterious contact. "You say it was a man who met you?"

"His voice was scrambled like it was on the call. He spoke to me through a speaker he set up in the middle of the floor. From the feedback, I'd say he was using a wireless microphone tied to a voice scrambler to talk to me. But I'd still bet prewar money it was a man."

"And what did this man tell you?"

Meisner leaned back onto the building and lit up a cigarette. He took a long drag and said, "Mainly that you're missing the point of all this, Lieutenant."

Deacon looked at him, irritated. "And what exactly is the point?"

"That the benevolent justice system of the territory is anything but. Oh, it may look all warm and fuzzy on the outside, and the people will tell you they're God-fearing and happy as clams. But on the inside, where no one can see, that's where the real barbarism lies."

Deacon crossed his arms and leaned back on a jointed pipe. "Biblical laws are pretty absolute. Jews didn't fuck around back then when it came to keeping the peace."

Meisner huffed. "They weren't interested in keeping the peace back then any more than the leadership is now. They're interested in obedience, a populace that does what it's told with no dissension. Those old rites of execution were written thousands of years ago to scare the unruly hordes into submission. When you make the punishment far worse than the crime itself, criminals tend to think twice about doing whatever it is they're thinking about. There was no such thing as petty crime back then. You were damned sure going to lose a body part or two if they didn't kill you outright. Generally speaking, it's a completely effective deterrent. Watching someone be publicly tortured and dismembered has the added benefit of scaring the shit out of anyone who might consider doing something criminal in the future. The trouble with that kind of justice system is that it isn't justice; it's terrorism."

"Your contention is that E-Rep is terrorizing its citizens into obedience?"

"Fear thy God, Lieutenant. And if he ain't around, fear us. Those killings were executions already sanctioned by the Ecclesiastical Republic. Your victims would have died anyway after penance was administered. Your executioner just went old-school, like the good book says."

"E-Rep is disavowing any connection to these killings. It doesn't butcher its criminals according to Scripture—you know this. They're executed peacefully by lethal injection," Deacon said, robotically repeating the company line toed by all law enforcement when speaking to the press. "Lesser infractions are committed to rehabilitation and reconditioning, then returned to society as productive citizens."

"That's what the press releases all say. I know, pal, I helped write them back in the day. And with an election coming up in a month, you can bet the E-Republic is pumping that bullshit through every news pipe and public channel it can."

Meisner could see Deacon was losing patience. "I interviewed one of their so-called rehabbed citizens for the network a couple of years ago. Poor slob fell asleep driving home from a bar. Took out a kid and his grandmother without even knowing it. They tested his blood alcohol at the scene, so they knew he wasn't legally drunk, and the bar confirmed he only had one beer. He'd been working all day and was just dead tired. It was an accident, plain and simple, and the driver was all tore up over it. The unauthorized taking of a life is an automatic death sentence down here, but since he was genuinely remorseful and legally sober, they sentenced him to R&R as atonement. I first met him outside the courthouse awaiting his trial. Aside from being an emotional wreck, the guy was genuinely sorry and horrified by what he'd done. A real straight-up, good guy." Meisner took a long drag from his cigarette and continued. "I caught up with him after the trial, about four days after his release from rehab. Had his certificate of good standing on the wall and had been deemed a saved citizen. I barely recognized him. This guy was six feet, two ten easy. Solid as a rock. But he was at least fifty pounds lighter and sat there twitching like he had a case of St. Vitus's Dance. Every time he answered a question, he'd look over into an empty corner like he was being watched. Kept whispering Scripture under his breath and tugging a rosary around his fists so tight his hands were white. A month later he stepped off the curb into the path of an oncoming truck. The coroner ruled his death an accident despite several witness statements that he deliberately stepped in front of that vehicle."

Deacon stared into Meisner's eyes, hoping against hope. "You think something went wrong during his rehab?"

"Quite the contrary; it was a complete success. It just has a rather unfortunate and fatal side effect." He pulled a data pad from his pocket and tossed it to Deacon. "See for yourself."

Deacon scanned the list of names, dates of sentencing along with their offenses, causes of and dates of subsequent death. He'd seen it before, but because of the restrictions on access to sentencing records, he hadn't been able to correlate the sentencing dates. His worst fears were realized when he saw his son's name.

"The fact is that every person who has ever been given R&R as penance has either died or is going to die, some sooner rather than later but all of them for sure, and no one will even notice."

"What do you mean sooner rather than later?" Deacon asked him.

"Some people take longer to implode than others, but they all ultimately pay the same price. There's a reason penance is performed in secret, away from the prying eyes of witnesses, and it isn't out of respect for the condemned or because faith is a private matter, either." Meisner leaned in and quietly said, "There are worse things in heaven and earth than are dreamt of in your philosophy, Lieutenant."

Deacon felt a chill run down his back. *Oh God, Neville,* he thought.

"Why haven't you told the story then?" Deacon asked. "What you have is circumstantial, but it's enough to launch a federal investigation for human rights violations. Why haven't you exposed the truth about all this?"

"Because printing it would be considered heresy under the law. Even if I applied for asylum in federal or Constitutional territory, they'd be forced by treaty to extradite me to face trial, with or without proof. No matter how hard the Feds fought for me or delayed extradition, it would still happen. And you and I both know how that trial would end."

Deacon's thoughts drifted back to Neville, and he absently said, "The Council acts as the hand of God to bring his justice to the world."

Meisner looked at him. "Lieutenant, do you really think an omniscient deity who could throw down thunderbolts to incinerate his enemies, rain down fire and brimstone to destroy a city, and flood the entire surface of the world to eradicate sin needs us to exact justice in his name? Those men are not delivering God's justice, Lieutenant, they're torturing the faithful into obedience." He stared into Deacon's stunned face and said, "You're chasing one man who's executing people already condemned to die at the hands of a group of men who kill with impunity and without remorse. What you need to ask yourself is, whose is the greater sin?"

5

The mass shooting at the high school finally broke wide, keeping the news feeds fully engaged. Thanks to a gag order instituted by the Justice

Ministry, not one station mentioned the grisly murder of a priest. The promise of an exclusive to Buck Meisner ensured his temporary cooperation and silence. Markham and his deputies had their hands full with the Davis case and gave Deacon full control of the murder scene. The lack of attention was a much-needed relief, but the team knew it wouldn't last. Eventually, word would circulate about the murder and the press would descend like hungry wolves. But that wouldn't happen until they'd peeled every last strip of meat from the bones of the LaGrange massacre.

Burke worked as quickly as possible gathering evidence from the crime scene and, for once, didn't object to having help. Digger had the body carefully extracted and most of the tank deconstructed and taken back to the lab. He worked feverishly through the night as the team labored through the evidence upstairs.

"You were right, Digger, the man was a member of the clergy," Joyce said into the mic. From his console in the morgue, the portly coroner smiled with satisfaction. "Austin Goodwin, current pastor of St. Anthony's church, recently relocated to Atlanta after a couple of decades serving the good people of "Mt. Olivet" in Talladega. Married with two children, family lives in Bremen."

"That's not all," Meisner added, walking into the pit. "Here," he said, tossing a wrapped package to Deacon. "I found this in my mailbox this morning. No return address, but I think we both know who sent it."

"One of your adoring fans?" Deacon said as he opened the plastic outer bag.

"I don't give anyone my home address. Not even the rags I freelance for know where I live. It's safer that way."

"I take it there are also no security or surveillance cams nearby for anyone to tap into," Deacon remarked.

"As I said, it's safer that way."

"Did you touch it at all?" Deacon asked.

"Nope. Picked it up with a pair of pliers and dumped it in the plastic bag. Came straight over here."

"Deacon handed the package off to Burke, who'd already gloved up. He pulled out a data pad and handed all the containers to Corbett, who immediately began scanning them for any trace evidence. It was coded with the Ecumenical Seal and certified by the current Director of Archives, Monseigneur Martin Eddings.

"This pad's legit," Burke announced. "It even has an Ecumenical Seal laser-etched into it, and the data's heavily encrypted."

"How long will it take you to crack it?" Deacon asked.

"Give me a few minutes," Burke said with a smile. Fifteen minutes later, an uncharacteristic "FUCK!" echoed across the pit.

"Having trouble, Burke?"

Burke looked up at Deacon, feeling more rage than embarrassment. "It's got some serious military-grade encryption, boss. Whatever's on here, they didn't want anyone accessing it without direct authorization. This could take days."

"Or you could just use the decryption phrase that came with the pad," Corbett suggested. Everyone turned to stare at him, and he ran the casing across a microscope. Tuning the lens to the highest resolution possible, he pulled up a series of characters finely etched into the frame:

"יְהַב חָכְמְתָא לְחַכִּימִין וּמַנְדְּעָא לְיָדְעֵי בִינָה"

Burke smirked and said, "Nice try, Corbett. The darned things are made in Israel. That's probably just the manufacturer's name in Hebrew."

"No it's not," Joyce interjected. "I grew up reading Hebrew. This is close, but some of the letters don't make sense."

"It's Aramaic, actually," Corbett told them. "It says: 'Who gives wisdom to wise men and knowledge to those who know understanding.' It's a passage from Daniel 2:21." Deacon stared at him evenly. He swallowed but couldn't seem to find his voice, so he commandeered Burke's console and keyed the sequence up in Aramaic. Within seconds, the Penance List for the Ecumenical Council with the names and punishments of all the condemned for the past six months filled the screens. Deacon raised an eyebrow at Corbett. "It . . . it's like you always tell us, boss. You have to think like your

273

enemy to defeat him. If this guy is totally into old-school biblical retribution, why wouldn't he go old-school on the passcode?"

Deacon smiled broadly and nodded to where Corbett sat trembling. "Outstanding job, Corbett." He then turned to Burke, who sat chewing on his lower lip and looking wounded. "Nice to know someone's been paying attention around here."

"Is Austin Goodwin on that list?" Joyce asked over his shoulder. Corbett inhaled her sweet perfume and scanned the list.

"He sure is. He was reassigned a month ago but was scheduled for a level five penance starting next week and lasting a month."

Elli looked to where Deacon sat. "What the hell could he have done to deserve such a horrible death?"

Deacon had a pretty good idea. In the old days, church officials used to rotate their own through parishes to avoid discovery for child molestation and sexual assault. Despite the decades of outcry against such cover-ups, it was still rare for a member of the clergy to be remanded to custody. Such things were considered extreme crimes in the territory today, but the new church still looked after its own image.

"Joyce, pull up the dates of his service at Mt. Olivet and cross-reference them with any hospital admissions for children under the age of fifteen." She had the list compiled within a minute, and it was extensive.

"If you're thinking child molester, you're casting a wide net," Joyce told him. "Burning was only used for a pretty specific subset of crimes. You need to tighten the parameters."

"How so?" Deacon asked her.

"From what I remember, burning was reserved for those who committed adultery with the daughter of a priest or for instances of incest. At least, that's how it was in the Old Testament."

"The new one wasn't quite so specific," Elli offered. "But those crimes would definitely qualify. And Goodwin had a daughter."

Deacon thought for a moment. "We need to find out if it was in fact his daughter or the daughter of some other clergyman in the area. You two dig around and see if you can find anything tying our victim to molestation or incest." He looked toward the deputy. "Tanner? Tanner?"

Tanner had been absently watching the news reports on Mona. "Does Mona's name appear anywhere on that list?" he asked quietly.

Corbett read through the names and said, "Yes, she's here but not as part of a criminal proceeding. She's listed as a voluntary commitment and was assigned a level four penance."

"That means any crime given rehabilitation at a level four or below isn't a death sentence," Elli said.

"That's helps us whittle the list down a bit, but it's still pretty long," Joyce told them.

"I have a cousin who's a Bama state trooper, and Olivet's in his jurisdiction," Tanner said. "He might know something about Goodwin."

"That's great, but don't tell him why we need to know. Just tell him you're there on E-Rep business that's highly confidential. In the meantime, let's dig up everything we can on Goodwin and his daughter."

"Can I talk to you for a second?" Meisner whispered to Deacon while Joyce assigned the parishes to the team to investigate. Deacon followed him to an unoccupied corner, where he pulled another package out of his coat. "This was also attached to the package, but it was specifically marked for your eyes only."

Deacon took the plastic case carefully. It contained what appeared to be an unmarked video disk. He opened the confidential file and removed the disk, which had a note attached beneath it. The author left it unsigned, but the message was written in tidy script by a hand that trembled slightly.

"Wirz isn't telling you everything"

Deacon shot Meisner a questioning look, but the journalist simply said, "I don't know what's on it. I never looked. But I get the feeling you might want to find some place private to watch it."

Deacon examined the strange disk. Its companion bore the seal of the Ecumenical Council along with a printed warning about the contents being classified at the highest levels. This disk had no such warnings or declarations.

Laser-printed along its edge was an inscription that read "PENANCE #126455-8987." His hand started to tremble as he recognized the number. He'd written it over and over again on every E-Council correspondence he'd written over the last few years. It was Neville's sentencing number.

6

The Penance List contained the names of those that had been sanctioned by the church within the last six months, along with the names of the primary witnesses in each case. Each person's sins and the biblical passages violated were listed next to the criminal codes. The list was ordered by severity, with the most heinous convictions at the top. No one was surprised to see poor Ellory Bainbridge there. Adultery was akin to murder in the eyes of the new church. Even less surprising was the startling percentage of female names present. And in almost every case where the convicted was male, a female was named as a co-defendant. Very few male names appeared unaccompanied. In each case, the level of penance assigned corresponded to the severity of the crime itself, with the highest numbers given to the most severe cases. Tanner was able to confirm that a level seven penance was the highest punishment. It had been given to Janine Turnbull, her fiancé, and Ellory Bainbridge. The method of delivery for such penance was not detailed in any other way.

Joyce shook her head as she read the list, knowing that they would all become members of a statistical horror that no one would notice. "I wonder how many of them will end up dead in the next ninety days," she remarked.

Elli cringed at the thought of more unexplained deaths being coldly cataloged. "Agnes, can you run a comparison of this list against the death certificates issued within the territory?"

Agnes ran the comparison in less than a minute. The four oldest names on the list belonged to three women and one man that had died. Two of the women died due to aneurisms; the third had a heart attack. The man had stepped out into traffic and been hit by a truck. They'd all died three months after serving penance.

Elli felt her heart sink but kept reading. A third of the way through the list she said, "I know some of these people."

"Do you know them well enough to help us sort out their sentences?" Deacon asked.

"I suppose," she muttered. Elli didn't like the idea of airing the dirty laundry of her friends and acquaintances, much less spreading innuendo and rumor, but Deacon reassured her that the information would be kept confidential and not tracked back to her in any way. "This name," she said, touching the screen. It immediately linked to the territorial registry and displayed the current stats for the person, along with a photograph. "She's a nurse in the children's ward at my hospital, works with the new admissions. Her daughter recently went missing. She told everyone the girl eloped with some man the family disapproved of, but there were rumors about the girl's sexuality. Scuttlebutt has it that she jumped the gender train north."

An image of battered old Pastor Cooper sweeping broken glass from his altar popped into Deacon's head. Everyone knew the stories about the Underground Railroad that had been resurrected during the war. The Ecclesiastical government deemed it a criminal organization whose sole purpose was to aid and abet criminals and deviants escaping God's justice. The more rabid believers within the territory often joined volunteer enforcement units to help bring it down and curry favor within the leadership.

"They must have suspected the mother of helping her daughter flee prosecution," Joyce told them. "They probably have her on the list for pickup and interrogation before sentencing."

"That's not exactly a crime worthy of fatal biblical punishment, especially without the daughter's conviction. I think it's safe to say this woman's not a potential victim of ours."

"At least we know we're on the right track," Joyce told him as she scrolled down the columns. "Bainbridge and Dockweiler are on the list along with Goodwin, so for now, our theory holds."

"Agreed, but this list is stolen evidence, which means we can't use it to prosecute. We need to find a connection outside of this list." Deacon looked up and then rubbed his eyes. They'd scoured Meisner's apartment complex all morning for any possible trace of his mysterious benefactor and come up empty. Daylight was now fading, and he was exhausted. "It's late. Let's call it a night, and we'll pick this up first thing bright and early."

The gathering broke up, and Joyce watched her partner shuffle off down the hall. There was another name that she'd recognized on the list but dared not mention it. She was sure it was the first one that Deacon had searched for.

7

Elli took a gulp from the tumbler of ice and bourbon and winced. It was that nasty apple-flavored variety that had reappeared recently and tasted even worse than the standard variety her father favored. But it did the trick. She took another gulp, not caring that the taste reminded her of the rotten apple she'd bitten into as a teenager. Warmth flooded her system, pushing back at the shock that had begun to manifest. The alcohol fumes burned away the stench of stewing organs from her memory, but it did nothing to purge the image of the man in the vat with the smoke pouring from his mouth, a crucifix dangling from his neck. She took one more gulp shook her head. She needed to forget. She needed to focus on something else, anything to drive it from her mind.

She heard the refrigerator door shut and the hiss of escaping gas from a bottle opening. Tanner was pouring himself a beer. She watched him in the dim kitchen light, looking more frayed than usual. The crime scene had disturbed him but not as deeply as poor Mona's death. Yet through it all he maintained his calm resolve. He had followed Deacon's every instruction to the letter and still found the strength and chivalry to drive Elli home when she couldn't do it herself. Now he puttered around her house locking doors and windows, turning on lights and adjusting the temperature, all to make her feel comfortable and safe. His uniform was wrinkled and stained and his short hair a little disheveled, but he remained devastatingly handsome and somehow innocent-looking.

She closed her eyes and sucked down one of the larger ice cubes left in her glass, trying to calm the bourbon fire in her belly. But it wasn't the bourbon making her feel this way—it was Kyle Tanner. *You're being ridiculous,* she chided herself, but the feeling only intensified. *It's just a perfectly normal reaction to a traumatic event,* she reasoned. *You've experienced a terrible shock. He's here creating a safe environment and looking after you, so you're aroused by the posttraumatic safety he's providing. That's all it is, absolutely normal.* She ran through the psychological papers she'd read on posttraumatic sex and did everything she could to convince herself that her reaction was logical.

Then Kyle sat down next to her on the couch. Their eyes didn't meet; he didn't even acknowledge her. He just sat there peeling the label off the neck of his beer bottle, staring into the head as it dissipated, looking lost and alone. "I've never seen anything like that before," he said quietly. "Things like that aren't supposed to happen here."

Elli's body shuddered slightly at his vulnerability, making her feel even more ridiculous than she already did. The boy was ten years younger than she and as far removed from her socially as a person could get. "It shouldn't be happening anywhere, Kyle, to anyone," she told him. "But he must have been guilty. Otherwise, he wouldn't have been convicted."

"My buddy over in Olivet said there were rumors about Goodwin's daughter. The girl started to miss a lot of school due to an unknown illness once she hit junior high. She stopped hanging around with her friends and shut down socially. Her parents told the school counselors that the depression was a result of her illness, so no one really questioned it. Everyone just respected the family's privacy."

"Agnes said he'd been transferred from his home parish last month and was scheduled for reconditioning, whatever that means."

Kyle took a long swig of beer. "It means a complaint came through official church channels, but nothing was ever proven. Without a confession, a witness, or a victim, all they had was an unsubstantiated accusation, so no prosecution took place. To save face, he agreed to undergo reconditioning to avoid prosecution."

Elli reached for the bottle of bourbon and poured herself a little more of the vile liquid. "If that's what he did, someone must not have wanted him to get away with it." She took a sip. "I'm not so sure I disagree with him."

Kyle turned to see her staring into her glass, the amber liquid swirling around the last glob of unmelted ice. He reached out and laid his hand on her arm. "Elli, you can't possibly believe this is justice. This isn't what we're about. This isn't God's way."

"Isn't it?" she asked as her eyes grew glassy. "Since this whole investigation started, I've seen and learned things about us that I never imagined were happening, and I'm not so sure this isn't justice. If Goodwin is guilty, doesn't he deserve this? Don't any of us deserve this?"

Kyle took the glass from her and grasped her hands gently, trying to calm her. She went on. "I saved a boy's life after his parents told me to let him die. That it was his time to go because God expected it. But justice wasn't served until he later hung himself, and I was punished for denying God that death. I committed an act of defiance, and I could be next on his list."

He reached up and brushed a tear from her face. "You committed an act of compassion," he whispered to her. "And I can't imagine God would punish you for saving one of his children. It's your calling. It's what you were born to do."

The bourbon fire flared in her gut as her mind screamed *put your lust in neutral, Doctor, you're drunk off your ass.* But she didn't care. She knew the kiss was coming even as her soul shouted out that she was an unmarried woman and committing a sin. *It's just a kiss, stuff it.* But it was more than just a kiss. It was long and lingering, wet and wonderful. Liquid napalm poured down her throat, drowning out the alcohol fire. The heat was unbearable, and Elli fell into it without restraint. She lost herself in his embrace and the all-consuming heat that melted them both together. The weight of his body over hers pulled at the obscure memory of her only two other sexual encounters. Awkward rites of passage during college in the Constitutional territory that she had never revealed to anyone but God. The hours in confession afterward, the self-imposed penance that drove her to bury herself in her studies, surging to the head of her class. It was a last-ditch effort of her learned guilt to forestall a mortal mistake.

She'd beaten her soul up relentlessly over those two instances, but neither had equaled the intense passion and ecstasy she was experiencing now. The last thought she had before losing herself to Kyle completely was, *If I'm destined to be punished eternally for my sins, I'm going to make sure I've earned it.*

Suffer My Children

1

Deacon sat in his empty office, staring at the data disk in his hands. The room was neat but barren since he spent nearly all his time either out in the field or in the pit working a case. The cleaning staff kept it tidy just in case he needed a nonthreatening place to interview someone or have an off-the-record conversation. Still, a light puff of dust floated free of his chair when he sat down. His stomach rumbled, reminding him that he'd forgotten to eat all day, but he ignored it. He was sure that whatever was in the file wouldn't be compatible with food. The data was a visual record of the treatment and rehabilitation protocols for Neville MacNair as dictated and compiled by Dr. Cyrus Canton and staff. He opened the massive file and hit play.

"Day 1: Dr. Stanton Evaluation. Patient 782094, involuntarily detained and committed by family with the blessing of the Ecumenical Council for detoxification and deterrent therapy for drug abusers and criminals. Patient has a years-long history of drug use and petty theft, which resulted in several incarcerations for lesser offenses and minimum time served. All such punishments have failed, as have Constitutional efforts at rehabilitation. Patient exhibits a severe lack of respect for authority. He is arrogant and adamant in his belief that his strength of will can overcome any treatment we administer and that we are wasting our time. Patient repeatedly challenged the medical staff to do their worst, insisting that he would prevail. The anger and defiance displayed upon intake is common among involuntary transfers; however, it is amplified by the patient's dysfunctional relationship with and animosity toward his father, a high-ranking federal law enforcement official. It is therefore recommended that this patient be enrolled in the most stringent and invasive conversion therapy program available for unrepentant addicts and repeat offenders.

"Day 5: Dr. Stanton Observation. Patient continues to exhibit symptoms of withdrawal from drug use. During stage one of withdrawal he experienced chronic nausea, sweating and diarrhea. These were prevalent during the first two days after intake but have diminished to sporadic levels.

Patient progressed to stage two of his withdrawal and began experiencing abdominal pain and muscle spasms, which continue to escalate. These continued throughout days three and four, culminating in several seizures overnight. When patient was lucid, he screamed due to the physical pain. He continued to curse his father during the most severe bouts of pain and subsequently begged his attending physicians to provide drugs to alleviate it while offering false prayers as recompense. All such pleas have been refused. The patient is currently in his most weakened state of defiance due to withdrawal. He still experiences physical pain but is too exhausted to lash out. With the information gained through observation of the patient during this purge, we have gained the information necessary to construct an effective psychological deterrent to his addictions and behavioral deformities. It is hereby recommended that level five reprogramming begin immediately."

The observations were clinical and detached, as if the person dictating them were observing a rat in a research trial. It was hard to believe that they were describing the horror and pain that a human being experienced during detox. The subsequent videos, however, brought it into full relief. There was no doubt about the depth of suffering or the amount of pain and disorientation the young man was experiencing on the cold floor of the cell. He lay there in his own vomit and waste until an attendant with a hose came in once each day and hosed him down with icy water. A band of readings flowed down the left side of the screen, indicating the temperature and humidity inside the cell. After each dousing, the temperature of the room was adjusted, and the patient's shivering grew stronger to maximize his pain.

On day 6, the treatment began, along with its firsthand visual documentation. The patient was cleaned thoroughly and dressed in hospital greens. He was wheeled into the treatment room on a gurney and strapped down onto a table with indentations that cradled his head, buttocks and feet. His ankles and arms were strapped down, and a fleece-lined collar was placed around his neck and secured to the table. He was barely conscious. The temperature in the room was raised to a comfortable level, and soon the patient began to relax and nod off for the first time in days. While he napped, the doctors adjusted the settings for the table, which was embedded with electrodes. A metal circlet was attached to his head and strapped down beneath his chin. When they were certain he was sufficiently restrained, a curved screen was lowered so that it hovered just above his face, obscuring his view of the room. The lights were lowered and a nurse stepped forward with a pneumatic injector. She pressed it to the patient's neck and activated it.

The effect was immediate. The patient was fully awake within seconds as the artificial adrenaline coursed through his veins, lighting them up like napalm. The overhead screen flickered on, and a stream of images began to flow. They were muted and showed people using drugs and smoking substances. Some hallucinated. Some slowly writhed while others staggered and fumbled their way around. The images amplified the cravings the patient had been fighting throughout his withdrawal until his mouth became dry with need and his pulse beat with the power of his addiction. He struggled to free himself from the table, even lifting his head toward the screen as if he could smell the fumes, desperate to reach for the images before him.

The doctor activated the first switch, and every electrode within the table erupted with energy. The patient's scream was blood-curdling. No agony he'd experienced during the past week came close to what he now felt. Every muscle in his body tensed. Had he not been strapped to the table, he could have snapped his spine with the ensuing convulsion. It lasted only five seconds, but to the patient it seemed to go on forever. When it stopped, he collapsed onto the table in tears as a voice crawled into his ears and asked, "Do you want the drugs?" In his pain and confusion, he answered "yes." This, too, was typical, the doctor explained in the voiceover. When treatments commenced, patients still clung to the addict's notion that more drugs would cure the pain they were feeling. Once again the electrodes fired, this time with a higher intensity. The patient screamed, and the images flowed. When it ended, he was again asked, "Do you want the drugs?" and again, the answer was yes. The scene was repeated three more times. The first time, the patient fainted, but the nurse was ready with her injector to bring him back. The third time, he flatlined. A resuscitation team came forward and stabilized him, then the treatment resumed. The fourth time was the turning point. The patient screamed in agony and when asked the question again, whimpered "no." The images slowed, and the next time the electrodes were fired, the charge was considerably less. The patient was asked a fifth time and a sixth time. Each time, the charge was weakened and the answer was "no." By the tenth firing, the charge was negligible, but the answer remained "no."

The patient fainted and was allowed to sleep for an hour. When the treatment resumed, he was asked the question, but only an insignificant charge was inflicted. This went on for hours. Whenever he hesitated, the charge would increase until the question brought about an immediate denial. The treatment ceased around midnight, and the patient was left to sleep until the next day. On day 7, the patient was again asked the question and answered no. He then began to twitch on his own, a learned response that was reinforced to make him ready for the next phase of treatment. Day 8 was a day of rest, it being a Sunday. There were no treatments, only hourly visits from attendants who brought food and water and encouraged him to read the Bible in his room. At some point during each of these hourly visits, the caregiver would casually ask, "Do you want the drugs?" and the patient would answer no and twitch reflexively.

Day 9 commenced with a therapy session with the court-appointed psychiatrist. The video continued as the detached clinician questioned the patient, who, with his drug habit now firmly in retreat and his belly full, had regained some of his former arrogance.

"So, Neville, the doctors tell me you've made great progress. You've beaten your addiction in only a week." The patient looked at him wearily and huffed. "Is that all you have to say? You've been set free. You are no longer its slave."

The patient laughed contemptuously, shook his head and said, "Am I supposed to praise God because his overseer freed me?"

"It is through His grace that you have been set free, my son," the doctor explained. "I am merely His deliverer, if you will."

"Well, halle-fucking-lujah!" the patient responded. "Maybe if you free enough of us, he'll set you free one day. Until then, I guess you just have to be content with those steak knives, eh."

The doctor leaned forward on the desk and spoke in a fatherly tone. "My boy, you have been listening to propaganda. No one is a slave in the territory. We created this paradise in praise of God and all of his children. We are here by choice."

"No, you aren't," the patient told him. "I am the one who had a choice. I chose to do drugs. It was my choice to be what I was. I knew the risks and I took them. I made myself what I was. Y'all step in line with your so-called God because you have no choice. You are what you are because He tells you what to be."

The doctor sat back, unsettled, and then explained, "We are people of faith, Neville, as is your father. Our leaders and holy council guide us in living the way the good Lord intended. We do His good works and live by His will because we know it is our salvation, indeed the salvation of all mankind."

"You do His work because you're afraid!" the patient thundered back. "You're afraid of how he'll punish you if you don't do what he commands. That is why you obey the Lord." He watched the doctor clench his jaw and then said, "You're more a slave than I ever was."

"That's not true," the doctor answered sternly, but the patient was undeterred.

"It's always been true. Since the minute you raised your hands to him, it's been the truth you won't admit. It's that way here on earth, and it'll be that way throughout eternity. You are His slave. The only thing that ever helped you forget what you really are was enslaving MY people. You treated us like animals, abused and degraded us. You set a definition of slavery so horrible that it defied belief. All so you could convince yourselves that you were something greater."

The doctor's face began to darken, but he remained silent as the patient continued. "But then my people were freed. Lincoln done freed the slaves! Suddenly you all had to face the truth of what you really are, and you just couldn't face it."

The patient sat back as he watched the doctor's knuckles turn white on the stylus he was rubbing between his thumb and forefinger.

"So here we are. Once again, I'm freed, but you still fighting a war based on a lie you tell yourself. And your God loved you so much, he gave you a new Massa. One who could feed your self-delusion. He sent you rich, white one-percenters to convince you of your righteousness, and they sent you to work in their fields until there were no fields left to plow. Then they sent you to war to take from those who opposed their tyranny, and you bled and died for them. Now they are kings of their own country but, you still turning those empty fields in the name of faith, afraid of the overseers. Afraid to defy your

Massa lest he cut you down." The patient smiled and leaned in closer. "I'm free, but you still a slave. And no matter how many niggers you kill, you'll still be one."

The stylus snapped and the doctor said, "I think that'll do for today." He signaled the orderly to remove the patient. When the room was clear, he pressed a button on the desk and dictated, "The patient retains his defiant and deviant behavior even after successful purging of his addiction. Recommending commencement of Phase Three to begin immediately."

2

Deacon stopped the video and could hear his heart beating loudly in his ears. He'd been unknowingly holding his breath and exhaled sharply. As the air flowed painfully into his lungs, angry tears ran down his cheeks. He'd seen enough junkies in his long career go through withdrawal and recovery and knew it was an ugly process. But he wasn't prepared for the electroshock reinforcement. It had obviously been successful without any visible side effects other than a minor, reflexive twitch. But this was his son, not some nameless drug addict picked up in a sweep. He closed his eyes and steadied his breathing. Nothing he'd just seen had any connection to the hallucinations and paranoia that Neville suffered during his last few days. Whatever had caused it had to be a part of the Phase Three treatment. He wasn't sure he was ready to see what had been done to his boy, didn't think he had the strength. Steeling himself, he resumed the playback.

Once again, the treatment room came into focus. The attendings with their hypo-injectors all stood around the electrified table, ready to begin. A loud commotion could be heard outside of the room as Neville was brought in. The first time he'd been in this room, he'd been barely conscious and too weak to resist. This time, he was fully aware and robust. Deacon could hear his protests muffled by a struggle through the closed doors.

"What the hell you doing? . . . You said I was cured . . . Let go of me!"

The attendings reflexively stood back as the orderlies dragged Neville into the room and strapped him down once again. It was no easy task and they took more than their share of punches before succeeding, but they were hulking men and used to such resistance. Neville struggled against his bonds, uttering a string of curses, but everyone stood silent and waited. The door opened, and the psychiatrist entered with his evaluation pad and a brand-new stylus. He approached the table and stared down at Neville with an icy smirk.

"Welcome to the final phase of your addiction purge, Neville."

Neville glared up at him and hissed, "I'm not an addict anymore. You said so yourself. What the hell are doing to me?"

"Enlightening you, my boy," the psychiatrist responded. "Addictions such as yours are fed by weaknesses in one's character. Weaknesses that exist due to a lack of faith. As long as these defects exist, we cannot guarantee that you will not relapse into destructive behavior, and we can't have that. We take our responsibility to our citizens very seriously." He signaled to the nurse beside him, and she handed him a hypo-injector.

"What is that shit?" Neville demanded.

"Faith, my boy," the psychiatrist told him. "Within this vial is the breath of God. You will once again hear the voice to which you have become deaf. You will see his angels and know they surround you every moment to help you stand against temptation. You will hear His word, feel his embrace, and see his glory every day of your life from this moment on."

Neville struggled, gurgling "no . . . no . . . no" as a massive orderly clamped down on his head and wrenched it sideways. The injector struck, and instantly the breath of God surged through his bloodstream, lighting every nerve it touched on fire. As he tensed and writhed, the curved screen dropped once again and blurred, frantic images flowed across it. The psychiatrist then closed his eyes, spread his arms wide and began to speak.

"And He summoned the crowd with His disciples, and said to them, 'If anyone wishes to come after Me, he must deny himself, and take up his cross and follow Me.' For even the Son of Man did not come to be served, but to serve, and to give His life a ransom for many."

The voice droned on, delivering scriptures on sacrifice, redemption, and damnation while the breath of God burned through Neville's body, causing him to shudder and weep continuously beneath an onslaught of avenging angels and burning bodies of the unrepentant. Specific sounds and images began to repeat over and over and the voices began to whisper, but all Deacon could hear was his son's trembling voice calling, "Daddy . . . I'm sorry . . . help me . . . save me."

Deacon dropped his head on the desk, choking back his sobs. He'd committed his son to save him from an inevitable overdose only to deliver him into the hands of a worse fate. This was why Neville had not been able to forgive him. He had chosen to accept the assurances of the Council despite his own doubts about their motives, and it had destroyed his only child.

He wept uncontrollably, all the grief he'd refused to feel for four years bearing down on him with the force of a hurricane. A distant chirping sound struggled to break through the torrent, but grief kept its grip. It wasn't until his sobs turned into dry heaves and his tears were spent that he realized he could still hear the annoying chirp. He reached into his pocket, pulled out the blinking comm line and slipped it over his ear.

"MacNair," he responded in a low, shaky voice.

A peculiar buzz came over the line, which morphed into a voice barely recognizable as human. "The Lord is my shepherd; I shall not want," it said.

Deacon's chest turned to ice. "Who the hell is this?" he whispered coldly.

"He maketh me lie down in green pastures. He leadeth me beside still waters. He restoreth my soul," the eerie voice droned.

"You have no soul, you maniac," Deacon spat into the line. "You're not doing it to expose that injustice. You're just a cold-blooded killer doing the Council's dirty work."

The voice curdled and bubbled. "He leadeth me in paths of righteousness for his name's sake. Even though I walk through the valley of the shadow of death, I will fear no evil."

"You better fear me, you son of a bitch," Deacon snarled.

The voice hesitated but then said, "I will fear no evil, for thou are with me, Lieutenant." Deacon sat holding his breath, waiting. A sigh crept over the comm line and the voice continued. "You think me monster, but you've seen the true face of evil. You knew it the minute you played back those sessions."

Deacon bolted from the chair, desperately looking around the room. His hand crept to his weapon. He knew he was alone but still felt eyes peering at him from far away, slithering along some remote, electronic tether, examining every crack in his soul.

"Your son was not innocent. None of them were. They brought their sins to the house of the Lord because the Father of mercies and God of all comfort comforts us in all our affliction. Yet they were not comforted. They were tortured in His name by a man of God who fancies himself a god and seeks to remake the world in his own image."

"Wirz . . ." Deacon muttered coldly.

"O star of the morning, son of the dawn! You who have weakened the nations! You who have declared, 'I will ascend to heaven above the heights of the clouds; I will make myself like the Most High.'"

"He instituted the R&R Protocols and started brainwashing people. But why?" Deacon asked.

"My name is Legion, for we are many," it answered.

"Foot soldiers," Deacon told the voice. "He needs foot soldiers to carry out his plans."

"Very good, Lieutenant. My faith in you was not misplaced."

Deacon tapped his finger on the desk as his mind rapidly put together the pieces. He took a deep breath and then muttered, "'For whatever is born of God overcomes the world; and this is the victory that has overcome the world—our faith.' He doesn't want to take over the territory; he wants to take over the Cadre."

"Why rule one kingdom when you can rule them all?" the voice gurgled. "What do you know of the brotherhood?"

"I know you're one of them," Deacon told him.

"Do you now?" the voice asked.

"You think helping me resolve my son's death will make me sympathetic to your little quest? That I won't come after you just like the rest of them?"

"I have said these things to you, that in me you may have peace," the voice offered. "But I understand your need for retribution."

"This isn't about retribution. It's about justice for the people of the territory. It's about saving their faith."

"Then in this we are kindred souls, Lieutenant. Look not upon me as thine enemy, for I am the way, and the truth, and the life. At least, for now."

Silence flowed from the comm line as the distortion ceased, and Deacon could hear a strange, grinding metal sound in the background. The line suddenly went dead, and he was left standing in his office, shivering as if death itself had run its icy fingers down his spine.

3

The gravel drive wound up through a half acre of wooded countryside. It was just long enough to allow someone to slip into a distant time and forget the sprawling Atlanta skyline hidden behind it. Elli drove toward the sprawling house, following the small solar lights that lined the drive. The house itself was dimly lit except for two rooms: the upstairs salon off the master bedroom and the downstairs study. Even after being out of her runway profession for years, her mother still kept to her beauty routines, a complicated process that could easily take hours if she were left undisturbed. Elli could practically smell the lemongrass and lavender of her mother's boudoir as she entered the house. As comforting as it would be to wrap herself in her mother's delicately scented embrace, she instead followed the sounds of her father's voice to his study. Here the aromas of fine bourbons and cold pine logs awaiting the first winter chill floated in the air, making her feel safe. She lingered in the doorway as her father finished his phone call.

Only an hour earlier she'd been staring at the ceiling of her bedroom as Tanner snored softly beside her, the warnings of her teachers about the dangers of sin banging a loud "WE TOLD YOU SO" in her brain. Since childhood, she'd been schooled that sin was not a stepping-stone you could jump on and off of at will but a path with few exits. And once you started down that path, it would only lead you further astray. Like every other child, she'd viewed such warnings as she did algebra: something you were forced to learn but would never use, no matter what they told you. Lying there in the dark, the irony of that attitude bore down on her. Not only had she used algebra on many occasions in her life, she was now traveling the path from one sin to the next with no end in sight. And it had all started with Toby Holmby. Although she still didn't consider her actions sinful, the church declared her defiance of God to be a punishable sin. Since then she'd lied to the Council about the progress of the investigation, questioned the motives of her spiritual leaders openly, and just had the most amazing sex she'd ever had in her life with a virile young man to whom she was not married. Her entire existence was going up in flames and she had no idea how to stop it. She'd snuck out of the apartment so as not to wake Tanner. The e-drive in her car had made no noise when she started it, and she'd waited until she backed out into the street to shut the door. Now here she stood in the foyer of her family home in the heavily wooded suburbs of Tuxedo Park. Waiting and hoping that her father wouldn't be disappointed at the sinful mess his daughter had become.

Quentin Hollister disconnected the comm line and looked up to see Elli standing forlornly in the doorway. No matter how old his daughter got, he always saw the awkward little girl with long legs under a mop of unruly curls when he looked at her.

"Hey, Sweet Pea!" he said adoringly as he went to embrace her in his customary bear hug. "What brings you out here? Not that seeing you isn't an utter delight."

She hadn't spoken to her father since her sentencing. She'd been far too embarrassed. Elli sank into his arms and lingered in the warmth of his chest. As tall as she was, her father still dwarfed her slender frame.

Quentin caressed her hair. "We're long overdue for a heart-to-heart, don't you think?"

Elli looked up into her father's concerned face. She'd never been able to hide anything from him, but something in his expression said he knew more than she was willing to share. Council edicts and judgments were strictly sequestered even from family members, but Quentin Hollister was a senior Senator with considerable power.

"I take it they told you," she said.

"Not everything. Just enough to keep me informed in case of any possible political repercussions prior to the elections."

Elli dropped her head back onto his chest and mumbled, "I don't know what to do, Dad, and I need your help."

He led her to the couch and sat next to her with his arm gently wrapped around her shoulder. "I'm forbidden from publicly condoning what you did to that little boy," he told her. Elli's face pinched in slightly as she closed her eyes. It was the same expression her mother made when she steeled herself for a dressing down that she had no intention of accepting. He lifted her chin to look into her eyes. "But I want you to know how damned proud I am of you for doing it."

Elli stared at her father, feeling both horrified and relieved. But would he be so proud of her once he knew what she had discovered?

"Dad, I need to tell you some things, and I need you to explain them to me." She paused. "I need you to be straight with me about them because . . ." she couldn't say what she wanted to say, that if he lied to her it meant he was a willing participant in something she couldn't even contemplate.

"Okay," Quentin told her. "Tell me everything, and be as honest with me as you want me to be with you. Don't leave anything out, and don't sugarcoat it. Deal?"

"Deal," Elli answered.

They'd been saying this to each other all their lives whenever they needed to have serious conversations, and neither of them had ever been disappointed. Elli told him everything, beginning with the sentence imposed on her by the Council and their threat of revoking her medical license if she refused to cooperate. Quentin's blood boiled when he heard how they'd threatened her, but he let her continue. She explained her assignment to the task force and what was expected of her. She told him about the murders and exactly where they were in the investigation. He listened without interrupting, and it was well after midnight when she finished. It was only when he got up to stretch that she faltered.

"I've discovered some things, Dad. Things that the public doesn't know but I think they should. If it's true, it means we've been led down a path we never intended to go, and people are dying for it."

"Does this have anything to do with the Council and its mandates?" Quentin asked her. She started to respond but he held up a finger to his lips. Quentin had long suspected that the Council monitored not only its members and employees but the Senate itself. He walked over to the sound console and tuned to a special station playing old country music. It was a pirate signal set up by a group of disgruntled hackers in the early days of the Republic. It originated in federal territory, so the Council had no way to shut it down, and it transmitted a hidden low band of white noise guaranteed to confuse any listening devices in the room. Not many people knew about it, but those who did put it to good use. Patsy Cline filled the room with her laments about the insanity of love, and Quentin led Elli to a bench close to the speakers.

"We can talk freely now, but keep it as short and simple as you can."

Elli shook her head and handed him an evidence pad that showed all the information she'd discovered regarding the convictions and subsequent deaths. She explained the data quietly as he read along with her conclusions. When he finished reading, she asked, "Did you know about this, Dad?"

Quentin stared at the reader before him for a minute and then said, "Yes."

Elli's face went white with shock, but Quentin held his hand up to quiet her. He wrapped her in a bear hug and whispered, "Don't investigate this any further. Let it go, Elli."

She pushed back from his embrace, noting the look of determined panic in his eyes. "That may not be possible," she said as she rose from the bench and faced the cold fireplace. "The team believes these murders are an attempt to expose the truth about what the Council is doing, that someone affiliated with the Council is directly responsible."

"All the more reason for you to get out now," he told her.

Elli looked at him suspiciously. "If I ask to be removed from the case, I'll have to submit myself for reconditioning."

He jumped up and grabbed her shoulders. "I don't ever want to hear you say that again."

"Why? You're afraid they'll do to me what they did to all these other people, aren't you? That I'll end up dying mysteriously because I dared to do what was right instead of what was ordained." Quentin didn't say anything. He just stared deeply into her eyes as she spoke. "You always taught me to stand up for those who couldn't stand up for themselves. How can you expect me to turn my back on them to save myself?"

He reached up and caressed her face. "Because I am not Abraham, and I'd never sacrifice you for anything."

4

It was just before dawn when Deacon arrived at the Hollister estate exhausted and angry. He didn't want to be here, but Elli had called and begged him to come. The revelations about Neville's fate had left him in no mood to play politics, and he struggled to contain his animosity as he waited for the gate to open. He breathed into his hand and winced. He'd broken down and had the drink he'd promised himself not to. He'd given in to a weakness the director had warned him to avoid. But he didn't feel weak. He felt pissed, betrayed, and furious. The alcohol had burned through the initial grief and guilt and left him seething. Angry enough, he hoped, to do what needed to be done. He pulled a pack of mints from the center console and chewed a handful, then drove onto the grounds.

The lights were all off except for the study on the ground floor. Elli was waiting for him, shivering in the frigid predawn air.

"Thank you for coming," she muttered as she led him into the house. They made their way into the study where Quentin waited. He stood respectfully when they entered, but instead of greeting Deacon warmly, he raised a finger to his lips and electronically closed the shutters against the coming dawn.

Tuning the radio station to its pirate signal, he said, "Now we can talk."

Deacon smiled as Hank Williams's voice invited them all to go honky tonkin'. "Never would have pegged you for a rebel, Senator," he remarked.

"I guess after a hundred seventy-one years, it's still in the blood. But you didn't come here to discuss American history, did you?"

"I came here because your daughter asked me to," Deacon answered, glancing toward Elli. "Although she hasn't explained why."

Quentin poured coffee for the three of them, but Deacon refused, not wanting to douse the firestorm in his heart.

"I told him about the research Joyce showed me: all the convictions and the subsequent deaths the Council is responsible for," Elli explained.

Deacon shot her a withering look and then said to Quentin, "If you've called me here to express your moral and political outrage at our findings, I'm not interested."

"I called you here to warn you," Quentin told him. "Your little research project goes deeper than you know. You keep investigating this and you're going to put your entire team in danger, a team that at the moment includes my daughter. So, you see I have a vested interest in your dropping this. We appreciate your concerns, but it's territorial business. Let us handle it."

"Let you handle it?" Deacon shot back as he closed in on Quentin. "And just how long should we sit on this and wait for you to handle it? How many more innocent people have to be tortured and die, Senator, before you handle it?"

Quentin shook his head in contempt. "Sounds like you've been drinking the Kool-Aid, Lieutenant. Nobody's being tortured here." He inhaled the minty whiskey fumes on Deacon's breath. "Or maybe it was something stronger than Kool-Aid."

Deacon struggled to keep his rising fury in check as Quentin sat down behind his desk.

"You've been listening to propaganda. I thought you were smarter than that."

"Propaganda, is it?" Deacon said, leaning over the desk. He pulled Neville's transcript disk from his pocket and slid it into the reader. "Allow me to show you propaganda." He entered the Aramaic security codes, and the official Ecumenical records played across the desktop as Elli and her father watched. He didn't want to see it again and tried to tune out the droning conversation between Neville and his doctor by standing in front of the fireplace. But when his son's voice screamed out in terror and called for him, he gripped the mantel tightly. From the speakers embedded in it, Patsy Cline lamented that she was falling to pieces each time someone spoke a loved one's name. He pressed his forehead painfully against it, wishing she'd shut the hell up.

When the playback stopped, Quentin pulled the disk and examined it. The laser-etched Ecumenical Seal told him it was authentic. Elli sat beside her father, rubbing the tears from her eyes. Quentin was now visibly sweating and asked in a trembling voice, "I take it this young man is your son?"

"My son. My child, whom I entrusted to your government and the church to help save. This is how they helped him." Deacon walked back to the desk and stabbed a finger at the disk. "This is what they did to him. And he's not the only one."

"What happened to your boy?"

"He killed himself," Deacon said for the first time in four years. "Said he couldn't stand to live one more day while ghosts haunted him and destroyers stalked him. He couldn't face each day with them threatening his soul if he slipped up again. That's what your so-called rehabilitation did to his mind. Left him haunted and terrified until he had to take his own life to escape it." He looked down to where Quentin sat rubbing his lips. "Just like the hundreds of your faithful citizens who hoped for forgiveness for their transgressions, he was sentenced to an intolerable living hell whose only escape was Hell itself." He cocked his head slightly. "You had no idea this was happening, did you?"

"No," Quentin said shakily. "R&R is considered the purview of the Ecumenical body. The elected government only passes the laws dictating what is and is not a crime according to biblical precedent. The Council has full and complete authority to dispense that justice however it sees fit."

Deacon shook his head and looked away. Quentin pressed on. "The only condition to allowing them full autonomy was that any terminal punishments had to be reserved for terminal crimes, those wherein a life was lost with intent. Those executions had to be performed in the most humane and respectful manner possible."

"They agreed to play nice, and the Senate gave up oversight of the process."

"Yes," Quentin answered as he stared at the disk on his desk. "Archbishop Wirz heads that division with their full confidence. May I ask how you got your hands on this?"

"It was sent to me by the serial killer we've been hunting. Whoever he is, he has access to the Council's most classified edicts. He may even be on the Council himself. And he's decided to dispense the Council's justice the way the Old Testament says it should be done." Deacon watched the blood drain from Quentin's face. "Apparently, he finds it more humane and respectful than your rehabilitation." Deacon reached down and picked up Neville's disk, wiping it clean. "I can't say I disagree with him."

"How can you say that?" Quentin gasped. "You're telling me you think this . . . this inhuman monster is doing his victims a favor?"

"AT LEAST THEY DIED CLEAN!" Deacon yelled, slamming his fist on the desk. "At least they were given the chance to confess and receive absolution before they died. Their souls were sent to God absolved of their transgressions and free to enter His kingdom. They weren't left to suffer in pain and agony with no choice other than to face eternal damnation in this life or the next!"

Quentin shrank from Deacon's fury and sank into his chair. Johnny Cash began to wail that he had fallen into a burning ring of fire. But while his love kept going down, down, down, Quentin felt the flames burning higher by the second.

Deacon gathered his temper and took a deep breath. "Know this, Senator. I will find the murderer who's killing your people. And then I'm coming for the son of a bitch who tortured my son, even if I have to burn your Eden to the ground reach him."

As he walked away, Quentin said, "You may get your man, Lieutenant, but you'll never reach Wirz. He has unprecedented control over the Council and the support of a rogue faction with unlimited resources. Resources that can make someone disappear without a single question being asked. He'd take out your entire team before you even got close."

"Then I suggest you start praying, Senator, because Armageddon is coming."

5

"Looks like you had it pegged just right, Lieutenant," Tanner told Deacon and Joyce. "Pastor Goodwin's daughter missed a lot of school this past year, supposedly due to some medical issues. No hospitalization records exist, but she spent a lot of time at home. When she did come back, she started getting into arguments with her teachers and a couple of fights with her friends. Dropped her P.E. classes and started losing weight. One of her teachers thought she might have developed an eating disorder, but when the school nurse tried to talk to her about it, the girl pulled away. Wouldn't let the nurse touch her at all."

"Classic signs of abuse in adolescents," Joyce added.

"She isn't the only one, either. There were a couple of other students, boys, who exhibited the same behavior. They didn't go to the same school, but they were also members of Pastor Goodwin's congregation."

"And no one investigated these incidents any further?" Deacon asked.

"The families of all the known students were questioned, but none would even consider implicating the church. They all just stuck with the same excuse about teenagers going through some sort of phase, like it was normal. Without a formal complaint, there was nothing that could be done."

"Well, somebody complained because Goodwin was scheduled for rehab."

"They were most likely ordered by the Council to keep the matter private, probably with some promise that Goodwin would be removed and treated for his tendencies," Joyce added.

Deacon shook his head. For the last seventy years churches across the country had been pulling this same shuffle on unsuspecting parishioners. It wasn't until Catholic dioceses across the nation were held accountable that the laws were changed to forbid the sheltering of predator clergy. But now that the church was in full control of half the population, the need to show a bright and shiny face to the world had become even more imperative, and no hint of impropriety could be allowed to be known.

"Tanner, take the names on the Penance List around the Talladega area. Talk to anyone whose crimes might be high-profile enough to be a target, but steer clear of anyone affiliated with the church directly. I don't want the Council getting wind of this."

"What should I tell them when they ask how a state cop knows about a confidential sentencing order?"

"Tell them the truth, that you're working on the joint task force investigating the murders and there's a possibility that they may have been targeted. You're just there asking questions to make sure that if they're in danger you can provide protection for them and their families until the killer is caught. If they want to know how they were targeted, just tell them you can't discuss that without endangering the investigation and that your sole priority is their protection. Keep them on your side and talking."

"Is Det. Bachman joining me, or should I wait for Elli?" Tanner asked.

"Dr. Hollister has family matters to attend to," Deacon told them. "It's doubtful she'll be returning to the investigation. That leaves us down by one, and I need Bachman on another matter. We need to find the next victim before our killer has time to act, so get busy."

Tanner left reluctantly. He wanted to ask about Elli, but MacNair looked exhausted and in no mood to talk. He'd woken up alone in her apartment with a note that was short and sweet: *Went to talk to Dad about something. Catch up with you later.* It even had a little heart drawn over the "i" in her name. A completely girlie thing that had made him blush. Now she was gone and not answering her phone. He tried calling her again as the cruiser sped south through the clapboard houses dotting the flat Alabama countryside.

With Tanner safely out of range, Deacon retreated to his office with Joyce on his heels. He didn't speak until they were both safely locked in and the standard surveillance monitors turned off.

"What's happened, Deke?" she asked. "You show up looking like you haven't slept in a week and send Tanner out alone in violation of our orders with no explanation. Then you tell us the doc isn't coming back but you won't elaborate. What the hell is going on?"

"They killed him, Joyce," Deacon told her wearily.

Exhaustion and grief settled onto her partner like a lead shroud as she sat across from him and listened.

"They killed my boy just like they did the others. They were supposed to help him find his faith again," Deacon muttered. "God was supposed to give him the strength to fight his addiction and make him whole again." He pulled Neville's disk from his pocket and handed it to her along with a set of earbuds. He couldn't bear hearing it again.

Joyce plugged into the console and watched the recordings. As Joyce watched the playback silently, he closed his eyes and thought of Elli. He'd left her standing at the door of the estate that morning, appalled by what she had witnessed and uttering hollow apologies. Apologies from someone who had chosen ignorance as a way of life. He knew he was being unfair to her, but there was no room in his burning heart for forgiveness, not today at least. Today he had two madmen to stop. One wielding fear, obedience, and the word of God on an unsuspecting populace, turning those he could not control into helpless weapons of mass destruction. The other using those same holy words to lay bare the cruelty that underpinned a common belief system and the hypocrisy of its literal applications. Both belonged to the same extremist group, and each committed heinous crimes for their own purposes. And each believed unconditionally that his cause was just.

Deacon's mind twisted itself into a Gordian knot. Stopping the executioner wouldn't stop the killing; he'd made that obvious. It would just make such actions more "palatable" to the populace and allow Wirz to continue his plans for a new world order. So why bother stopping the killer? Maybe he should just let the man keep killing and bring it all crashing down. Maybe the killer had the right idea. Maybe this is how to stop the Cadre once and for all. Maybe, maybe, maybe his mind pondered in an endless loop.

You're trying to sympathize with a serial killer to justify exacting your revenge.

He tried to drown out his rational mind by reasoning with it.

Wirz was just as big a butcher as the killer, probably more so because he tortured with impunity, he offered. Quentin's warning about pursuing the archbishop popped up from his memory. Wirz had unlimited resources and could make someone disappear without a trace, he'd said. For Deacon, it was a hollow threat at best. The South had been steadily trying to kill him since the first shots of the war. Anything that mattered to him had been buried in a grave behind a white picket fence in the Huntsville Memory Gardens.

Wirz isn't your target, his mind whispered. *He's committed no crime under the laws of the territory, and his actions are sanctioned by the Ecumenical Council. You're fucked.*

"Dammit!" Deacon hissed aloud. There had to be a way to take them both down.

Eventually, Joyce pulled the buds free from her ears and sat back rubbing her eyes as if she could remove the horrors she'd just witnessed from them.

"I know I wasn't around when you lost your son, Deke, but I don't understand why you considered the Ministry an option to helping Neville," Joyce said gently.

"We had no choice," Deacon explained. "My wife would put him in treatment centers and he'd relapse. The army had rehab programs for active-duty soldiers and their families. We went through all of them. None of them took, mostly because I wasn't there to reinforce it. By the time the war ended, he was spending all his time with his junkie friends in Chicago. Then I got appointed to federal service and moved us back down here to my home state. I forced him to come, hoping the distance would help. He just found new friends and better drugs. We tried everything available. There was just nowhere else to turn." He dropped his head and took a deep breath. "When every door is closed to you, God will open a window. All we had to do was look for that open window and not be afraid to crawl through it. That's what our pastor always told us, that God would always be the last refuge for his children in their time of greatest need. I gave my son to God in order to save his life. Instead they tortured him to death." He wiped his eyes as rage began to overtake his emotions.

"You have to forgive yourself, Deacon. You didn't know this was happening. None of us did."

"God was supposed to save my child, hallelujah!" he chuckled in disgust. "I guess he's cured as fuck now." Joyce stared at him, trying to fight back her own well of pity. "I don't know," Deacon muttered. "Maybe Burke and all his atheist friends are right."

"God didn't do this, Deacon," Joyce told him sternly. "Did you see God anywhere in that treatment room? The Ministry did this. God had nothing to do with it. We need to punish these men."

"I can't," he told her. "The Ministry was just following established territorial law in its actions. They are legally innocent of any crime, and my hands are tied."

She leaned back in her chair, gently rubbing the Chai around her neck as she watched him. Even in his darkest moments, she'd never known Deacon to abandon God outright, and it frightened her.

"There's more," he muttered. "What I'm about to tell you is top secret. I'm violating a presidential order by telling you this, but you need to know."

She sat up straight and listened intently as Deacon laid out everything he had been told about the Cadre and Wirz's involvement with them. She grew increasingly stunned as he told her what he'd discovered about their influence in territorial and world politics. But when he told her that their killer was also one of them, she got up and began to pace nervously as she pieced things together.

"You're telling me that you've been investigating E-Rep for the White House because the FBI stumbled onto a hack and uncovered a secret organization operating there?"

"Yes."

"And this hacker stole a bunch of documents, including the Penance List we were just given, meaning our killer and the hacker are one and the same." Deacon nodded. She continued to pace. "The Cadre operatives in E-Rep don't want the Feds investigating the murders because they're afraid we'll stumble onto the organization's existence as well. So they file a demand for jurisdiction to keep us out." She looked over at Deacon. "But they didn't count on you fighting for the case, so they sent over two completely unqualified representatives to derail the investigation."

"That's what they were hoping for," Deacon said, smiling up at her. Joyce had always been a top-notch detective with a keen mind, but he was impressed with how quickly she connected the dots. "They picked Tanner right out of the academy. They knew he didn't have the investigative training to do anything more than observe and report but would do anything to prove himself. They underestimated his intelligence." He paused for a moment. "We all did."

"And the doc?"

"Dr. Hollister was convicted of violating religious law. Remember the Holmby boy's suicide?"

"That was her?" Joyce exclaimed.

"Yep. She's here because Wirz gave her a choice: face reconditioning or serve as their eyes and ears and provide eyewitness testimony that we violated the rights of their citizens and/or tampered with evidence. Basically, the Council blackmailed her into serving."

Joyce suddenly felt ashamed for being so hard on Elli. "I think I owe the doc a huge apology," she said. "And Wirz is a leading member of this Cadre?"

"According to the hacked files the FBI recovered. He was their chief recruiter in Rome until he was appointed to a junior post in the Ecclesiastical Republic. From there he began grooming and recruiting local politicians and appointing other Cadre members as positions became available. After the untimely death of his predecessor, he gained control of the Justice Ministry and replaced the entire staff with operatives. From there, it's a short hop to the judiciary and full control of the entire legal system."

"Making Wirz the most powerful man in the government," she replied bitterly.

"This is why the killer sent me those transcripts. He wanted me to know that Neville was another of the penitent deaths. It's all connected: the executions, the brutality, the misogyny. It leaves the means and the authority to kill anyone with impunity in the hands of one man while leaving the Ecumenical Council and the Church to take the fallout if it goes bad."

"That doesn't make sense," she countered. "Wirz is on the fast track to the highest position on that Council. He's practically guaranteed to be appointed high bishop when the current one steps down or dies. Why would he destroy the Council when he's destined to lead it?"

"Because the Council is just a means to an end. It's not his ultimate objective."

Joyce stared at him. "Then what is that exactly?"

Deacon looked at her evenly. "He wants to take over the Cadre." When her eyebrows shot up in disbelief, he added, "Wirz said something to me during our meeting. He said, 'For whatever is born of God overcomes the world; and this is the victory that has overcome the world—our faith.'" He looked into Joyce's eyes and said, "Why lead just one country when you can lead them all?"

"It still doesn't add up, though. This Cadre has been operating in secret, staying very well-hidden for decades. They like operating behind the scenes. Why would they let Wirz put that all at risk?"

"Because they don't know what he's really up to. If they did, they'd put him down."

"And the Svengali complex? What possible reason could he have for brainwashing the populace?"

"Even a despot needs an army," Deacon explained. "He's creating an expendable supply of preprogrammed soldiers ready to do his bidding at a moment's notice and timed to explode before his secret's discovered. Remember Mona Davis? A seventeen-year-old girl with no formal firearms training suddenly turns into a crack shot after reconditioning. She goes on a rampage, calmly picks off every potential witness to our case, and is immediately killed by police without defending herself. He could send the faithful across the globe disguised as territorial missionaries and ambassadors without anyone suspecting they were programmed assassins."

"But why destroy the government he's seeking to control?" she asked.

"History is full of people who rose up through the ranks only to destroy the governments they work for: Hitler in Germany, Castro in Cuba, Trujillo in the Dominican Republic, Mussolini in Italy. These men started at the bottom and worked their way into power through political or military systems. And they didn't stop when they got to the top. They seized total control, abolished the allegedly failing systems of government, and set up dictatorships, all with the approval of the people. Wirz is no different."

"So why did our killer turn on them if he's one of them?"

"I don't know," Deacon said, throwing his hands up in frustration. "I have absolutely no fucking idea. Maybe he got passed over for promotion. Maybe he didn't get his Christmas bonus. Maybe he found out his gold watch was a knockoff. Or maybe, just maybe, he's become a true believer."

"You think he's gone native?"

"It's possible," Deacon told her.

"And this is the only way he could express his disappointment?"

Deacon laid his hand on the data pad containing Neville's sentencing records. "His reasons don't matter. What matters is that we have to stop him. And the only way to stop him is to take up his cause."

The Blood of God's People

1

Chaos captured the airwaves in the days following the shooting at LaGrange Academy. The survivors and their parents gave endless interviews on national news describing the carnage. The parents of the victims appeared lost yet stalwart in their grief, devastated but secure in the knowledge that their children now sat at the right hand of God. There were the usual comments about poor Mona Davis. Everyone considered her to be a good girl with no previous issues or disturbances. Everyone had something wonderful to say about her, which was why no one believed she would do something so horrifying. Mona's father gave a particularly tearful speech about his child and how she had been coming along so nicely in recovering from the loss of her boyfriend. He remained as mystified about her behavior as everyone. When asked how she got her hands on such a powerful gun, Mona's father proudly stated that he was very strict in his household about his weapons. He'd given Mona all the proper training on the safe use and storage of the gun but also that such things were off-limits to her except in an extreme emergency. One daring reporter asked why the gun was so readily accessible and not locked away, to which Mona's father replied, "If it weren't readily accessible, how the hell could you protect yourself from an intruder?" Throughout the interviews, Mona's mother remained in seclusion. The school was closed for the rest of the week, and Halloween celebrations everywhere were canceled. The entire territory went into a state of mourning as the dead were remembered fondly and buried with all the pomp and circumstance befitting the martyrs they'd become.

Abel watched it all from the monitors in his studio with the sound off and the closed captions on. The gallery was surprisingly busy given the recent tragedies, but with the High Holy Days less than a month away, everyone was getting ready. Marshall had been true to his word, and the family portrait bookings were piling up fast. Everyone wanted to capture that perfect family picture to grace their holiday cards and party decorations, and Abel had become the one to hire. They would sit dressed in their finest clothing, hair and makeup perfectly applied, and project perfect smiles and perfect posture to form a delightful image of the perfect family. This was the image they would send out into the world for all to see. And it couldn't be further from the truth. Inevitably, at the end of every shoot when the last light dimmed, a collective release would flow from their faces and reality would once again assert itself. Their portrait would become the embodiment of an unattainable dream, a stark reminder of what they once sought to become.

It was a full three days after the Davis shooting that news of the third victim finally hit the evening news. The gallery only had a couple of patrons, so Abel turned up the sound. The anchorman reported the murder from his desk in a somber fashion. There were no pictures from the crime scene or on-scene interviews. Only a smiling picture of the latest victim to fall prey to the as-yet-unidentified killer and a stern warning to be cautious and vigilant until he was caught. Abel shook his head at the apathy being displayed. Austin Goodwin, a loving father, husband, and loyal voice of God had been silenced by a follower of Satan. Calls for prayers for the family and those who loved him went out on the heels of demands for justice from the federal task force that had done nothing to keep him safe. Just another day in the territory. There was no mention made of the fact that the voice of God had been using his voice to bugger little children. Not one person spoke up for his poor daughter who'd suffered his attentions in the dead of night with a gag in her mouth. No church official spoke up to say that they were aware of his proclivities and were taking steps to rectify him. The voice of God would forever be praised as a victim of evil instead of what he truly was.

"Excuse me," a mousy voice said, startling Abel from his anger. He turned to see a young woman holding a marble crucifix with a rose embedded in the center. "I'd like to know how much this is?"

"Of course, my dear," he told her as he examined the piece and swiped through a catalog on his data pad. He already knew the price but used the pretense to examine the woman more closely. She watched the news feed as he pretended to search. Her hands trembled, and she clenched them repeatedly on the counter to stop the shaking. Her makeup was a little heavy for such a pretty face, but it couldn't hide the dark circles under her eyes or the slight twitch that crept into one corner of her mouth whenever the words "sin" or "evil" were uttered during the broadcast. She'd been reconditioned. All the signs were there. Judging by the way she fought the tremors in her hands, he guessed she had no more than a month or so before she imploded like all the others. "Is there something wrong, dear?" he asked quietly.

She turned and dropped her eyes quickly. They were moist and darted back and forth as she struggled to respond. "No, it's just . . . the news is so terrible." She dug her fingernails into her palms, and they began to bleed slightly. Her left hand bore the telltale tan line where a wedding ring once rested. Its pale, slightly greasy shine indicated that it hadn't been gone long.

Abel knew there was much more than the news bothering her, but he also knew that she'd been reconditioned not to reveal it. Prying would only cause her great distress and might push her over the edge. He surmised that she was either legally divorced or recently widowed by an abusive husband, the latter most likely. If she were in fact a widow, it was clear she didn't mourn her husband's passing and most likely had a hand in it. The self-defense would have been justified, but she still would have to atone for his death. Whether the hell she had been living was worse than the hell she had been delivered into was a truth she was still coming to terms with.

She stared past him and muttered, "Just feels like God's given up on us sometimes. Maybe we should all just give up."

He reached out and grasped her hands securely within his own. She pulled back at first but then relaxed as he looked into her eyes. "God only gives up on you when you do." He smiled compassionately. "You can still hear His voice if you try. You've only forgotten how to listen."

Her smile was pitiful but overflowed with gratitude for his kind words. He released her hands. "Let me polish this up for you. It'll just be a minute. And don't worry about the price—we'll work something out."

He walked back to his workbench and put the marble sculpture into the engraving machine. He entered the code for Psalm 9:10 and watched as the machine laser-imprinted the words onto the crucifix. He polished the sculpture and returned with a taffeta ribbon and an embossed box. The bell on the door tinkled as the remaining shoppers left, leaving them alone.

"May I ask your name?"

The girl hesitated but then answered, "Rebecca Tully."

He handed her the marble cross. "Rebecca, whenever you feel as if God has abandoned you, I want you to look at this and remember these words."

Rebecca looked down at the inscription, and as she read it aloud, tears began to fall from her face. "Those who know your name trust in you, for you, LORD, have never forsaken those who seek you."

Abel reached out to caress her cheek, then grasped her face fully, pulling her attention to him. Staring into her eyes, he said, "You know what the Lord asks of you." Her pupils suddenly grew wide. "Go and do his bidding."

Rebecca turned and walked out of the gallery into the night. There was no longer any doubt she'd been reconditioned. She responded to the trigger phrase immediately. Whatever she'd been programmed to do she would now do without hesitation.

Abel closed and locked the gallery door, watching as the girl walked away into the dark, offering a prayer for her soul, hoping that it wouldn't be in vain. The unveiling was to take place in three days, and he had to be ready. Pulling up the security feeds in his office, he replayed their conversation, stopping the playback to capture images of Rebecca's face. Such a wealth of pain and suffering floated in her tears and haunted expression. Her reconditioning should have erased the horrors of her abuse and returned her to society as a healthy, happy servant of God and a good citizen. Instead, Wirz had stripped her of her free will and turned her into an abomination. Obedience had been hardwired into her brain and faith made a weapon. She could be used and discarded as the archbishop saw fit. The girl would have made a fine addition to his collection if he'd needed one, but his final subject had already been chosen. Abel poured himself a rich burgundy as Wallace Milton's fire and brimstone speech bleated from the news feeds on the overhead monitor.

2

"You have to do something!" Milton shrieked at Wirz. "Public opinion is shifting, all because of Hollister and his bleeding-heart equality politics. We've lost the support of five senators so far, and three more are wavering. If we lose them too, the bill will fail, and I'll be a laughingstock."

Wirz watched him pace, growing more and more irritated. For all his expertise as master manipulator of public opinion, the man was a completely spineless narcissist. "Then your upcoming dedication speech should be the perfect opportunity for you to turn things around, show a united front to the public between you and Hollister. That should put you back on track."

"Haven't you been listening?" Milton sneered. "Hollister is voting against the bill! Do you think he's really going to stand on that stage and not speak out?"

"Leave Quentin to me," Wirz advised. "You won't have any resistance. Just get your ass on that stage and do your job."

Milton stood trembling with rage but didn't leave. Wirz shot him a warning look. "Anything else?"

"My son," Milton told him. "You promised me you'd have him extradited before the election. There's only a month left."

"That release is contingent upon your performance until then," Wirz reminded him. He watched Milton cringe. "We wouldn't want him to have any further misfortunes during his remaining incarceration."

Milton nodded slightly and then beat a hasty retreat. As soon as the door shut behind him, Wirz's comm line hummed. He slammed his hand on the connection button. "This had better be urgent."

"Yes, sir," his head of security responded. "We monitored a visit by Homeland Security Services to Senator Quentin Hollister's residence two nights ago. We've analyzed the surveillance feeds for the three hours they were there, but there was too much interference from inside. Some sort of masking signal. It stopped as soon as they left."

Wirz's irritation swelled and formed a burning ball in his gut. "And the hacking investigation?"

"We've identified the source code used to access the system. It belonged to your predecessor, sir. It must have been used by someone attached to his service. We've begun conducting interrogations of all previously assigned personnel. It won't be long now."

Wirz closed the line and stared at the desktop where the Ecumenical Seal twirled serenely against a bloodred backdrop. It wouldn't take his team long to find the person if he were indeed among the former employees of the Hand, but it would amount to nothing. Meeks would never give his passcodes to anyone under any circumstances and would have personally dispatched anyone caught or even suspected of using his passcodes. The man had been a consummate professional. An example to every member of the Cadre of dedication and precision at its highest standards. It was the cruelest of ironies that Wirz had been the one to retire him with extreme prejudice.

Wirz had been Meeks' protégé and actually missed his old mentor. An interesting mix of cold practicality and endless empathy. Whether his target was the most reprehensible degenerate or an innocent toddler, he would act with the precision of a surgeon, striking without hesitation or regret. And yet he always went to great lengths to ease, if not eliminate, the suffering of those necessary targets that he deemed worthy of compassion. Unlike his mentor, Wirz felt nothing for his targets. Ten years of study in the Vatican had taught him that they were nothing more than mistakes that God had neglected to remove. To him, they were less than human. Obstacles that needed to be removed quickly for the agenda to continue. Meeks had warned him that his pathological indifference would be a problem and cautioned that arrogance was humanity's most fatal flaw. Perhaps if he had taken Meeks's words to heart instead of humoring the old man, his first kill order would have gone better. In his haste to prove his mentor wrong, he'd rushed the elimination, exposing both of them to local authorities. Meeks had taken a bullet to the shoulder saving Wirz, even though standard protocol was to erase him. His empathy earned him a titanium plate in the shoulder and a stern rebuke from the leadership. Wirz had spent the remainder of his career being the best Cadre operative possible to repay that kindness, even when charged with Meeks' elimination.

He spent months working with Meeks observing him before engineering his death, which was no small feat. The result had been quite a bit of genius that not only earned him high praise from his superiors but gave him the perfect catalyst to assume Meeks's position and endear himself to the populace. It had been, in his mind, a work of art. He had no doubt that Meeks himself would have praised his work had he not been its subject. Meeks had been quite the connoisseur of art. He'd collected a substantial amount of it during his lifetime. Wirz had curated its donation to the Ecumenical museum upon his death. Some of the work had been done by

Meeks himself. The man had nearly as much talent as any of the old masters he admired. Despite the dropped shoulder he earned saving Wirz's life, he had steady, delicate hands and a keen eye for minute detail. It gave his work a most lifelike and emotional dimension.

The smile of reminiscence relaxed from Wirz's face and began to quiver as he stared at the blank red screen. Meticulous, eye for detail, dropped shoulder. A consummate professional who would kill without hesitation anyone who discovered his access codes. The words dragged through his thoughts like a rusty anchor. Wirz shook his head to drive the forming notion away. The old man had lost faith in the Agenda, that's all. Probably part of the reason the Cadre had ordered his retirement. But he couldn't force the idea into retreat. It fought through every rationalization he threw at it until it slammed into his conscious mind like a bullet.

"No," he whispered. "No, no, no, no . . ." he muttered as he called up the legal records and death certificates of the former Hand to the High Archbishop. Tunneling through file after file of accident reports and investigative files, he found the coroner's reports for the victims and scrolled through them until he found Meeks. He read through the report, noting the limited amount of detail due to the condition of the badly burned corpse. No identifying marks due to the lack of skin. Dental records provided only a 70% match—again due to the condition of the corpse and the high-intensity burn. He didn't realize he was sweating. Height, weight, age were all a match. DNA was impossible to verify. Beads of sweat began to bounce off the screen in the desk as he inched closer to the end of the report. An old break in the victim's leg suffered in a skiing accident two years prior to his death was noted. He had no idea Meeks had taken up skiing, but they'd been apart for several years before reconnecting. There was some arthritic damage to the one joint they had been able to retrieve, but this was pure speculation. All in all, the identity of the victim had been to declared a 95% match to the Hand, and the report ended with a positive identification. He reread it again and again, each time feeling the dread sink deeper and deeper into his soul. It wasn't there. It had never been there. And he had never bothered to look for it until now. The titanium plate was gone.

Arrogance is a fatal flaw, and yours will be your undoing. Meeks' words came through loud and clear as he held his breath. He'd accepted the report as accurate, never once considering that his efforts might be unsuccessful. But the one piece of evidence that would have made the report a 100% match wasn't here. He'd been outmaneuvered, and his mentor had survived. He also knew without a doubt that the man was coming for him, and this time, there would be no empathy to save him.

3

November blew in with cold winds and frigid nights. By day the southern sun shone down, breaking up the daily cloud cover, but its light was cold, devoid of any warmth. Within a month there would be snow in the capital. The square was packed to capacity with the faithful, including a sizable number of Atlanta's most elite citizens, and everyone was bundled warmly in their winter best. Broadcast crews were set up around the perimeter and at the central dais where the new statue would be unveiled: a gift to the congregation of Saint Michael's Cathedral for its steadfast work in bringing the word of God to the Republic. The spacious church held a thousand people, and its services were broadcast live every Sunday. It catered to the spiritual needs of Atlanta's wealthiest citizens and had figured prominently in every election since the founding of the Ecclesiastical Republic.

Wallace Milton made the rounds in the crowd, shaking hands and begging for support. He had bags under his eyes, but no one noticed when he squinted, and the redness of his face was attributed to the wind chill. He'd spent the previous night working on the dedication speech for the tightly covered statue behind him, a work of art created to remind the faithful of the wages of sin and the disobedience of wayward wives, Lot's wife in particular. It was the perfect representation to drum up support for his Family Preservation Act. The wealthy supported the bill as long as it left them in total control of the territorial resources. Marrying off their children to one another to consolidate power was a game they'd been playing for centuries. But there had been considerable pushback from the working class. Mothers, and quite a few fathers, didn't like the idea of mandating marriage and children over education and career for one gender and not the other. They clung to the old American premise that their daughters could aspire to be more than just housewives yet still maintain a family. The poor saps even believed that women actually had a voice in policy matters, thanks to the sprinkle of old crones currently sitting in the Senate. *If they only knew how invisible those women were*, Milton mused.

He looked around the crowd and saw Caulder Wirz oozing his way among the affluent. They fawned over him as if he were the Pope, kissing his ring and being humble and contrite. It was an impressive show even if it was total bullshit. None of them liked Wirz one bit. In fact, most of them were terrified of him. But Wirz was the one who bailed them out of penance every time one of them did something stupid. He was known as the patron saint of fat, lazy, rich, perverted assholes and performed miracles for them every day. He also knew all their dirty secrets, which meant he owned them. If he wanted support for something, he got it, or heirs and relatives started to disappear. These last few days, Wirz had been incredibly testy. The man had been snapping at people left and right with zero patience for any sort of resistance, humor or irritation. During their meeting last night, Milton had joked that Wirz should go get laid and work off some of his pent-up anger. Wirz didn't find it funny and stabbed Milton's desk with a letter opener hard enough to split the wood, just barely missing Milton's hand. Even his pet police dog, Markham, was maintaining a healthy distance, working security with his deputies around the perimeter. Whatever bug had crawled up Wirz's ass was chewing away with a vengeance. Milton intended to give him as wide a berth today as possible.

Conspicuously missing from the ceremony was Quentin Hollister. Ordinarily, it only took one member of the Senate to perform a dedication, but this was Quentin's congregation, and people were wondering why he wasn't making the presentation. Wallace made up an excuse that poor Quentin had suddenly taken ill and asked the congregation to pray for his swift recovery. Wirz fumed openly at the announcement, turning nearly purple with rage and disappearing into the church. Truthfully, Wallace couldn't be more pleased with his absence. He preferred not having to share the stage with a raging lunatic like Wirz or a sanctimonious prick like Quentin. Especially when one of them was adamantly opposed to the legislation he was trumpeting. Maybe Quentin's absence had something to do with that little talk he'd had with Wirz. Milton smiled at the thought of the two men he hated most in the world coming to blows. At the very least, Quentin was sure to feel Wirz's wrath for disobeying him, and that made Wallace smile even more.

On the outskirts of the crowd of parishioners, the photographer stood taking wide-angle pictures of the spectacle. He wore typical working-class clothes, and most people assumed he was part of the media crew. They walked by, waving and clowning it up for the camera, assuming the images would be broadcast live. He merely smiled at them as they moved on. The wealthy gathered like expensive bric-a-brac near the podium where they could be admired and appreciated. He remained far enough away to be nondescript but still close enough to capture their arrogance when the opportunity arose. Despite his attempts at anonymity, eventually someone recognized him. Marshall, whose wife he had immortalized on her birthday, arrived late and hurried through the crowd. The man was shoving his way through and blundered right into him, knocking the camera from his grasp. As only the wealthy can manage, Marshall offered an apology wrapped in antipathy, not for the collision as much as for the existence of the lesser person in his path. But upon recognizing who he had just plowed into, he cried out in joy.

"Abe, old buddy! You here on business or pleasure?"

The photographer thought quickly. "Purely business, old friend, but as you know, my business is also my pleasure. I'm working on a fresco for the capitol building. I was thinking a depiction of the statue towering over the adoring crowd of the faithful might be a great image, but that, of course, will depend on how these shots come out."

Clapping him on the back, Marshall said, "If there's anybody that can turn this crowd into a work of art, it's you, my friend." Moving off, he called out, "And if you need another setup, a bunch of Senator Milton's supporters are getting together for a fund-raising brunch after the ceremony. Maybe you can recreate the Last Supper or something."

Abel waved back as his friend disappeared giggling through the crowd. He was mildly intrigued by the idea. Wallace Milton surrounded by his adoring constituents at a long table. Holding court as he awaited his fate come the dawn. Assigning these wealthy hedonists to the positions of apostles around their savior would be a fascinating psychological endeavor, one that he was sure would be lost on them entirely. Milton would no doubt wallow like a pig in a muddy pond at the idea of being portrayed as a modern-day Jesus. He'd probably request the finished piece be permanently hung in the Senate chamber itself as a tribute for all he had done for the Republic.

Abel aimed his camera at the podium where Milton and his entourage waited for the mic test to finish. *One cannot receive glory before repentance, Senator Milton*, he mused, looking at the temperature gauge on his phone. It was still chilly, but the temperature had been steadily rising over the past hour, which guaranteed the unveiling would be a spectacular show.

As Abel swept the stage, a familiar face appeared in his lens. Buck Meisner oozed among the elite, following Milton at a discreet distance but always within earshot. His hair was darker and he seemed to have dropped a few pounds, but it was definitely Meisner. He skulked nearby, mining statements from the new southern nobility as they publicly declared their loyalty to Milton and the Republic. After his last ambush, it was as close to Milton as he would ever get. Abel snapped a few stills of Meisner as he worked the crowd. It was obvious he wasn't paying attention to any of them. While his hand-held recorder captured the banalities of the rich, Meisner's brain absorbed every word Milton uttered nearby. The old boy was craftier than Abel had given him credit for. A skill for which he would be well rewarded today.

A loud warning tone sent everyone scrambling into position, and an old man in a cream-colored suit and red tie took the stage. This was Pastor Emoline of St. Michael's cathedral, a jovial ball of a man with a stringy comb-over who presided over the weekly broadcasts. People often referred to him as the Easter Bunny, given his penchant for polyester pastels and oversized Gucci loafers. He took the stage and smiled broadly, baring two unusually oversized buck teeth, and called the crowd to order. With a flourish of praise and a sly request for more contributions, he introduced the next Savior of the Wepublic, the Honowable High Senator Wallace Milton. As the crowd applauded and cheered, Milton strode to the mike as if he'd just won the national presidency.

"My fellow citizens!" he cried to thunderous cheers. "We are here to dedicate this gift to the church of St. Michael's for all the great work it has done to guide the faithful into the arms of our Lord Jesus Christ and to thank them for their commitment to the word of God and to our Republic."

More cheers, more blathering, more campaigning, love of God, love of country, blah blah blah. Abel tuned out as much of it as possible as he snapped away. He'd heard these same words for months in one form or another. It was all pomp and distraction. A misty rain began to fall, but only the expensively coiffed took heed and covered up. Then the crowd got quiet as Milton began to speak of the importance of family and the need to nurture it in every way possible. Abel listened as Milton spoke of the holiness of marriage and the sacred duty of motherhood as the cornerstone of the teachings of Christ. Abel was curious how he came to that conclusion since, in Christ's time, his disciples and leaders were men. Women had no more significance than cattle and were valued in terms of how many sheep they could be sold for. Then Milton began to speak of the great responsibility of women as guardians of the future generations of the Republic, of the need for their adherence to, and teaching of, the wages of sin and devotion to God and Country so that future generations would know the wrath of God protected them from the spread of evil. The crowd cheered even louder. Milton threw his arms high and wide, and they thundered their adoration as if Jesus himself had returned. The cameras ate it up.

Milton reached for the curtain behind him and yelled, "I dedicate this statue to the glory of all women of the Republic!" In one movement he pulled the cover down and whirled it around him like a prized bullfighter taunting a bull. An exquisite sculpture of Lot's wife turned toward Sodom pining for her life of sin glistened in the warming air. The crowd cheered and applause thundered as the photographer snapped away. The applause dwindled quickly, though, as the realization of what was actually on the pedestal sank in. Every third or fourth picture captured emotions evolving from righteous adoration to shock and then abject horror. It took nearly a minute for the first scream to penetrate the crowd. Milton's entourage searched frantically for a gunman as Markham raced toward the stage, but it wasn't a shooter that had spooked the crowd. One of the guards took a step back and slipped in something on the stage. He looked down at the thick pool of red and stumbled back. He followed the shock of the crowd as they fled the statue of the hapless wife of Lot. Instead of a marble effigy, a pillar of salt stood melting in the fall rain before their eyes, gazing back toward Sodom as rivulets of blood and fluid oozed from her decaying eyes and hands.

4

The sky was beginning to mist over the quaint suburbs of Calhoun as Deacon stood on the tiny steps of Roberta Lee's home. The nurse had been reluctant to discuss her daughter or her own possible conviction with a federal officer, but she recognized Elli from work. The entire hospital knew how she'd saved the Holmby child. Although they were expected to publicly support the Ecumenical Decrees on the treatment of terminal patients, most of Elli's fellow caregivers privately stood behind her decision. In Roberta Lee, Elli had found a kindred spirit who understood the impossible choice she'd been faced with and supported her.

Deacon's comm line began to chirp, and he left Elli and Roberta to say their goodbyes privately. He picked up the call inside the cruiser, but at first all he could hear was chaos and Markham shouting to his deputies, "Get them under control! Get these people under control!"

"Markham, what the hell is happening!" Deacon shouted at the console.

"I need you at the St. Michael's dedication now. Your murderer just struck in the middle of a press conference!"

"Secure the area. I'm on my way," Deacon ordered and then cut the line. Leaning out of the window he shouted to Elli, "Hollister, get in here now. We've got an emergency."

Elli gave the woman's hand a final squeeze and raced to the cruiser. She'd barely gotten in when Deacon gunned the engine and shot out into traffic with the emergency lights blazing. "What's happening?" she asked as Deacon set the cruiser to a code three response and the sirens blared.

"Markham called. Our killer just struck again, and the crime scene is active. We have to get to St. Michael's while the evidence is still fresh."

"St. Michael's in Atlanta?" she stammered. "That's my church," she muttered. Her eyes went wide a moment later. "Oh god, my father. He was supposed to co-chair the dedication ceremony."

Deacon could see she was about to fall apart. "Keep it together, Doc. We don't know the situation or who's been hurt. Markham and his men are there keeping everyone safe, so don't borrow trouble you don't have."

Elli shot him a look of pure panic. She knew how he felt about Markham's skills, so his assurances were hollow at best.

He switched on the commlink to HQ and called Agnes. "Agnes, get the team into tactical gear and get them to St. Michael's. We've got another victim."

"Already on it, boss. We had the ceremony on the vid," Agnes told him. "We started packing up the van the moment things went to hell."

"Good girl. Is Tanner back yet?"

"Not yet, boss. He's still in Tuscumbia tracking down his lead from the list."

"Get him turned back and headed to the scene. We'll meet him there," Deacon ordered and disconnected the com. To his right, Elli was frantically calling her father, to no avail. His comm was turned off, and not even his personal secretary knew where he was. She threw the phone across the dash in frustration as the car sped through traffic. "Elli, just because you can't reach him doesn't mean he was hurt. It's pandemonium there right now. Security's first priority would be to get the dignitaries to safety."

She rubbed her face roughly. "He was scheduled to be there to speak at the dedication with Milton. Even though he opposed the new legislation Milton was presenting, he would never disappoint the congregation. Not with something so important to them."

Deacon tuned the onboard communications system to the local news. Elli watched it, becoming more agitated as the cameras captured crowds of people racing from the church and lines of deputies trying in vain to control them. Her hands were shaking as she gripped the overhead handhold against the vehicle's speed.

"Did Roberta tell you how she smuggled her daughter out of the territory?" he asked, trying to distract Elli from panicking.

"What?" Elli stammered.

"Did Roberta tell you how she got her daughter out before the territorial police could arrest her?" he asked, much more slowly and forcefully.

"Yes. There's an underground network for refugees operating in the territory. When someone needs safe passage, they leave a sign at a drop location. They're picked up at a remote site by a boatman they call Charon. He sends them on down the river to a depot somewhere."

Deacon smiled at the irony. In Greek mythology, Charon was the ferryman who carried the souls of the dead to Hades, and sly old Pastor Cooper had been fascinated with Ancient Greece and its gods as a young man. That he now took up the mantle of ferrying persecuted souls to new lives of peace was poetic. "Did she tell you where this place was?"

"No," Elli answered. "She didn't want to put her contacts in jeopardy. Apparently, the Underground Railroad still has a lot of work to do yet." She gripped the overhead bar as the vehicle swerved through light traffic on I-75. "I promised her we'd let her know if anyone started asking questions about it because of the investigation so she could warn them." She hesitated and then added, "I also told her we'd help get her out before the Council came for her. I figured we owed her that much for interrogating her."

Deacon looked over to where Elli sat staring at him hopefully. "That's a promise we'll keep," he told her. A smile crept onto her worried face.

5

Wirz had been snarling orders into his phone in the empty rectory when the panic started. Hollister had dared to defy him by skipping the ceremony. To the Justice Ministry, his absence amounted to nothing more than a slight embarrassment and Milton had, as usual, used it to his advantage. But it was defiance nonetheless and could not be tolerated. Wirz had invested significant resources into Wallace Milton, but with Milton's sinking poll numbers, Quentin Hollister was the popular favorite to replace him. That meant bringing Quentin into the fold, either willingly or unwillingly. Since he'd chosen the latter, Hollister had to be taught a significant lesson.

Wirz had just dictated the details to his operative when the screams became a chorus. He looked out toward the courtyard and saw the security team surround Milton and hustle him off the stage. The crowd was clawing its way over folding chairs and trampling its slower members under a stampede of leather heels.

"Change of plans," he said into the phone as he hurried out of the church. "Get to St. Michael's immediately. Consider this a level one threat."

He closed the line and raced down the stairs. The noise was even louder in the vestibule where several attendees had taken refuge. He sped past them out onto the breezeway just in time to see Milton diving into a limo, followed by his entourage. The car sped away, careening off of two smaller vehicles and nearly hitting one of the sheriff's deputies. The press corps had surrounded the stage, and every camera was buzzing at light speed where the bleeding statue had begun to run under the morning mist. As he worked his way through the journalists, a layer of salt broke away from one delicate hand of the statue. It revealed the graying, mottled skin of the corpse sealed within.

Searching the crowd for Markham, Wirz found him shouting to his deputies, attempting to gain control of the chaos. He grabbed the man's uniform and whirled him around.

"To hell with the civilians. Cordon off this area as a crime scene immediately and get these reporters the hell out of here!"

The menace in Wirz's voice and enraged flush to his face was enough to snap Markham back into focus. He shoved past the archbishop, grabbed two of his deputies, and began forcing the reporters out of the courtyard and away from the crime scene. Wirz waved to his own security staff and ordered them to help. He stood alone in the courtyard, staring at the ghastly statue as a faint memory crept in. He'd seen this type of work before. The memory was fleeting and disappeared as fast as it landed, but it confirmed he'd been right. The sound of federal sirens in the distance was getting closer. MacNair and his team must have been nearby when the call went out, which didn't leave him much time to act.

He returned to the vestibule and ordered the resident clergy to evacuate the church and not return until cleared by the federal authorities. Retrieving his data pad from the office, he called up the network connected to his flock and waited for the red lights to populate. He needed someone nearby, someone inconspicuous. By the time MacNair's team began to deploy, he'd found just the soul he was looking for.

Deacon ran to the courtyard with Elli on his heels. Burke deployed the forensics team, hobbling along on a cane and setting the perimeter. Agnes shadowed Joyce into the courtyard, mindful of Deacon's warning to remain in sight of an armed officer at all times. As beautiful as the sculpture had been, it was eroding in the mist and beginning to lose shape. Agnes had a tent deployed within minutes and, by the time Digger arrived, had the entire stage enclosed. He was red-faced from his dash across the compound with his equipment, but he still managed a maniacal grin as he stared at the statue. Snapping on his gloves, he ran his fingers delicately along the arm, admiring the work, absently licking his face when rainwater dripped onto his cheek.

"Salt!" he cried out as the taste exploded onto his tongue. He picked a crumbling layer off the statue and rubbed the substance between his fingers. It granulated and then dissolved. "Mediterranean sea salt if I'm not mistaken."

"Why would he encase a body in salt instead of plaster?" Agnes asked.

Deacon bent down and read the plaque at the base of the statue. "'But Lot's wife, behind him, looked back, and she became a pillar of salt.' Whoever this woman was, she was a harlot and a sinner, married to a good and just man but unable to resist the temptations of Sodom and Gomorrah."

"I need to get her to the morgue as fast as possible," Digger said. He scurried around the statue, taking readings and examining it. "Before the coating melts completely and destroys all possible evidence."

Burke's bots went into high gear, taking readings and collecting evidence at breakneck speed. Agnes was running DNA samples through the system, hoping to get an ID before the body was fully exposed and moved. Elli watched them as they worked, unable to do anything but stare at the ghastly spectacle on the stage. She wondered if the poor woman had been encased while still alive, as Lot's wife had been.

Deacon listened patiently as Markham described the unveiling ceremony and the subsequent chaos, bouncing from horror to fury as he spoke. "What the hell kind of monster does this to a young woman?" he spat at Deacon. "You've been investigating this mess for two months and you've turned up nothing. Meanwhile my people are being butchered here."

"And we've never had a crime scene as fresh as this one until now," Deacon offered. Looking into Markham's flustered face, he said, "Don't go to shit on me now, Markham. I need your help. If I have to go through official

Council channels to request access to records, it's going to cost us time, and that means he gets away AGAIN!"

"If you're asking me to defy the orders of my own government—"

"I'm asking you to get me what I need right now," Deacon said desperately. "Find out who the artist was, who ordered this statue made, who delivered it. I need names, purchase orders, bills of lading. I need the names of any workers or subcontractors that have had anything to do with this thing, and I need them fast. You can get that for me right now without having to wait weeks for an Ecumenical Request Form." He stared at Markham while the man chewed his lip. "Dammit, you're a cop, Markham. And I'm asking you as a fellow officer to help me find this killer before anyone else gets hurt."

Markham took a few deep breaths and steadied himself. He'd been ordered not to cooperate beyond the minimum requirements and adhere strictly to the laws of interterritorial evidence retrieval. But as a sworn officer of the law, he couldn't stand by any longer while his people were brutally murdered, no matter what the Council said. "I'll have it to you by tonight."

As Markham walked off muttering prayers to God for his career, Wirz sat inside the rectory whispering to a disheveled man with wide, vacant eyes. He'd been attending the ceremony with his sister and her children and got separated from them during the stampede to escape. Wirz found him huddled along a staircase and hustled him back to the office to speak with him. An hour later, Wirz left the man sitting inside the church basement staring at the walls, muttering Wirz's instructions to him and cradling a high-powered rifle with a telescopic sight.

A Prayer at Gethsemane

1

The team had the site packed up and cleared by the time the sun had set. Tanner had been out of range most of the day and was headed back to Huntsville to meet them. The church would remain closed off as a crime scene until Deacon gave the all clear. Markham had ordered it. True to his word, the sheriff had every conceivable document available along with a list of names in Deacon's hands by the time the evidence vans pulled out. Chen's techs were already running down names and arranging for warrants. For the first time on this case, Deacon felt ahead of the game. He would have to send Markham a real thank-you when he got back to HQ, but first he had to find Elli. Everyone had been so busy with the body that no one noticed she'd disappeared. An usher had caught sight of her earlier hurrying into the church, and Deacon eventually found her kneeling in a small alcove off the main chapel in silent prayer.

The only light came from the flickering candles, giving Elli an angelic and tragic glow. Her eyes were dry and puffy, and the tiny trails of smoke from the candles irritated them. She'd held it together all afternoon while the team worked to free the body from its pedestal. She'd even managed not to scream when it cracked and slumped over onto the stage. But when the salt encasing the victim's face popped off, she found herself staring into the poor woman's milky, wide-eyed expression. She tried desperately to gain control of her rapidly shattering emotions as she prayed. Her life had become a series of grisly deaths, each more horrific than the first. And it showed no signs of stopping. She felt lost, her faith battered and bruised with every new discovery until she sat on the brink of abandonment. She looked up at the gentle, carved arches retreating into the darkness, imbued with faces of the apostles, the savior, and Mary Magdalene. She used to feel comforted by those faces as they watched over her. They assured her that she was not alone, even in her most desperate moments. Tonight, they felt cold and indifferent, their ears closed and hearts hardened. They stared down blankly, seeing nothing more than a simple human unworthy of their time and attention.

She lowered her head and prayed with trembling hands for the victim, not that it would do any good. There was no provision of faith for the saving of one who had died. For a person whose life had ended, their fate was already sealed and judgment was inevitable. It was too late to do anything about it. Whatever sins this poor young woman had committed in life would mark her throughout eternity. She would have no opportunity to atone for them or confess. She'd been robbed of that by a monster. But Elli wanted to try. Someone had to, even if it was only a sign of respect for the deceased. The victim's family was most certainly being notified at this moment. At least they would have closure. But closure was the one thing Elli wouldn't have this night, not physical or spiritual. Not after everything she'd seen and learned.

The words of the Council rang like a church bell in her ears: *It does not serve God to interfere in his divine judgment. We must accept his condemnations as people of faith.* They'd made their position clear. The dead were beyond their purview, and their executioner was an irritant at best. Like the statues above her, they wouldn't be of any help. Her only purpose on the task force was to offer as little assistance as possible and provide information on its progress, or more accurately its lack thereof. They knew she wasn't a qualified forensic investigator, and that had been the entire point: to give them time to hide and to plan, to manipulate the information to their own selfish ends.

Deacon entered the church and walked down the pews until he spotted her. She'd told him that this was her favorite place to be as a child and that she often still came here after a daunting hospital shift to pray for those she had lost and for those she had saved. To give them into God's hands once she had done his will on earth. He was loath to intrude on her privacy, but she'd run from the churchyard in such a state of panic, he feared for her sanity. He crossed himself humbly at the altar before quietly joining Elli in the vestibule. He lit a candle in the rack and then knelt quietly next to her, whispering a prayer for the victim.

Elli sniffled and rubbed her face to shake off the puffiness. "I'm a little surprised to see you here," she said.

"Because all us liberal sinners shun the Almighty and revel in the destruction of morality?" he asked. "I've heard all the rhetoric about us federal citizens. I thought you would know better than that."

"I didn't mean to imply that at all," she said defensively. "I graduated from Johns Hopkins. I spent most of my adult life in the Constitutional states. I just meant that—"

"That prayer wasn't something we routinely engaged in?" he said. Elli dropped her eyes, embarrassed that the old prejudices still managed to rear their ugly heads even after years of living among them and learning otherwise. Deacon wasn't angry or disappointed. He just smiled. "I have been known to pray when necessary. You see, me and God have a very special relationship. He accepts me for what he made me and expects me to do the same." He stared up at the figure hanging from the cross. "We just happen to be having a disagreement at the moment. I'm not perfect, Elli, and I don't pretend to be. I am a messed up, cursing, drinking son of a bitch with an ex-wife who couldn't take being married to one and a son I wasn't much of a father to. Can't really blame her." Elli uttered a small laugh. "I don't get to places like this much, so I confess my sins as I go, usually over a shot glass on my living room couch. The good Lord knows more heinous and disreputable things about me than anyone on earth because I don't lie to him. More importantly, I don't lie to myself. I'm pretty sure He forgives me."

She looked up to see him eyeing her with compassion. "How long have you been a cop, Deacon?" she asked.

"Not including my military service, thirty long-ass years," he replied. When he saw her cringe, he offered a "scuse me" to the faces hovering above.

"So you've dealt with murderers and psychopaths for a long time. You've seen men and women blowing each other up over everything and shooting innocent people just because they believe something different than you do." She paused. "I don't know how you stay sane and can still believe in God."

"My mother taught me that the good Lord never gives you more than you can handle," he offered.

Elli jumped up and cried, "I can't handle any more, Deacon. I can't!"

"Elli, calm down. It's okay. Just talk to me."

"No, Deacon, I can't deal with this. If God exists, then how can he let this keep happening? This isn't justice—this is cold-blooded murder." She was full-on rambling as she paced the vestibule. "And the Council just sits there and does everything it can to keep us from stopping it. They act as if it's nothing because they view it as justifiable. This isn't God's judgment. This is evil!"

"Elli, they're just men with power looking out for their own interests."

"Men with power?" she demanded. "Those men represent the combined faith of the Ecclesiastical territory. They are my religious leaders and the wardens of my faith. They're supposed to be the people who guide us and teach us how to be righteous, and they're covering for a murderer!"

She picked up a Bible and threw it at the altar. It crashed into several communal chalices, sending glass shattering all over the floor, but thankfully missed the lighted candles nearby. As she searched for something else to throw, Deacon grabbed hold of her arms and tried to restrain her.

"Calm down, Elli, before you set the place on fire," he told the struggling girl.

"I don't care!" she snarled back. "Let it burn. There's nothing here. There's no God watching over us. Just a bunch of power-crazy old men using us to do their dirty work, and I'm tired of it. I'm tired of praying for nothing. I'm tired of staring at mutilated bodies, and I can't do it anymore!"

Elli dissolved into a flood of tears and pain, and Deacon held her tightly. She cried for everything she'd been taught that now seemed only a pack of hollow lies. She cried until she had nothing left and was empty inside. Her life suddenly seemed meaningless, as if everything she had ever accomplished was only to keep her busy during her mundane existence, a way to pass the time until she, too, crumbled into nothing. And all the while Deacon held her.

When the tears and anger finally ebbed, he took her face into his hands and looked her firmly in the eye. "Elli," he said sternly, "don't ever say that. Don't deny God, and don't deny your faith."

"I don't have any left," she said wearily.

"Yes, you do," Deacon told her. "Do not let them rob you of your faith, Elli, because then they will own you. They win. They will turn you out as an example of how the godless states converted you into a nonbeliever and use you to further their own agenda. You will become their tool in this, and they will use you to destroy everything."

He lowered his hands and stared her squarely in the eyes. She looked into his calm face and said, "You still believe, don't you?"

He exhaled and smiled ever so slightly. "Yes, Elli. Yes, I do. Because faith in God is not predicated on the evils that men do; it's about the good they do in His name. It's about what He EXPECTS us to do for him. And I will continue to hunt this killer down and stop him because THAT is what God expects me to do."

Elli stared past him into the darkness of the vestibule with its flickering candlelight. "I don't know what He expects me to do anymore."

"I think He expects you do what you have always been called to do: save lives. It may not be the way you've been trained to do it, but you can still help. I need you. I need you to help me because you're the only person I can trust in this. Can you do that?" Deacon asked.

She took a deep breath and wiped her runny nose on the sleeve of her sweater. She only nodded, but Deacon let out a sigh of relief.

"We need to connect Wirz definitively to these murders and publicly expose what he's doing to people. It's the only way to stop him and end these killings," he said.

"I'll try," Elli responded shakily.

Deacon enveloped her in a bear hug that lifted her off her feet. When he set her down, they headed for the front entrance of the church, and Elli felt her spirits slowly returning. They were halfway down the center aisle when the first shot rang out. It hit Elli squarely in the back just to the right of her spine, taking her down immediately. The second shot hit Deacon as he turned to grab Elli, clipping his left temple. They both went down, but Deacon managed to roll and pull his gun with his right hand. He peppered the balcony with gunfire until his magazine was empty, but no other shots rang out. A door banged to the rear of the building, and Deacon crawled to where Elli lay. She was barely breathing, and her pulse was thready as he attempted to stop the bleeding in her chest.

He punched his comm link and yelled, "This is Deacon MacNair, service number 1227855. I have an officer down inside St. Michael's cathedral at 3756 State Lane Road and a wounded civilian. Send police, fire and rescue immediately. This is an active shooter crime scene. Repeat, this is an active shooter crime scene." He disconnected the call and said to Elli, "Hold on, kid, I'm not going to let you die. Do you hear me? I am NOT going to let you die."

2

Sirens wailed and lights flashed. There were shouts and people in uniforms running. Rooms came and went, the chapel, a vestibule, an emergency transport, a hospital corridor, a trauma room. All the images swirled around each other in a dense fog, moving out of order in slow motion as if time itself had broken down. At some point there were screams and wails of anguish that cut through the terse orders of the triage teams and surgical staff, and every now and then a familiar voice floated through the din to reach Deacon's ears. He tried to reconcile the input, to somehow put the confusion in order. The cries of anguish had to be for Elli. She had a loving family, parents who worried for her safety and survival. He had no one who cared that much for him. He taken his fair share of bullets since his divorce, and the only people who had ever shown any interest were his teammates. He was sure the familiar voice had been Joyce. It was so hard to be sure with the pain meds surging through his veins. The din subsided once his wound was patched and the room went silent. He had to have been unconscious for a time because the window showed a pitch-black sky. He was still disoriented when he pulled his clothing from the cabinet and stumbled down the hallway to Elli's room. An image of her lying there hooked up to every imaginable machine while a torrent of doctors worked on her teased his subconscious and he stumbled away. Guards. There should have been armed guards at both rooms. Where were they? Flashing white lights and a chorus of shouted questions and demands. Joyce's voice boomed over it. The press trying to get pictures and official statements. He stumbled away again toward a side entrance. Biting cold and distant chaos gave way to silence. An avatar enticingly asked a destination. He muttered an answer and then slipped under the waves of mental fog and into darkness.

Deacon shook his head and looked around the church alcove, wondering how the hell he'd managed to drive here. His head still throbbed from the gunshot wound. He remembered slipping out of the hospital. He remembered borrowing a police cruiser and driving out into the night, but the trip here was a blur. He had hazy images of pulling off the road at least twice to close his eyes against the onslaught of dizziness, but he remembered nothing else until he opened his eyes sitting on the pew and staring at the wooden floor.

Pulling himself up to a sitting position, he cradled his head in his hand. It was still dark outside, but it had to be edging toward dawn. It was chilly in the chapel, but he didn't feel it. In fact he felt slightly warm. Logic told him that it could be a sign of infection. He hated hospitals, but this was one of many reasons he should never have left. But in the depths of his foggy brain another reason floated into focus. Elli. He'd left Elli behind, something he'd sworn to her he wouldn't do. No, not to leave her behind. He'd sworn he would not let her die, and now she lay in the intensive care unit with a gunshot to the back, barely hanging on to life. There was nothing he could do for her; the doctors and surgeons had taken up the fight now. But he'd run and left her behind to fight alone.

A wave of sobbing threatened to overtake him as he slid off the pew and sank to the floor. He fought back the tears with spears of anger. Anger at the Cadre, anger at himself, anger at God. Whatever it took to fight them. In the end some tears had managed to escape. They flowed down his cheeks as he stared at the ever-stoic statue of Jesus offering his generic, one-size-fits-all expression of support. It hadn't changed since Neville's death. It still never gave him any answers. All it ever offered were questions. Why did you do what you did? Do you think you did the right thing? Was that the moral and Christian thing to do?

Deacon began to laugh. "All those powers and you're nothing but a shrink. A goddamned good-for-nothing shrink." He rubbed his head. "If you think you're gonna hand me a bill for this lifetime of spiritual therapy when I reach the pearly gates, you can cram that bullshit up ya ass."

"That's no way to talk to your Lord and savior, son!" Pastor Cooper's surly voice echoed. Deacon hadn't heard the old preacher come in. Cooper strode down the aisle intending to box Deacon's ears until he got close enough to see the bloodstains on his clothes and the soaked bandage on his head. Cooper helped pick him up from the floor and settled him into a pew.

"What are you doing here at this time of night, old man?" Deacon asked quietly.

"I heard a car pull up and saw flashing lights across the street. Thought someone might have broken in and tripped the alarm. I didn't expect to find you here." He retrieved a bowl from the altar and several clean silks used during services. Filling the bowl with holy water from the font, he cleaned and dressed Deacon's now-bleeding wound as best he could.

"I doubt holy water is gonna do much good at this point, preacher," Deacon chided him.

"I suppose not, but it can't hurt," Cooper told him. "You mind telling me what the hell happened tonight and why you are bleeding all over my church and cursing the Lord?"

"Sorry about that," Deacon told him. He told the old man about his conversation with Elli and the subsequent shooting at the church. He hesitated when Cooper asked him who he believed was responsible and why. The last thing he wanted was to put Cooper in danger, but the old man was adamant. When he finished, he hung his head and said, "I guess I didn't have anywhere else to turn."

Cooper sat back with a kindly smile. "The Lord's house is man's refuge from those who would do him harm. He's always here when you need him."

"How can you still believe that?" Deacon asked quietly. "With all that's going on in the territory and all the wrong being done, how can you still believe he gives a damn what happens to us?"

"Why wouldn't I? You still do. Otherwise you wouldn't be here." Deacon smiled up at him, conceding the point, but Cooper could still feel him slipping away. "You need to understand something about the good Lord, son. He's not here to solve our problems for us. He's here to help us make the right decisions to survive, to have the will to fight and to grow. He is our strength to keep fighting. And he will always have our back when we feel we just can't fight any longer."

"Is that what He told all those people who died at the hands of white nationalists during the war? What He tells all the non-whites in the territory who hide in fear of what their new slave masters will do to them if they disobey?"

"Those people who died were fighting for what was right. It was their fight to fight, not God's. He knew they would have to decide for themselves what path to take, and they knew they might have to make the ultimate sacrifice to do it. Their deaths were an abomination before God, but he rewarded their faith in Heaven." Cooper took a breath while he let Deacon absorb his words. "The people in the territory who cower in fear of their faith have chosen to do so. They have not yet found the strength of God's will to fight back against their oppressors. That will is not something God can give you. It has to come from within. You have to be ready to accept it, embrace it, and accept the consequences of using that strength before you can truly become one with it."

"What about your son Chet and his partner? All the gay parishioners that used to attend services here? They fled to the north rather than face judgment at the hands of the Ecumenical body."

Cooper exhaled and closed his eyes sadly. "That was a matter of survival, not choice. They would have been put to death, and that was unacceptable."

"Why?" Deacon asked him. "The Bible's pretty clear about homosexuality. Most people have accepted the written Word as fact. They turn a blind eye to what E-Rep does because of it. But you, a man of God, helped smuggle them all out before they could be judged."

Cooper gave him a puzzled look that said "Who, me?" but when Deacon stared back, clearly not buying it, he said, "Yes, I defied the Council. And yes, I smuggled those people to the Constitutionalists."

"You defied the word of God."

"I defied the judgment of men," Cooper responded. "The Council was created to weigh the confessed sins of a man against his good works in the name of the Lord and assign penance accordingly so that he or she could atone. Those people were good Christians and did good works for the community. They attended church regularly, were charitable toward their fellow man and were law-abiding citizens who did no harm. Yes, they were sinners, but who among us is not? Their sin was against God, not man. We are all taught to love one another regardless of our faith, race or persuasion, for we are all God's children. They sinned in their relationships with a member of the same sex, but they did so out of that love. And in this, we are not fit to be their judges. Only God can judge them. And when they stand before him, they will have to take that up with him."

He rose from the bench and lit a large white candle in the center of the altar. "My sin was defying the Council for what I believe was a great wrong, and I will stand before God and answer for that. But I will stand before Him with a clear conscience and a pure heart for my actions, and if He judges me harshly, I will accept that judgment, knowing I did what I felt was right."

He sat back down next to Deacon. "Whatever you do in this lifetime, do what you know in your heart is right. Follow your faith. Don't fear defying the Council."

"Even if doing it violates religious law?" Deacon asked him.

"Religion is a construct of men, not God. There is nothing holy or sacred about it. Whatever grace we give it comes from us, and it only serves man's adoration of himself. Faith can't be found in a book. Faith is intangible, a spiritual connection to something unseen yet deeply felt. If faith is telling you that what you are doing is right, then you must do as faith tells you. And if committing a sin is the only way to accomplish that, then do it with a pure heart and a pure objective. Don't worry about what a bunch of old men misreading a two-thousand-year-old book tell you is right or wrong. Do what your faith tells you to do. God knows your heart, and He will judge you accordingly in the end."

"Is that what you tell your parishioners?" Deacon asked.

"With every breath I take," Cooper told him. "I tell them what I am telling you now. We all live in THIS world, and this world isn't black or white, right or wrong. The world has grown and changed, and sometimes we have to make sacrifices because there are no absolutes. So don't be afraid to piss God off if you know what you're doing is right. Sometimes doing the wrong thing for the right reasons is the right thing to do."

Deacon thought for a moment. "I'm going to have to fight these men on their own terms, and it's going to take down a lot of people. It could destabilize the territory."

"If that's what it takes to expose the evil among us, then that's what you have to do. Don't worry about the territory. Eden will rise again. But we can't fix what's broken until we bring it into the light."

3

Quentin Hollister sat in front of the roaring fireplace in his library, a glass of whiskey in his hand. The storm outside beat a steady cadence on the tall French doors. He didn't hear it any more than he felt the heat radiating from the fire or the whiskey burning a trail down his throat. This room had been his inner sanctum since childhood and had served him well during his time in the Senate. His father had told him that a well-provisioned library, one worthy of hosting heads of state and dignitaries from around the world, was the hallmark of sophistication and class of a southern gentlemen. A place where a man could plan the course of his life among the histories and philosophies of those who had shaped his moral fiber and stimulated his mind. Some of the most important decisions in history had been made in rooms like this, his father had told him. He hadn't left this room for two days.

Many of the books on the shelves had been there since his great-grandfather's day and were considered rare collectibles. They had been added to over the years and culled carefully as the times changed and each new generation took up residence. But the essence of history and the gentility of those storied days still remained. This room, unlike any other, had the ability to remove the stresses of his day and the doubts of his heart. And to make the process more effective, a carefully curated cabinet of the finest whiskey and liquors from around the world provided an impetus of clarity for his mind. But tonight, even the silky smoothness of a fine Tennessee whiskey couldn't reach deep enough into his soul to cleanse it or burn hot enough to chase away the darkness. He gulped the remainder of his drink, feeling it scorch his throat, and refilled the glass from the decanter at his feet.

They tried to murder my child, he thought as he stared at the dancing flames. He took another gulp and then wrapped his arms around his torso as it burned holes in his empty belly. Quentin was not the type of man to succumb to emotion. He had been stoic when the sheriff appeared in his office to inform him that his daughter had been shot. He'd been cool as ice as he stood in the intensive care ward and listened as the doctors described her condition and her chances of survival. He'd been calm and controlled when he'd called his wife Stella to give her the news. And he'd been a bastion of strength as he coordinated the security arrangements for his daughter's hospital room and the very best of doctors to treat her. But as he sat in front of a fire he couldn't feel, drinking booze he couldn't taste, surrounded by a storm he couldn't hear, he shivered with cold and eventually began to weep.

The attack hadn't been a random robbery or some accidental shooting as the news reports were broadcasting. It had been an assassination attempt, pure and simple. Whether the assailant had intended to kill her or MacNair was still not known, but the message to Quentin was crystal clear: The Cadre would stop at nothing to preserve control of the Republic. What made matters worse was that one of his colleagues and trusted peers had been responsible. MacNair insisted that there was no clear evidence to indicate the direct involvement of anyone in the Senate, but there was enough circumstantial evidence to connect a few high-ranking members of the Ecumenical Council to that rogue organization. MacNair had asked for his help with the investigation despite having no rock-solid evidence, and he'd hesitated. Though he knew what MacNair had uncovered was true, he'd refused to commit. His cowardice had nearly cost him his daughter's life.

Stella opened the door to the study without knocking. She'd just spent the day at her daughter's bedside and was completely exhausted. Her makeup was old and there were streaks on her cheeks where her tears had left rivers in her foundation. Her hair was damp from walking through the rain, and her dress was ruined. She went to the sideboard and poured herself a hefty glass of brandy, preferring it to the whiskey that Quentin favored. It burned like Greek fire growing as it touched her insides. But that endless heat left her cold.

Quentin didn't even acknowledge her presence as she kicked her heels off at the door. Even without them she was statuesque, as slender as she had been during her runway days with legs that still gave Quentin chills when she walked.

"How is she?" Quentin mumbled.

"She's alive," Stella told him. "Not that anyone expected her to survive, but then she's always had her daddy's iron will."

Quentin laughed softly. "I think she gets her iron will from you, my dear. She's always favored you in everything. You know, she told me once when she was little, she wanted to grow up to be just like you." Stella let the compliment pass unanswered.

"How could you let this happen?" Stella snarled.

Quentin looked up from where he sat. "What the hell are you talking about?"

She threw the glass past him into the fireplace. The last of her brandy sprayed, causing the flames to flash. He jumped from his chair to keep from being singed.

"You could have stopped them." She stood face-to-face with Quentin, the accusation in her eyes boring through him. "They've been after you since the beginning, Quentin, but you always refused them. You wanted to be the voice of compassion and leadership the country needed to see, the one man who could bridge the gap between the Constitutionalists and the citizens of God. You could have revealed their involvement with the Council years ago and stopped them."

"You want me to expose them? Just like that?" he thundered back. "I should just destroy the holy Council that guides our entire way of life?"

"YES!" Stella screamed.

"The Council is not to blame for the manipulations of these operatives. They're trying to protect the territory and its faith."

"Oh, please!" she retorted. "They're nothing but a bunch of old men drunk on power and scared their little secrets will get out. They pretend to be pious and righteous in the light of day because that's what it means to be an Ecumenical Leader. You have to set an example for the people to follow so they can adore you and bow down to you. But turn out the lights and they scurry like the cockroaches they are. Milling about with their paid whores and selling their souls to the highest bidder."

Quentin looked at his wife with sympathy. "You don't understand. They aren't the ones who did this. There are others in the shadows controlling them, manipulating them. Their organization is ruthless and will stop at nothing to keep their grip." He waited for Stella to calm down. "Do you remember what happened to Spurlock?"

Stella grabbed the decanter from the sideboard. "You mean the fool who drove his car into the Chattahoochee and killed himself, along with the half-naked whore he was with?"

"Yes, and it wasn't an accident," he told her. "This is what they do. This is how they deal with people who get in their way." He glanced past her toward the family photo on his desk, to the smiling face of his daughter Elli. "I resisted them as much as I could without destroying our way of life, and they tried to kill our daughter because of it." He collapsed into the chair and stared into the fireplace.

Stella walked over and sat on the arm with her back to him. "We can send her up north. We can get her out of their reach . . ."

"Their reach is everywhere. There is no place where she'll be safe. They're in every dark corner of the country."

"Then turn on the lights, Quentin," Stella muttered. "You can't stand by any longer and play it safe and diplomatic. Let the sun in and run them into the light." Quentin looked up as she turned to face him. "You can't kill a cockroach until you can see him. Then you squash him until there's nothing left."

He rubbed his hand along her thigh and stared lovingly into her face. "You were always the strong one," he told her. "You gave up everything to come here with me, to raise our family, to support my career. Look where it got us. I've lost you and almost lost our daughter."

She slid down into the chair next to him and snuggled into his lap. "You didn't take anything from me," she sighed. "I came here because I believed in you and what you wanted to achieve. Somewhere along the way, you just forgot who you are. You became one of them and left us behind."

Quentin closed his eyes. She was right. He had forgotten who he was. He had allowed the culture of power to poison his life. He'd become weak and succumbed to temptations like most of his colleagues. Walking with God by day and lying with Satan at night. There had been a number of women over the years and more than enough influence peddling that he'd turned a blind eye to. By the time he realized the depth of the infiltration, it was too late to intervene. Exactly when it had happened he had no idea, but his lack of resistance had now cost him nearly everything—and no secret organization was responsible for that. "I'm so sorry I failed you," he whispered.

Stella's heart cramped with guilt as she thought of the men she'd often sought comfort with and the fact that her iron will came to her in a liquid form these days. "What are we going to do?" she asked quietly.

Quentin didn't answer.

4

Deacon tried to sit up but groaned aloud as his brain shifted in his wounded skull. A strip of anesthetape filled with timed-release painkiller was plastered over the wound, but he still felt dizzy and weak. He'd been hunched over the surveillance feeds from the church for hours looking for suspects in the case and now for the assassination attempt on Elli and himself. Joyce smothered him with coffee, food, and anything else he needed. She even made him lie down on the sofa in his office every hour to make sure he rested. It annoyed him endlessly, being treated like some fragile old man. It had been years since a woman had tended to him like this, not since his marriage had crumbled. But as irritating as it was, he was deeply grateful for it.

Burke ran the crime scene investigation in connection with Markham's deputies and was doing an exceptional job. Any contempt Burke held for the locals had died the moment Elli was shot. The need to find the shooter had broken through his massive superiority complex and allowed the potential Deacon had always seen to come forward. He dumbed down the procedures for the locals with no condescension, allowing the two factions to work together seamlessly, and acted in every way a leader. Deacon walked past and patted him confidently on the shoulder. Despite the pain, Burke didn't wince this time.

Joyce kept him apprised of every tiny development they uncovered, but it wasn't much. Clues that she would normally have gushed about she delivered with calm reflection, always noting if, when, and where they were worthy of pursuit, trying valiantly to fill his shoes.

"Is that really how I sound when I'm in charge?" he snickered.

"Right up to the point where you lose it, start quoting Scripture and calling people cocksuckers in the most polite and professional manner," she replied calmly, tossing a pillow at him before leaving.

He reloaded the feeds from the beginning and continued to search, making notes of individuals that appeared to fit the killer's profile. He had no clue about the identity of the assassin, but he was positive the two were not one and the same. He'd made it halfway through when his comm link chimed. The harsh beep sent his ears ringing until Agnes's soft voice informed him that he had a call on a secure line. She patched it through as Deacon removed his earpiece and set the unit on speaker. The last thing his aching head needed was a phone call beamed directly into it.

"MacNair," he muttered.

"I've been looking for you everywhere, MacNair," Markham's voice boomed out. Deacon lowered the volume. "You were supposed to be under guard at the hospital, but they said you signed yourself out against doctor's orders. I thought you were dead."

"You ain't getting rid of me that easy, Markham," Deacon told him. "I've been looking for the shooter, but we haven't identified him yet."

"That's why I've been hunting you down. We found the guy already."

Deacon sat up much more quickly than his brain would have liked, and his eyes shot open. "You have him in custody?"

"Sort of," Markham told him. "He's dead. One of the maintenance crew gave us a description of him leaving the chapel just after the shots rang out. We caught up with him this morning. Tried to bring him in for questioning, but he put the barrel in his mouth and pulled the trigger before we could arrest him. Kept babbling on about angels demanding his sacrifice before he blew his head off."

"Who was he?" Deacon asked.

"Nobody, and I mean that literally. Charles Butler Wickham. Had one prior for getting drunk one night and giving his wife a black eye about eight months ago, but other than that he was a clean, churchgoing good old boy. Worked at a brewery over in Woodstock." Deacon pulled up the Penance List and searched for the name. He found it in under three seconds. "The rifle's ballistics match the slug we pulled from Dr. Hollister, but unless you've been withholding evidence about your suspect or ruthlessly pissing off my citizens, MacNair, I have no idea why this man would want to kill you."

"I do," Deacon muttered.

"Well, by all means enlighten me," Markham said snidely.

"It's his reconditioning," Deacon told him. "Contrary to what the media is reporting, he wasn't making any political statement, and he wasn't crazy or depressed. He did it because someone brainwashed him to."

"What the hell are you talking about, MacNair?" Markham asked.

"You have access to the current Penance List, right?"

Markham hesitated. "Yes. It's my job to schedule the pickups."

"Look back at your records. You said he had a domestic violence conviction about eight months ago. He underwent reconditioning as penance. Whatever they did to him, they programmed him to take orders and then self-destruct like some sort of time bomb before he could be captured and questioned."

"I think that bullet may have dug a little deeper into your skull than we thought, Lieutenant," Markham said evenly.

"Listen to me, Caleb, please. Pull the list and check the names. You've had a rash of accidents and suicides over the last couple of years. People who did things completely out of character and who had no reason whatsoever to take their own lives. Good people. It's the one thing they all have in common."

The line was quiet for a minute, and then Markham quietly said, "Lieutenant, I'm gonna say this as a fellow police officer. You need to get back to the hospital and have the docs look at you. You may be suffering from PTSD, and you shouldn't be up."

"Dammit, Caleb, it wasn't his fault!" Deacon yelped before pulling himself back. "Wickham is innocent. And so was Mona Davis." Deacon waited, but all he could hear was Markham's heavy breathing. "They did it to her, too, Caleb," Deacon said sympathetically. "If you hadn't shot her, she would have killed herself because they've all been programmed to not leave witnesses. You didn't have a choice. Both of you are as much victims of this as Wickham. It wasn't your fault."

Deacon waited as Markham's deep breathing continued, now with an anguished hitch. "What you're saying is that the Council is responsible for this. You're accusing my government of murdering its own citizens."

"You and I both know who's directly responsible for this, Caleb, and it isn't the government," Deacon answered. "I don't know if or how many of the other Council members are working with him and I won't make unfounded accusations, but you're a cop, Caleb, a good cop. These are your people. Elli is your people. I can't believe you'd let this go on and turn a blind eye to it."

After a minute, Markham said, "I'll have the body transferred over to you for examination along with the slugs. I don't know how long it'll take the Council to find out about the transfer, but you better be prepared for a shit storm when they do."

The line went dead and Deacon closed his eyes. He'd just tipped his hand to his opponent in one of the biggest poker games ever played. He prayed he'd made the right move.

5

Deacon wasn't the only one scanning the security feeds. Wirz replayed them over and over, but unlike MacNair, he prayed he wouldn't find who he was looking for. The crowds were unremarkable, filled with the wealthy patrons of the diocese surrounded by the poor working class, all straining to get a glimpse of the pageantry. The media crowds milled about carrying equipment and live streaming the event across the country. Then the chaos erupted and everyone stampeded away from the stage in every direction. He stopped playback and requested the feeds from the day before and the morning of the dedication. Milton had been conspicuously AWOL since fleeing the scene three days earlier, and he wasn't taking anyone's calls—probably cowering somewhere with a bottle. He'd have to arrange for Milton's son to lose a leg this time instead of just breaking one. That should bring old Milton out of hiding.

As Wirz waited, he looked over the bills of lading, the commission contract, and anything related to the installation of the statue. The documentation listed it as a gift from an obscure church in Italy to its unofficial sister in the Americas. The artist's name retrieved very generic background information, detailing a hermit of sorts with great skill and no photographic evidence whatsoever. Hallmarks of a fictitious identity. His name was attributed to a substantial body of work that literally existed nowhere. Not one piece could be found exhibited in any museum or public place anywhere in the world. All of it was in the hands of private collectors that occasionally listed the pieces for substantial amounts of money. Wirz had no doubt that every private collector was as nonexistent as the artist himself. He contacted the shipping company and learned that the delivery and setup were meticulously arranged through third parties run by what turned out to be a series of shell companies. All in all, the entire effort was untraceable, and the gift from fellow worshippers was a lie.

The screen peeped and the feeds from the day before the ceremony began to run. Two hours into the feed, a black truck arrived and a very nondescript man in a work jacket and steel toe boots entered the church, followed by a man in coveralls. Both wore baseball caps and neither removed them when entering the church, a sin Wirz would have had them reprimanded for at length. They both came out followed by the bishop when a large delivery truck pulled up an hour later. They were still wearing their hats, and Wirz muttered a curse as he watched all three follow the delivery truck into the courtyard. He watched the installation of the statue, which was unremarkable. The crew did an exceptionally careful job with the piece. The man in the work jacket supervised them closely to make sure nothing happened to the statue, inspecting it at every stage to ensure its condition and somehow managing to avoid looking into the monitor. Four hours later, the statue stood in the courtyard as the tarp was secured to handles installed in the base to keep it safe. The bishop shook the hands of every man and blessed them each for the fine work they did. Only the man in the work jacket remained behind to make sure the statue was safe and secure from prying eyes and mishaps. Before leaving, he took the bishop's hand in both of his and gave it a simple shake. This was not the greeting of a simple citizen of Eden. Working-class men always gave their boldest southern handshake to the clergy, often shaking the elderly member's arms so hard their entire bodies shook. Only men of the cloth greeted each other by grasping one hand with two.

Wirz zoomed in tighter, but the man in the work jacket kept his back to the monitors wherever he went. He knew how to evade identification. He let the playback resume until the man left and ran the feed rapidly to the hours before the ceremony the next day. His comm line chirped insistently, but he ignored it. He watched as the maintenance workers came in early to clean the courtyard and set up the chairs and stage. He watched as the media crews came early to stake out their camera locations and set up their equipment. He watched Markham arrive with his deputies and set up security for the event. Eventually people began to arrive, the wealthiest being fashionably late to make a grander entrance for the cameras. It wasn't until the stragglers, the freelance journalists, began to arrive that he noticed something strange. As they passed through the checkpoints, each one showed his badge and was searched until the one and only Buck Meisner showed up. He couldn't find his badge and then argued with the officer checking through his bag, causing such a ruckus that it took three officers to search it and then clear it. No one noticed the man with the camera move quietly past the melee and join the crowd of photographers. Wirz stopped and replayed the incident twice. Each time, the man slipped quietly by, keeping his head low and his identity obscured. He had a press badge hanging from his neck, but it was conveniently obscured.

Wirz froze the clearest image of the man as he passed behind the officers and then pulled the cleanest image he could find from the delivery feed. Viewing them side by side, he had no doubt that this was indeed the same man, but the face was obscured in both images. Only the body and build were visible, and they were nearly identical. It would be an extreme stretch of the imagination to believe the man was Harrison Meeks. He was much leaner and more muscular than he remembered, but that could easily be attributed to a steady exercise regimen. His hair was kept covered by a ball cap, as was most of his face. Wirz needed more if he were to be certain.

He returned to the feed from the ceremony and looked for his subject. In every place the photographer appeared, he faced away from the monitors or held his camera up to obscure his face, just as any professional assassin would. Wirz's frustration was humming like an electrical tower when he realized he'd been looking for the wrong thing. He restarted the feeds, running through them from the installation all the way through the mayhem, watching intently for his prey. An hour later, he sat back in his chair as the color drained from his face. In every instance, the man kept his right shoulder dropped, supporting everything with his left side.

A shriek of anger erupted from Wirz as he sent a stack of data pads crashing into the wall. The commotion was no doubt heard across the entire floor, but his aides knew better than to enter his offices without permission. His temper was as legendary as the God of the Old Testament, yet he stared at the door until he was satisfied no one would disturb him and then began to pace and grumble. Outsmarted by an old man who'd long outlived his usefulness; played by the mentor who taught him everything he knew.

Apparently not everything . . .

He stared out the window overlooking the capitol grounds. If the Feds got to Meeks before him, they would put an iron wall of protection around Meeks until trial. And once they discovered who he really was, Meeks would never see the inside of a prison cell. He'd be granted immunity from prosecution and would expose the Cadre to the entire world. He'd disappear into witness protection, and Caulder's life would be over. If the Cadre found out, they'd mobilize every operative to hunt Meeks down and erase him and any federal agent that got within a mile of his true identity. They'd make him disappear, and the case would go cold. The outside world would learn only that the killer, under his current alias, had been stopped. The Council would make some sort of statement alluding to the hand of God putting a stop to his crimes, and people's faith in the leadership would be reaffirmed. It was the better outcome, but Caulder's life would still be over. His failure would be laid bare and his immediate retirement set in stone.

There was only one way he would survive. He had to find Meeks before anyone else could and eliminate him. He settled into his office chair and fired up the encrypted communications network. It was time to start cleaning house.

6

Sunday services had ended at the territorial cathedral and news crews gathered on the capitol grounds. It was unusual for a senator to make a statement to the press on a holiday weekend and especially not on a day reserved for worship. But it was noted that today's gathering was sanctioned by the Council as a public service message and that all networks were expected to attend. This, of course, meant that every journalist within a hundred miles was also present, including the ever-intrusive Buck Meisner. The rumor mill had been churning in high gear with theories about the sudden disappearance of Wallace Milton. Everyone expected him to give a heartfelt and yet utterly political speech about what he'd been up to and why. But when Quentin Hollister approached the dais to address the crowd with Kyle Tanner at his side, a palatable tension began to form.

Quentin stepped up to the podium and glanced toward Tanner. The deputy had refused to leave Elli's hospital room. It was only after a contingent of federal officers took his place, and at Elli's insistence, that he agreed. Kyle took a quick look at the security contingent and nodded that all was ready. Quentin stepped up and engaged the microphone.

"Good morning," he began reservedly. "I'd like to apologize for disturbing your observances on this holy day and offer thanks and blessings to everyone watching and listening throughout the territory. May God protect, preserve and bless you all."

In accordance with custom, everyone present repeated the blessing back to him.

"It is with great regret that I announce that, due to personal and familial circumstances, High Senator Wallace Milton has chosen to resign his position and discontinue his campaign for election to federal office."

Pandemonium instantly broke out as questions were shouted from the crowd. It took several minutes and the assistance of Ecumenical Security for him to restore quiet before continuing.

"In the event that High Senator Milton were elected to federal office, it would be my duty to step into his position in the Senate until the next scheduled elections are held. I will henceforth be assuming that duty, effective immediately."

Questions rumbled yet again, and security urged everyone to quiet down. Quentin stared at the data pad Wirz had given him. It contained a prepared speech outlining his dedication to continuing the platform Milton had been pushing. No one had seen or heard from Milton since his disappearance, and the Council remained silent. Quentin knew in the pit of his stomach that Milton would never be found. He relocated his stopping point and prepared to speak. A vision of his daughter lying in her hospital bed listening to him recite this litany of fear and oppression caused him to hold his breath. The silence became deafening as Quentin turned the pad over. A minute later he began to speak.

"Much has been said over the past few months about the threat the Constitutional territory represents to our new Eden. It has been proposed that our representation in the affairs of our great country is being marginalized and suppressed because of our adherence to Scripture. But nothing could be further from the truth."

Listening from the recesses of the capitol balcony behind the lectern, Wirz dug his fingernails into the carved wood railing as the crowd below murmured in confusion.

"If we have suffered from isolation, it was not at the hands of our fellow Americans. It is because we have imposed it upon ourselves out of fear and hubris. Since its creation under God, America has stood for personal liberty and religious freedom, and we exist as a country today because of that great belief. We formed our territory to offer the faithful a place of salvation. A place wherein they could live under the grace of God, free from the threats that exist in our sister territories and the temptations of unregulated liberty. But in our desire to create utopia, we have failed."

The crowd rumbled, but every person within earshot of the broadcast suddenly went silent as he raised a hand and continued to speak.

"We are all given a destiny in life by our Creator, and it is up to each of us to discover what that destiny is and make a path to it. No man can or should dictate the destiny of another human being. That is a power belonging solely to the Almighty. Only God himself can dictate what that destiny is for each and every one of us. Only He can tell you how to serve him. And only you can know His desire for you. Therefore, as my first official act, I am withdrawing the Family Preservation Act from consideration by the Senate."

The crowd erupted yet again, but Quentin was able to quiet them without force. "I encourage each and every man and woman of the territory to serve God however they are called, whether as doctors, lawyers, firefighters or teachers, or as mothers and fathers of generations yet to come. Only you and God can know, and only you and God will know, when the time is right for you to embrace that role. Whatever your path and however you serve God and your fellow man, I ask that you do it with the love and mercy that are the embodiment of God Almighty. I ask that you serve all mankind, believers and non-believers, equally without judgment or fear as Jesus taught us. To do so is to exist in a state of grace. That is what God wants for us, and I assure you that we, your leadership, stand ready to assist you and guide you on your journey. Questions, please."

As a thousand questions bombarded the new high senator, Wirz sank back into the shadows, his scowl mutating into a tight grin as he spoke quietly into his comm line. He didn't need to witness the aftermath of his orders, so he made his way down to the underground garage.

The police tried to control the crowd and direct the questions, but they were outnumbered by press. Even Quentin's pleas for order went unheard. It was only after the shot echoed across the plaza that the cries subsided. And then the screaming began.

7

Elli clutched her mother's hand as the two of them watched the press conference in horror. She desperately searched for her father's face in the panicked crowd, but all she could see was a pile of policemen, shielding what she dreaded was her father's body. The network had switched from a live feed of the podium to the stampeding crowd fleeing the scene, but the main feed to Elli's hospital room came directly from the Homeland Security cameras. They remained trained on the steps of the capital as more and more agents and police surrounded the staging area. Commands were shouted into earpieces and guns were drawn. The huddle of agents and officers grew more agitated as they called for assistance. When several of them moved aside to make room for the rescue crews, she caught a glimpse of blood-spattered uniforms. Stella gasped and whispered, "Oh God, Quentin," but Elli couldn't speak. She gripped her mother's hand even more tightly and tugged fiercely at the crucifix around her neck, its chain digging into her skin.

On the steps of the capitol building, Deacon and Joyce watched as Kyle Tanner's blood gushed onto the marble. The bullet had taken out his carotid artery, and no matter how much pressure they applied, it was impossible to stop the flow. When the medical team arrived, they took over, but even they knew the deputy wasn't leaving these steps alive.

Around the scene a wall of agents blocked the view, keeping Senator Hollister from the sniper's line of sight. He was no doubt long gone, but Deacon knew they wouldn't stop another shot if he decided to take it. The slug had torn through one of the columns behind them, leaving a star-shaped pattern around a large hole. He'd seen this type of damage before. The bullet was a high-velocity round capable of penetrating at least two people before it even slowed down and lodged in the body of a third. It had been one of the military's preferred weapons during the war. He turned to Senator Hollister and said, "Sir, we need to get you out of here. We cannot let anything happen to you."

"I'm staying," Hollister said as he cradled Tanner's head in his lap. Kyle Tanner had taken a bullet meant for him and now lay bleeding to death on his thigh. "This should have been me," he said as Kyle glared up at him.

Kyle tried to speak through the blood filling his mouth, but Quentin couldn't understand him. He leaned closer, and Kyle grabbed his hand tightly. "Fight for us. Don't let them win," he gurgled and began to wheeze. The paramedics pushed the senator back and pressed more firmly on the wound as sirens wailed ever closer, but the deputy never had a chance. Kyle Tanner's eyes went wide and blank as the ambulance entered the gate.

"He's gone, Senator. Please, let's get you out of here and under cover," Deacon told him. This time Quentin obeyed. The entire entourage moved in a fast, tight huddle into the building and to an anteroom with no windows reserved for private consultations.

Joyce's comm link chimed and a call was patched in from Angel's Mercy Hospital. "Deacon, it's the senator's wife." She handed the line over to Hollister, but before he could answer, Deacon said, "Just tell her that you're uninjured and safe, that the person hit was one of your security detail. Keep it short, and tell her that you have to go and to give no details to anyone, especially not the press."

Quentin shook his head and accepted the call. He retreated to a corner where he could reassure Stella and his daughter with some privacy. A knock at the door caused the entire room to draw their weapons as the intercom was pressed.

"It's Markham," the voice called from the box. "The scene's been secured, and I need you out here."

Deacon turned to Joyce. "Keep him in here and don't let anyone else in until I make sure it's secure." He slipped out the door, not moving from it until he heard the locks reengage behind him. Markham was red-faced and angry to the point of tears, but he kept it in check. His uniform bore the bloody imprint where a hand gripped the shoulder and then smeared down across his chest.

"I've raised that boy his entire life. I'm the only daddy he ever knew."

Despite his intense dislike for the man, Deacon felt nothing but sympathy for him. When a fellow officer is killed, no matter the agency, it's felt throughout them all as if he or she were one of their own. "I'm sorry, Sheriff. Tanner was a good man, and he didn't deserve to go out like this."

"He was a kid. He had his whole life ahead of him," Markham told him. "The academy was supposed to help straighten him out, make him stand up for himself, but he just wouldn't toughen up. I thought if I gave him to you for a few weeks he'd be pissed enough to gain some guts."

"He had guts and then some," Deacon said. "That boy had integrity and dedication. You should be proud of the job he was doing."

The first tears crept down Markham's face. "Whatever you need, doesn't matter. You'll have it. You just find the son of a bitch who did this and make sure that cop-killing motherfucker gets caught."

Deacon nodded. "It might mean going further than you're willing to go." He waited until he was sure Markham was listening. "There's more than one madman at work here, and we have evidence that it involves members of the Ecumenical Council and the Senate. It's a major threat to the territory, but I can't stop it alone."

Markham dropped his eyes slightly and looked beyond him. It told Deacon that Markham knew more than he was letting on, but now that it had turned personally deadly, the man had a choice to make. Markham looked past the doors to the red stain on the marble outside. A stretcher was being maneuvered down the stairs, and as it was tipped, a bloody arm fell and hung limply from under the sheet. He looked back at Deacon. "You swear to me you're not doing this out of revenge for your boy, that you're really here to help us."

"I'm giving you my word as an officer of the law. I'm here to protect these people, and I'll do whatever it takes to do it."

Markham looked hard at Deacon's eyes. Every racist thought he had nurtured since before the war screamed out to him not to believe it. *You couldn't trust a nigger* was what his daddy had always told him. He'd followed in Daddy's footsteps and joined the sheriff's department with that in mind. Even years later and with more than a few African American friends, that motto still kept his feelings for them at arm's length. His superiors and his benefactors in power had used it as a mantra to keep him motivated for years, and he'd done some unbelievably shady shit for them in return. But Deacon wasn't a superior, a benefactor or a friend: he was a fellow officer, and Markham knew what determination and honesty in a cop looked like. He closed the door on his daddy's specter, if only temporarily, and said, "I'll handpick the officers. You just tell me when and where. We'll be there to take care of business."

Deacon held out his hand, and Markham gripped it.

PART 4
A Requiem for Justice

Blessed Are Those Who Mourn

1

The attempted assassination of Senator Hollister sent shock waves throughout E-Rep territory and cast a dark shadow over Thanksgiving celebrations. Speculation and conspiracy theories dominated the talk shows, and pulpits trumpeted the arrival of Satan in the new Eden. Pundits pondered the political implications of the disappearance of one territorial candidate and the attempted murder of his possible successor, and Washington was ablaze with representatives demanding action. Deacon heard none of it. He simply sat in the president's study waiting for the delegation to leave. His mind was back in Georgia, in the chapel of a large Atlanta church, a small group of sheriff's deputies wearing dress uniforms huddling in the front pews. Elli sitting in a wheelchair next to her father, looking pale and weak with only her eyes betraying the strength she possessed. Law enforcement from every precinct in two states filling the remaining rows, leaving the press to pack every other available space to the rafters. In the streets outside, crowds of people fighting for a glimpse of the spectacle and a chance to be on TV.

The honor guard was simple but dignified. There were no ridiculous sprays of flowers or ornamentation. It was a somber and stately service. The Council had sent people to officiate but Markham refused, insisting instead that the family pastor give the eulogy. The pastor's words were heartfelt and left not a dry eye in the house. Deacon had never seen more men in tears in one place in his life, except once on a bloody battlefield outside of DC.

President Turnouer sent Marine One to fetch him and gave him no chance to refuse, so he had to skip the graveside services. He didn't really need to be there; having attended so many military funerals, he had the routine memorized. He also knew the cemetery well, having buried a few friends there over the years. The dirt paths that wound their way through the old family plots would be icy, so they'd have to step carefully in the procession. It would be a slow and steady slog, but military and law enforcement shared a common grace when carrying the body of a fallen brother or sister. At the graveside, Psalms 23 and 27 would be recited, perhaps followed by Ecclesiastes 3:1-8. There'd be the traditional 21-gun salute. Then everyone would say their final goodbyes and the casket would be lowered into the cold, laser-cut winter ground. As Tanner's only living relative, Markham would be accepting the flag. Later tonight the grave would be filled in, and Kyle Tanner would rest for eternity in a backwater cemetery next to his mother, grandfather, and nine obscure Confederate ancestors. Even though he would miss it, Deacon could still feel the finality and sorrow.

The doors opened and a Secret Service agent ushered him into the Oval Office. The last meeting he'd attended here revealed to him a dangerous foe he wasn't allowed to confront, only observe. This time, he'd be leaving with a license to kill. No bargaining, no compromises, just the authority to act with extreme prejudice. Thanks to Neville's rehabilitation records, it took less than half an hour to make his case and even less time to secure the warrants.

December had brought cold, ice and flurries to the south, but Marine One cut through them, cleanly delivering him back to Huntsville. Instead of reporting in, he climbed into his cruiser and headed east toward the outskirts of Atlanta. He knew that a federal arrest warrant would be useless without the support of local law enforcement, and there was only one person he had any chance of convincing. He made his way through the aging row houses along Daniel Street until he found Sally Markham's shotgun two-story. It was a modest clapboard structure with aged brick facade and a front porch surrounded by a carved wood balustrade. The front yard contained a few dead rose bushes and even deader grass sprouting weeds, and it was no wider than the narrow house itself. In fact, the entire plot couldn't have been much more than a hundred feet across and five hundred feet long. All of it surrounded by a rusted iron fence. Sally Markham was long dead, and her only son Kyle had just been buried less than a mile away. To Deacon, the entire plot resembled a lonely family crypt where only ghosts remained.

Deacon walked up the gravel drive next to the fence and climbed the porch as quietly as possible. He stood listening for a minute to the cold wind moaning across the eaves before knocking softly. Heavy footsteps shuffled across the floor inside, eventually stopping behind the front door. When it opened, Caleb Markham stood staring at him with a beer in hand and glassy eyes. He hadn't told anyone where he was going but said nothing when he saw Deacon, just hung his head and stepped aside as Deacon came in.

The living room was simple, homey, and dusty from an absence of inhabitants. Old pictures had been scattered across a low wooden table. Pictures of Sally and her boy from the day he was born right up to his academy graduation picture taken less than a year ago. Several empty beer cans spilled from a small wastebasket, and the only light came from a weary fireplace where a pine log too old and tired to pop burned away. Caleb waved Deacon to a comfortable chair as he lowered himself unsteadily onto the couch. Without speaking, he pulled another can of beer from a cooler on the floor and offered it to Deacon, who politely declined. Markham popped it open and took a long drink before staring down at the pictures on the table again.

"None of this was supposed to happen, you know," Caleb muttered. "We just wanted to live simple country lives." He pulled the black tape from the badge hanging on his open shirt. "This shit's what we wanted to leave behind. It's why we fought the war. Got tired of all the killing and dying and people just being assholes to one another. It's easier being apart, being with your own. Not needing to worry about how anyone else feels about nothing or that they might be offended. No political correctness to watch out for or feelings to hurt because everybody's the same and wants the same thing." He took another swallow and burped quietly. "At least that's what we told ourselves."

Deacon didn't want to argue with the man, especially since he was halfway to drunk and still armed.

"You know, I've read Scripture all my life and gone to Sunday school like every other good southern boy out there. I used to feel uplifted and safe. God's eyes looking down on me, watching over me. The Word's the same, but now it don't mean the same. His eyes, they don't protect anymore; they wait. They wait and they wait for you to fuck up just a little bit, and then they take you. No confessions, no apologies, no forgiveness." He looked into Deacon's eyes but then lowered them again.

"I played my part the way I was expected to just to keep those eyes off of me. To survive. I tried to teach Kyle to do the same, but I couldn't tell him the whole truth because I knew it would put him in danger. I suppose I have you to thank for enlightening him."

It was a cheap shot, but Deacon didn't rise to it. "Couldn't be helped," he answered quietly. "But I did everything I could to keep him out of harm's way."

"Hell, I suppose I had it coming after the way I treated you," Markham told him. He leaned forward. "You know, when I was a kid, I had friends who were black, brown, and everything in between. Never brought them home, though. Only the white ones were welcome. Daddy taught all us Markhams that you couldn't trust niggers or wetbacks as far as you could throw them, but they had their uses. Wasn't till I was older that I understood what those uses meant. Didn't seem very Christian-like to me, but it was made very clear that what is and isn't Christian was way above my pay grade. Sheep don't tell the shepherd where to graze unless they want to end up as lamb chops."

Markham's eyes grew watery as tears began to form. "That old fuck was so proud when I got my badge. Thought I joined the force to follow in his footsteps, keep the colored folks in their place." He drained the can and dropped it onto the growing pile in the basket.

"Do what is just and right; rescue the oppressed from the power of the oppressor. Don't exploit or mistreat the refugee, the orphan, and the widow. Don't spill the blood of the innocent in this place."

"That Jeremiah really knew his shit," Caleb chuckled.

Deacon smiled sympathetically. "I can help you do what is just and right, Caleb. But I can't do it alone." Markham shot him a defeated look. A look that changed to confusion when Deacon handed him the e-warrant. He read through it, shaking his head.

"You'll never get within ten feet of Wirz to serve this. His security forces won't allow it. Where you gonna find someone stupid enough to take them on?"

Deacon stood up slowly. Looking down at Markham, he said, "I'm here, aren't I?"

2

It was cold in the square, vicious and unforgiving, but she had to sit down. The ground had iced over the night before, and the meager sunlight had turned it to a muddy slush. It was the worst place for her to be during her recovery, but Elli didn't care. She sat on the small bench fully bundled against the cold that still worked its way beneath the layers. It crept into her back, wrapping itself around her wounds and stabbing her cruelly. The pain sometimes brought tears to her eyes, but she let them fall without any outward reaction. Some part of her felt that she deserved their torture for Tanner's death. She'd begged him to stay close to her father because she didn't trust anyone else to protect him. He'd promised her he would, and that promise had left him bleeding out on the steps of the capitol.

She'd barely made the funeral. She hadn't been formally released from the hospital and was only allowed to attend on the condition that she remain in a wheelchair and return immediately when it was over. She'd gone wearing hospital scrubs underneath a heavily insulated full-length coat that hid the IV still embedded in her arm and the automatic dispensers strapped to her waist. It had been a warm day and she'd been doped to the gills when the entire county turned out to pay their respects. The IV was now gone, as were the auto injectors, but the gunshot had left her weak and hobbling on a cane when she had the strength to stand.

Her parents were mortified when she told them she wanted to visit Tanner's gravesite alone. Quentin demanded that she be surrounded by armed guards, but she refused. They argued and fought but eventually compromised, and the guards remained at a discreet but effective distance. She couldn't see them but knew they were close, actively watching everything and everyone around her. By the time the cold began its assault on her joints, she'd forgotten about them entirely.

She pushed herself up from the bench slowly, grimacing as her muscles howled in protest. Grasping her cane, she walked slowly down the street. It was deserted, which she'd expected. Snow had an apocalyptic effect on Georgians. They hunkered down like a bunch of sinners facing the rapture itself. Only two businesses were open: a restaurant emitting the most enticing aromas and an art gallery. Ignoring her rumbling stomach, she continued to the gallery. The picture window there held three moderately sized paintings and a shelf of small sculptures. All were exquisitely crafted, but one drew her attention. It was a small memorial wreath wrapped around a carved cross. The flowers had been airbrushed to pale perfection, appearing almost lifelike, but the cross itself was smooth and angular. So like Tanner: a spray of tenderness fearfully clinging to the rigid expectations of life. It was just what she needed.

She opened the door and was greeted with a rush of warm air. The interior was comforting, with soft yellow bulbs and the scent of oil paint and gardenias floating throughout. It took only moments for the warmth to seep into her bones, and she relaxed for the first time since the shooting. There was no one in the gallery. Why the proprietor had bothered to open on such a day was a mystery, but she was grateful for it. She hobbled over to the counter where a laptop computer displayed the news feed without sound. She didn't need to hear what they were saying. The pictures of her father were enough.

Looking around once more, she called out "Hello!" A door to her left banged open, startling her, and she dropped her cane. An older man of average height hurried over to her, apologizing endlessly.

"I'm so sorry, my dear. I'm afraid I was restocking the studio and didn't hear you come in," he gushed. When she bent to pick up the cane, he grasped her arm and said, "No no no no, dear, let me do that. You just keep yourself steady." He picked up the cane and led her to a small bench. He held her hand like any proper southern gentleman and settled her comfortably. "Please have a seat. I know how inconvenient it is to suffer a disability. May I get you a warm cup of coffee?"

"Oh, no thank you, I don't want to be any trouble," Elli said, looking into his kind face. A long scar trailed down his cheek, giving his refined good looks a rugged charm. There was something oddly familiar about him, but she just couldn't place it. "I wanted to inquire about the memorial piece I saw in your window."

"It's no trouble at all," the man told her. "Why don't I get you that coffee and we can talk about it. Cream and sugar?"

"Yes, please," Elli told him even though she usually drank it black. She watched him walk back to the rear studio and noted the pained drop in his right shoulder. He must have been in some sort of accident, she thought. It certainly explained the long scar and his doting over her like a wounded bird.

He came back deftly balancing a tray with cups in one hand and a steaming pot in the other. He swung his wounded leg out to kick the studio door shut. The movement sent a gush of air from the back room flowing into the gallery. The gust was as cold as the park had been, refrigerated, and carrying an odd scent of brine that reminded her of her grandmother's pickling marathons. He handed her a cup, filled them both, and sat down next to her.

"My name is Abel Jennings. I'm the proprietor slash artist in residence. And you are?"

"Ellinore Hollister," she replied with a faint smile. "Your work is lovely."

"Thank you, Miss Hollister," Abel told her. "You were inquiring about a memorial piece. You've lost someone recently?"

Elli's smile faltered just a bit and her eyes became misty, but she choked her emotions back. "A very dear friend. He passed away just a short while ago. The cross with the roses in your window reminded me of him, and I thought it would be a nice keepsake to place at his gravesite."

Abel smiled warmly and patted her hand. He retrieved it from the window and held it out for her to examine. It was even more beautiful up close. The cross was alabaster marble edged with strips of burnished aluminum, and the rose crown was so delicately carved it nearly seemed alive. There was a square indentation in the center of the cross where something could be inscribed, and she ran her fingers over it, picturing Kyle's sparkling eyes.

"Perhaps there's a personal message you'd like to inscribe for your loved one?"

The question caught Elli off guard. She'd only met Kyle three months ago, and despite one night of intense passion, she barely knew him. Still, it had been enough for her to fall in love. There were so many things she wanted to say, but it would take a memorial the size of the Vietnam Wall to hold it. How could she possibly put a lifetime of possibilities into that tiny square?

"I will sing of your strength; I will sing aloud of your steadfast love in the morning. For you have been to me a fortress and a refuge in the day of my distress."

"What?" Elli muttered.

"It's a passage from Psalm 59," Abel told her. "Judging by the sad look on your face, it seemed appropriate."

Elli stared at him in confusion but then said, "It's lovely. I think it would be perfect." A lone tear crept down her cheek, and Abel reached up to wipe it away.

"I'll need a few minutes to inscribe this. Please help yourself to more coffee and relax." He carefully took the cross from her hands and returned to the studio.

Elli refilled her cup and sat with it between her hands, the steam caressing her face. She wanted to close her eyes and fill her heart with the sensations of Kyle's hands on her body, but the very notion brought forth waves of intense pain. She gulped the coffee, letting it scald her throat, and then rose slowly. Her security detail had positioned itself outside the gallery on the sidewalk, and the agent in charge shot her a questioning look as she passed the door. She signaled him that she was fine, and he resumed watching the streets outside. Wandering around, she examined the photographs and paintings hanging on the walls. Each one detailed a moment in an anonymous life but somehow managed to tell an entire story in that moment. One picture in particular held her attention. It was of a priest kneeling at an altar, his arms thrown wide and head tilted back, bathed in the sunlight streaming through a stained-glass window. It was meant to depict devotion and divinity, but what it really exuded was a far different story. Abel Jennings had a marvelous eye.

The door to the studio opened, and Abel returned with the plaque mounted and the cross properly polished. "Thank you so much. It's perfect," she told him quietly.

Abel peered at her closely. "Is there something amiss? I can still change it if you're having second thoughts. The cement hasn't dried yet."

"What? Oh no, it's absolutely perfect. It's just"—she looked around the gallery—"it seems like such a waste of appreciation buying something so mundane when I see all these incredible portraits. I'd expect to see such marvelous work in an art gallery in New York or London, not some local suburb."

"It's my pleasure and I appreciate the compliment, my dear, but not everyone has your taste in art, and a man must make a living, after all." He watched her examine the priest portrait closely. "What is it about that picture that you find so intriguing?"

"The misdirection," she said without turning around. "He appears to be praying in celebration, but if you look closely at his face, you can tell he's in pain." Abel moved closer and she pointed to the priest's face. "The tear streaks on his cheek and the hardness of his eyes. You can feel the hurt emanating from him. Almost as if he's kneeling there not in prayer but demanding why God let whatever happened to him happen. It's more accusation than adoration."

"You have an amazing eye. Not many people would have been able to see the pain beneath the obvious symbolism. Are you an artist?"

"No," Elli told him, blushing. "I certainly don't have the talent to do this. I'm a doctor."

"That would explain your keen eye for detail. It's refreshing to meet someone with the ability to see beneath the I of faith to the humanity beneath."

A chill began to creep back into Elli's body, but this time it wasn't from the cold outside. A thousand random images flickered in her memory, trying to form something important. She followed the man back to the counter where he wrapped the cross gently in velvet and stowed it in a gift box. As he worked, she looked around again at all the beautiful work. "It's all so beautiful and yet so full of loss."

"The very embodiment of a life of faith," Abel remarked, handing her the box.

Time slowed to a crawl as she reached for it. Her mind felt as if it were pushing through quicksand, struggling to reach the shore. She paid for her purchase and thanked him for his kind words, but that sucking feeling remained. Whatever it was, she knew it was urgent, perhaps even a matter of life and death. But the harder her mind pushed toward solid ground, the further that ground moved away.

"It was my pleasure, and I hope that I will see you in my gallery again soon." His eyes were warm and appreciative and his hand comforting and tender as he shook hers. But when they touched, her internal barometer dropped like a stone.

The gallery door opened and the head of her security detail stepped in, nodding to her cautiously. At his appearance, Elli released Abel's hand. She thanked him and hobbled to the door, followed by the agent. Once outside, the agent signaled the car and helped her inside. They pulled away, circling the park before heading south toward the Atlanta suburbs. Elli watched the gallery fade into the distance like a retreating tornado and felt her internal pressure equalize.

3

The cemetery was deserted and silent. An odd mix of old and new. The outer graves were flat and the headstones featureless where the new arrivals now lay. They surrounded the more elaborate graves and monuments from the early days of the country. Flamboyant angels and intricate statues proclaimed the final resting places of the honored dead in the crypts beneath. The vast family crypts nestled in hillsides were adorned with long lists of names and dates covering the last two centuries. Ledgers of death spanning generations, always with room for more to come.

Elli made her way carefully through the markers and into this older part of the cemetery. She didn't know how far back Tanner's family extended, but it warranted him a spot closer to the center. Markham had seen to that at least. The trees were bare and dripping from the melting slush, and her cane sank precariously into the wet ground with every step. The trip took much longer than she expected, but she eventually found the Tanner family plot behind a rusty iron fence. There were only twelve graves, but each declared a long life span. None of the Tanners had passed before the age of ninety except for three Confederate officers who died in battle and one child whose marker indicated death by tuberculosis. Kyle had been laid to rest next to his Confederate ancestors. The shiny new marker seemed out of place beside the lichen- and dirt-covered headstones of his forebears, but he belonged next to those who'd given their lives in the line of duty. Elli made a note to thank Markham for his thoughtfulness.

She set the package she carried on a nearby marker and removed the carved cross. It took a bit of maneuvering for her to lean down and set it at the base of Kyle's marker, but she managed without falling. It sparkled in the sporadic sunlight, making the entire scene even more macabre and unbearable. When she couldn't stand it any longer, she dug the toe of her boot into a slushy pile of leaves and dirt and sent a spray of rot across the marker, dulling its shiny exterior. A fitting testament to a life stolen for no good reason.

The cold began to seep into her bones again, warning Elli that it was time to leave. The rusty gate groaned in protest at the disturbance of the dead as she made her way back to the car. She lost her footing in a puddle and flopped against a large oak. Muttering curses, she righted herself and saw that she was not alone. A solitary woman stood staring down at a lonely, unadorned marker. Elli recognized her from the news and knew that the solitary grave she watched over could only be poor Maniac Mona's.

It would have been a gross violation of southern manners to intrude unannounced or unpermitted, so she made her way carefully to the grave and cleared her throat. The woman looked up and Elli smiled. The woman didn't react, just turned back to stare down at the grave at her feet.

"If you're here to mock my child, I think she's had more than enough of that, if you don't mind."

Elli felt ashamed and blushed deeply. "I would never do that to your poor daughter," she told the woman. "I met her briefly. She was a lovely girl. Please accept my condolences on your loss. She didn't deserve this."

The woman looked up again, but this time her face was streaked with tears and bore a look of gratitude. A look that Elli saw in the eyes of her most terminal patients when they knew a lonely end was near and were thankful for any kindness they received.

"She wasn't crazy, you know," the woman told her. "My little girl was so smart. She got accepted to a school up north, you know. I was going to send her there next year." The woman suddenly darkened. "I shouldn't have waited."

Elli watched the woman's face harden and noticed the expansive bruise on her cheek for the first time. "Did your husband do that?" she asked sympathetically.

"He recites Proverbs with every stroke," she muttered sourly. "It is his duty to chastise an unruly wife." She fought back the tears and bit her lip. "I didn't want this for my daughter."

Elli felt her anger rising. She'd heard this from so many women in the territory, and it made her sick every time. Her profession forbade her from interfering since the Church considered it a private matter between spouses. "It's still abuse," Elli told the woman. "It's not my place to say and I apologize if I've offended you but . . . I'm sorry. It's none of my business."

"I appreciate your concern," the woman said quickly. "Not many women would have had the nerve to speak up that way, but I suppose any woman strong enough to defy the Council would certainly not fear telling the truth."

Elli was stunned and fumbled over what to say next.

"I know who you are, Dr. Hollister. Marjorie Holmby was an acquaintance of mine. A stupid, blind woman if ever there was one, but she is the friend of a close friend, so I was obliged to humor her." Her face became hard and her stare as cold as ice. "I wish you'd met my Mona sooner. Maybe she'd still be alive if . . ." Her voice cracked as cold, angry tears trailed down her cheeks. She choked back her grief and fought the breakdown as hard as she could.

Elli reached out and grasped her hand. The woman returned her grip with a fierce intensity. They stood staring down at the gravestone for a time, sharing that desperate grasp until a rumbled of thunder echoed in the distance.

"God must be angry," Elli muttered quietly. "That's what my momma always used to say. That when the Almighty was angry, he would rumble and complain, and if people didn't listen to why he was angry, he would sit down and cry in sadness, and his tears would become the rain."

"My momma told me that God rumbled because people wouldn't listen. That the storms were his rage at our stupidity." She clenched Elli's hand even tighter. "The more we turn his words into weapons, the more he's gonna scream and rage until he finally just gives up and wipes the world clean of us. Kinda gives new meaning to global warming, doesn't it?"

Elli stared at the woman, and a smile crept onto her face despite the pain forming under her grip. "Your momma sounds like a woman to be reckoned with."

"She was. Her name was Eve. Mine's Catherine, by the way."

Elli took the introduction as an excuse to wrench herself free of Catherine's death grip and extended a handshake instead. "Pleased to meet you, Catherine."

"My Mona never really got to know her. My husband didn't approve of strong-willed women. I snuck her out as much as possible and took her to her Grandma, but it wasn't nearly as much as it should have been. He was of the majority opinion that Eve was weak and pathetic and the cause of all the sin in the world."

"That is what they've taught us for thousands of years," Elli responded. "The so-called weaker sex."

"They're wrong, you know," Catherine told her sternly. "Adam was the weak one. He wanted to stay in paradise all pampered and taken care of by God. Never exploring, never aspiring, never growing. Just a pampered, weak little boy always clinging to his daddy throughout eternity, having everything handed to him and being attended to by a woman. Pathetic. Eve was brave. She was the one who had courage. She wanted to know the world our Father created for us so that she could be the best steward of his gifts that she could possibly be. She ate from the Tree of Knowledge to become the protector of paradise and sacrificed her immortality to become all that she was capable of becoming so that we all could become what we were meant to be, His greatest creation." She looked down at Mona's headstone. "I tried to teach that to my daughter so she could go bravely into the world, but she was so desperate for her father's love."

"It wasn't her fault," Elli told her, grasping her hands. "You can't repeat what I'm about to tell you to anyone, understand?" Catherine shook her head. She knew the importance of the confidentiality of women in the territory. "You daughter was innocent. Mona was every bit a victim of a murderer as those she killed. They did this to her during her reconditioning. Used her as a weapon."

A look of desperate hope crept onto Catherine's face. One that hadn't been there since long before her daughter's funeral. Elli reached out and stroked Catherine's bruised face. "I promise you the men responsible will be brought to justice and your daughter will have peace in heaven."

Elli left Catherine smiling gratefully over her daughter's grave. As she hobbled back toward the car, she had no idea how she was going to make it happen, but she knew she wouldn't stop until it did. Even if it cost her everything she had.

4

The car was quiet and warm and gave Elli a chance to absorb everything that had occurred: paying her respects to Kyle, the haunting conversation with Mona's mother, the intriguing encounter with the artist in his gallery. They orbited her conscious mind like angry planets fighting the suction of a dying star. She'd been sidelined from the investigation for weeks but still remembered the last conversation she'd had with Deacon. He'd come to see her the day after Tanner's funeral. It was the lowest she'd ever seen him. He apologized endlessly for leaving her at the hospital and not returning. He hated himself for putting her in harm's way and announced his intent to have her honorably discharged from the investigation, having served her penance. She wouldn't hear of it. Her heart was still raw from the service, but she wasn't going to let anyone stop her from finding Kyle's killer.

She couldn't bear returning to her apartment. Kyle's scent was still everywhere they'd made love. Instead, she returned to her father's house, the only place of comfort left in her newly brutal world. A cold burst of air swept over her as the driver opened his window to confirm his identity at the front gate. The chill cut through the warm miasma of images in her brain, grinding it to a halt. Kyle's headstone floated starkly in her mind. A simple monument in a barren plot, surrounded by snow and melancholy. The ornate, flowered cross she'd purchased lay propped against the base, the lone artistic touch in the gray tableau. A delicate piece of work bearing a meticulously engraved personal message from her to him. A bold statement of her feelings for a man she was certain she loved.

She closed her eyes tightly as Ellory Bainbridge's naked body swam into view, the imprint of her unborn child bruised into her torso. *Personal.* Kevin Dockweiler's corpse crucified in the hall of worship appeared next. *Artistic.* Austin Goodwin kneeling in penitence, smoke pouring from his screaming face. *A bold statement.* The statue of Jessica Glick glistening in the morning rain as the salt melted away, exposing her cadaver beneath the beautiful sculpture. *Meticulous.* "My God," she whimpered as it all came together. The studio had been filled with clues. His paintings, his sculptures, the beautiful photographs. The way they captured the hidden pain and suffering of each subject without detracting from the beauty of the work itself.

The driver opened her door and reached in to help her. She hadn't even noticed the car rolling to a gentle stop. Muttering curses, she shoved his hand away and grabbed her cell phone. Her heart beat loudly in her ears as she waited for Deacon to answer.

Deacon was working with Markham at the assassination site, but the shooter had left no evidence behind and no witnesses to identify him. Unlike the man who'd shot at Elli, the assassin responsible for killing Tanner had vanished without a trace. A careful review of the available broadcast and surveillance feeds pinpointed the shooter's location but also confirmed to them that Tanner wasn't his intended target. The deputy had stepped in front of Senator Hollister to push back an intrusive cameraman, and it had cost him his life. The senator had openly declared his defiance to the Ecumenical Council on a live broadcast, and a contingency plan had been activated. This wasn't the work of one of Wirz's unwitting soldiers; it was a professional hit gone wrong. And it left Markham feeling even more enraged at his nephew's senseless death. The two of them had just climbed into a federal cruiser when Deacon's comm line began chirping with the emergency signal. Dispatch routed a call from the Hollister home through the onboard communications display.

"Elli, what's wrong? Are you okay?" he asked.

"I know who the killer is!" she shouted.

"I'm here with Sheriff Markham, Elli. Say that again slow and easy," he told her.

"I know who's been doing the killing. I met him this morning. I stopped in a shop to buy something to put on Kyle's grave, and I met him."

Deacon and Markham stared at each other and then Markham asked, "How do you know he's our man, Doc? Did he say something to you to give him away, or did you see something?"

"Nothing specific while I was there, but after I left, I remembered all of the pieces he had on display. There's a picture of a man, I think he's priest. He was kneeling with his arms wide, crying and looking up, begging for absolution. I'm positive it's a picture of our fourth victim, Pastor Goodwin. It looks a lot like him. And there's some smaller sculptures in one of the cases that are modern interpretations of religious works. I'd swear that one of the crucifixions was sculpted to resemble Kevin Dockweiler."

Markham shook his head. Elli's intuition wouldn't be enough to get a warrant or even justify a search or detainment. "If we go in there without cause," Markham said quietly, "we could spook him, and we'd never catch him. We need something concrete."

"Deacon, he fits the profile the department worked up to a tee," she said. "Older, well-educated, highly skilled and knowledgeable in art, extremely fit. And he really is an artist. I stumbled into his gallery accidentally and spent time looking at his work. I'm telling you, Deacon, this is our guy. If you'd met him, you'd know it like I did."

"Where is this place, Elli?" Deacon asked as he activated the onboard mapping system.

"West Park Square, across from the park. The guy's name is Abel something, and he has a long scar down his face."

"Markham and I are going to check him out. You stay put and don't leave the house until you hear back from us."

Deacon disconnected the line and Elli sat back, breathing heavily. When the driver reached for her a second time, she allowed him to escort her into the house, where she curled up in her father's favorite chair, shivering. She'd just spent time with a serial killer they'd been hunting for weeks. She should have felt triumphant or at least relieved. But all she could think of was the warmth of his hands cradling hers and the icy chill they created within her soul.

5

Markham brought up the information on the gallery and performed a deep search on the owner. A photo of Abel Jennings popped up while his vital statistics scrolled down the right side of the screen. His bio was that of a proper, world-traveled gentleman. Educated in the States, his degrees were in art history and theology, though he'd studied the former abroad and written for some lesser-known art journals. He'd been in business for a little over a year, and he supported his shop with private commissions. His business books were clean and tidy with no strange entries or untoward purchases, and his personal financials were just as unimpressive. A little too unimpressive for Deacon's taste. He contacted Agnes, who had Corbett do an analysis of the public data. They had nearly reached the gallery when the results came back. Despite a carefully constructed history, prior to two years ago, Abel Jennings didn't exist.

Two blocks from the gallery, Deacon pulled over and parked behind a liquor store. Turning to Markham he said, "We need to play this very carefully. If Elli is right, this man is a professional killer." He hesitated and then added, "And he most likely belonged to the same organization as Wirz."

Markham started to object, but Deacon cut him off. "Don't ask me how I know, Caleb, because I can't tell you. Just don't drop your guard for a second. I don't want your death on my conscience."

Markham swallowed his pride and said, "If you're right and we go in there asking questions, he'll know we're onto him. But I think I know how we can throw him off." He logged into the state police briefings from the previous day and scrolled through the current notices posted by E-Rep. "If we were looking for someone else, say his probable next victim . . ." Deacon smiled as he followed Markham's train of thought. "We just need to find the right one."

They scanned the list together until they found a likely candidate. A young widow named Rebecca Tully had been reported missing when she failed to fetch her children from daycare. No one had seen her in over a month, and many already suspected she'd fallen prey to the killer. Deacon opened the sentencing files and found her name associated with an accidental death. She'd been exonerated in the shooting death of her husband but still found culpable for the circumstances that led to it. She'd been bound for reconditioning and released only two months ago.

Armed with data pads showing Rebecca Tully's profile, they went door-to-door, working their way toward the gallery. With the Christmas season in full swing, several shoppers were picking up trinkets, and they waited until the crowd thinned before entering. They split up and worked their way toward the register, being as gracious as possible while showing Rebecca Tully's picture to each shopper, asking if by chance they had seen her. Markham was intently examining the painting of the priest Elli had warned them about when a voice startled him.

"I hope you have a good reason for harassing my customers, Sheriff."

He turned to see Jennings, hands clasped behind his back, dressing him down like a grade school teacher. Markham pulled himself up and said, "I do, sir, and I'm sorry that we've disturbed your business, but we're looking for a missing young woman." He handed Abel the data pad with the girl's picture on it. "She's a mother, and we'd like to get her home to her kids by Christmas, so we're asking everyone if they may have seen her."

Abel recognized her immediately. Even though he wasn't responsible for the girl's disappearance, he wasn't surprised by it. She'd been nearly catatonic when she'd entered his shop. The subliminal trigger he'd used had obviously worked. "I'm sorry, Sheriff, but I don't recall seeing the girl in here. I hope she hasn't met with any unfortunate circumstances."

"We're hoping the same, sir, and I hope you won't mind if we keep asking your customers."

"Of course not, Sheriff. Please continue, and if you like I would be more than happy to post her image on the monitor here in case anyone that comes in has seen her."

Markham thanked him and shook his hand. It was warm and friendly, but it still left him with a chill. "I notice that you have security cameras around your shop. Would you mind if we looked through the feeds? It's possible that she may have come in and left without being seen."

Abel smiled. "You may indeed. Just let me finish up with these patrons and I'll show you to the office." He returned to the register and went through the line as quickly as southern etiquette would allow. The security feeds had been scrubbed of any trace of the woman, so he had no concern that the police would find anything. And even though he was suspicious of their motives, he relished the opportunity to mentally fence with them.

Deacon had been watching the interaction while talking to customers. He'd also been making note of the artwork and sculptures on the shelves and walls. The wailing priest definitely resembled the late Pastor Goodwin. Though he didn't see the crucifixion that depicted poor Kevin Dockweiler, he did find a sculpture of a woman prostrate before an armed avenging angel, begging for absolution. The woman looked a great deal like the salt-cured Jessica Glick recently discovered in the courtyard of St. Michael's. He joined Markham at the register as the last customer left the shop. Together, they followed the mysterious Abel Jennings into the office where he reloaded the security feeds for the last three weeks. As they watched intently, Abel quietly questioned them.

"Does this have anything to do with the monster that's been preying on our territory, if I may ask?"

"Not yet," Deacon answered. "We're working very hard to make sure that doesn't become a reality."

Abel hugged himself and relaxed his face into that of a concerned bystander. "I hope you catch him quickly, Detective. This is a time for the celebration of Christ's birth. We shouldn't be cowering before Satan and his minions and hiding in fear."

"We're doing everything we can to catch him, and I can give you my word that we won't rest until he's caught." He gave Abel a reassuring smile and inhaled deeply, unsettled by a strange scent in the air. "If I may ask, what is that scent?"

"A mixture of frankincense and cedar with a touch of myrrh. I keep it simmering in a small bowl beneath the air conditioning system during the holidays. I like to use little touches to provide the right atmosphere for holidays. In the time of Jesus, these particular fragrances were very prevalent in every holy place. It helps people to connect emotionally to their biblical history."

"You study ancient history?" Deacon asked politely. He knew it was a dangerous question, but the feeds were nearly done running.

"I'm more of an enthusiast than a scholar," Abel answered judiciously. "Most of the commercial work I do is religiously based, and people tend to trust the observations of an artist when he can throw in some carefully curated trivia to give the work some mystery."

Deacon edged out a little further on the ledge, easing his grip. "Your work seems to depict a lot of suffering and sacrifice."

"Faith is suffering and sacrifice," Abel told him. "Our savior suffered so that mankind would be forgiven. He was sacrificed so that we could attain divinity. I would be doing Him an injustice to dilute what He experienced for the sake of a contrived harmony."

"Even during a celebration of his birth?"

"This isn't a Hallmark shop, sir," Abel told him evenly. "We take our faith quite seriously here. I strive to show it the proper respect."

Deacon looked into his eyes and nodded. "My apologies if I've offended you. Your work is extremely impressive, regardless of the topic. You have quite a multifaceted talent."

"No offense taken," Abel told him. "I'm afraid I've spent far too much time justifying my work to people who are incapable of appreciating its significance. It's refreshing to meet someone that recognizes the painful nature of belief."

Deacon felt his shorthairs tighten as he nodded his acceptance of the apology.

The three of them exited the office to a gallery filling once more with Christmas shoppers. Deacon had never been more grateful to be surrounded by a crowd and didn't exhale until he was once again standing in the frigid air of a Georgia winter.

Markham had to rush to keep up with Deacon but finally caught up as they reached the cruiser. "Elli was right," Deacon told him. "That's our man."

"How the hell did you come to that conclusion?" Markham asked. "I didn't see anything in there or on those feeds that looked suspicious. The guy cooperated and even offered to help."

"You should have spent more time looking at his art," Deacon said, scrolling through the pictures he'd quietly snapped on his phone as he questioned the customers.

"I saw that picture the doc said looked like the preacher," Markham told him. "It looked like him for sure, but it also looked like half a dozen guys I see at the truck stop every day."

Deacon climbed into the cruiser and synced his phone to the holographic onboard display. When Markham got in, he zoomed in on the body of the man in the painting. "Do you see these marks on his neck and the ones on his wrists?" Markham leaned in close and squinted. Deacon shot him an irritated look and waited for Markham to swallow his macho pride and take out his reading glasses. As the near-sighted sheriff looked closer, Deacon said, "Those marks match the ones on the victim's body perfectly, not just in location but in size, shape and definition, as if they were painted from still life."

"I'll have to take your word for it. I'm afraid I haven't been reading the detail reports you've been submitting very closely." He looked up and blushed. "Wasn't exactly supposed to be helping you solve this if you recall." Deacon started the cruiser and gunned it out into traffic, slamming Markham back into his seat. "What the hell are you doing? If that's our guy, let's go back and arrest the son of a bitch. Why are we leaving?"

"Because he's already chosen his next victim," Deacon said, turning on the emergency lights and winding through cars. He pressed a button on the display to bring up a grid of the photos he'd taken and chose one. It filled the display, drawing a muttered "fuck me" from Markham.

"I'll call ahead and try to warn her. Get some cars over to the house."

"I've been trying since we left," Deacon told him. "She's not answering, and neither is the senator. All the communication lines to the area are down."

"Well, shit put your foot down, boy, before I have to appear before a committee meeting!"

Deacon gunned the accelerator, ignoring the automated speed warnings from the onboard avatar. "You and I are going to have to have a serious discussion about race relations between fellow officers when this is over."

Markham didn't know how much he'd pissed off Deacon and didn't care. He'd take whatever ass-kicking he deserved if it got the man to drive faster so that the vision of Elli Hollister bound over an open fire wouldn't come to pass.

6

Police cruisers and unmarked vehicles littered the property around the house. Deacon and Markham had both deployed officers throughout the grounds and put Det. Bachman in charge of internal security. Joyce wandered through the large estate, making sure everyone was accounted for and every possible entrance secured. No one could enter without a biometric scan, and no one could leave without a minimum four-man armed escort. The Hollister estate was officially on lockdown until further notice.

The Hollisters sat silently in the dining room in front of a large meal. Elli's mother insisted she eat heartily and often after collapsing in the study, but she only picked at her food, flicking the fried okra into her Brunswick stew. They were two of her favorites, but she had no desire to eat. She only took a bit whenever her mother looked at her with concern. Stella herself sat chewing the same bite of food she'd taken five minutes earlier, swallowing only after it had turned to a tasteless mush. Quentin ate very slowly, having no more appetite than Elli but not wanting to disrespect Stella's efforts. His wife had always cooked her way through stress, and tonight she'd outdone herself. They were safe, but no one felt that way.

Joyce wandered into the dining room after her latest rounds, and Stella graciously insisted she join them. The detective tucked into the mouth-watering food without hesitation as her eyes constantly darted to every window and doorway. It wasn't often that you pulled stakeout duty and got a spread like this.

Halfway through the meal, Elli suddenly said, "This doesn't feel right."

"What do you mean?" Joyce asked, mopping up her stew with a fluffy biscuit.

"This. Us being targets," she told her. "We don't fit the profile. We aren't on any sanctioned lists and haven't committed any sins that require punishment."

"You're forgetting about the Holmby boy. You were punished for defying God's will," Joyce explained.

"I didn't defy God's will," Elli responded. "I defied his parents' will to let their son die. The church punished me to placate the beliefs of extremists and appear to remain unbiased. It was politically motivated. That's not the same thing."

Joyce forgot about the food and listened intently.

"Saving lives is my calling. It's what God has always wanted me to do. I'm doing His will every time I save a life. When there is no longer anything I can do to keep death from happening, that's when God's will comes into play. At that point, it's up to Him, out of my hands, and I take a step back. If He truly meant for that boy to die, he would have died regardless of my efforts."

"What about the painting of you Deacon saw in the gallery?" Joyce asked.

"It may not be what he thinks," Elli said, rising and hobbling to the library. She returned with a pristine copy of the Old Testament and opened it to Leviticus 20. "Corbin told us that the Bible has very specific instances in which a person can be put to death. Adultery, for instance."

"Ellory Bainbridge," Joyce muttered as she read over Elli's shoulder.

"Bearing false witness; that was Kevin Dockweiler's sin," Elli continued. "There are a bunch of others: sacrificing your seed to Molech, cursing your mother and father, homosexual behavior, sleeping with your wife and her mother, bestiality, blasphemy, witchcraft. It's a pretty well-defined list, but defying God's will isn't on it."

"The priest committed incest with his daughter," Joyce added. "That's definitely in the top ten."

"What I can't figure out is how the last victim fits. The story of Lot's wife isn't an act of sin like the others."

"We haven't been able to make it fit either," Joyce answered, opening her data pad. She pulled up Agnes's research on the Glick woman. "She was the wife of an Amish church elder. Cared for her aunt and was a well-liked member of her church with a solid reputation for helping her congregation. She was the daughter of a pastor back in Kansas before she moved down here and married. Apparently, she was living a double life after her marriage. Burke was able to find several witnesses near her aunt's hometown that know her to be quite a party girl."

"Wait," Elli told her. "I read something about the daughter of a priest." She flipped back through the pages to Leviticus 19 and said, "Yes, here it is. The daughter of a priest is to be burned if she prostitutes herself. Maybe that's what the painting meant."

Joyce shook her head. "Jessica wasn't burned; she was encased in salt rock. It would mean our killer changed his methods, and that's something this guy doesn't do. Every murder reflects the sins of its victim." She read further into Jessica's history in Kansas and stopped. "She worked the bars pretty heavily back in Kansas as a teenager, as well, and there was an investigation into her father on charges of child endangerment. The case was never resolved because Jessica moved down here and married. The charges ended up being dropped."

"What were they?" Elli asked.

"He was part owner of one of the bars she worked and was charged with prostituting his kid."

"You must not defile your daughter by making her a prostitute," Elli read aloud. "But it still references burning."

"'She has done an outrageous thing in Israel by being promiscuous while still in her father's house,'" Quentin interjected. "'She shall be brought to the door of her father's house, and there the men of her city will stone her to death.' It's not Leviticus, it's Deuteronomy 22:21."

"Jessica Glick was encased in stone. Salt rock, specifically, but it was still rock of sorts."

"And she refused to give up her previous sinful life when she married and left Kansas. She looked back, so to speak. Thus she remained sinful and was turned into a pillar of salt," Elli explained.

Joyce looked around the room, then grabbed her phone as she walked out. The Hollisters all followed her into the living room as she spoke to Deacon.

"Deke, we were set up. The picture you saw was a bait and switch. It belonged to the fourth victim." She set the phone on speaker so that everyone could hear them. "It referenced one of the sins she was guilty of, but she was executed accorded to her original sin, which follows the rules of biblical law. Her father prostituted her out as a child back in Kansas."

"You're sure about this?" Deacon asked.

"Positive. It's all there in Agnes's background research. That means there's only one punishment left unperformed. Beheading."

"Beheading was reserved for murderers and subverters of cities," Deacon said. "It's a safe bet none of the Hollisters is guilty of murder. And unless the senator is leading his people astray . . ."

"That would depend on who you ask. I try to follow the Lord's word, but the Council has its own interpretation of that," Quentin said.

Deacon hesitated and then hissed, "Shit! He's saving the best for last. He's going after Wirz."

The Horn of Gabriel

1

The whiskey felt like liquid gold in his belly, but Milton kept it to just two shots. Just enough to keep up his courage while he packed. Two sets of three passports each for himself and his son—one federal, one Constitutional, and one international, each in a different name—went into the duffel bag over the false bottom containing half a million in US currency. Most of his wealth had been stashed in offshore accounts years ago, the access codes to them cleverly buried in the identification numbers of the fake passports. Two weeks' worth of clothes and a shaving kit later, he was ready to roll. He loathed leaving behind the trappings of a wealthy politician, but he didn't need much to replace it all where he was going. The only thing he couldn't leave behind was the last family photo he'd taken with his wife and son. He slid it into a ball of underwear and crammed it to the bottom. He'd smuggled half a million in diamonds back from Nigeria once in a bag of dirty underwear on a bet. His durable old tighty-whities suited him just fine because TSA agents hated searching them.

The cell phone vibrated insistently, but he ignored it. The national elections were set for mid-January to give the voters time to recover from the silly season. He'd gone underground after Thanksgiving, but apparently his extended holiday vacation to reflect and pray for the Lord's wisdom and support wasn't fooling anyone. He knew Wirz was looking for him, but if Wirz was now taking out federal agents, things had gone from bad to shit. It would only be a matter of time before someone came for him, and he wasn't sticking around until then. Only one thing left to do before he disappeared into the Caribbean sunset: make sure Pete was safe. Tossing the buzzing phone into the fireplace, he pulled out one of several burner phones and called an old friend in the capitol. Within an hour Pete would be transferred to a medium-security work facility for first-time offenders, and his file would be digitally erased. By the time Pete arrived at the institution, his entire identity would have been replaced with that of a low-risk addict due for release in seven days. A week after that, he would be on a plane to Belize. Wirz wasn't the only one with friends in low places.

He called for a car and ordered it to meet him at the gate of a house a quarter mile away and then stomped the burner phone into a pile of debris. He scooped up the pieces and threw them into the fireplace next to his official phone but didn't stay to watch them burn. He was out of shape, and the trek to the nearest neighbor's front gate left him red-faced and out of breath. He still beat the car by a good twenty minutes. From there, it was a short drive to DeKalb and a private jet to St. Petersburg. After that, a Caribbean island with no extradition.

On the seat next to him sat a Bible. By law they were provided in all transportation for hire. He picked it up, rolled down the window and tossed it out onto the road. Let the poor saps who still believed in God's little paradise use it. To hell with God. His soul had been damned long ago, and he intended to happily spend the rest of his life on a tropical beach indulging in whatever vices he saw fit to enjoy along with his degenerate son.

He looked up to see the driver observing him in the rearview mirror. "Don't worry, pal, I'll buy you a new one," he said, folding up a wad of bills and stuffing them into the window crack.

The driver resumed watching the road and said nothing. He knew the man wouldn't say anything. This particular service catered to the elite and knew how to disguise their customer logs and still stay aboveboard. They got paid ridiculously well for providing clandestine transportation to important clients. Milton sat back and soon found himself very sleepy. They were still a couple of hours from DeKalb, and the booze was beginning to hit him hard. He drifted off as the car sped north on Buford Highway through tree-lined neighborhoods.

He came to as the car bounced over a wide set of tracks and noted that the sun was coming up behind them. The airport was nowhere in sight. The road was not the paved roadway of the city but a wide dirt track lined with trees. And they were headed in the wrong direction. Panic surged through his hangover as the car slowed. If Wirz's people had found out about his escape plan, he was as good as dead. The car came to a stop in front of an isolated farmhouse. As the driver got out and walked toward it, Milton pawed through his duffel, digging out the gun he'd stowed in it along with a two-inch wad of hundreds. Maybe he could buy his way out with a guarantee of his silence. It was a long shot, but he was willing to try the carrot. If not, the stick would suffice. In either case he intended to fight for his freedom. He was breathing heavily when the driver returned and opened his door, standing aside.

Stepping out of the car, Milton looked at him and said, "I know your bosses probably told you to bring me out here and put a bullet in my head, but there's no need for that."

The man just stood there calmly and said nothing.

"I have no intention of telling anyone anything about your organization, Wirz or anything else. All I want to do is disappear quietly and never set foot in this country again." The man still didn't react. He showed the wad of bills to him. "I've been a loyal servant to your ideals, and I don't intend to betray that. I'm just asking you to get me to the airport so I can disappear, and I'll make it worth your while."

The driver stared for a moment and then removed his cap. He regarded Milton with a compassionate look and said, "Senator, I'm not here to turn you over to the Cadre. I believe in you, and I'm here to help free you from their influence."

Milton was confused but kept his grip on the gun in his coat pocket.

"You were elected to serve your people. In that service, you were led astray and as a leader led your city astray. Because of their control, you broke your covenant with your people. I am here to avenge you and yours for their betrayal."

Milton was confused even more by the way the driver smiled at him but wasn't about to look a gift horse in the mouth.

"The airports are being watched," the driver told him. "You would never have made it out of the terminal if you'd gone there. Thankfully, I have an escape plan that they won't be able to follow." The driver walked toward the house's open door, indicating that Milton follow him.

Milton exhaled and followed. He stuffed the wad of bills back into his pants pocket, thinking that he'd just saved himself a hundred grand, but he kept his grip on the gun in his other pocket just the same. They walked into the house, and the driver closed the door behind them. The electric lights weren't on, but ancient gas lights threw dark shadows around the comfortable front room. There was a soothing odor in the air that he couldn't identify. Heady, like the haze you'd smell in an underground dispensary. It made him light-headed, too light-headed to remain vigilant. Maybe that's why he loosened his grip on the gun and rubbed his eyes instead of using his other hand. Maybe that's why he was suddenly reminded of his grandmother's wake and the incense that floated through every room to make sure the smell of death wasn't noticeable. Maybe that's why he didn't notice the gleaming sword in the driver's hand until it was too late.

2

Crowds surrounded the Capitol Basilica shouting and jeering as the emergency session of the Senate met. The elections were a month away, and with Senator Milton missing, another had to be selected to replace him. The vote took less than an hour as there was only one clear successor. The few radicals that put themselves forward to be chosen were easily dismissed, and the succession was swift and undeniable. It was the last thing in the world Quentin Hollister wanted, but with Milton's disappearance he had no choice but to accept. Archbishop Wirz watched the session from the balcony, accompanied by a contingent of personal security. The outcome was expected but not unmanageable. He knew that as long as Hollister's daughter was vulnerable, the senator could be controlled. He left quietly as the final certification was underway. On the floor below, Hollister watched him leave as he stood with one hand on a Bible and the other raised to take the oath of office.

A contingent of sheriff's deputies surrounded the angry crowds and kept them behind barricades. Markham had pulled every available officer and some from private firms to make sure that no more innocent blood was spilled on these steps. The marble sparkled in the midday sun now that Tanner's blood had been scrubbed away, but he could still see every puddle and drop as if it were fresh. He'd stuck tight to Wirz since the gallery encounter, watching and waiting. It was only a question of who would strike first. That question was answered when three federal cruisers pulled into the civic center. The flashing lights turned into the main entrance. They drove slowly through the crowds and waited for the barricades to open for them. Markham radioed his men to let them through.

The crowds of territorial believers howled even louder as the vehicles pulled directly up to the steps of the Basilica and parked in a row. Their cries turned to jeers and insults as Deacon and Joyce exited the vehicles with four federal agents in tow. They waited at the bottom of the stairs until they saw Markham come out and then slowly walked up to meet him below the podium. The sheriff had hardened considerably since his meeting with Deacon. The stiff lines in his jaw and tightness of his shoulders revealed the stress the man was under. Neither smiled when they met, just stood looking at each other in silent understanding of what was about to happen. They waited silently until the doors to the general assembly chamber opened and Archbishop Wirz came out to the podium, followed by his security contingent, to make the announcement of succession.

Wirz strode up to them looking mildly annoyed. Ignoring Deacon entirely, he turned to Markham and said, "Sheriff, you were ordered to clear these steps of any disruptions. Why are these people still here?"

"These people are exercising their right to be heard, Your Excellency. We do still have that right here in the territory last time I checked," Markham told him defiantly. "We have kept a clear perimeter for the leadership, sir. They're in no danger."

Wirz shot him a devastating look. "Then why are there six federal agents standing on my steps?"

Deacon stepped forward as Joyce handed him a data pad bearing the Presidential Seal. "We're here to serve a federal arrest warrant," he said, staring Wirz coldly in the eye. "If you prefer, we can do this inside."

Wirz huffed condescendingly. "You have no authority to serve a federal warrant on territorial soil, Lieutenant. Warrants have to be submitted to the territorial embassy and processed through legal channels." Smiling coldly, he said, "I'm afraid you've wasted a trip."

Senator Hollister had been listening from the wings and walked up to stand next to Wirz. "I'm afraid he's right, Lieutenant. You have no authority to execute warrants without the consent of territorial law enforcement."

Deacon's eyes went wide with surprise. The last thing he had expected was for Hollister to defend the man who tried to murder his daughter. Beside him, Wirz smirked in satisfaction.

"You have no authority to serve anyone here, Lieutenant." Hollister handed the warrant to Markham and asked, "Am I right, Sheriff?"

Markham looked through the warrant and said, "Yes, sir, you are indeed correct. No federal officer may arrest a territorial citizen without due process of territorial law enforcement." Deacon and Joyce were momentarily stunned. Then Markham turned to Wirz and said, "But I can."

He reached for his handcuffs as he stared into Wirz's angry eyes. Wirz clenched his jaw and said, "You do this and your life will end."

"My life ended the day you murdered my sister's boy on these steps. I think it's more than fitting that yours should end here too."

Wirz smiled devilishly and clasped his hands behind his back. "What happened to Officer Tanner was a tragedy. The act of a brazen and cowardly assassin whom you should be busy hunting down instead of harassing the leadership." He ran his hands along the buttons on his titanium wristband as he spoke until he felt the one he was looking for. "But if you insist on perpetuating this assault on our very way of life"—he pressed the button on his wrist and stepped on the power switch at the foot of the pedestal, and his voice boomed across the courtyard—"Arise! For this matter is your responsibility, but we will be with you. Be courageous and act."

The crowd cheered in solidarity as several among them suddenly froze and dropped their signs. They stood staring for a few seconds and then began to push slowly forward. People continued to cheer until the first gun was drawn. Their cheers changed to shouts of confusion and outright screams as everyone realized what was about to happen. An officer stepped up to the barricades as the first armed man approached. Holding out his hand, he gave the man the usual warning: "Hold on there, mister, just put that gun down. This is a peaceful demonstration; there's no need for violence." He never made it past the word "just." The man put a bullet squarely between the officer's eyes, sending the crowd into a frenzied panic.

People scattered in a screaming stampede while several members of the crowd pushed forward, firing at Deacon's team and anyone that tried to stop them. Deacon and Joyce dove for cover while Markham threw Senator Hollister to the ground. They scurried behind the pillars, returning fire as they groped their way to the stairs, unfazed by the hail of bullets. The federal marshal to Deacon's left took a bullet to the chest and went down. But Joyce took the shooter out with a head shot. The rest just kept coming.

"They aren't even taking cover!" she yelled over to Deacon as she returned fire.

Deacon shot the nearest assailant in the leg, hoping the wound would snap him out of whatever control he was under. The man simply rolled over and continued to fire. Deacon's next shot was to his chest. "Just keep shooting!" he shouted back to Joyce. "They're all being controlled. You can't stop them!"

Markham heard him and began taking kill shots. Two women and three men went down before he ran out of bullets. As he ducked behind a post to reload, he looked up to see Wirz calmly walking across the lobby toward the elevator bank. He turned to where Deacon was crouched and yelled, "Lieutenant! Wirz is getting away!" Deacon pivoted to look as the elevator doors closed on the archbishop. "Get after him. I'll cover ya!"

Deacon waited until Markham began shooting and ran toward the door. He made it just as he heard Markham holler out in pain. He'd taken a round in the shoulder but was still fighting back. Deacon leveled his weapon from the door and took down Markham's shooter, then ran into the capitol after Wirz.

3

"Seal the building," Wirz told his security staff as he pressed the elevator button. As the doors closed, they took up positions on either end of the lobby, setting up a kill zone. Cadre operatives didn't need to be told to use deadly force. The car rose silently while Wirz composed the press releases in his head. A group of loyal territorial citizens took up arms to defend their beloved leader against a fascist takeover. Martyred in the name of God as warriors defending his children, they would be guaranteed sainthood. That would be the official position of the leadership, but social media would be the battlefield. By now there would be a least a dozen amateur videos of the approach of the federal officers and the chaos of the initial shots. No one would care about the truth. No one would even know.

The doors opened and he strode down the hall to his office, where two aides waited outside. One he dispatched to the Ecumenical Hall across the compound with his carefully crafted story and instructions to make a public announcement. The other followed him in, standing watch just inside. Wirz waved a hand across the top of his desk, and live feeds began streaming across every screen. He smiled as he watched the media broadcast the very images that would catapult him into the high archbishop's position. Media was such an amazing thing. More powerful than any political party and more widely heard than any corporate sponsor, it shaped the world within nanoseconds. He opened his carefully curated archive of interviews and selected a series of stories. It was widely known that the federal government strenuously objected to the use of conversion therapy on citizens. They took every opportunity to denounce the practice on the world stage and vilified the leadership for using it on territorial citizens. But Wirz didn't need a preprogrammed army to defend him. Within an hour he would have a million social lemmings around the world spreading horror stories of the coup and defending the children of Eden in an attempt to justify their own liberal views, all without the help of reconditioning. And the world would howl in protest.

The real concern was the Cadre leadership. They had a very specific timetable set aside for their great Agenda and didn't take kindly to that timetable being fucked with. He would have to assure them that his contingency plans had been put into action for their protection and assure them that the outcome would guarantee them anonymity. As long as he stayed in control, they wouldn't recognize his assumption of power until it was too late.

After securing his office and uploading all his confidential files to a private server, he looked up to where the attendant stood guard and said, "Have the car brought round to the back of the garage, and make sure we aren't followed."

The man didn't move.

"Unless you've suddenly gone deaf, I suggest you move quickly."

The man only smiled.

Wirz's eyes widened as stared deeply into the man's face. He'd aged a bit. Crow's feet had sprung up around his eyes, and his skin had the pallid hue of someone who avoided sunlight. His physique had changed as well. He no longer sported the extra pounds of a bureaucrat. His body was now lean with sinewy muscles that belied his age. A long scar ran from his temple down across the bridge of his nose, trailing back toward his left ear. No doubt a result of the accident. The scar had marred his face substantially, allowing him to hide in plain sight for two years, but Wirz had no doubt who the man was.

"The works in your gallery are signed Abel Jennings," Wirz told him. "Perhaps a more fitting alias would have been Lazarus."

The man only smiled sweetly.

"Lazarus spent four days in a tomb only to rise at the behest of Jesus." Wirz cocked his head and asked, "How long did you lie in your tomb, Meeks?"

"Considerably longer," he replied.

"And the, uh . . . scar?" Wirz asked, running his finger across his cheek.

"A steel body panel in the wreckage. I was told I nearly bled to death from it before I was rescued. An ugly reminder of the incident, but I'm thankful to those who left it there."

"And who should we thank for your miraculous resurrection?" Wirz asked sarcastically.

"There were many, although the Almighty deserves most of the credit."

"You were never a true believer, Harrison. You and I both know that," Wirz said. "You played your part well, but your faith was never with God."

"I guess I've matured. I've learned that belief in a better world and belief in God are not the same, but they can coexist," Meeks said, walking slowly away from the door.

"Is that what your activities are a result of? Maturity?"

"They were acts of mercy, Caulder. Not that you would understand the concept."

"I'll have you know that I am the very voice of mercy on the Council. It is my pleas for compassion that have saved the lives of our citizens in the face of certain death."

"You certainly made it appear that way, but we both know that your mercy is far more torturous and just as deadly as any penance the Council would have given." Meeks cocked his head. "How many of those you've saved have survived your mercy?"

Wirz smiled coldly. "The current survival rate is 89%, although that number changes drastically upon activation. Until then, the penitent live perfectly normal lives in complete service to God."

"Until that faith shreds their minds and turns them into tortured animals desperate to escape it."

"Sacrifices to the greater good have always been necessary. You once understood that."

"I understood what I was indoctrinated to understand, just as you were," Meeks told him. "The greater good was the Agenda, or have you forgotten?"

"The Agenda was a pipe dream. A cowardly approach to world economic stability that would never have achieved its goal."

"The goal was more than that. The need for peaceful coexistence under our complete control without the threat of war. The balance of a global economy where no one nation prospered at the expense of another and each would bear responsibility for the safety, security, and prosperity of its neighbors. Infiltrating the ranks of faithful believers around the world gave us access to certain cancerous individuals and organizations we would otherwise never have been able to reach. Faith was merely the catalyst that allowed us to implement the dream."

"A dream nearly a hundred years in the making and not yet achieved," Wirz scoffed.

"Patience is our strength, Caulder. Man himself took 300,000 years to evolve into his present incarnation. One cannot remake the world in a day."

"God managed it," Caulder remarked with a smile.

Meeks shook his head and regarded his protégé with pity. "I recall us once having a very spirited discussion on the impact of Einstein's theory of relativity on the biblical interpretation of time."

"I was much more naïve then," Wirz told him. "With all due respect to Einstein, time is relative to the necessity of faith. And right now, if you will excuse me, mine is rather limited."

Meeks glanced toward the bulletproof windows overlooking the courtyard. They muted but could not block the sounds of gunfire. "No need to rush. The Feds seem to have their hands full at the moment." He walked closer to the desk with his hands clasped behind him. "You've strayed from the path, Caulder. And we both know how the Cadre deals with those who stray."

Wirz began to push buttons on the desk's surface while reaching for the gun strapped just beneath it. The holster was empty, of course. Meeks would have searched the office when he arrived. It was standard operating procedure for cornering a target on their own soil. He balled up his fist and shook his head. "You were the greatest of us before you were retired. A knife so keen it left no scar on the world no matter how deep the wound."

"That was our purpose, you and I. The Cadre's surgical tools created to remove those diseased people of society that threated the Agenda. We offered them a choice: be a part of the new world order, stay out of its way, or remain a problem. If they made the wrong choice, we didn't wait for the world court or a corrupt government to quantify the threat. We acted cleanly and precisely, without hesitation."

"And how does your newfound savagery serve your faith and that purpose?"

"What you see as savagery is a reflection of your cruelty, Caulder. You play God with the faithful. You manipulate the minds of the penitent to create the illusion that they can be saved and their sins forgiven. Then you leave them to die by their own hand, damning them in eternity. I lay their sins bare. I help them to atone and absolve them of sin so that they will know eternal peace with God."

Wirz began to laugh and shook his head. " And which God would that be?" he asked, his eyes taking on a frantic glow. "Remember Genesis

3:22, my friend. Did not God say, 'Behold, the man has become like one of Us, knowing good and evil'? Us, not Me. Us. The Bible itself declares that there are many other gods in the universe and also that we are now their equal." He moved the toe of his boot to a small button on the side of the desk leg and pressed against it, setting off a silent alarm. Leaning across the desk, he sneered, "I am the only god these faithful need absolution from. I am the only god they need serve, and they die in service to me. The faithful are my legion, and I will use them to make the world in my own image."

"And they say I'm insane."

"You are insane, my old friend," Wirz sneered gleefully. "You brutally execute people in the name of an invisible god invented by a desperate man thousands of years ago while spouting platitudes about mercy and compassion. The fiction of a lost soul wandering the countryside searching for a reason for his pointless existence."

"Is that how you truly see Christ?" Meeks asked, inching closer. "As a wandering mad man suffering an identity crisis?"

"No, no, old man. Jesus was far greater than that. He was the first God born of man. He was a visionary. He concocted the meaning of life and then sold it to an entire race. He gave them purpose and hope where they had none. Encouraged people to abandon their wealth and power to Him and take up the cause of humanity, inducting them into the grandest pyramid scheme ever to grace the planet. Jesus was no madman, Meeks. He was the Bernie Madoff of the first century. The first incarnation of P.T. Barnum. A con man who believed his own lie so completely that he brought about his own resurrection. He was a miracle, the inspiration that sent men like Houdini on a quest to prove their own immortality. To this day, his worshippers hunt down and recruit others to take up his cause and give beyond their capacity to give. All with the promise that the more minions they recruit, the closer they will come to their invisible God in the afterlife. The machine Jesus set in motion still churns its way through the population with an insatiable appetite. And every culture on the planet has recreated what he set in motion. New name, new rules, new rewards, same system."

Wirz pulled himself back from his vision and refocused his wild eyes on Meeks. "Unlike Jesus, however, I don't believe the con. I know that the purpose of existence is whatever purpose we give it. And my purpose isn't to worship the invisible but to be worshiped. The Bible says that I AM as God. And I shall give the minions something tangible to pray to. Something real that they can touch. Something they will have no doubt possesses the power to change their lives."

Meeks slipped the weapon from the hem of his coat as Wirz raved. "The Cadre will never allow you to attain your goals. The Agenda forbids it."

He cocked his head and looked at Meeks curiously. "Have you forgotten that you were retired because you lost faith in that Agenda?"

"I was always a believer in the Agenda. It was you that I lost faith in. Unfortunately, I couldn't convince my brothers to see the corruption you infected these people with and the threat you'd become to us all."

"They believe completely in me," Wirz said confidently, easing his personal sidearm from his sleeve. "And I will change their Agenda, or my minions and I will sweep them from the surface of the Earth. Like God in Noah's time. The choice will be theirs."

"No, Caulder, it's time to return Eden to those whom it was intended to shelter and drive out the snake once and for all," Meeks said, raising his weapon.

4

Deacon rounded the corner of the lobby and ducked just as shots chipped away at the marble pillar to his left. The security guards had him in a solid crossfire and there was no way he would get to the elevator without being hit. He returned fire and crawled into the shadows behind a long planter. From there he could see that there were four armed men, and they had every possible escape route in their sights. Every time he shifted position, shots rained down on him, leaving him grazed and bleeding in several places. There were doors evenly spaced around the rotunda, but they were sealed flush with no handles. Only legislative personnel or E-Rep law enforcement could open them, and they were the ones currently trying to kill him.

The chaos outside continued as more police from every agency joined the melee. Deacon scuttled between the planters toward the front entrance but was driven back each time. He'd just emptied his last magazine when the front doors burst open. Bachman and Burke pushed in, firing high along the balcony, while a considerably wounded Markham made his way along the planters toward Deacon. Tossing him his territorial ID and a loaded weapon, he yelled "GO!" and drew a second weapon to cover the lieutenant.

Deacon crawled to the first door and pressed Markham's badge to it. It slid open silently, revealing a staircase. He dove through as the first E-Rep shooter was knocked from the railing. He reloaded as he took the stairs two at a time. At each floor, he could hear the emergency warnings directing everyone to the evacuation corridor, which kept the civilians out of his way. At the last landing, he crouched low to one side of the door and swiped Markham's ID. He waited for nearly a minute before entering the main corridor. All of the senators' offices were shut. He made his way slowly down the curved hallway to the Ecclesiastical Seat.

Four guards had been posted outside, and all of them were dead. All four were still armed, and each had his throat cut. Only a highly trained assassin could have killed four armed men, and that meant Jennings was already here. Deacon stared at the door, and for the first time in his career he hesitated. His sworn duty was to save the life of Archbishop Wirz. But he'd promised his son that he would end the man who tortured him even if it cost him everything. Save the devil, save yourself. Kill the demon, save your soul. He'd already decided Wirz had to die, but Wirz's life at this moment was in the hands of a killer calling himself Abel Jennings. A killer Deacon had also sworn to apprehend.

Give Jennings his chance, his conscience whispered. *Let him take your vengeance and then capture him. Keep your hands clean.* Deacon gritted his teeth and snapped his head back against the wall with a thud. It was the perfect solution. His duty to his country and to his son would be met, and his career would be safe. He could finally be at peace. All he had to do was wait. He closed his eyes and tried to picture Neville's face, but it wasn't his son that came to mind. It was the hollow, indifferent eyes of a wooden figure dangling from a cross that stared back at him. No longer blandly returning his glare, those eyes bore down on him now. In them, he saw the answer he'd been demanding of his savior for the past five years. Deacon reached out and waved Markham's ID across the door with little hope that it would open. Wirz wouldn't have been stupid enough to give a lowly pawn access to his private chambers. Whether by design or divine intervention, the lock disengaged, the door slid open, and Deacon charged in, gun raised and ready.

The artist, Abel Jennings, the man formerly known as Harrison Meeks kept his gun trained on his protégé. He'd disabled the alarm system in Wirz's office and knew there would be no help coming for him. Wirz, however, had been expecting a contingent of security personnel to come through the door and was shocked when Deacon rushed in ordering both men to disarm and raise their hands. He grimaced but then smiled at Meeks.

"It looks like your time has finally run out." Glancing toward Deacon he said, "I believe this is the killer you've been searching for, Lieutenant."

"Put the guns down and raise your hands, both of you!" Deacon ordered.

Wirz shot Deacon a disgusted look. "I knew you were too weak to do what needed to be done," he sneered. "But I will not fail in my mission." He tightened his grip and leveled the weapon at Meeks.

Meeks never took his eyes from Wirz but spoke quietly to Deacon as he kept his own weapon on target. "So whoever knows the right thing to do and fails to do it, for him it is sin. You know the right thing to do, Lieutenant."

"I know you murdered innocent people who didn't deserve to die for their sins, no matter what your objective was," Deacon answered evenly, and Wirz smiled a wretched smile. "I'm sure you've killed thousands more in your lifetime pursuing that damned Agenda of yours. But that's for the law to determine, not me."

"I will gladly bear judgment for my sins, Lieutenant," Meeks answered. "My actions were for the greater good of all mankind. To bring peace to this world." Looking hard into Wirz's smug expression, he said, "But as a man of God, I cannot allow this abomination to go free."

"I, and I alone, act with the authority of the Almighty," Wirz sneered. "It is I who will lead the faithful and bring the world to God."

"Shut it, Wirz," Deacon snapped. "There's a special place in hell waiting for you, and I'm going make sure you don't miss your flight."

Wirz shot him a malicious grin. "I acted with the authority of the laws of my territory and with the Council's blessing. I and I alone have returned the faithful to a state of obedient grace, and my followers will never allow you to arrest me." He chuckled as he watched Deacon struggle to decide his next move. "You can't take us both in, Lieutenant. You only have two options, so which will it be? A serial killer who tortures and maims his victims, or the freely elected official who brings order and obedience to God's kingdom?"

"Both options leave me with a murdering bastard roaming free," he said. "Then again, I could just let him kill you, then take him in." He smiled viciously at Wirz. "Kind of solves both issues." He glanced toward Meeks and added, "Who's to say he doesn't escape on the way in or meet a mysterious death on his way to prison? He is after all, a master assassin." Wirz's smile shriveled as Deacon spoke. "You see, Wirz, my options get better and better every minute as long as I let you die first."

"You'd throw your career and your life away to satisfy your thirst for vengeance?" Wirz asked. "Vengeance is mine; I will repay, saith the Lord. You have no right to avenge your boy upon me."

"I have every right in the eyes of the law and in the eyes of God," Deacon told him as he lowered his weapon. "'Let every soul be subject to the governing authorities. For there is no authority except from God, and the authorities that exist are appointed by God. Therefore, whoever resists the authority resists the ordinance of God, and those who resist will bring judgment on themselves.' You need to read up on your Romans, Wirz. All governments of man exist by the grace of God, and that means your ass is mine."

Wirz howled in rage and swung the barrel of his gun toward Deacon, who dove out of the way, giving Meeks a clear shot. Both weapons fired simultaneously. Deacon felt a round streak past his neck as it blew out the door frame. He rolled and came up just as Meeks' shot slammed into Wirz. The archbishop flew back and crashed into the glass table, shattering it into deadly shards.

Meeks advanced on Wirz until Deacon said, "Hold it," and took aim. "Drop the weapon and step away."

Meeks ignored him and knelt next to Wirz. "You'd be wise to let me finish what I started, Lieutenant. You could walk away clean knowing your boy had been avenged and his torturer punished."

"And I suppose I'm to take your word for it that you won't kill anyone else."

Meeks looked up at him with apologetic eyes. "My work here is done. But I can't in good faith guarantee my skills won't be required elsewhere. We have a world to save, you and I."

"The only thing I need to save the world from is you and your people," Deacon told him. Now drop the weapon and back away."

"Have you forgotten? My people tried to murder me," Meeks told him. "I can help you expose them. There are thousands of them you don't even know about. I can lay them all at your feet if that is what you desire. Make you a hero, the savior of America. All I ask is that you let me remove this evil from our midst once and for all."

"Who were you?" Deacon asked. "Before you became Abel Jennings."

Before Meeks could answer, a large glass shard swung through the air and sliced upward across his throat. Wirz lunged at Meeks with a howl of rage, and the two tumbled into the growing pool of red at their feet. The two men struggled until Meeks began to tire from blood loss, and Wirz pinned him to the floor. Pulling Meeks' gun from his failing grip and placing it against his temple, Wirz snarled, "This time, old man, there won't be any resurrection for you."

Deacon fired, hitting Wirz squarely between the eyes and sending him sprawling back onto the bloody floor. "This is MacNair. I'm on the top floor in the Ecumenical Seat. I need paramedics and medical transport immediately," he said into his comm link as he huddled over Meeks. Grabbing the sash from Meeks' uniform, he tried to apply pressure, but Meeks stopped him.

"Don't bother, Lieutenant. I'd much prefer to die on my own terms than in a prison hospital."

Deacon looked down at him with a scowl. "I should let you die. You've earned that. But you still have to face justice in this world before you answer for your crimes in the next." He pressed the sash into Meeks' throat and secured it around his neck.

Meeks closed his eyes and whispered, "For the LORD is a God of justice. Blessed are all who wait for him." Deacon felt him go slack and released the tourniquet.

A group of loud voices erupted from the stairwell down the hall. Deacon grabbed his weapon and made his way toward it. There was still gunfire coming from below and no way to tell who had arrived. He positioned himself in a small alcove and sighted down the hallway. As the group rounded the corner, he took aim but pulled up short when he heard Joyce Bachman calling out for him.

"Over here!" he yelled back as Joyce hurried toward him with a contingent of federal officers, local deputies, and medical personnel. "Down there, end of the hall," he said as Joyce and one of the technicians checked him for wounds. "It's over," he told her. "Got 'em both."

Joyce smiled at him and wiped a streak of blood from his forehead. "You should have waited for backup," she chided. "At least then you'd have witnesses to make it justifiable."

"That asshole stood in front of a crowd of hundreds on live television and called them to attack federal officers executing a legal arrest warrant. I think I'm covered as far as witnesses."

"Yeah? Well, that asshole was second in command of half the country and a religious leader. The press is going to hand you your ass on this one."

"Well, hell, they don't have to take my word for it. Just ask the other guy back there in the robes with the slashed throat what happened."

"What other guy?" Burke asked, emerging from the archbishop's office. Deacon bored into Burke with an annoyed look that quickly melted into dread as he charged past him. The massive puddle of blood still congealed around Wirz's body, but there was no sign of Jennings. A quick search of the room uncovered one bloody handprint on the wall behind Wirz's desk, but no other sign of the man remained.

5

On Deacon's orders, the officers immediately began the search for Jennings, but Deacon knew they wouldn't find him. Burke's wonder bots discovered a hidden door beneath the bloody handprint, no doubt placed there for emergencies or in case Wirz's true allegiance was ever discovered. The blood trail led to an underground parking lot, but no vehicle was found. The man had disappeared even though there was little chance he could survive his wounds. Staring out across the Huntsville grounds to the old launch platforms, Deacon was sure that whoever Abel Jennings really was, he was still out there.

The team had finished processing the evidence and been sent home to enjoy a long week of rest with the president's congratulations on a job well done. Only Agnes and Joyce remained.

"Beware wise men bearing gifts," a soft voice called out to him. He looked up to see Agnes and Joyce sauntering over to him, grinning like a pair of Cheshire cats.

"I don't think anyone could mistake you two for men," Deacon complimented Agnes. "Any plans?"

"We Buddhists are totally down with Jesus, so the sky's the limit, and I have about ten parties to hit this week."

Deacon reached out and took her hand. "You did a great job as usual. Go enjoy yourself, and I'll see you in the new year."

She pulled him into a tight hug. "Do me favor and don't spend Christmas alone."

"I'll try not to," he replied, smiling down on his diminutive investigator.

She gave Joyce a similar embrace. As she reached the door, she said, "By the way, your bet with Burke is technically a draw since neither of you figured out the identity of the killer."

"What the hell does that mean?" Deacon asked.

"Ask the woman who did," she said, grinning as she left the two of them alone.

Joyce smiled at him, waggling her eyebrows. "You figured it out?" he asked.

"You could say that," she answered. "It's worth at least a week of meals at The Colonnade. Now, shut up and pay attention. I have places to be."

"I thought you Jews didn't believe in Jesus and the virgin birth."

"We don't. That's why we celebrate Hanukkah, which is what I should be doing instead of paperwork," she groused, handing him the finalized report. "I'm missing my mother's latkes and my dad's killer barbeque brisket for this."

"It's greatly appreciated," Deacon replied, slipping the pad into its dock.

"Digger was able to confirm the presence of a second assailant in the office from the blood pool, so you're covered. But you're never gonna believe who Abel Jennings really is."

He raised an eyebrow as she mischievously reached across the desk and tapped the display control.

"Meet your master assassin. The one and only Harrison Meeks, well-beloved Hand to the High Archbishop tragically killed by a drunk driver on the Tybee Bridge three years ago."

"You're shitting me!" Deacon exclaimed.

"Oh, it gets better," Joyce said, pulling up additional files. "Archbishop Meeks had quite a history of service in Rome and across Europe and a robust education in both theology and art. Possesses PhDs in both subjects. His entire career has been dedicated to religious service and the preservation of conservative morality. He even taught three years at Yale Divinity in New Haven. He left the faculty after serving in the war as a chaplain and subsequently took a position with the Ecumenical Council, where he rose to fame and glory. Everyone expected him to be appointed high archbishop when the current one retired."

"I met him years ago during the formation of the Territorial Charter," Deacon muttered, remembering the genial, open-minded man everyone believed would be the future of Eden. "You're telling me that he dedicated his life to the service of God, taught theology, served as a chaplain during a war, and somehow managed to become a sadistic master assassin? That doesn't make any sense."

"That's because it's all fake!" Joyce told him, calling up a series of old photographs. "I had Corbett do a deep dive on Meeks's whereabouts after leaving Yale. He served in the Constitutional army for the first three years of the war but then left to join the delegation to Rome. He volunteered to be part of the peace talks to end the war." She reached across the screen and pulled an Italian police file to the forefront. "A month after arriving in Italy, he went to Venice for a little vacation and was involved in a boating accident. He spent four months in a hospital there undergoing surgery and rehab and rejoined the peace talks after he recovered. That's the official bio. But local police reported a body that washed up on shore that same day matching Meeks's description. That man died as a result a boating accident too but had to be buried as a John Doe on Sant' Ariano. The city reopened the old ossuary after about a hundred years of nonuse because of the overflow on San Michele."

She pulled up the photo of the body and placed it next to Meeks's faculty photograph. The resemblance was remarkable. Then she added a photograph of Meeks from the final days of the peace talks and one taken upon his elevation to archbishop years after. They all appeared to be of the same man.

"We pulled Meeks's medical records from just before his transfer to Rome. He had no physical injuries other than a couple of shrapnel scars from a landmine. But when he was admitted to the hospital in Venice after the accident, doctors noted the presence of a titanium plate in his shoulder from a previous injury. An injury there's no record of anywhere."

"If this man isn't the real Harrison Meeks who the hell is he?" Deacon asked with a sinking feeling.

"Unknown," Joyce told him. It was the first crack in her smile that day. "Every DNA trace possible was run, and we couldn't find a match anywhere. Meeks's available medical records date after the war, and they all match this guy's current DNA profile. It's only when we compared it to his enlistment testing prior to the war that the results came back unmatched. We know he assumed Meeks's identity when the real Meeks died. He may even have had engineered Meeks's death, but there's no way to prove it. We may never know who this guy really was."

Deacon stared at the mosaic of information and pictures and scowled. The solution to his case was no solution at all. The killer would be classified a John Doe, and until they could find his body, he would remain a mystery. "I think we can call this one solved," he groused. "And The Colonnade's on me, for all of us. Close up shop and head home. Enjoy your holiday."

"Thanks, boss," Joyce replied, feeling equally disillusioned. As she retrieved her jacket and purse from her desk, she said, "Merry Christmas, Deke."

Deacon smiled back and said, "Chag same'ach" in a decidedly mispronounced Alabama drawl, drawing an incredulous smile from his partner.

As the day inched toward dusk, snow began to fall, lightly coating the campus. Deacon made his way slowly down the winding paths to his car. There was a sense of closure when you solved a case, not unlike the closure that grieving families felt when a criminal was convicted and justice finally served. But he didn't feel it this time. The killer had been mortally wounded. Medical professionals examining the amount of blood loss declared that the suspect could not have survived his wounds. And although his body had not yet been found, the case had in fact been solved. Publicly, he'd been identified only as Abel Jennings. Since Meeks was also a false identity, the Senate and the Council saw no reason to publicly destroy his legacy. Harrison Meeks would remain a figure of inspiration to the children of Eden. His true identity had been deemed classified by the White House as the investigation into the Cadre was now firmly in the hands of the FBI and CIA and Deacon was released from his obligation. There was nothing left to do but put it behind him, if he could.

He reached the cruiser as the last of the light sparkled on the accumulating snow and was pleasantly surprised to see Elli waiting there for him. She looked healthy and rested, thanks to her mother's robust cooking. She still had her cane, but she was no longer hunched over or struggling to walk. The light seemed to have returned to her eyes but not entirely. There would always be a cloud over them for Kyle.

He hugged her fiercely, drawing a distinct "umph" from her as he squeezed her chest. "Merry Christmas, Doc. How the hell are you?"

"Better and better every day," she told him. "The Council has declared my penance served in full and my license to practice reinstated. I am officially off your service."

"Well, I for one am sad to see you go. You would make a hell of a detective, Doc."

She smiled warmly. "I think my calling lies elsewhere." She dropped her eyes for a moment, then said, "My father sends his many thanks and wants you to know you can count him as a friend. If you need anything, just call him."

"I think the senator is going to have his hands full in the next few months," Deacon replied.

"That's certainly an understatement. There's a reformation happening in the capitol. The high archbishop resigned this morning along with a few of the older members of the Council, and several of Wirz's appointees seem to have gone AWOL. The remaining members have decided to hold open elections in the spring to replace them. They feel letting the people decide who represents them in faith would go a long way toward restoring trust."

"The rats are deserting the sinking ship, but there could still be others hiding in plain sight. Your father's going to have to be very careful who he trusts."

"That's one of the reasons he wants to keep in contact with you. We don't have the resources to properly screen the new candidates. He's hoping you could put in a good word with Washington to help us get it right this time." Elli saw a familiar tightness in Deacon's expression and shifted tactics. "You'll be pleased to know that the R&R Protocols have been suspended and the rehab centers shut down while the Council investigates. The Senate is retasking them to help the people who were reconditioned. They can't undo the damage that was done, but they'll give them all the help and support they need to live a normal life for as long as possible." She looked into his scowl and said, "I know we have a long way to go, but please have a little faith in us."

Deacon stared down into her kittenish eyes and his scowl disappeared. It was no mystery why Kyle Tanner had fallen for her so quickly. "I have all the faith in the world that you will succeed, Doc, and I pray that you do."

She grinned broadly and gripped him in a bear hug. "Can you come to Christmas dinner?" she asked. "My mother is rediscovering her love of cooking, and there'll be plenty."

"After the reviews Bachman gave, I wouldn't miss it," he said, kissing her forehead lightly.

And the Just Walk Still

The graveyard was clean and well-kept. The grass was mown evenly and maintained a deep green glow despite the scattered snowflakes. It would turn brown and go dormant soon, but no one would notice. Snow would cover its dying corpse, leaving the cemetery tucked under a crisp, white blanket. It would sleep along with all the other corpses lying beneath it, hidden from the world. But unlike the bodies it entombed, the green would return with the spring thaw and welcome the bereaved and lonely. Enticing them to sit among the tombstones and reminisce with the dead while the grass beneath their feet measured them in anticipation. People didn't think of scenes like this when they thought of the Deep South with its sweltering, humid heat and hurricane floodwaters. It happened more often since the war. The changes wrought by man's weapons of destruction had altered the landscape and the weather as well. Cities of the dead now occupied more space than those of the living, and they inevitably drew the snowfalls of mortality every December.

Deacon felt more relaxed here than at T-Bone's on a Saturday night. There was no lament of jazz to soothe his nerves. Sound here was muted by the fog and snowfall and wouldn't carry. No blue-brown haze of rich tobacco clogged his lungs. The air was too cold and sharp. No amber liquid sent waves of napalm to his heart to burn away the demons. Instead, the warm tears on his cheeks burned trails into his skin as the ghosts they carried away blended into the melting snow at his feet. He hadn't been here in a long time. Protected by a crown of moss, the tombstone still looked new. Perhaps it hadn't had enough time to be battered by the elements or abused by people with no respect for their purpose. His heart knew otherwise. It looked pristine because it was at peace finally. *He* was at peace finally. He knelt down and brushed the name clear. Neville Martin MacNair.

"I've done right by you, son," he whispered. "They'll never hurt anyone again."

He touched the stone with his bare hand. Where he should have felt cold and dampness, he felt only warmth. He stood there for the better part of an hour crying the demons from his soul, and when he left, he was no longer himself. He walked the paths through the tombs, encountering only one other person kneeling at a headstone. They didn't acknowledge each other, but a slight frisson of shared grief flared as he passed by.

It was a two-hour drive back to Atlanta on icy roads, and he'd promised Elli he wouldn't be late. He made his way back to the cruiser but stopped short when it came into view. A large, gold box tied with a brocaded red velvet ribbon sat on the hood. He approached it cautiously. On top was a cluster of mistletoe in which sat an envelope imprinted with a verse from Jeremiah:

"But the Lord is with me as a dread warrior; therefore, my persecutors will stumble; they will not overcome me. They will be greatly shamed, for they will not succeed. Their eternal dishonor will never be forgotten."

Deacon hands shook as he carefully untied the ribbon and lifted the lid. He pulled aside the red tissue paper and stared down at the contents. He stumbled back from the box, the envelope gripped in his hand. Nestled inside the rose-colored paper was the head of Wallace Milton, a crucifix tooled into his forehead.

Breathing heavily, he opened the card. It contained a photograph of him kneeling in the snow in front of Neville's grave, his hand placed lovingly on the stone. It had been taken only minutes ago. Inside the card in tight, clean script was written:

"Behold the atonement of one who would lead the children of God astray and into the arms of sin. Welcome to the revolution, my friend. The fight is far from over."

April 23, 2020

AUTHOR'S NOTE

My many thanks to my editor, Kerri Miller who gave my manuscript her very best spit and polish. To Jeff Bringle, I am thankful for your beautiful art and pragmatic vision during the journey. To all my friends and family who have pushed, prodded, teased and nagged me endlessly to keep going, I am eternally grateful for every one of you. My undying gratitude goes to the outstanding creative talent of the Relax and Write family and our amazing mother, Maia Danzinger. Without each of their incredible talents and endless support through the toughest and darkest times we face, this book would never have come to light.

To my readers, I would like to say that although this is a work of fiction, it is not entirely outside the realm of possibility. Zealotry and extremism are invading every aspect of our lives, even our faiths, and pulling us further from God than we have ever been. It is my hope that such a future as I have envisioned, never comes to pass. We all can, and must, share this country and this Earth. It is vast enough for each person to live their own truth peacefully alongside their brothers and sisters with love and respect. To that end, I hope that each and every one of us finds his or her own truth within our own hearts and uses it to right the injustices, heal the pain, and live in peace and love the way God meant us to.

ABOUT THE AUTHOR

Dina Ritz lives in Los Angeles, California with her menagerie of critics. She loves to explore her rich, family history in New Orleans, Louisiana, and the myriad of "what-ifs" that creative fiction allows us to imagine.